D1093726

# ATLAS
## OF THE
# BIBLICAL
# WORLD

Perga in Pamphylia. *A striking carving from the theater at Perga, where Paul and Barnabas landed from Cyprus, and where they later "preached the word" during the first missionary journey (Acts 13:13–14; 14:24–25). It was a port to the east of Attalia (the modern Antalya) on the south coast of Anatolia.*

# DENIS BALY AND A. D. TUSHINGHAM

# CONSULTANTS

R. P. Roland de Vaux, O.P.
*Professor, École Biblique
et Archéologique de
St. Etienne Jerusalem*

Richard N. Frye
*Aga Khan Professor of Iranian
Harvard University*

Michael Gough
*Professor of
Early Christian Archaeology
Pontifical Institute of Medieval Studies
Toronto, Canada*

Basheer K. Nijim
*Chairman, Department of Geography
University of Northern Iowa*

David Oates
*Professor of
Western Asiatic Archaeology
Institute of Archaeology,
University of London*

# ATLAS
## OF THE
## BIBLICAL
## WORLD

THE WORLD PUBLISHING COMPANY
NEW YORK

*Published by The World Publishing Company*

*Published simultaneously in Canada*
*by Nelson, Foster & Scott Ltd.*

*First printing—1971*

*Copyright © 1971 by The World Publishing Company*

*Library of Congress catalog card number: 71-107641*

*Printed in the United States of America*

**WORLD PUBLISHING**
**TIMES MIRROR**

# CONTENTS

## Maps in Color

## Black and White Maps

*Color*

**PHOTO-GRAPHS**

*Black and White*

# FOREWORD

The title of this atlas which I have been asked to introduce to the public is significant: it is an *Atlas of the Biblical World*. The people of the Bible knew that the country which they occupied, the land which God had promised to their fathers, was only a small part of a "world," which had long been for them the whole of the known world. This world corresponds more or less to what we call the Middle East. Despite much variety and contrast, it has certain common geographical features: its inhabitants had developed independently, but they had had economic and cultural connections, and had been the actors in a partly common history, which is the most ancient history that we can write. Israel was a latecomer to this world, occupied only a small part of it, and played only an insignificant role on the political scene and in the development of material progress. We must place the land of the Bible, the "Holy Land," within this geographical framework in order to understand, as Israel understood, the unique character of her spiritual calling: "For you are a people holy to the Lord your God; the Lord your God has chosen you to be a people for his own possession, out of all the peoples that are on the face of the earth. It was not because you were more in number that the Lord set his love upon you and chose you, for you were the fewest of all peoples" (Deut. 7:6–7).

The second novelty of this atlas is that the maps, except maps 30–35, have been prepared, and most of the text written, by a professional geographer. Professor Denis Baly has already published an excellent book on the geography of the Bible about a decade ago.[1] It is true that the historical and political geography, which has the chief place in other biblical atlases, has not been neglected; the maps which deal with this aspect of geography reflect the results of the most recent research, together with the uncertainty that is still attached to certain identifications. Of the two chapters written by Dr. A. D. Tushingham, one illustrates the mutual contribution rendered by archaeology and geography, and the other proposes a reinterpretation of the ancient topography of Jerusalem, which, even if it is not yet definitive, has been made necessary by the recent excavations. All this was to be expected. However, most of the maps, and the larger part of the text, are concerned with the truly geographical features—structure, relief, climate, vegetation—which determine the natural regions and govern man's activities, the use which he has made of the soil, and the course of his routes.

This emphasis is justified, for a knowledge of the physical and human geography is indispensable to the historian and the biblical scholar. The fundamental characteristic which continually influences the life and history of the land of the Bible is its lack of unity. Relief, soil, and climate are continually varied. It is divided into four parallel zones, stretching from north to south, which are themselves subdivided. The dry dunes of the Philistine coast in ancient times were succeeded by marshes in the Sharon plain; the Cis-Jordan plateau is dislocated by the transverse folding of the Negeb, and interrupted by the collapse of the Plain of Esdraelon, while in the Judean hill country the crest forms

[1] Denis Baly, *The Geography of the Bible* (New York: Harper and Row, 1957).

the dividing line between the cultivated land and the steppe. In the central Rift Valley, the Jordan drains the Huleh marshes but cleaves the Ghor without watering it, and flows from the well-stocked Lake of Galilee to the completely sterile waters of the Dead Sea. On the Trans-Jordan plateau the rich fields of Bashan are contrasted with the rocky wastes of Edom. These contrasts are even more marked when one travels from west to east. From Jaffa to Amman is only 115 km. (72 mi.) as the crow flies, but the traveler leaves the coast plain for the uplands of the Shephelah and then the highlands of Judea, which reach 1,000 m. (3,300 ft.); from Jerusalem to the Dead Sea he drops 1,200 m. in 25 km. (4,000 ft. in 15 mi.), and then Amman, only 40 km. (25 mi.) to the east, is 1,500 m. (4,900 ft.) higher. He passes from a humid and temperate maritime climate to Jerusalem's dry and more extreme continental climate (but with the variety that one associates with more temperate regions), and then to a tropical climate at Jericho. He first crosses a zone of Mediterranean agriculture, with wheat, vines, and olives, but after Jerusalem he sees no more vineyards and oliveyards, and soon no more plowed fields. As he enters the Jordan Valley, the tawny wilderness of the Ghor, the rich oasis of Jericho, and the still surface of the Dead Sea seem like the landscape of another world. On the other side of the valley he meets wheat and barley again, but few vines and almost no olives, and Amman marks already the edge of the desert.

The natural conditions thus divide the country into a mosaic of little regions, which have different ways of life and divergent interests. This separatism is strengthened by the difficulty of communication. The principal roads follow the physical features from north to south, but the transverse routes, which might have helped to relate the different regions to one another, are precarious, and have always played a secondary role. These circumstances of physical and human geography have conditioned the daily life of most of the inhabitants, in the period of the Old Testament as well as that of the New. Apart from the capital cities, Jerusalem and Samaria, the "cities" were no more than villages. The farmer lived from his field and his flock, which he and his family tended together. Other needs were taken care of by the village craftsmen, or perhaps those of a neighboring village, the potter, the weaver, the carpenter, the mason, and the blacksmith, who worked with their sons, or with a few employees. There was no large-scale industry. Nor was there any important

trade, and such trade as there was, apart from that in purely local products, was conducted by foreign itinerant merchants, usually Phoenicians. The bonds of family were strong, and the traditions of clan and tribe persistent. The central government did not interfere very much, except to collect taxes in kind, and recruit young men for the army. Local affairs were managed by a council of elders. The divisions of the country and the lack of good communications meant that people traveled little.

This cantonal type of life had important political and historical consequences. Before the institution of the monarchy under Saul, the tribes pursued separate goals. Unification took place under David, but did not survive his successor, Solomon. After him, until the fall first of Samaria and then of Jerusalem, Israel in the north and Judah in the south were two separate and often hostile states, and the kingdom of Israel was torn apart by intertribal rivalry. The only firm and durable link was that of religion, and it was this which made out of "all Israel" one people, and out of the country the land of the Bible.

The last contrast—and not the least—which this country presents is the disproportion between the meagerness of its natural resources and the greatness of its spiritual destiny. This is the mystery of God. The very poverty of the country prepared its vocation. A man could not grow rich there, but the soil, with a little work, would provide all his daily needs. Such an existence, in the bosom of the family, without needless luxury, encouraged the development of a more personal type of life, and the recognition of the true human values. Greece had similar conditions, with poor soil, varied relief, and poor internal communications, and it also produced the highest achievements of the spirit. Yet this simple life was not guaranteed merely by man's activity. It depended on the rain, which made the harvest sprout and the pasture grow green again. But this rain was always uncertain, and one had to beseech God that it might fall in due time and in sufficient quantity. So the country led man naturally to the supernatural. The Bible, written there, preaches the sanctity of poverty, which is wealth.

This sanctity was preserved by isolation. The heart of the land of the Bible, the central highland, lies aside from the great trade routes, and it was not directly coveted by the great powers, who fought for mastery and were interested only in control of the strategic route along the coast. The people of the

Bible could live in peace, turned toward their God, if they did not interfere in the quarrels of their rich neighbors; the Prophets, who opposed the human politics of the kings, were defending not only the religion of the people but their very existence. The insignificance of the country, as well as its poverty, prepared it to receive and guard the message of God.

In return, this message has transformed it. One can neither visit nor live in these mountains and valleys, these plains and deserts, without being reminded of the Bible: Elijah on Mount Carmel, Abraham and Lot at the Dead Sea, Abraham and Sarah at Mamre and Hebron, David and Solomon at Jerusalem, Ahab and Jezebel at Samaria, and Jesus at Bethlehem, at Nazareth, and beside the Lake of Galilee. In traveling these roads, one follows the footsteps of the Patriarchs, the Prophets, and Jesus. The land is saturated with the prayers of the faithful of ancient times, and those of the pilgrims of all ages, of all those who believe in the one God of the Bible. The land helps us to understand the Bible which came out of it, but the Bible also gives to the land its own meaning, and makes it dear. It is in every respect "the Land of the Bible."

ROLAND de VAUX, O.P.
(Translated from the French)

# PREFACE

This atlas has been taking shape over a long period of time. It was first conceived in 1960, when I had the opportunity to revisit the Middle East, and travel widely in regions which I had not known before at first hand. I undertook this study because I was becoming increasingly aware, in my teaching and elsewhere, that to know only part of the Middle East was to misunderstand it. The actual work on the production of the base maps for the atlas began in the early part of 1965, and in 1966–67 I visited the Middle East again, for the purposes of extensive field research, made possible by the generosity of a Ford Foundation grant, administered through the Great Lakes College Association, of which Kenyon College is a member. On this occasion I had my own car, and drove well over thirty thousand miles. I was able to visit a large number of regions which I had not previously known, and also to study many of them at different seasons of the year, under varying climatic conditions. There were, it is true, a variety of obstacles, and plans had to be changed from time to time because of political conditions, "wars and rumors of wars," and sundry acts of God, such as snowstorms at Petra, ferocious floods in the mountains, and devastating sandstorms, but never at any time did my wife and I receive anything but help and kindness from people of every nationality, in every country that we visited. Without this unfailing and ready assistance from everyone we met, rich and poor, "a great multitude whom no man can number," the work could never have been done. I cannot let the atlas appear in public without recording my heartfelt gratitude to all of them.

A work of this kind cannot possibly be the production of one man, and from the beginning it has been a cooperative effort, involving constant consultation between the World Publishing Company, Jeppesen and Company, who were the cartographers, and Dr. Tushingham and myself. Particular thanks are due to Père de Vaux for his kindness in writing the Foreword, and to the distinguished scholars who formed the Editorial Board, and who criticized both the maps and the text before they took final shape. Their help and suggestions were invaluable, but any faults that still remain, of course, must not be laid at their door.

Certain goals have directed the formation of this atlas from the beginning. First, it should always move from the greater area to the smaller. What should be borne in mind at all times and be presented first of all is the Middle East as a whole; then the various major regions within the Middle East should be considered; and only thereafter should attention be focused upon the tiny area in which most of the events in the biblical record took place. This was done deliberately so that Palestine should be seen in perspective, and that the reader might grasp something of the feelings of those who looked out at the world from the Palestinian hills, and found themselves saying continually, "We seemed to ourselves like grasshoppers, and so we seemed to them" (Num. 13:33).

Second, it should make available to the reader of the Bible, and also to the more serious student, geographical information about the biblical world which is not easily obtainable elsewhere. The production of physical maps of the Middle East is a highly complicated business because of the large number of sources from which the information must be gleaned, the varying reliability of the information, and, from time to time, the flat contradiction that exists among the sources. One cannot, of course, stipulate in advance what kind of geographical information is going to be useful to biblical studies, and to try to do so would be prejudicial in the extreme. Some may be tempted to think, for instance, that information about structure and geology is less likely to be valuable than information about climate. However, it is impossible to know before one begins. The fact that the Cenomanian limestone normally carries a thicker forest cover than other types of Middle Eastern rock means that a knowledge of the distribution of this type of rock helps us to plot with more accuracy the extent of the ancient forests, which have now in so many areas completely disappeared.

Third, the reader should be given every assistance to *visualize* the environment, and as far as possible place himself within it, so that he may look at it as an insider and not an outsider. The relief map bases were drawn by Hal Shelton of Denver, on the basis of information collected and compiled from a large number of sources by Jeppesen and Company, cartographers, and of my own research, especially into problems of geology, landforms, and natural vegetation. A great deal of this information came from field studies. The production of these relief maps has been a fascinating task, and all of us who have been involved in it venture to express the hope that these maps are the most detailed and most accurate maps of this kind that have ever been published of the Middle East. All the photographs in the book have been taken specifically for the atlas, and the color plates are designed to assist the reader in his interpretation of the maps. For this purpose most of them are accompanied by an inset, taken from the relief map, showing the region where the picture was taken.

Roughly half the black and white maps are concerned with further interpretation of the environment, thirteen are historical maps of the type more usually associated with biblical atlases, and seven deal with the development of the city of Jerusalem. Except where they are discussed in the text, each is accompanied by an explanatory section. Fuller explanation is given of the two maps of the natural regions of the Middle East and of the Levant (12 and 13) in Chapters Four and Five.

In two important subject areas it was felt that more detailed information was essential: the problems of the climate, on which in the last resort all life in the Middle East must depend; and the results of the recent excavations in Jerusalem, which have so greatly increased our knowledge of the ancient city. The climate and its effects are discussed in Chapters Two and Three; and for Jerusalem we have been fortunate in having the help of Dr. A. D. Tushingham, Chief Archaeologist of the Royal Ontario Museum, Toronto, which collaborated with the British School of Archaeology in Jerusalem, and the Ecole Biblique et Archéologique de St. Etienne in Jerusalem, in the Jerusalem excavations. As Associate Director of the expedition, Dr. Tushingham has had the benefit of the advice of the Director, Miss Kathleen M. Kenyon, for which he expresses his deep appreciation. For those interpretations, however, which must be based on literary rather than archaeological grounds, Miss Kenyon must be absolved from all responsibility. Map 29, The Site of Jerusalem, together with the discussion of this in the text, is a joint production, though Dr. Tushingham has been the final authority on all matters concerning Jerusalem. Maps 30 through 35 and their accompanying description, which show the historical development of Jerusalem from Canaanite days and constitute one of the most important features of this atlas, are entirely his work. These maps were drawn by Mr. Claus Breede, Scientific Il-lustrator in the Office of the Chief Archaeologist of the Royal Ontario Museum, under Dr. Tushingham's direc-tion. Dr. Tushingham has also written the first chapter, Archaeology and Ancient Environments.

My most sincere thanks are also due to the follow-ing: to my wife, both for helping with the indexing and for patiently allowing the atlas to take first place in my thoughts for the last three years; to Mrs. Haldeman, for typing late at night, and on high days and holidays, to enable me to meet successive deadlines; and to the following members of my class on the Middle Eastern world, who gave up a lot of their spare time to helping with the indexing of the maps: Bernard Dale, John Fallat, James Fine, Jeffrey Goldberg, Kevin Horrigan, Edwin Mills, Alexander Yearley.

DENIS BALY
*Kenyon College, March 1969*

# PROBLEMS OF NOMENCLATURE

Nomenclature is a matter on which, unfortunately, great offense may inadvertently be given. First, there is the question of spelling, to which, it must be frankly admitted, there is no entirely satisfactory solution. For biblical names, the Revised Standard Version of the Bible has been our authority. For Arabic and Persian names, where there is the problem of an entirely dif-ferent script, it was decided to adopt a simplified trans-literation that would convey to the uninstructed reader some idea of the correct pronunciation with a mini-mum use of diacritical marks, which many tend to find confusing. We would have preferred, of course, to make a full use of such diacritical marks, but we felt that they would hinder the use of this atlas by the general public. Turkish, however, now uses the Latin script, and so for Turkish words the Turkish spelling has been adopted, even though this involves the use of one or two letters unfamiliar to those who know only English. For the regions now within the U.S.S.R. and elsewhere, the new edition of *The Times Atlas* has been our guide. This unfortunately results in our having to write "Kızıl Irmak" in Turkey and "Kyzyl Kum" in Russian Central Asia, but this could not be avoided. It seemed better to use the spelling that would enable the reader to find the places mentioned on other standard atlases as well.

The second problem is that quite a number of geo-graphical names have become in the Middle East a matter of acute political controversy. We have tried, as far as we possibly can, to avoid the use of such words, and have chosen, for instance, to call the eastern moun-tain region of Turkey the "Urartu Region" instead of the "Armenian Region," as it is more familiarly known to geographers. However, the use of the name "Ar-menia" as a province of the Persian Empire and later a kingdom cannot be avoided, nor, of course, can the name "Israel" be avoided in any biblical atlas. There-fore, to prevent all possible misunderstanding on this matter, it is necessary to state clearly that this is a historical atlas, and that such politically "hot" names are used only in a historical sense. *They are never used in a modern political sense at all, and should not be understood as expressing any political opinion today.*

1. Royal hunt in Persia. *This carving at Taq-i-Bustan, near Kermanshah, is Sassanid, and therefore post-biblical, but it shows well the stags being herded into the enclosure for a royal hunt. Wild animals were far more common in biblical times than they are now, and these royal hunts symbolized the triumph of order over disorder. Josephus tells us that Herod the Great once killed forty animals in one day.*

# ARCHAEOLOGY AND ANCIENT ENVIRONMENTS

## Chapter One

Whatever success man has had in modifying and adapting to his own desires the physical world in which he lives, he is not—and never has been—completely the master. At most, he has been able to achieve a compromise between the Eden he has fervently wished for and the hard facts of life. The reason is not simply a matter of means, that is, of possessing the tools and techniques by which his environment can be manipulated. It is, rather, a matter of imagination, of fulfilling a recognized need, of discerning a potential advantage to himself, of weighing the benefits against the cost, and of exerting the energy and the capital (his own or his community's) to achieve the desired end. In the past, control of the environment was often fitful, stultified by the lack of adequate tools, sporadic as need or desire rose and fell, and often frustrated by the unexpected results of interference in the processes of nature. It is the same today, as man for the first time begins to exploit the age-old resources of the Sahara, the Arctic, and the oceans. We may generalize and say that the measure of man's advance towards civilization has been largely the amount of control he has exercised over his environment.

The archaeologist, as a student of the human past, must therefore have a clear understanding of the world in which man lived. The further he pushes back into the history of mankind, the more necessary such understanding becomes. In prehistoric times, man's choices of food and shelter, tools and weapons, clothing and adornment, even of fears and hopes, were largely determined by the natural conditions in which he found himself. But even after he had built cities and founded nations, when his very visible achievements appeared to proclaim his growing mastery of nature, he was still capitalizing on the physical advantages and minimizing the disadvantages of the particular area or location in which he found himself. He built his home and his city where there was water (from rainfall, lake, or stream) and adequate food (wild or domesticated); his roads and bridges allowed him to follow only more easily the valleys and easy passageways already provided by nature through otherwise impassable ranges of mountains or dry desert; his mines and dams existed only where the earth's crust, in its configurations and content, provided resources which he could harness.

The archaeologist must therefore learn from the natural scientists, the topographers, the climatologists, and many other specialists the ancient environmental conditions of the region in which he is working. As a matter of fact, the answer to the question perennially asked of archaeologists—"How do you know where to dig?"—can often be most easily framed in terms of ancient topography and environment. Assuming that many of the natural features existing today also characterized the ancient landscape, the archaeologist may seek that combination of natural phenomena which would encourage man's early settlement in a certain area or his later building of an important city. Were there wild cereals or animals which could have been domesticated? Were there a good water supply and raw materials from which tools and weapons could be made? Or, if the archaeologist is interested in discovering an ancient center of commercial, diplomatic, military, or cultural importance, he will study the natural physical factors which would favor trade and intercourse,

1

whether they be local sources of wealth (rich farms or grazing lands, minerals, and other natural resources) or good communications (streams, passes, and roads giving access to other cities and sources of raw materials).

Having narrowed down his field to a few important possibilities, he will then study carefully the remains—mainly pottery—of the various settlements in the immediate area, to discover which of them was active in the period for which he seeks information. His excavations can then confirm his choice (or lead him to make an attempt elsewhere) and produce the evidence he desires.[1]

But if the archaeologist must be a student of ancient topography and environment, he is also a teacher. Landscapes may have altered in many ways over the centuries, especially if man has been present in them. The archaeologist, in fact, in his study of ancient man is really deriving his information about him in large part from his artifacts—his handiwork—and these consist in large part of his efforts to modify the world about him. As we study the works of his hands we can infer much about the unmodified natural environmental factors of that district. The Palestinian hill country is pockmarked with rock-cut cisterns; these reflect directly the fact that this region in past ages—as still today—was not well provided with springs or dependable streams. To live there, man had to learn to conserve the winter rains for the long dry summer. The great terraces which today climb the slopes of many of the hills in the lands of the eastern Mediterranean have not only required much outlay of energy and time for their creation and maintenance; they have also changed the contours of the hillsides and halted or delayed the erosion that would otherwise have taken place. The demonstrable fact that they (and other moisture and soil-retaining structures) have existed for many centuries is direct evident for ancient erosion, with all its implications for ancient forest cover (or lack of it), amount of rainfall, and the local flora and fauna. Such deductions permit a reconstruction of the ancient physical setting.

A good example of this is tree cover. In Palestine and Trans-Jordan today there are only sporadic patches of forest, even though modern governments have been attempting to reforest the slopes of dry hills to conserve moisture by checking runoff, and thus also to control erosion. The Bible, however, refers to forests in the hill country of central Palestine (e.g., I Sam. 14:25–26) and of Trans-Jordan (II Sam. 18:6,8) and to the jungle of the Jordan (Jer. 12:5; 49:19; Zech. 11:3); the impression is that these districts were more wooded than they are today (Josh. 17:15–18). There is little doubt that man is partly responsible for this deforestation. He used wood for building material and for fuel (for cooking, heating, firing of pottery, smelting and working of metals), and cleared original forest cover to obtain fields on which he could plant food crops. His goats would destroy young trees and prevent natural reforestation. His taxation systems and other economic programs may have discouraged the planting of trees.

The process of deforestation is sometimes vividly illustrated by archaeology. The upper parts of tombs of the first half of the third millennium B.C. and earlier at Jericho have been eroded completely away—a direct result, it appears, of the destruction of the trees in the region, which allowed the winter rains and winds to scour away topsoil and soft, chalky subsoil unimpeded.[2] The deforestation of this part of the Jordan Valley seems to have taken place between 2600 and 2300 B.C. In the hill country, the process took much longer. As we have already seen, there is literary evidence that this region was still wooded when the Israelites first began to settle it, and excavations indicate that before this time there was wood for building—at least for wooden posts to support roofs that were also partly constructed of wood. When Solomon required large quantities of cedar for his building projects, however, he had to make arrangements with Hiram of Tyre and send work gangs to the Lebanon to cut it (I Kings 5:1–14). While, in this particular case, the use of cedar may have been an indication of Solomon's exotic tastes and the preference of his Phoenician architects, it is a fact that under the monarchy stone piers replaced wooden posts for supporting roofs, a practice which may suggest a serious shortage of timber.

Not only the amount of wood available for man's use but also the types of wood reflect changes in climate or other environmental conditions. The charred wood in the late eleventh century B.C. destruction of Tell el-Ful (most probably the site of Gibeah of Saul) included cypress and pine, while the wood used in the reconstruction of the eighth century was almond. Pre-

---

[1] See, for instance, Sir Leonard Woolley, *A Forgotten Kingdom* (London: Penguin, 1953). pp. 1–23.

[2] Kathleen M. Kenyon, *Archaeology in the Holy Land* (London: Ernst Benn, 1960), p. 130 ff.

sumably, the coniferous forests of the earlier period vanished during the following three centuries. Even where the wood itself has not been preserved—or is in too poor a condition for analysis—pollen can provide many of the answers. It is very resistant to decay, and, when it is found in samples of soil taken from strata of known date and is analyzed, it can add much to our knowledge of the variations, from place to place and from time to time, in vegetation cover, a knowledge which in turn can be interpreted in climatic and general environmental terms.

Animal bones can provide similar evidence. The excavations of the caves of Mount Carmel, in addition to documenting the early history of man in Palestine over many thousands of years, produced faunal remains which demonstrate changes in climate—rhinoceros and hippopotamus reflecting a warm and damp climate, gazelle a dry period.

Food grains and animal bones can be studied and identified, and the proportions of wild and domesticated varieties worked out. Such research can lead not only to a broader understanding of the processes of domestication but also to the identification of the natural flora and fauna of a region at a particular period. It is fortunate that Near Eastern archaeologists have begun to collect, in a far more systematic fashion than formerly, samples of soils, bone and plant fragments and the like, and even to engage as part of their regular or occasional staff palaeoecologists, whose special skills at analysis and interpretation of such materials can throw so much light on the physical milieu in which man built up his cultures in various regions at different times.

The improvement of excavation techniques and the availability of new chemicals which can preserve in the field very fragmentary and perishable remains have both contributed greatly to the new flow of information. A good example of this is the recognition and preservation of woven material—basketry, matting, and textiles. Although, in many cases, the organic substances may long since have disappeared, their imprint on the soil about them can reveal the methods and patterns used by the ancient craftsman and, in many cases, the materials he used. The knowledge of the source of the fibers, once more, can suggest the environment in which he was working. Reeds and rushes imply water in some abundance—in backwaters or marshes of perennial streams—for both growth and working. If the textile is linen (from flax), again there is evidence of plentiful water, not only for the cultivation but also for the separation of the fibers from their

pulpy stems. If the yarn is wool, identifiable as from sheep, goat, or camel, there is a clear reflection of the climatic conditions which would favor such animals.

Man early learned to exploit the rock beneath his feet. His cutting and quarrying operations are evident in many places, and he obviously learned quickly which types of stone were most useful for his purposes. Clayey mud was used for bricks; purer, cleaned clay was manufactured into pottery. He learned to make plaster for surfacing his floors or for lining his cisterns in order to make them watertight. Beautiful pebbles early attracted him as ornaments for his person. Later, malleable materials such as copper or lead could be cold-worked for the same purpose. The development of metallurgy and the manufacture of tools and weapons, harness fittings, receptacles, ritual equipment, and the like created a tremendous demand not only for raw materials but also for the skills which could convert them into useful and beautiful objects. Archaeology can document the processes of manufacture and, most importantly for geographical studies, indicate some of the sources of the raw materials. The study of the ancient copper mines and refineries of the Arabah south of the Dead Sea has a direct bearing on the study of the geology of the region, and can provide a picture of an ancient terrain in which outcroppings of copper or the green dye of its oxides marked the hillsides. Such resources afforded valuable trade goods which could be exchanged by the local inhabitants for other desired products from abroad. The salts and bitumen of the Dead Sea and the turquoise from Mount Sinai are other examples of valuable products which gave an economic importance to areas otherwise desolate and sterile. Exotic materials—that is, materials not native to the districts where they have been found, such as obsidian, malachite, ivory, or certain types of shell—document ancient trade routes and, indirectly, the economic geography of the ancient world.

Negative evidence from archaeological excavations is also at hand, although not always easy to interpret or evaluate. If a city which prospered in the past because of an adequate water supply, proximity to trade routes and good fields, and possession of a strong defensive site suddenly ceases to be occupied, there must be a reason. Sometimes, it is not difficult to see what happened. Earthquakes could wreak havoc; it is probable that the first period of the Essene monastery at Qumran came to an end because of the earthquake which occurred in the spring of 31 B.C. Certainly, the evidences of great cracks in baths and cisterns and the subsequent abandonment for a generation would point in this direction. Enemy action, too, could destroy a city. However, after both natural disaster or human destruction, the innate advantages of the site would probably lead to its rebuilding and reoccupation very quickly. But what if, for no obvious cause, a good site is abandoned, perhaps for centuries? The reason, again, may be economic or political. The great entrepôts of Petra and Palmyra or the trade cities of the Negeb survived only while the trade routes provided the conditions for their prosperity. Political considerations could mean the disappearance or, at least, the descent into obscurity of an earlier capital or administrative center. In such cases, archaeology can document the fact of a break in occupation, but this fact will have no necessary implications for topographic or environmental change. The reason for the break may not be local but a result of the impingement of foreign political or economic factors and decisions on the local situation.

But there are other occupational lacunae which appear inexplicable, and, recently, several new answers have been suggested. One such break in occupation occurs at Tel el-Far'ah, the site of Tirzah, capital of Israel under Baasha and Omri before Samaria was built (I Kings 15:33; 16:23–24). This city occupied an easily defended hill in a rich countryside plentifully supplied with water. Why then should it reveal a seven-century gap in occupation, beginning about 2600 B.C., when other towns were flourishing? It has been suggested that the water, which still spreads out in shallow flats, became a breeding ground for the anopheles mosquito and produced malaria in the district. Why should Jericho, so old, so rich, and so well-endowed with water and food, suddenly cease to be of importance about 1350 B.C.? Its destruction, by the Israelites or other enemies, cannot explain why it was not immediately reborn to another period of flourishing activity. It has recently been suggested that a slight shifting of subterranean rock layers may have directed into the great spring radioactive water, whose mysterious results in producing sterility could only be interpreted as the working of a curse (Josh. 6:26; I Kings 16:34; II Kings 2:19–22). This hypothesis might well have been tested during the excavations, if anyone had thought of it. Human bones in the tombs might have betrayed the radioactivity. Samples of soil might have revealed its presence or absence, but such samples would have to be selective if they were to tell the true story—for example, they would have to be taken from levels occupied immediately before the break in occupation. If it could be proved that malaria in one case and radioactivity in the other were the reasons for breaks in

occupation at these sites, such evidence would have important implications for our understanding of the ancient physical environment.

Similarly, the remarkable preservation of perishable materials, such as wood, textiles and matting, flesh, and so on in the Middle Bronze Age tombs at Jericho has suggested that hydrocarbon gases percolated into the tombs and inhibited decay. The position of Jericho in the Great Rift Valley makes such a hypothesis worthy of serious consideration, and, if it can be demonstrated, such effluvia from subterranean depths may have produced other effects on the natural environment of the Jordan Valley which have not yet been considered.

Already, the study of human bones and teeth from ancient tombs has shown that the early population of Palestine suffered from many of the diseases we know today, such as rheumatism, osteitis (possibly the result of leprosy, syphilis, yaws, or tuberculosis), and dental caries. So far, however, it has not been possible to produce clear evidence of the types of epidemics that probably decimated the population from time to time. One may suspect, when tombs are found with many burials made apparently at the same time and without evidence of bodily injury, that such epidemics have occurred but unless the diseases attacked and left traces of their attack on teeth and bones (normally the only parts of the body preserved), archaeology cannot at present do more than guess at the identity of the disease. Likewise, the environmental factors which might have facilitated the rapid spread of such diseases must remain unspecified.

It is obvious that the potential of archaeology for defining local, and peculiar, ancient environments has hardly been touched. It is probable that, in the future, archaeologists will take far more samples of soils, ash, the air in tombs, the bricks and mortar of buildings, the plaster or beaten earth of floors, the stains left in receptacles, and many others—samples which scientists will analyze and from which they will derive information of kinds that are at present unimagined and that have a bearing not only on our understanding of man's life at far-off periods but also of the world in which he lived.

Such archaeological evidence as we have described has often only a rather indirect bearing on our comprehension of the environments in which early man lived, and its full relevance may be seen only in years to come. But there is one aspect of ancient topography where archaeology provides first-hand evidence: the identification of ancient sites, ancient roads, springs, and other natural or man-made phenomena.

The Bible contains hundreds of place names. For many of them, there is no problem of identification. Jerusalem, Bethlehem, and the Jordan River pose no problems. The Old Testament "Sea of Salt" or "Sea of Arabah" is easily identified with the Dead Sea. Amman has reverted to its ancient name (Rabbath Ammon) after a period under its Greek name of Philadelphia. Samaria is better known locally today as Sebastia, the name given to it by Herod the Great in honor of the Emperor Augustus (Greek *Sebastos*). The Sea of Galilee (John 6:1) has had many names: Chinnereth (Num. 34:11), Gennesaret (I Macc. 11:67; Luke 5:1), Tiberias (John 6:1; 21:1), but there is no room for confusion.

The names of some biblical places are only slightly concealed under the modern Arabic forms. Dibon, capital of Moab, is today Dhiban; Hebron is al-Khalil, "the Friend" (of God), i.e., Abraham; Bethel is Beitin; Bethany is al-'Azariyeh, probably a corruption of the name of Lazarus; Gibeon is al-Jib; Gerasa is Jerash; Gezer is Tell Jezer.

Other names, however, do not so easily allow of identification, and, in some cases, one can be led astray by apparent likenesses of ancient and modern nomenclatures. Where was Megiddo situated, Lachish, Kiriath-sepher, Gibeah of Saul, Mizpah, Shechem, Ai, Gihon, Capernaum, Gadara, Bethphage? These are all places that played a more or less prominent role in the biblical story, but no modern place names provide a clue to their whereabouts.

The solution to such problems must depend on a two-pronged approach—one documentary, one archaeological. Every text referring to an unknown location must be perused very carefully to reduce every possible clue as to its whereabouts. Was it on a road between two other known places? If so, are any distances given? Did it function as a border post? If so, where and at what period? Was it on the line of march of an invader, was it a center of some manufacturing enterprise, did some event take place there which provides a hint as to its location and the time when it was occupied?

It is probable that such information will give a strong indication that the place in question was situated within a rather circumscribed area. The archaeologist must now search carefully within this area, seeking a site, perhaps no longer occupied, which fits all the information at his disposal. He may find several possi-bilities. A more intensive study of the remains on the surface, particularly of the pottery sherds scattered about, will give him a strong indication of the periods at which each site was occupied. He may, at least tentatively, eliminate those sites which were not occupied at the time when the documents indicate that the city or town he seeks was inhabited. Finally, only careful excavation can answer the question—and then, perhaps, not definitely. He may discover that the site excavated fulfills all the requirements of location and occupational history, and he may then say that there is high probability that he has identified the site of the ancient town. Absolute proof can come only from the discovery of written records—perhaps nothing more than seal impressions with the town's name, ostraca (writing in ink on a potsherd), or the like. Unfortunately, Palestine has preserved few written records of the past in its soil,[3] and we are left, in most cases, with a degree of probability, greater or less, for the identification of an ancient site with a ruin existing today.

However, even the "almost certain" identification of ancient place names permits a reconstruction of the political and economic geography of past ages. We can identify the routes of travel and trade, of cultural diffusion and conquest, which were in use at different periods; we can trace the boundaries of tribal districts, of independent states and imperial provinces; we can understand why certain towns flourished in one period and declined in another. Such information will, most commonly, document and illustrate the activity and decisions of men rather than the features of the natural environment; but, where our knowledge of the past does not permit us to explain such facts on political or economic grounds alone, it may be possible to predicate environmental causal factors. But in itself, the very ability to locate on a map the sites of ancient settlements and named natural features is a contribution to historical topography.

It is probable that the contribution of archaeology to an understanding of ancient topographical and other environmental features will become greater as the excavators realize the importance of the evidence that they can produce and as professional geographers recognize the manner in which archaeology can not only discover but also date the changes which a landscape in all its aspects can undergo over the millennia.

---

[3] The scrolls and other documents on parchment or papyrus found in caves near the Dead Sea and elsewhere since 1948 are an important exception to this general rule, but the rule still holds. One would have expected to find, at least in Jerusalem and Samaria, inscribed stelae, archives, and other such materials, but they are conspicuously lacking.

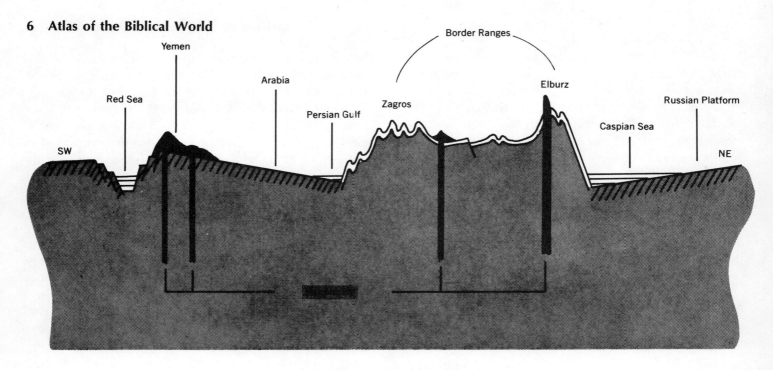

**The structure of the Middle East.** This is a generalized diagram and is not drawn to scale.

# STRUCTURAL ELEMENTS OF THE MIDDLE EAST

## Map 1

There are three types of mountains in the Middle East: *folded mountains, block mountains,* and *volcanic mountains.*

**Folded mountains** are what their name implies, mountain ranges created by the folding and compressing of the relatively soft sedimentary rocks as the result of extreme lateral pressure. The great mountain ranges of the world are mainly of this character. The exact causes of their formation are not known, but the generally accepted theory is that there are two vast blocks of very ancient, very hard rocks (or *horsts)* separated by a great trough (or *geosyncline),* into which sediment from the two horsts was washed down over the space of millions of years. In the Middle East, the northern horst was the Siberian shield, underlying the great plains of Russia and western Siberia, and the southern horst was the Afro-Arabian shield, which today forms almost the whole of Africa and Arabia. Between them lay the great trough of Tethys, whose remnants may be seen in the Mediterranean, Black Sea, Caspian,

and Persian Gulf. For some undetermined reason the two horsts moved toward each other, and the sediments formed in the trough between them were compressed and folded up, very much as a thick carpet is folded if pressure is applied from the two sides. Great blocks of more ancient material, which were more resistant to folding, were often carried up with the folding.

**Block mountains.** The pressures of the orogeny, or mountain-building, were so gigantic that the shields themselves, resistant though they were, were tilted and even bent, and when the pressure became too great they cracked and broke. Sometimes the shattered blocks were pushed upwards between parallel cracks or faults to form block mountains, and elsewhere they dropped downwards to form rift valleys. Such mountains differ from folded mountains in that they are usually not so high, and they tend to have relatively level, plateaulike tops. Block mountains and rift valleys characterize the Arabian peninsula and northeast Africa, especially along the Red Sea region.

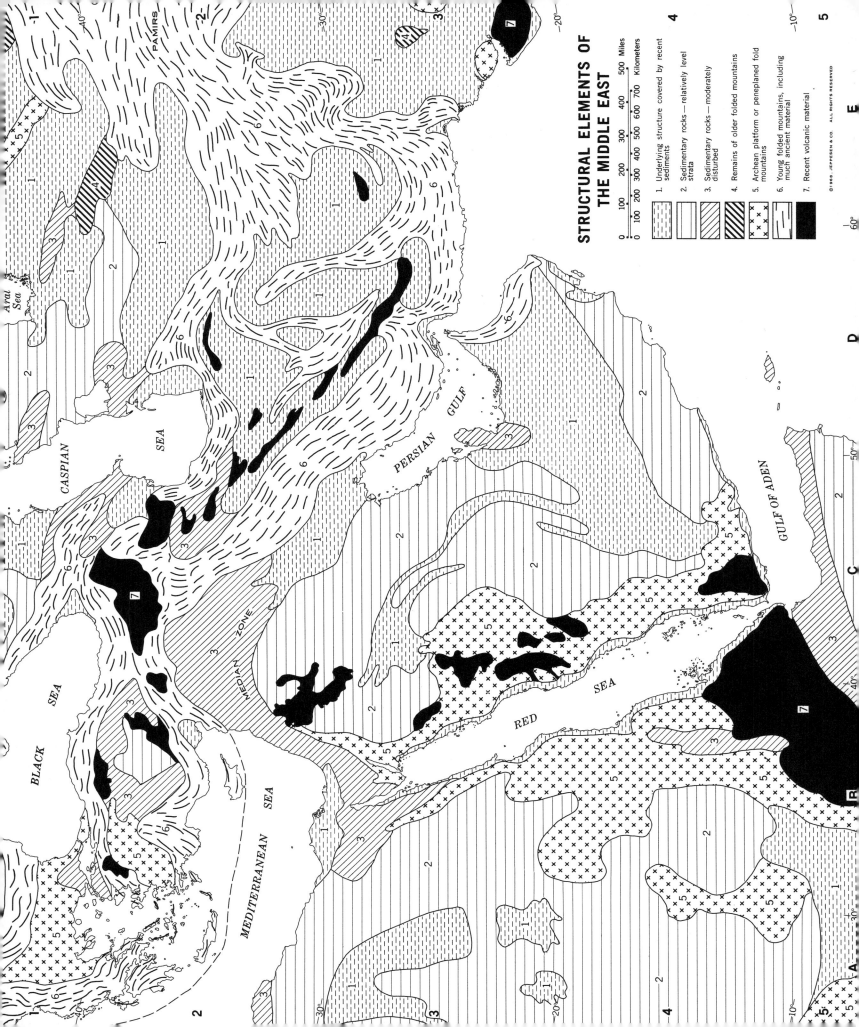

# STRUCTURAL ELEMENTS OF THE MIDDLE EAST

1. Underlying structure covered by recent sediments
2. Sedimentary rocks — relatively level strata
3. Sedimentary rocks — moderately disturbed
4. Remains of older folded mountains
5. Archean platform or peneplaned fold mountains
6. Young folded mountains, including much ancient material
7. Recent volcanic material

500 Miles
100 200 300 400 500 600 700 Kilometers

ARAL Sea

CASPIAN SEA

BLACK SEA

MEDITERRANEAN SEA

PERSIAN GULF

RED SEA

GULF OF ADEN

PAMIRS

MEDIAN ZONE

**Volcanic mountains** may be associated with either of the two former, where material from deep down in the earth was pushed up through the cracks made during the orogeny. Sometimes the lava has flowed out over enormous areas, and sometimes there have developed the towering, conical mountains which one normally thinks of as volcanoes (Plates V, 14).

Orogenic activity in the Middle East is not yet finished. Earthquakes occur, especially in northern and eastern Turkey and western Persia, where they can be exceedingly severe. In the Palestine and Syrian region of the Levant coast they are less frequent, and normally less severe, but about once every thirty or forty years they can be disastrous. The volcanoes are all believed to be extinct, though this is not absolutely certain, but they were certainly active in Arabia in medieval times, and the last eruption of Mount Ararat in northeastern Turkey was on June 20, 1840. Hot springs are frequent in many parts of the Middle East.

The pattern of the Middle East structure is somewhat as shown in the accompanying diagram. In the north central section of this map are the great folded ranges. These tend to form a double line with between them a high, greatly disturbed plateau, formed of a block of more ancient material, though covered by more recent sediments. The two border ranges twice come together: in the high Urartu region between Turkey and Persia, where there has been much volcanicity, and again in the even higher Pamir mountain knot in the extreme east, the so-called "roof of the world."

The intermontane plateaus are far from simple. In both there are extensive lava flows, and the Persian plateau is interrupted by tilted block mountains and hills, as well as by transverse folded ranges.

On either side of the folded mountain region is a trough, occupied in the north by the Black Sea, the Caspian Sea, and the Aral Sea, and in the south by the Mediterranean and the Persian Gulf. Four out of five of the great river systems, the Tigris and Euphrates, the Indus, the Amu Darya (Oxus) and Syr Darya (Jaxartes), flow in these troughs. Only the Nile is different, since it follows what are apparently cracks in the African plateau.

The region of the Levant coast and the Mesopotamian trough has been called by W. B. Fisher the Median Zone. This is a region where the rigid underlying platform has prevented true folding, but where the effect of the orogeny has been felt in the rippling of the sediments which lie on top of the platform. The hills and mountains are seldom high, just topping 10,000 feet in the Lebanon though usually lower, and they tend to parallel the line of the high, folded ranges north and east of them. The determinative factor seems to be faulting, and so these are essentially block mountains, outlined by faults, but with folded sediments on top of them.

The Afro-Arabian platform is in this region largely covered by later sediments. It is broken by the gigantic rift of the Red Sea and by the Gulf of Aden rift, which joins the Red Sea at right angles. These form only one section of the enormous rift valley system which extends from the borders of Turkey, through Lebanon and Palestine, and continues into the highly complicated lake region of East Africa. The highest parts of the platform are the two sides of the Red Sea, where the fault scarps drop precipitously into the sea. They reach their greatest height in Abyssinia and southwest Arabia, where there has been tremendous volcanic activity.

## GEOLOGY OF THE LEVANT SIMPLIFIED

*Map 2*

In principle, the geological history of the Levant is fairly simple. For millions of years the region formed the coast of the great continental block of Afro-Arabia, with the shoreline, very roughly speaking, more or less about where it is at present. This did not, however, remain constant, for there was a slow process of uplift and depression, whereby the edge of the continent was sometimes lowered beneath the waters of the sea and sometimes raised above them. During the prolonged periods of inundation marine sediments, especially limestone and chalk, were deposited, and during the periods of dry land sandstones were formed, suggesting conditions of a desert character even then.

The very ancient pre-Cambrian platform that formed the Afro-Arabian continent has been exposed in the extreme south of the Levant, on either side of the Gulf of Aqaba, though, as may be seen from Map 1, it is exposed over a very much wider area in Africa and Arabia on the two sides of the Red Sea. It is composed of very ancient, hard, metamorphic rocks, and ancient volcanic material. In the Aqaba region it is mainly granite.

For our purposes, the history of the Levant may be said to begin, millions of years later, with the Jurassic period, during which time most of the Levant was dry land, and immensely thick beds of sandstone were laid down, usually a dark red, though sometimes white, yellow, or purple in color, often known as *Nubian sandstone.* This was laid down on top of earlier limestone, which cannot be shown on a simplified map of this kind but which is exposed in the west of the Lebanon mountains and in the canyons that cleave the edge of the Trans-Jordanian plateau. The sandstone is widely exposed in the extreme south of the Levant and along the edge of the Trans-Jordan plateau, especially along the edge of the Wadi Arabah in the south, and the east of the Dead Sea, as well as in the lower Jabbok Valley. It is in this

rock that occur the old copper mines of the Arabah, at Punon (Feinan) and elsewhere. It is exposed also in the Lebanon and Anti-Lebanon, and in the Nuseiriyeh Mountains to the north of the Lebanon. On the seaward side of the Lebanon it carries the characteristic umbrella pine, which is normally found on the sandy soils of the coast.

With the following period, the Cretaceous, there began an extensive invasion of the land by the sea, which reached its greatest extent in the Upper Cretaceous, and the Eocene period which followed. During the Middle Cretaceous was formed the massive *Cenomanian limestone,* whose steep cliffs and deep gorges are such a striking feature of much of the Levant. This rock forms the heart of the Judean region, and of Ephraim to the north of it, where its tendency to stand up in forbidding cliffs greatly aided the defense of the hill country. It also forms much of Gilead and the headland of Carmel. Farther north it is typical of parts of Galilee, of very much of the Lebanon and Anti-Lebanon, and of the difficult western slopes of the Nuseiriyeh Mountains. In the hills that splay out northeastward from the Anti-Lebanon this limestone is exposed by erosion in the middle of the anticlines or upfolds.

The Cenomanian limestone forms admirable building stone, and is widely used for this purpose. Indeed, the traditional method of building a house in Palestine was to quarry the stone on the spot, and then plaster the quarry, and use it for a cistern in which the rainwater was collected. In regions of adequate rainfall it breaks down into a rich *terra rossa,* of a reddish chocolate color, which is admirably suited to the growing of olives. It is certain that in these regions must have been the thickest woods and forests of the mountains before and during the biblical period, growing even as far south as the plateau edge of Edom, where they persisted until World War I.

The Upper Cretaceous was the period of the *Senonian chalk.* This is a soft

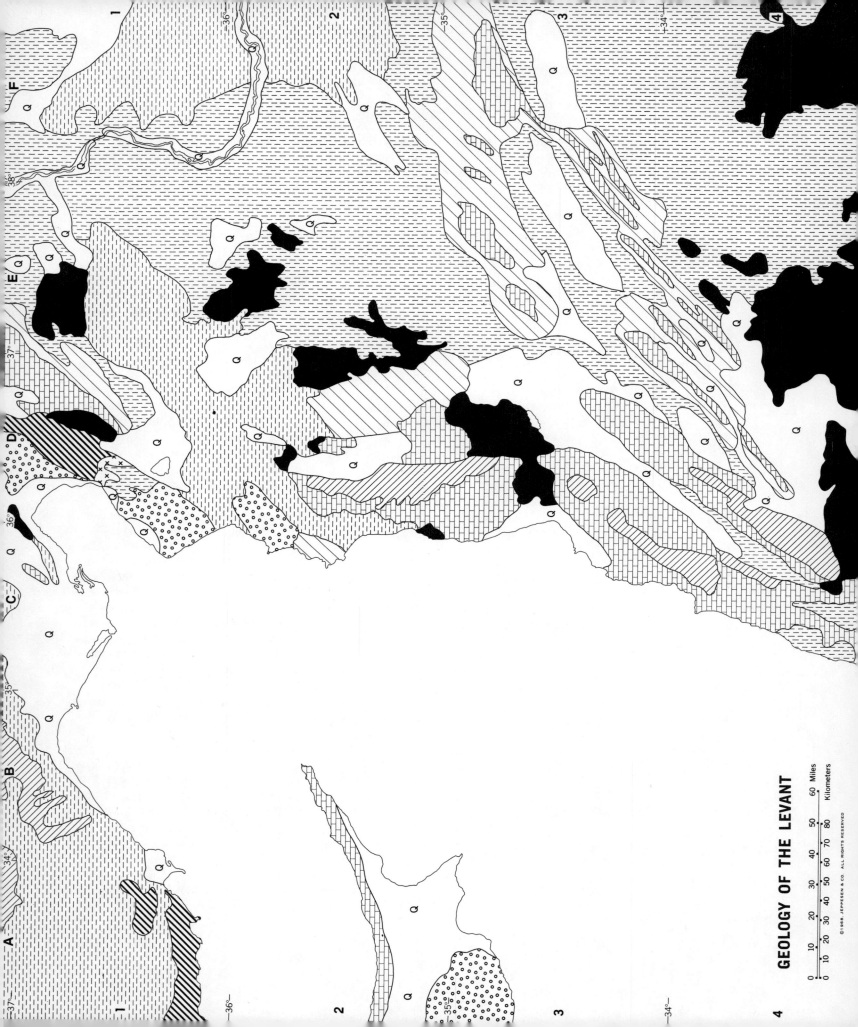

# GEOLOGY OF THE LEVANT

0   10   20   30   40   50   60 Miles

0   10   20   30   40   50   60   70   80 Kilometers

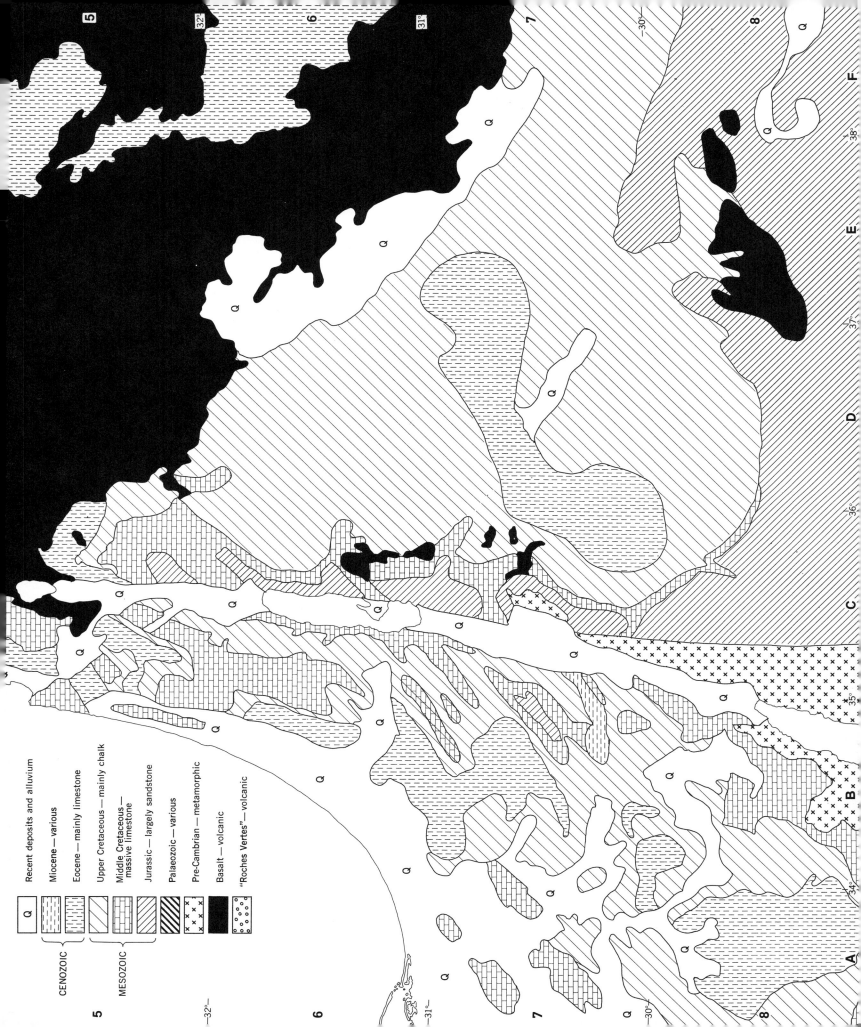

Recent deposits and alluvium

CENOZOIC
Miocene — various
Eocene — mainly limestone

MESOZOIC
Upper Cretaceous — mainly chalk
Middle Cretaceous — massive limestone
Jurassic — largely sandstone

Palaeozoic — various

Pre-Cambrian — metamorphic

Basalt — volcanic

"Roches Vertes" — volcanic

and an extremely porous rock, which is easily eroded and forms a poor and infertile soil. The characteristic landform is that of rounded hills. It is the combination of the porous chalk with the drought of the lee slopes that has produced the desolate Wilderness of Jeshimon, which protects Judah on the east. West of the Jordan it forms a narrow belt between the Cenomanian limestone and the Eocene limestone above it. When exposed, its soft nature led to rapid erosion, and along these valleys, which were unimpeded by rocks or dense vegetation, lay many of the important roads of Palestine. A narrow moat of chalk formed the western defense of Judah, but the penetration of Manasseh by chalk valleys was the reason for its vulnerability. On the Trans-Jordanian plateau, where the Senonian forms the major surface rock, it contains a large amount of flint or chert, which under conditions of desert erosion form a dense carpet of sharp, flinty pebbles. Hence the name Ardh es-Suwān, or flint country, for the area

west of the Wadi Sirhan. This was an important source of flint for tools and weapons before the introduction of metals.

The Eocene sea was fairly short-lived over most of the region, since the slow process of upward pressure which produced the great fold mountains of the north had already begun, and in fact the sea apparently invaded different parts of the Levant at different times during the Eocene period. The characteristic rock is a poor quality limestone, of much less value for building than the Cenomanian, and producing an inferior soil, unattractive for agriculture. The forests of the Eocene would have been generally a thick scrub, difficult to penetrate but of little value for lumber.

The gradual upwarping which was the beginning of the orogenic activity had already begun at the end of the Senonian, but it reached its maximum during the Miocene, and in the Pliocene which followed. Parts of northern Syria and southern Turkey were still under

water during the Miocene, and also the coast plain south of Mount Carmel. The *Mousterian red sand*, so valuable for the Palestinian citrus groves today, belongs to the Miocene period, but in biblical times it was little used.

Through the cracks in the earth's surface created by the intense pressure poured out molten basalt, to form the great lava flows of the plateau, which have in places dammed the rivers. The Lake of Galilee and Lake Huleh on the Jordan, and the Lake of Homs on the Orontes have all been formed by basalt dams. There are no lofty volcanoes in the Levant, though many low volcanic cones, of which the highest are in the Jebel Druze region.

The recent deposits of the Quaternary period are still being formed, both the alluvial deposits at the mouths of rivers along the coast and the desert deposits. These are partly mud flats formed by the washing down of the loose desert soil in the rare winter storms, and partly wind-borne loess.

# *Map 3* THE LEVANT RIFT VALLEY SYSTEM

The geological event which more than any other has determined the shape of Palestine and the Levant as we see them today was the shattering of the Afro-Arabian platform as a result of the tremendous orogenic pressures and tensions that produced the towering fold mountains of the Taurus and Zagros. A part of these fold mountains is to be seen in the north of this map, not only in the Taurus Mountains of Turkey, but also in the Amanus and Cassius ranges, which run out into the Kyrenia and Troodos mountains of Cyprus. South of these fold mountains begins the more rigid platform.

The shattering of this platform affected an area extending all the way from the borders of Turkey to the southern part of East Africa. It may be traced on a world atlas southward from

the Red Sea into Abyssinia, where it is obscured by the great volcanic mountains, through the double rift valley system of East Africa, easily visible, especially in the west, because of the two lines of long narrow lakes which encompass the broad, shallower Lake Victoria.

So vast a fault system is clearly far from simple, and it did not all take place at one time. The pressure seems to have begun to build up during the late Cretaceous period, but reached its maximum in the Miocene and succeeding Pliocene periods. The pressure seems to have come from the west-northwest and east-southeast, squeezing the intervening area into a series of parallel upwarps aligned in a north-northeast—south-southwest direction. With the increase of the pressure, the

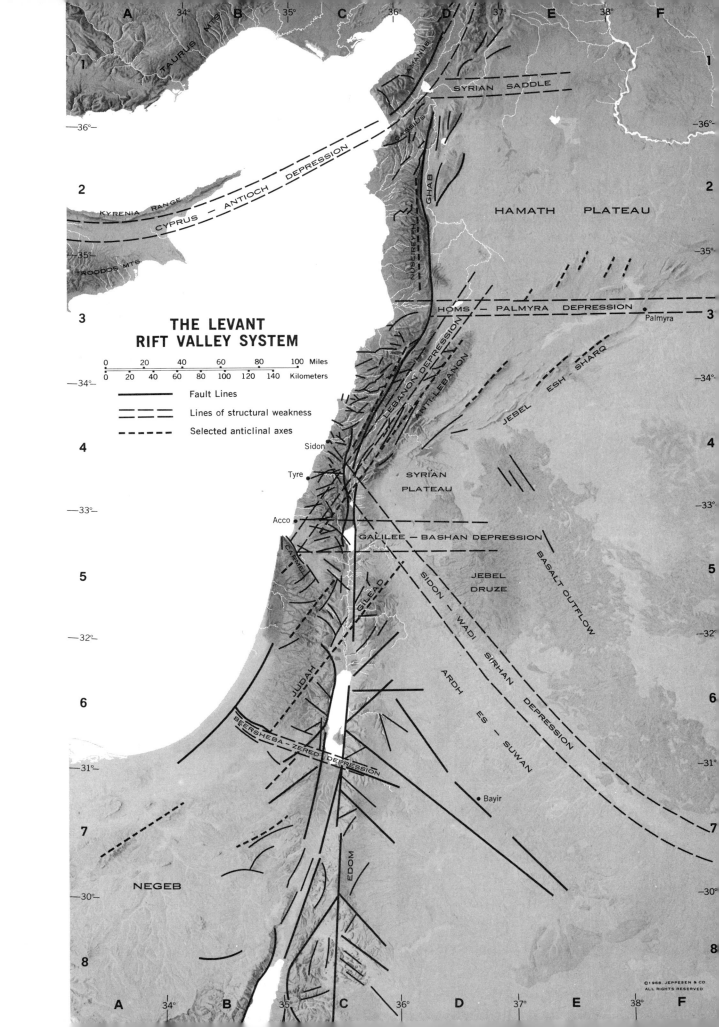

# THE LEVANT
# RIFT VALLEY SYSTEM

0    20    40    60    80    100 Miles
0  20  40  60  80  100  120  140 Kilometers

——————  Fault Lines

—  —  —  —  Lines of structural weakness

– – – – –  Selected anticlinal axes

A · B · C · D · E · F

TAURUS MTS.

KYRENIA RANGE

TROODOS MTS.

CYPRUS – ANTIOCH DEPRESSION

AMANUS

CASSIUS

GHAB

NUSEIREYEH

SYRIAN SADDLE

HAMATH PLATEAU

HOMS — PALMYRA DEPRESSION

Palmyra

LEBANON DEPRESSION

ANTI-LEBANON

JEBEL ESH - SHARQ

Sidon

Tyre

SYRIAN PLATEAU

Acco

GALILEE — BASHAN DEPRESSION

CARMEL

GILEAD

JEBEL DRUZE

SIDON – WADI SIRHAN DEPRESSION

BASALT OUTFLOW

JUDAH

BEERSHEBA - ZERED DEPRESSION

ARDH ES - SUWAN

Bayir

EDOM

NEGEB

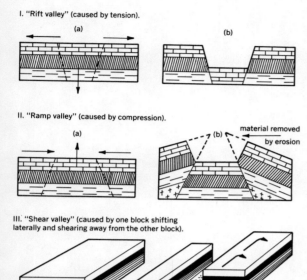

I. "Rift valley" (caused by tension).

(a)                                (b)

II. "Ramp valley" (caused by compression).

(a)                                (b)        material removed
                                             by erosion

III. "Shear valley" (caused by one block shifting laterally and shearing away from the other block).

**Three theories of the formation of the Jordan Rift Valley.**

strain upon the rigid platform became too great, and it broke. This did not happen all at once but over a prolonged period of time. In fact, it has not completely ceased even yet, and new, though fortunately minor, movements have taken place in recent years. Some of the faulting took place parallel to the alignment of the upwarps, i.e. north-northeast–south-southwest, but pressure from the west and east seems also to have been exerted, producing great faults which are aligned almost directly north-south, as in the Jordan Valley and the great Ghab fault of northern Syria. Here, the upwarp of the Nuseiriyeh Mountains is also aligned in a north-south direction.

Other fault lines developed at right angles to the main faults, and there are very evident structural depressions caused by faulting, which run both from West to East and more or less northwest-southeast. Sometimes these make a clear break across the mountains, as with the gap at the northern end of the Lebanon Mountains and in the Acco-Bethshan corridor, and sometimes they have produced merely a

lowering of the mountain ridge, as in the hill country behind Tyre and Sidon. Finally, there are "hinge faults," which curve off from the main rifts, as at the northern and southern ends of the Dead Sea.

There is still considerable argument about the formation of the Jordan Rift, whether it is a true *graben*—i.e., a valley caused by the pulling apart of sections of the block, and the dropping of the central section—or whether it was the result of upward compression, according to the so-called "ramp valley" theory. A more recent theory has argued for horizontal shearing, and the movement of the eastern block some 107 km. (67 mi.) northwards in relation to the western block. This theory has some attractions in the Palestinian area, where some important west-east faults in the western block would be continuous with similar faults in the eastern block, if the eastern block could be shifted 67 miles farther south, but it is difficult to fit it in with the situation farther north, since there is little evidence there of the compression that such a northerly movement must have produced.

However this may be, it is clear that we have today two major structural alignments in the Levant: north-south and north-northeast—south-southwest, with other alignments formed at right angles to these. Some clear zones of structural weakness, running more or less from west to east, divide the Levant into very distinct regions, which have been reflected in its history.

The most marked is the Homs-Palmyra depression, which extends all the way to the Zagros Mountains. On Map 3 it is shown by the line of Quaternary deposits. North of this is the Hamath plateau bordered on the west by the north-south Nuseiriyeh Mountains, with a steep eastern scarp created by the great Ghab fault.

South of the Homs-Palmyra depression the north-northeast—south-southwest alignment is dominant, the central valley between the Lebanon and Anti-

Lebanon being created essentially by a single great fault scarp on the eastern side of the Lebanon Mountains, the steep slopes of the Anti-Lebanon being caused by very sharply titled strata, though with the addition of minor faulting.

Farther south the pattern is more complicated because the two alignments are imposed on each other. The main direction of the upwarping which has produced the Palestinian highlands is north-northeast–south-southwest, as shown by the Judah-Gilead upwarp, with the Ephraim upwarp parallel to it to the northwest. Farther still, the headland of Carmel is really a continuation of the Anti-Lebanon–Galilee upwarp, though outlined by faults at right angles to this.

The great north-south Jordan Rift Valley with associated faults running parallel to it has cut right across this alignment, giving the Palestinian hills their familiar north-south direction.

Additional faultlines at right angles have produced both northwest-southeast and west-east valleys. Examples of the northwest-southeast alignment are the edge of Carmel and the Valley of Jezreel (the Acco-Bethshan corridor), which is continued southeastward in the fault wadi extending toward Bayir on the Trans-Jordanian plateau, and the Sidon–Wadi Sirhan depression. The Wadi Sirhan appears to be a true *graben*, i.e., a rift valley between parallel faults which has been covered with later sediment. It is continued in the line that marks the abrupt southern limit of the high Lebanon and Anti-Lebanon. In this section it is followed today by the Aramco pipeline.

The west-east alignment is evident in the Galilee-Bashan depression, which is imposed on and complicates the Acco-Bethshan corridor. It is responsible for the sudden steep escarpment (the esh-Shaghur fault) that marks the division between Upper and Lower Galilee, and for the basin of the Lake of Galilee, though here it is somewhat obscured by the basalt which has flowed into it.

# Chapter Two

# THE WORLD OF THE BIBLE

The "world" for any ancient people had a variety of meanings. First, it signified their own country, that area where their own laws prevailed and their own gods had the mastery, and it excluded everything that might be considered foreign and exotic, or in some way chaotic and threatening. In Arabic, the word *dunya* may still be used colloquially in this sense today. Second, it could mean for a sedentary people the whole world of agriculture and cities, but excluding the restless tribes of the desert and the mountains, who were thought to be by nature disorderly. Third, it could mean the whole inhabited world. Fourth, it could be all the dry land, everything that was not the heavens or the dread Abyss. In biblical Hebrew *eretz* could have all these meanings.

Something of the same ambivalence haunts us when we try to define in modern terms the "world" of the Bible. In its most restricted sense it is Palestine, or "the Holy Land," but even here the limits are far from clear. This "Holy Land" could be only the land which the Israelites effectively occupied, "from Dan to Beersheba," or it could be extended, as it was by some Israelite spokesmen in their more optimistic moments, to include all the so-called "promised" land, reaching according to some texts as far as the Euphrates in the extreme north and southward to the River of Egypt, the Wadi Ghazzeh entering the sea just south of Gaza (Gen. 15:18), or again it could be all the territory from Tadmor in the wilderness (Palmyra) to Ezion-Geber on the Red Sea, which the kings of Israel brought under their control in the brief moments of military expansion. These various "maps of Israel" have acquired new political significance in the arguments which rage about the existence and extent of the modern state of that name, and the arguments themselves illustrate how difficult it is to define the biblical Palestine. Probably, in popular usage, for most people "the Land of the Bible" would signify the settled regions on both sides of the Great Rift Valley of the Jordan and the Dead Sea, somewhat generally envisaged, with the northern limits at Damascus and Sidon, and the southern boundary at Beersheba, with an extension for the purposes of the Exodus story into the peninsula of Sinai.

There is no doubt, of course, that it was somewhere within these limits that the greater number of the biblical events took place, and this kind of concept of the land of the Bible is not unreasonable. Yet it is misleading, and to use Palestine as the starting point, as the *essential* land in relation to which the other lands are studied, is a serious mistake. If, in other words, our concept of biblical geography is that the lands outside Palestine have relevance only insofar as they have had an impact upon Palestinian history and thought, we shall see things out of perspective, and shall actually misunderstand this impact, which will lead us to misunderstand much of the Bible. If, because of either convenience or custom, we envisage Egypt, or Babylon, or Assyria as geographically marginal to the biblical world, we shall fail to grasp that these countries were not in the least marginal to biblical thinking, but loomed instead extraordinarily large. How could it be otherwise, when their armies marched and countermarched across the land?

It is easy enough to say that Palestine is no larger than the state of Vermont or the country of Wales, and book after book has used this illustration, but this does

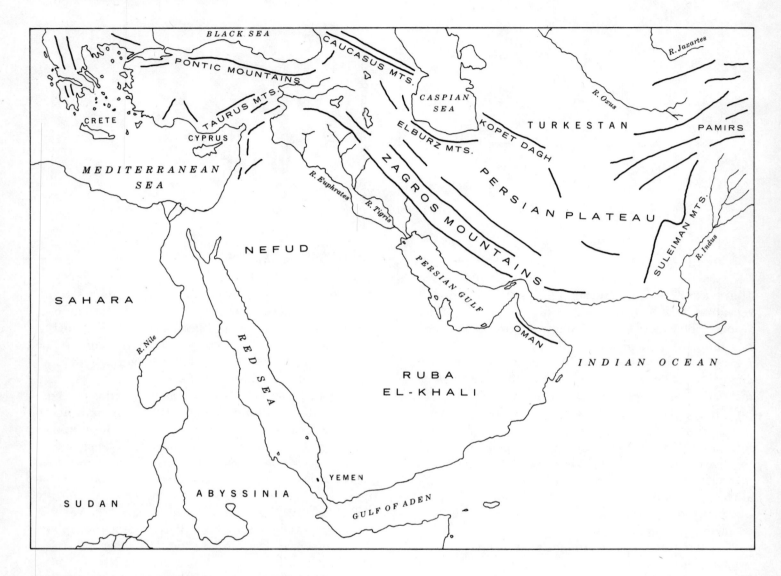

not help us to understand what it felt like to live in Samaria or Jerusalem, or perhaps in a little village like Tekoa or Ziklag. It throws no light upon the difficulties, possibilities, and frustrations of that situation, upon the political straits to which the governments were reduced whenever kings went forth to war, or the terrifying significance to Judah of the report that "Syria has signed a treaty with Ephraim" (Isa. 7:2), or the sense of appalled bewilderment which overcame men when the watchman saw approaching a troop of horsemen, and announced to the people that Babylon had fallen (Isa. 21:9), or why people wept in the streets when they saw the chariot which brought the dead body of Josiah back from the battle of Megiddo (II Kings 23:29–30; II Chron. 35:20–24). To understand all these things, to enter deeply into the hopes and fears of the Palestinian

people, to comprehend their actions, which to an outsider must often seem foolish and opposed to their own best interests, to take one's part in the urgent and often bitter debate between the prophets and the people, it is first necessary to come to almost every biblical passage with an intense awareness of the world outside.

The biblical "world," therefore, is more properly that whole area and all those people that the people of ancient Israel understood to have significance for them, whether as friend or foe, as a source of wisdom and understanding or as alien and dangerous. This area is, to all intents and purposes, what we would today call the Middle East, though by the New Testament period it had expanded westward to include all the Mediterranean. Physically, the limits of this area are reasonably well defined by sea and mountain. On the

# Maps I–III

The first three of the colored maps are concerned with the Middle East in general, with its climate, its landscape, and its trade. It is fitting to begin with a map of the annual rainfall, for water is everywhere the key to life in the biblical world, and very nearly everywhere the supply is precarious and deficient. So completely is rain the source of man's continued existence that the theme of "water = life" is woven into the fabric of all Middle Eastern literature, and is never far from the thinking of any of its inhabitants. For this reason the nature, distribution, and effects of the rainfall are the subjects of Chapters Two and Three.

Map II is somewhat of an experiment, because it is a map without names over the land. Geographical names are, of course, a necessary and convenient device, enabling us to identify and study the different phenomena of the environment. Indeed, from the first beginnings of human language man seems to have found names for those features of his environment which he understood to be significant. This last phrase, "which he understood to be significant," is, however, the operative one, for the giving of names always involves a process of division and selection according to some already formulated concept of the world. Thus, some societies, very often nomadic, have the most detailed identification of the various features of the landscape, whereas others have what seems to us a very defective system, and tend to use general terms for what other people would describe with great exactness. Dwellers in the alluvial lowlands sometimes have only a general name for a great range of mountains bordering the plain, and do not bother to identify each separate peak, even though these are clearly visible. In Israelite society the word ya'ar seems to have been used indiscriminately for what we would certainly wish to separate out into forest, woodland, scrub, wasteland, and so on, and is consequently of only small use when

we try to map the distribution of forests in biblical times. Similarly, in view of the difficulty of the identification of the Valley of Achor (meaning "the valley of trouble") in the wilderness of Judah, one is driven to wonder whether the name was used exclusively for only one valley in the region, or whether it was applied more generally, just as among the Palestinian Arabs of today quite a number of narrow limestone valleys bear the name "Valley of the Robbers." Changed conditions, as when a new society moves into a region, or moves from one region to another, may lead to the giving of names to features which previously were unnamed, and to the forgetting of identifications which earlier had been thought to be very significant indeed. Thus, the name Dasht-i-Kavir, which appears on all atlases as the name of part of the great Persian desert, seems to have been the creation of Western scholars of the nineteenth century. On the other hand, although it seems almost incredible to us that they can have done so, the Israelites appear to have completely forgotten which mountain was identified by the name "Sinai," for the geographical situation of Sinai was no longer significant to them after Mount Zion had become the goal of their pilgrimages.

Consequently, the biblical landscape has been allowed to speak for itself, to present itself to the eye quite unencumbered by any names, as something absolutely fresh, seen as a totality, entire and whole, with no attempt to distinguish and divide. It is seen as it would be seen from a spacecraft encircling the earth at a tremendous height, and the viewer is free to record his own impressions and make what interpretation of it he will. Subsequent maps will present the interpretations and the use which men throughout the centuries have in fact made of this world. It is portrayed as it would be seen in the growing season when it is at its most green. In the drought of summer, much that is green on this map would be brown.

Of course, it is impossible to present the landscape entirely freshly, for ten thousand years of settlement and history divide us from the pristine world, and the Middle East we would see from a spacecraft would be the Middle East as altered by the constant activity of restless man. Yet at this scale, if we eliminate the towns and cities, the general appearance would not be so greatly different, for it would be impossible to observe where cultivated fields had replaced the green of the natural vegetation. By the beginning of the biblical era, the limits of the deserts were in general roughly where they are now, and the steppes of today were steppeland then. One major difference, however, needs to be noticed: the forests have largely disappeared from vast stretches of the mountains. We must take account of a constant eating away of the forest, for fuel, construction, and shipping, and the cumulative effect of this over four thousand years must have been enormous. This has been greatly hastened in the last century and a half, and there is evidence that many mountainous areas in Turkey and Iran which are barren today were still densely wooded at the beginning of the nineteenth century.

The biblical world is one of great diversity and complexity, but one feature every part of it shares in common with the others: *constriction.* Constriction may be said, indeed, to be the essential feature of Middle-Easternness. The whole vast area is held as in a vise, within a rigid framework of mountain, desert, and sea. It is about as large as the continental United States, without Alaska—3,600,000 sq.

mi. (roughly 9,324,000 sq. km.), but no point is as much as 450 mi. (720 km.) from the sea, whereas Nebraska and the Dakotas are more than 1,000 mi. (1,600 km.) inland.[1] Towering mountain ranges and forbidding deserts cross it from west to east though the mountains are aligned more to the southeast, and the deserts to the northwest, so that they cross in what today we call Iran and Afghanistan. It is in the interstices between these three oppressive elements that for the most part men must live and move and have their being. Certainly all could be crossed—and were crossed constantly with a boldness that is nothing less than amazing when one considers the resources available— and certainly also men lived in both the desert and the mountains. Only the vast deserts of southern Arabia deserve the name of an absolute obstacle, though even this fantastic waste of sand and desolation is not impossible of negotiation.

Yet the greatest of concentrations of settled population were always between the mountains, the deserts, and the sea, for here alone was there room for maneuver and the possibility of growing enough food to support such a population, and the people who lived here feared the obstacles that hedged them in. The mountains, the deserts, and the seas so clearly lay beyond the limits of effective human life, as they understood life to be, that they could be given a place within the concepts of the civilized world only by saying that they were in some sense beyond meaning, and that they partook of the quality of disorder.

Both the desert and the sea were places where men must be constantly and restlessly on the move if they were to escape death.[2] Here, for the men of the city or the village, disorder prevailed over order, and meaning was submerged in chaos, so that one must sacrifice to the gods every time one ventured "outside the world." So also were the mountains terrifying, but the attitude of the plains-dwellers towards the mountains was somewhat ambivalent. Very often they had come originally from the mountains, especially in Mesopotamia, and so the mountains played a part in their folk-memory. But the mountains were feared, not because they lacked the means of life but because they had too much of it. From the mountains came the water which was life itself, often gushing out in mighty streams from mysterious limestone caverns (Plate 17), and from the same mountains came the sudden and destructive floods as well as the furious raids of the mountain peoples. The mountains were also clothed with forest, and the peoples of the plains both coveted and feared the forests. They needed the lumber and sent out military expeditions to acquire it, but the very luxuriance appalled them, for this profusion of vegetation imposed the same patternlessness and absence of clearly defined tracks and places of habitation, which so affrighted them in the desert and on the sea. Of all the fears of ancient man, this panic fear of forest is the most difficult for modern man to make his own. Yet it was very real and well-nigh universal. "The glory of Lebanon and Carmel"

[1] This is counting the Caspian as a sea, though technically it is an enormous lake, but the Great Lakes as lakes. This may seem arbitrary, but the Caspian is a vast single body of water, with an area of 169,300 sq. mi. (438,500 sq. km.) before its recent shrinkage, whereas the Great Lakes are five separate lakes, whose total area is only 95,170 sq. mi. (246,500 sq. km.).

[2] The role of the desert in ancient Israelite thought is well discussed by Shemaryahu Talmon, "The 'Desert Motif' in the Bible and in Qumran Literature," in *Biblical Motifs: Origins and Transformations,* ed. Alexander Altman, Philip W. Lown Institute of Advanced Judaic Studies, Brandeis University, Studies and Texts, vol. 3 (Cambridge, Mass.: Harvard University Press, 1966), pp. 31–63.

**1. Elburz Mountains in winter.** Although most people think of the Middle East as being mainly desert, high mountain ranges, often well over 10,000 feet, are found in the Caucasus, Eastern Turkey, Iran, and Afghanistan. They are thickly blanketed with snow in winter, and on the highest mountains the snow remains throughout the summer.

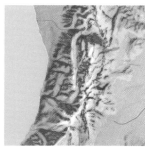

**II. Black Sea coast of Turkey near Trabzon.** Two regions in the Middle East have heavy rain all the year round: the southern end of the Caspian Sea in Iran, and the southeastern end of the Black Sea in northern Turkey. Both have a thick covering of warm temperate forest, with dense undergrowth.

# RAINFALL OF THE MIDDLE EAST
## ANNUAL

| Millimeters | | Inches |
|---|---|---|
| Under 100 | | Under 4 |
| 100–200 | | 4–8 |
| 200–300 | | 8–12 |
| 300–500 | | 12–20 |
| 500–1000 | | 20–40 |
| 1000–2000 | | 40–80 |
| Over 2000 | | Over 80 |

0   100   200   300   400   500 Miles
0   100   200   300   400   500   600   700 Kilometers

INDIAN OCEAN

PAMIRS

HINDU KUSH

THAR

River Indus

TURKESTAN

River Oxus

PERSIAN PLATEAU

ZAGROS MOUNTAINS

ELBURZ

CASPIAN SEA

OMAN

PERSIAN GULF

RUBA·EL-KHALI

ARABIA

NEFUD

YEMEN

CAUCASUS

URARTU

PONTUS

ANATOLIA

TAURUS

BLACK SEA

MESOPOTAMIA

River Tigris

River Euphrates

SYRIAN DESERT

MEDITERRANEAN SEA

RED SEA

EGYPT

River Nile

SAHARA DESERT

HORN OF AFRICA

ABYSSINIA

SEA

CASPIAN SEA

PERSIAN GULF

Strait of Hormuz

GULF OF OMAN

**THE MIDDLE EAST:
RELIEF AND VEGETATION**

0    50    100    150    200    250 Miles
0   50  100  150  200  250  300  350 Kilometers

©1968, JEPPESEN & CO. ALL RIGHTS RESERVED

# TRADE ROUTES
# OF THE MIDDLE EAST

• Sidon    Towns
———    Overland Routes
- - - -    Sea Routes

F

E

D

C

B

A

1   2   3   4   5

BLACK SEA

CASPIAN SEA

KYSYL KUM

KARA KUM

MEDITERRANEAN SEA

RED SEA

PERSIAN GULF

INDIAN OCEAN

RUB'A EL-KHALI

NEFUD

THAR DESERT

IRANIAN DESERT

TAURUS

CAPHTOR

KITTIM

MELUHHA?

SAHARA

ARABIA

Smyrna

Iconium

Sidon

Tyre

Damascus

Aleppo

Nineveh

Babylon

Ur

Susa

Ecbatana

Tabriz

Rhagae

Kashan

Isfahan

Yazd

Kerman

Persepolis

Meshed

Herat

Kabul

Quetta

Bokhara

Samarkand

Petra
(Sela?)

Dumah

Tema

Memphis

Thebes

Buhen

Napata

Meroe

Ptolemais
Theron

Muza

Sana

Marib

Muscat

Uqair

River Nile

River Euphrates

River Tigris

Greater Zab

River Tigris

Scale
Miles
0  100  200  300  400  500
0  100  200  300  400  500  600  700
Kilometers

20°  30°  40°  50°  60°  70°

10°

20°

30°

40°

50°

**III. Mediterranean vegetation in southern Turkey.** The south coast of Turkey is very different from the Black Sea coast in the north. Here the winter rainfall is heavy, but the hot drought of summer means that there is hardly any undergrowth, and the trees and bushes have small leaves to prevent evaporation.

**IV. Basalt desert of east Jordan.** This picture shows the barren landscape found in regions where the average rainfall is less than four inches a year. The rough, black basalt is a volcanic rock which formed an almost impassable barrier to trans-desert caravans. The yellow area is a mud flat, where the rare winter storms have washed sediment down into a depression. Similar landscapes are found in much of western Arabia.

embodied that *mysterium tremendum et fascinans* which men associated with the divine. Moreover, the mountains reared their heads toward that strange, but recognizably orderly, sphere of the sky, where the heavenly bodies moved with complex regularity. The mountains, therefore, were the abode of the gods.

Map III demonstrates how intricate was the pattern of the routes by which, from the very earliest days of human settlement, men exchanged the products of one region for those of another. Not all of them, it is true, were in use from the beginning, for greater sophistication and new methods of transport enabled men to venture along tracks they had not penetrated before. Nor were all these routes necessarily of equal importance at all times. The road from Susa to Persepolis, for instance, was really a creation of the Persian Empire.

In general, the roads follow the lines of least resistance, and the map makes clear that they run parallel to the mountain ranges rather than across them. The most important of all tended to be piedmont roads, following the spring line at the foot of the mountains and along the edge of the deserts. Among these we can include what later came to be known as the "Silk Road" from China through Samarkand, Bokhara, and Meshed to Rhagae (Reyy), close to the modern Tehran. Here it is divided. One branch followed the northern mountains through

Tabriz, and round the northern side of the Anatolian Plateau to the borders of Europe. Another, the "Golden Road to Samarkand," crossed the Zagros Mountains, by way of Ecbatana, Bisutun, and the Diyala Valley, to Babylon on the Euphrates. At Tur, near Meshed, the Silk Road was joined by what was really the continuation of the northern piedmont road—i.e., the road to India through Herat, Kabul, and the Kabul River down to India. Another pair of piedmont roads swung around the southern side of the Iranian desert. They entered the region through the Bolan Pass near Quetta, and then divided, because here there is an interior range of mountains. The northern line went through Kerman, Yazd, and Kashan, while the southern followed the interior valley to the south of this through Isfahan to Ecbatana. Yet another piedmont road was the "Royal Road" from Susa to Sardis, near Smyrna. This hugged the southwestern foot of the Zagros through Nineveh and north of Aleppo until it reached the extreme northeastern corner of the eastern Mediterranean. Then it climbed over the Taurus Mountains by the Cilician Gates. Herodotus says that it went around the northern side of the Anatolian plateau, but there was also an important route around the southern side of the plateau through Iconium. The last of the great piedmont roads was the Incense Route from southern Arabia to Petra and the Mediterranean.

The major rivers naturally provided important routes through the desert regions, and roads followed the courses of the Nile, the Euphrates, the Tigris, and the Indus, and the Arabian desert was crossed by a group of caravan routes following the wadi lines between the Nefud and the Ruba῾ el-Khali. Finally, a very important connecting road ran southwards from Aleppo across the Levant Bridge, through Damascus and the Palestine coastal region to Egypt. It was this road that joined the Nile Valley region with Mesopotamia and the north.

These were also the sea routes, following in general the coasts, and these seem to have been established from a very early date, for we know of communication by sea between the Harappa civilization of the Indus Valley and the Sumerian culture of lower Mesopotamia by as early as 3000 B.C. Indeed, it is essential to remember that in the Middle East the exchange of products is as old as settlement. Movement along the Silk Road to China goes back to Neolithic times, and the Neolithic painted pottery of the Yang Shao culture shows affinities with that of the Middle East. Evidence is beginning to appear for the possibility that ass-nomads may have regularly traded between the Levant and southwestern Arabia long before the taming of the camel in 1500 B.C. or perhaps earlier,[3] and in 7000 B.C. Jericho seems to have been in contact with both the Red Sea and the Anatolian plateau.

[3] *See p. 38.*

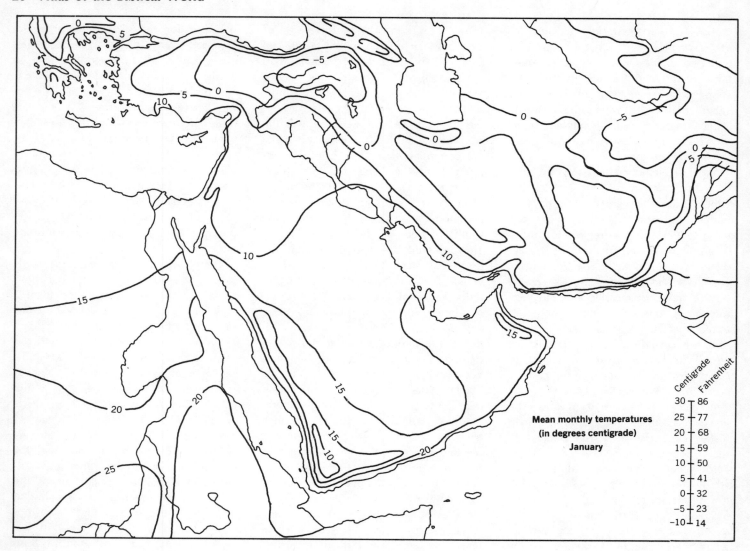

Mean monthly temperatures
(in degrees centigrade)
January

| Centigrade | Fahrenheit |
| --- | --- |
| 30 | 86 |
| 25 | 77 |
| 20 | 68 |
| 15 | 59 |
| 10 | 50 |
| 5 | 41 |
| 0 | 32 |
| −5 | 23 |
| −10 | 14 |

north, the boundaries are the Black Sea, the high barrier of the Caucasus, the Caspian Sea, and the deserts
which occupy the basin of the Aral Sea, the farthest
corner of the Middle East in the northeast being the
River Syr Darya, the Jaxartes of antiquity.

On the east, the limit is the beginning of the uplifted central section of Asia, the enormously high
mountain mass of the Pamirs and the Karakorams, both
of which lie certainly outside the Middle East. Farther
south, the curiously shaped Suleiman Mountains, with
their unexpected S-bend near Quetta, mark the border
between the mountains and plain in the east, and by
the passes across them, notably the Khyber Pass in the
north, invading hordes poured down to the rich lands
of the Indus. These fertile lands must be accounted
part of the world of the Bible, though marginal to it,
because from at least 3000 B.C. there was clearly com-

munication between the Indus and the lower Mesopotamian delta. After the establishment of the Persian empire, the rulers of the Persian plateau, whoever they
might be, strove to include within their dominions
these rich, irrigated lands, though not always successfully. This marked the limit of their ambitions, and it
seems to have been believed by many that the cultivated fields of the Indus marked the end of the inhabited world. Even Alexander, when his troops refused to
go beyond the River Beas, one of the tributaries of the
Indus in the north, apparently imagined that only a
very short distance would bring him to the farthest
point that he could go.

In the south, of course, all the way from the mouth
of the Indus to the Gulf of Aden, the border was the
Indian Ocean, and on the west the Nile and the
Mediterranean Sea. However, the western is the least

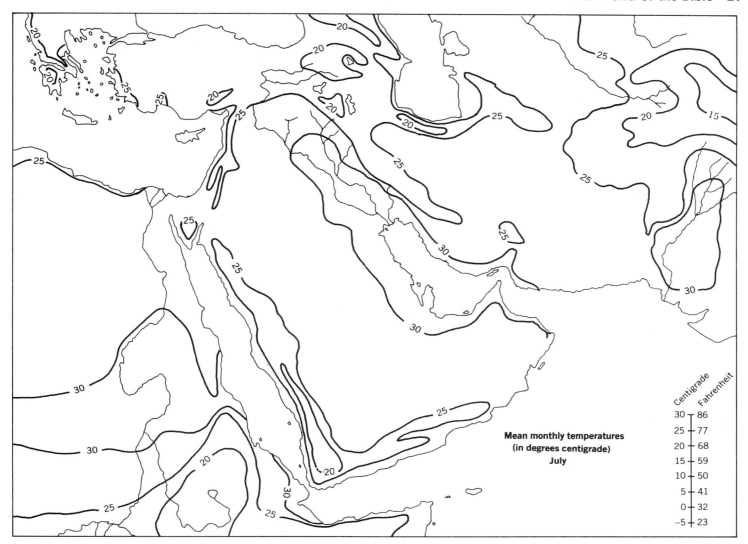

Centigrade Fahrenheit

**Mean monthly temperatures
(in degrees centigrade)
July**

| Centigrade | Fahrenheit |
| --- | --- |
| 30 | 86 |
| 25 | 77 |
| 20 | 68 |
| 15 | 59 |
| 10 | 50 |
| 5 | 41 |
| 0 | 32 |
| −5 | 23 |

clearly defined of all the boundaries, and it is far from evident how one should draw the line from the Nile to the Gulf of Aden. Probably the high volcanic mountains of Abyssinia should be excluded, but it is a moot point. The Ethiopia of the Bible refers rather to the Nile south of the Second Cataract, in what we should call the Sudan today, and there is very little, if anything, in ancient writings that clearly refers to these highlands. Some would place the Sumerian Meluhha or the Egyptian land of Punt amid the forested eastern slopes, but it is all very tentative. Others would identify Meluhha with Oman or now most probably with the Indus valley, and Punt with Somaliland. Yet we cannot altogether exclude the mountains from our purview, because, though the ancient world was not aware of this the floods of the Nile are the result of heavy summer rains in Abyssinia, and because from a very early date the

peoples of southwestern Arabia had close communication with the highlands immediately across the straits of Bab el-Mandeb. Perhaps it would be wise to draw the line from the Fourth Cataract to the straits so as to exclude the mountains from the true "biblical world," since they do not seem to have held significance for the remote Palestinians, but to include these mountains within the area that it is necessary for us to study.

Beyond the Nile and the Mediterranean coast lay the limitless desert and the sea, for neither of which did the ancient Jewish people have the least enthusiasm, but they could not avoid becoming increasingly aware of them, for the cultural expansion was westward. The Sahara, despite its oases, remained an obstacle, though it was constantly penetrated after the development of the west, but the Mediterranean Sea became in course of time an enormous lake, which was the center, rather than the limit, of civilization. The magnificent Minoan civilization had flourished in Crete (the biblical Caphtor) in the first half of the second millennium B.C., before the days of the Exodus, and Cyprus (the biblical Kittim) was noted from very early days for its copper, and was in close communication with Ugarit in northern Syria. Some scholars have indeed argued recently for a common origin for the culture of biblical Palestine and that of Homeric Greece, with Ugarit as the place where the stream divided. This may be, but the "coastlands" and "the multitude of the isles" remained extraordinarily vague to the people of Palestine, though they were frequently allied, and in very close touch, with the Phoenicians, whose ships ventured even beyond the Straits of Gibraltar. It was not until after the conquests of Alexander that the barrier was broken down.

In very nearly the whole of the Middle Eastern area the *basic* feature is a more or less serious rainfall deficiency, only the very limited regions of the Black Sea coast and the southern Caspian coast, both on the very edges of the Middle East, having no clearly marked dry season. So widespread throughout the Middle East are arid conditions that only two of the modern countries of that area are entirely without true desert: Turkey, and the tiny country of Lebanon on the Mediterranean coast of the Levant. It must be doubted whether there exists such a thing in the world as a region which has no rain at all, but in some parts of the Middle East rainfall is so appallingly infrequent that the yearly average comes very close to zero. Such areas are parts of the Sahara and the dread Ruba' el-Khali, or Empty Quarter, of southern Arabia. Inevitably, regions of this kind are without reliable records over a sufficient period of time to make it possible for us to arrive at a trustworthy average. However, the area of effective desert, where the rainfall is so irregular and unpredictable that cultivation without irrigation is quite impossible, is very much larger, and includes almost everything between 10 and 30 degrees of latitude. In Turkestan and on the Persian plateau, it extends far to the north of this.

We must except, of course, the mountain ranges which lie within every one of these desert regions. The mighty Zagros and Elburz, both rising well above 3,000 m. (10,000 ft.), have heavy rain and snow, and form entirely distinct regions of pleasant green. Indeed, on any mountainous district, however absolute the desert which surrounds it, there is always significantly

greater precipitation. How much exactly falls upon these intradesert mountains is far from certain, because once again we have practically no records for them, and the rainfall maps for such areas in this atlas can at best be only tentative. It is probable that any rain that falls within the 10- to 30-degree belt is extremely erratic in timing as well as in amount. Nevertheless, its effect and importance are undeniable. Near Bahrein in the Persian Gulf there are submarine springs of fresh water, supplied by rain which falls on the mountains overlooking the Red Sea, moving with incredible slowness through the porous rocks across the entire width of Arabia.

The mapping of rainfall in mountainous districts, even where one has plenty of information, is always a tricky business, because the totals vary so very greatly both with differences in altitude and with differences of orientation, the valleys and the leeward slopes having significantly less. This effect is exaggerated in the Middle East by reason of the marginal quality of the rainfall. Except only for particularly favored regions, such as all the Turkish coasts and the Caspian coast of Iran, we find ourselves moving away from the full effect of the mid-latitude cyclonic storms from which most of the Middle East draws its supplies, or in the south from the monsoonal rains of the tropics. Rainfall in such marginal regions often needs some extra triggering if it is to occur at all. This is frequently provided by the steep windward slopes of the mountains, forcing a rapid ascent and cooling of the humid air, with resultant precipitation which is, however, brought to a sudden end as soon as the air starts its descent on the other side. This rain-shadow effect is not only universal; it also produces major differences in the average rainfall on the two slopes, and it comes into effect with quite startling suddenness. The "carry-over effect" which is reported from more humid mountain regions, where the increased rainfall of the windward slope is continued for a little distance down the lee slope, is nowhere apparent in the Middle East, where the rainfall always decreases suddenly and sharply immediately the crest is passed.

Except for the coasts of the Black Sea and the Caspian, already mentioned, such rainfall as occurs in the Middle East is seasonal and for the most part confined to the winter months, but there is an amazing variation in the amount, extent, reliability, and distribution of this winter rainfall. The general rule is that the farther south one goes, the less assured is the rain and

# PERSIAN PLATEAU
# RAINFALL AND AGRICULTURE

—— 300 —— Annual rainfall Millimeters

Cereals

Riverine Irrigation — Dates

0   50  100  150  200  250 Miles

0  50 100 150 200 250 300 350 Kilometers

MOUNTAIN FARMING AND TRANSHUMANCE

SARDSIR OASIS CULTIVATION

SARDSIR MOUNTAIN FARMING AND TRANSHUMANCE

GARMSIR

LIMIT OF DATES

the longer the summer drought. Thus no place in Turkey has an absolutely rainless month, and the northern coast tends to have rain all the year, but as one moves southward along the Levant coast the gap between the end and the beginning of the winter rains gradually widens until when one passes the headland of Carmel the whole five months of May through September are usually completely dry. This five-month period of absolute drought characterizes, in fact, the whole of the ancient Israelite homeland.

In specially favored places such as Attalia (Antalya) or Anamur on the south Turkish coast, or Antioch (Antakya) in the extreme north of the Levant, the average annual rainfall may be as high as 1,000 mm. (40 in.) with, of course, very much more on the enclosing mountains, but on most of the Mediterranean coasts an average rainfall of over 750 mm. (30 in.) would be thought very satisfactory. Smyrna (Izmir), for instance, on the well-watered Aegean coast of Turkey, has an average of 693 mm. (27.7 in.) in the course of the year. Joppa (Jaffa) has on an average no more than 475 mm. (19 in.).

The mountainous region of southwestern Arabia is one for which information is at present still very defective, and until about a year or two ago might indeed have been reasonably described as nonexistent. The few travelers who had visited the Yemen came back with widely differing accounts of the climate—so different, in fact, that we can be fairly sure that there are broad variations from year to year, both in distribution and in amount. Now we have reason to believe that the heaviest rain comes during the summer months, from the edge of the monsoonal system, and falls mainly in heavy thunderstorms in the latter part of the afternoon. Over 750 mm. (30 in.) may perhaps be expected on the highest elevations, but in the valleys 500 mm. (20 in.) is a more probable figure. This summer rainfall extends, though in diminishing amount, along the west Arabian mountains, almost as far as Mecca, and eastward along the south Arabian coastal hills. North of Mecca the mountainous borders of the Red Sea receive some rain from the Mediterranean winter storms, and this determined the movement of the trans-Arabian caravans, lumbering northwards from Hazarmaveth (the Hadhramaut) and Sheba in the Yemen, laden with gold and frankincense and myrrh. They used the southern section in the autumn, when the wells would be full after the summer rains, and the northern section in the ensuing spring. Mecca, though no city was built there

until shortly before the time of Muhammad, was the region of waiting and assembly between the two seasons, and in consequence became the sacred area for the Arabian tribes. These errant cyclones of the Mediterranean winter sometimes penetrate the full length of the Red Sea and are responsible for the rare winter rain, or even rarer snow, which has occasionally been reported by visitors to the high Yemen. It must always be remembered that such visitors, before the revolution of 1962, were *very* few and far between.

In the other corner of southern Arabia, on the mountains of Oman, there seems to be no doubt at all that the greatest amount of rain falls during the winter months (perhaps as much as 500 mm. or 20 in. on the highest parts), as a benefaction from the Mediterranean cyclones which have passed along the Mesopotamian trough and received some rejuvenation in the Persian Gulf. A curious feature, which is worthy of study in the days when such study will be possible, is that there is some evidence that this rain is rather greater on the western sides of the mountains than on the seaward side. Whether these mountains obtain any rain from the summer monsoon is still a matter of dispute, and the general opinion seems to be that they do not.

Over the plateau of Anatolia and the Persian plateau, as well as the peninsula of Arabia, powerful high-pressure systems develop during the winter months, when the large land masses are notably colder than the surrounding bodies of water, and these form an obstacle to the eastward movement of the cyclones from the Mediterranean, which tend as a result to pass round them, along one of three corridors: the Black Sea-Caspian trough; the Syrian-Mesopotamian trough; or the narrow passage of the Red Sea. This high pressure breaks down only at the very end of the rainy season, when the summer heat starts to prevail. Consequently, on the edges of the Arabian and Persian deserts such rain as there is tends to fall in brief, torrential storms in the transitional periods, and particularly in March and April. The intensity of these storms is greatly increased by the rapidly rising convectional currents over the hot land. The southern edges of the Persian desert also seem to receive some rain occasionally at the height of the summer monsoon, in June or July. This is very irregular indeed, and very small in amount, but it does occur. Thus Kerman, during the seven years 1950–1956, recorded a small amount of rain in five out of these years, the greatest being 14 mm. (0.56 in.) in July of 1956. It must be remembered that all our records are for oases at the foot of the mountains, in a very marked rain shadow, and that we may with some confidence expect rather more in the high mountains that look down on them. It would not be more than a very occasional downpour even there, but could be important for replenishing the wells in an otherwise very dry region. The occurrence of this rare summer rain may be traced as far to the northwest as Isfahan, which in 1956 had as much as 45 mm. (1.8 in) in July, though that was a freak year. Records are very defective for southern Iran, but it would appear that these summer showers were more frequent in the 1950's than the 1940's, for in that decade we have hardly any evidence of them at all. All this suggests also that we should not entirely discount the possibility of occasional summer rain on the mountains of Oman.

The two great intermontane plateaus show a startling divergence from each other; in Anatolia the average rainfall nowhere drops below 200 mm. (8 in.), and is in general above 300 mm. (12 in.), but in Iran the greater part of the plateau receives less, usually very much less, than 200 mm. (8 in.), and only the mountains of the north and west have over 300 mm. (12 in.). Mirjaveh, in the extreme southeast of the plateau, has only 48 mm. (2 in.). In central Anatolia the rainfall increases in winter, with a maximum in December, but then the high pressure establishes itself, and the rainfall decreases, but rises again to a second and slightly greater maximum from late April to early June, the period known to the Turks as "the forty afternoons," when in Ankara a thunderstorm may be expected almost any day around 4:00 P.M.

Farther east, in the higher and even colder Urartu mountains, this double maximum is even more clearly marked, and the two maxima more widely separated. Thus Erzurum, with an average for the year of 476 mm. (19 in.), has 48.8 mm. (1.95 in.) in October, half this amount in December (24.5 mm. or 0.98 in.), but 78 mm. (3.1 in.) in May. The same effect is apparent in the high mountains of Iran, at Tabriz, Kermanshah, and Hamadan, and extends along the Zagros ranges at least as far as Shiraz, and probably very much farther, though evidence for this southeastern region is still hard to come by. Still farther east the effect is even more marked. At Kabul, just about 1,800 m. (6,000 ft.) above sea level, the total average annual rainfall is 332 mm. (13.3 in.), of which as much as 192 mm. (7.7 in.) may be

expected during the two months of March and April, when there tends to be a very sudden increase in the precipitation. At Kandahar, however, which is decidedly lower (1,150 m. or 3,450 ft.), the annual total is only 175 mm. (7 in.), and the maximum is in December (75 mm. or 3 in.). Unfortunately, figures for anywhere in Afghanistan are very scanty, and our information about the rainfall pattern in this eastern region is slight and unreliable.

Rainfall in most of the Middle East is not only restricted in amount and limited to one season of the year, but is also concentrated into a very few days, when there are likely to be torrential storms with extended dry periods between them. This concentration of the rain into only a fraction of the total number of hours in the year may, in fact, be said to be one of the most important features of the Middle Eastern climate, though it takes different forms in different climatic situations. Thus, in the Mediterranean coastal regions and on the coastal mountains, the cyclonic storms of winter deluge the land with rain for about three days, and every gully is choked with silt-laden floodwater, but then there is likely to be an interruption of at least a week and even sometimes as much as a month. Thus Attalia (Antalya) on the south Turkish coast receives its high total of 1,000 mm. (40 in.) in as few as 70 rainy days, mainly concentrated in the winter months. By contrast, Philadelphia, Pennsylvania, has a slightly higher total (1,078 mm. or 43 in.), and this is distributed over 124 rainy days. London, England, has very much less rain than Antalya (612 mm. or 24.5 in.), but as many as 168 rainy days in the year. Jerusalem, which has nearly the same annual average total as London—a fact which comes as a surprise to most people—averages only 50 rainy days. On the Anatolian plateau "the forty afternoons" of late spring and early summer, with their heavy thunderstorms in the late afternoon, have already been mentioned, as has also the tendency for the summer rain in southwest Arabia to be similarly heavy convectional rain in the latter part of the day. On the Zagros Mountains, and in eastern Turkey, the heavy rains of March and April are a combination of cyclonic and convectional, and may last for two or three days, during which the downpours are overwhelming. They coincide, it should be noticed, with the period of melting snows, and consequently the river beds and normally dry valleys are choked with far more water than they can easily carry, and the resultant floods often reach disastrous magnitude (Plate

7). It is not uncommon, even in these days of modern engineering and transport, for bridges to be swept away and roads undermined by these tempestuous waters, and in the ancient world, of course, their power for destruction would have been even greater.

The range of temperature in the Middle East is also extreme, partly because the farthest limits of the region extend from the latitude of Montreal to that of Nicaragua. Thus, in Turkey only the narrow coastlands of the Aegean and the Mediterranean are really hot in summer, Smyrna (Izmir) having an average temperature of 27.5° C. (81.5° F.) in July, and Attalia (Antalya) an average of 28.2° C. (84.6° F.) in the same month. The Black Sea coast is much cooler, the July average at Trapezus (Trabzon) being only 22.5° C. (72.5° F.), and Samsun only 1° C. (1.8° F.) higher. On the plateau, the average July temperature in the center, where the highest temperatures are reached, is around 23° C. (73.5° F.), which is decidedly cooler than much of the United States in the same period. In winter the center of the plateau has everywhere an average January temperature slightly below freezing.

East of Ankara the winter cold increases rapidly. Sivas has three months with an average below freezing, and Erzurum four. Erzurum has, in fact, only three months of the year (July, August, and September) when one can be certain that there will be no snow, and before the days of modern rapid transport one of the natural hazards plaguing the slow-moving caravans as they toiled over the high passes in this area for much of the year was frostbite. In the neighborhood of the large lakes the summer warmth is extended for a month by the moderating effect of the water.

On the Persian plateau, in Iran and Afghanistan, the temperature figures in winter are at first sight slightly surprising, for with the increased distance from the sea, increased altitude, and the more extreme desert conditions, one would expect greater cold than there is. It is true that Kabul has two months with an average temperature below freezing, but Teheran, Isfahan, and Meshed all have a January average temperature slightly greater than freezing, and Kerman, which is 1,830 m. (6,100 ft.) above sea level, has as much as 6.1° C. (43° F.) in January. In part, of course, this must be explained by the lower latitude, for the whole of the Persian plateau area lies south of Anatolia, the southern coast of the Caspian being about the same latitude as the northern coast of the east Mediterranean basin, but in part also it must be because the Iranian oases,

which are the only plateau stations where we have records over a sufficiently long period to allow us to arrive at even a tentative average, are all situated at the foot of high mountain ranges. We must therefore reckon with a marked föhn effect. This occurs when air that has lost its moisture on the windward side of the mountains moves down the lee slopes. The heating and cooling of dry air is much more rapid than that of damp air—i.e., roughly 10° C. for 1,000 m. difference in altitude (5.5° F. for 1,000 ft.), as compared with about 6.5° C. for 1,000 m. (3.5° F. for 1,000 ft.), and consequently unusually high winter temperatures may be expected at the base of the lee slopes of the Zagros and Elburz. When one moves out into the plateau, however, the cold is likely to increase rapidly, and it is probable that much lower average temperatures characterize the heart of the Persian plateau than are found in the bordering oases. Those who have flown in or out of Denver, Colorado, in winter may easily see a similar effect there. Denver lies in the zone that is warmed by the chinook, which is a föhn-type wind, and the lakes and ponds in the vicinity are normally ice-free, but in the eastern part of the state, away from the mountains, the lakes are frozen throughout the winter. That this effect pertains on the Persian plateau is indicated by the few figures that we have. Thus Seistan, well to the south, and only 600 m. (2,000 ft.) above sea level, has an average January temperature of 7.8° C. (46° F.), which is only slightly above that of Kerman (6° C., 43° F.), though Kerman is 1,830 m. (6,100 ft.) above sea level. A much greater difference in temperature is found between Kabul, about the same height as Kerman, and Kandahar, some 750 m. (2,500 ft.) lower. Here the difference is between −2.8° C. (27° F. and 6.7° C. (44° F.), showing the effect of the absence of the föhn winds.

Despite the föhn, plant growth tends to be twice interrupted on both the Anatolian and Persian plateaus, once by the winter cold and again by the summer drought. The most prolific growing season is that short period when warmth and rain come together in late March, April, and early May.

Above about 3,000 m. (10,000 ft.) the mountains are snow-clad throughout the year, and of course at much lower altitudes than this carry heavy snow in winter (Plates I and 14). As far south as Rabbah (modern Amman) snow occurs almost every winter, and the surrounding roads may be seriously blocked about once every five years, though this has been happening more

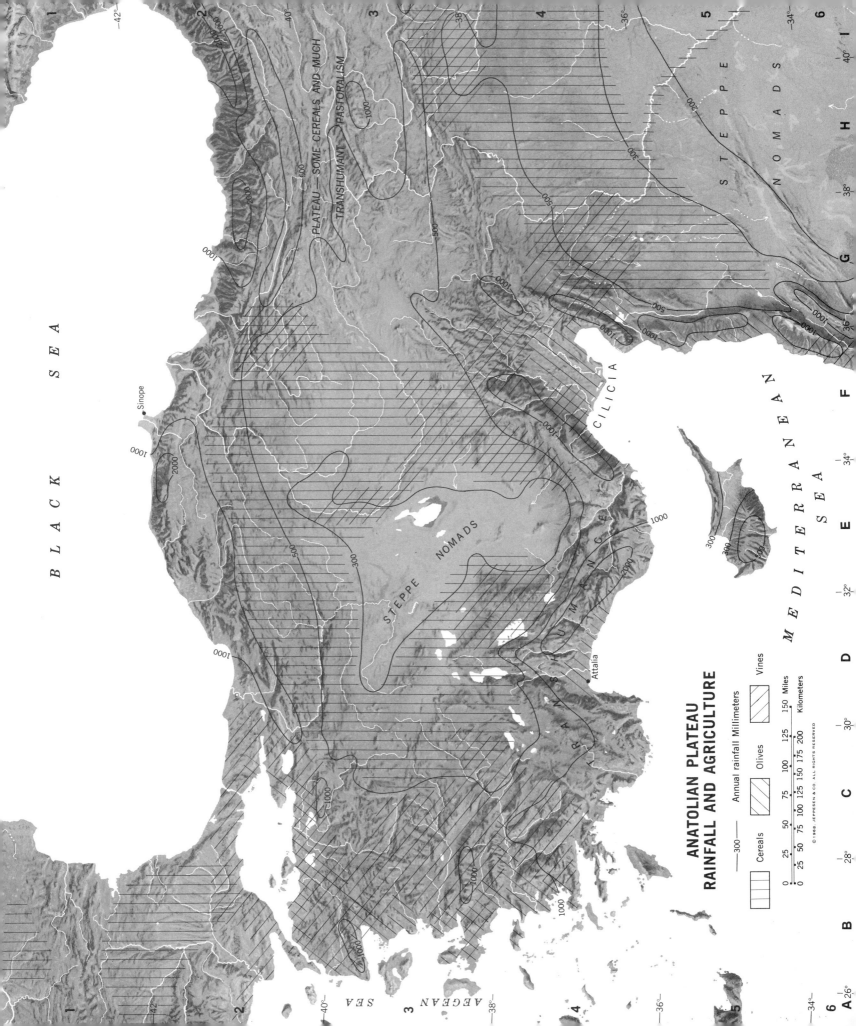

# ANATOLIAN PLATEAU
## RAINFALL AND AGRICULTURE

—300— Annual rainfall Millimeters

Cereals

Olives

Vines

Miles
0   25   50   75   100   125   150

Kilometers
0   25   50   75   100   125   150   175   200

BLACK SEA

MEDITERRANEAN SEA

AEGEAN SEA

STEPPE NOMADS

PLATEAU — SOME CEREALS AND MUCH TRANSHUMANT PASTORALISM

STEPPE NOMADS

NOMADS

CILICIA

TAURUS RANGE

Sinope

Attalia

frequently in recent years. At Mosul in 1924–1925 heavy snow fell, and lasted on the ground for a whole month, a phenomenal length of time, causing disastrous loss of life among shepherds and the destruction of thousands of sheep. The rare precipitation of the north Arabian desert not uncommonly falls as snow or sleet, and even at Baghdad puddles may remain frozen all through the day on the shady side of the street. "Snow upon the desert's dusty face" is by no means unusual, and the Arabian highlands overlooking the north end of the Red Sea are at times white with snow, and as mentioned above, some visitors have spoken of it in the Yemen. Frosty nights are no rarity even on the southern borders of the Arabian plateau. In general, the greatest extremes of cold come during the latter part of winter, when the effect of the penetrating seas and lakes is less. Snow in Jerusalem has been known as early as November, but it is much more likely after Christmas, and especially during February and March, and it is not unknown for the Easter ceremonies to be conducted in a snow-covered city, though admittedly this is a rare event.

The summer heat over very much of the Middle East can be ferocious, though it is modified throughout the interior by the much greater dryness of the atmosphere, and on the mountains by the altitude. In most desert areas the daily maxima may surpass 38° C. (100° F.), but the nights are cooler, and so the averages may be much less. Thus Rutba in northwest Iraq has 30° C. (86° F.) in July and August, but Riyadh in central Arabia has over 32° C. (90° F.) for the three months of May-July. It is rather cooler in August because of the onset of the *shamal,* or north wind. The heat is at its most unbearable along the humid coasts, and especially in the enclosed seas of the south. Thus the mouth of the Shatt el-Arab, where the Tigris and Euphrates flow together into the sea, has no less than four months with an average temperature over 30° C. (90° F.), and reaches 36° C. (97° F.) in both July and August, with very high humidity. Nowhere else attains quite these temperatures, though Muscat and the Red Sea shores run it close. Gwadar on the Makran coast is cooled in summer by the presence of the open Indian Ocean, and the hottest month is July, with an average temperature of 29.4° C. (85° F.), but shut off as it is from the northerly air masses, the summer lasts very much longer, and for seven months on end the average temperature is above 27° C. (80° F.). The Mediterranean ports are also hot and humid in the height of summer, though the heat is less prolonged. Thus Beirut has a monthly average of over 27° C. (80° F.) for only three months, with 27.8° C. (82° F.) in July; Antalya has only two months above 27° C. and Izmir just surpasses that figure in July and August. The decidedly cooler Black Sea coast has already been noticed.

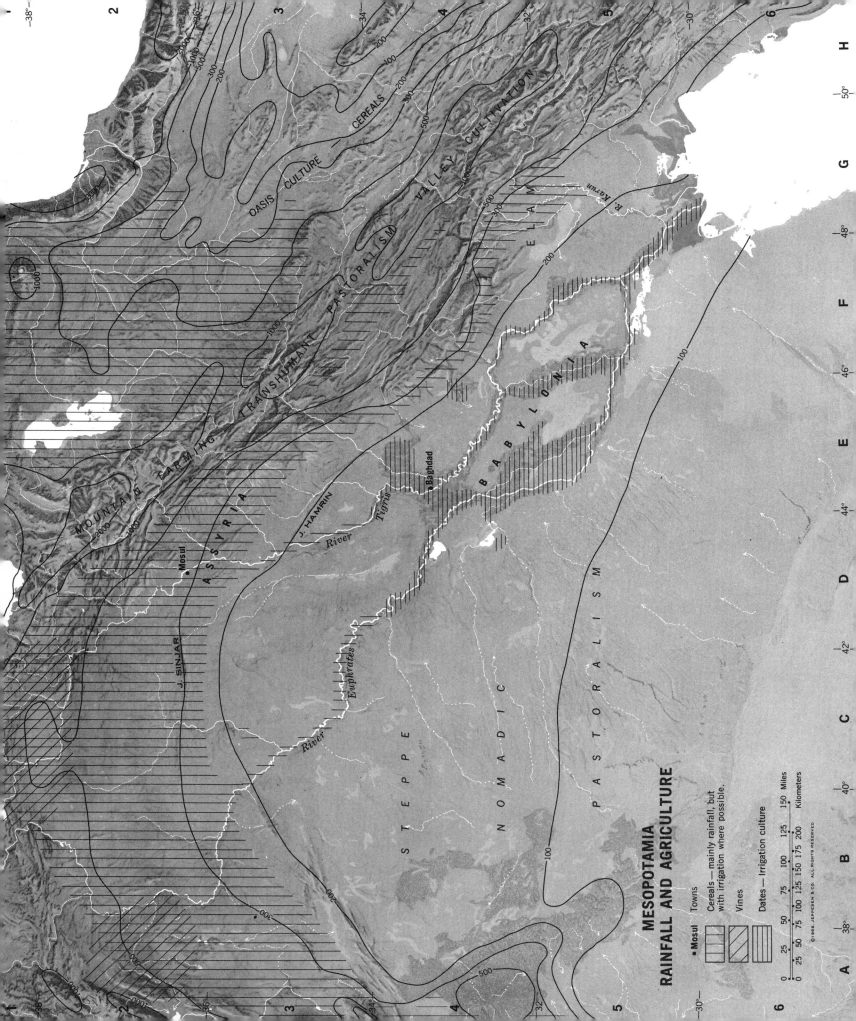

# MESOPOTAMIA
## RAINFALL AND AGRICULTURE

• Mosul  Towns

Cereals — mainly rainfall, but
with irrigation where possible.

Vines

Dates — Irrigation culture

0    25    50    75    100   125   150 Miles

0  25  50  75 100 125 150 175 200 Kilometers

MOUNTAIN FARMING

TRANSHUMANT PASTORALISM

OASIS CULTURE

CEREALS

VALLEY CULTIVATION

ASSYRIA

ELAM

BABYLONIA

STEPPE

NOMADIC PASTORALISM

PASTORALISM

J. SINJAR

J. HAMRIN

Mosul

Baghdad

Tigris River

Euphrates River

R. Karun

# THE LEVANT COAST RAINFALL AND AGRICULTURE

*Maps 7–8*

The Levant coastal region is a narrow belt of land between the desert and the sea, and is open in winter to the Mediterranean storms. Only in very restricted areas can river water be used for irrigation, though this is common in the narrow valley bottoms, and almost universally crops are dependent upon rainfall. The distribution and reliability of the rain is therefore a matter of great importance. The western highlands, so close to the sea, greatly limit the penetration inland of the winter rain, and except in the north the belt of land with sufficient rain for agriculture is seldom 160 km. (100 mi.) wide.

The rainfall is not only greater in the north; it is also more assured, lasts for a longer period, and extends much farther inland. In the extreme north there is on the coast no totally dry month, though the rain is concentrated in the winter period; in the interior the whole of the broad plateau of Hamath has sufficient rain for agriculture. To the south of this the Homs-Palmyra depression and the roughly parallel line of hills—e.g., Jebel Khanazir—form a distinct climatic division between good steppeland to the north and poor steppe and semidesert in the south.

In Palestine the rainfall is less, and also less assured, only Carmel and the highest parts of Galilee exceeding 1,000 mm. (40 in.). The rest of the coast plain and the highlands have usually just over 500 mm. (20 in.). In 1945–1946 the hill country of Judah just west of the Dead Sea had over 1,000 mm. (40 in.) of rain, but in the following year only

a little over 400 mm. (16 in.). South of Joppa (Jaffa) there is a very marked decrease. Generally speaking, all regions with over 400 mm. (16 in.) a year tend to have a January maximum, but where the average is less than 200 mm. (8 in.), the rain tends to come mainly in March and early April, with the breakdown of the Arabian high pressure system, though in good years the rain may penetrate far into the interior even in December and January.

Two areas have unexpectedly heavy rainfall: the Jebel Druze, southeast of Damascus, where the highest parts receive over 500 mm. (20 in.), largely as snow in winter, and the long tongue of greater rainfall extending southwards along the edge of the high Edomite plateau. In this area there are no intervening mountains to block the movement of the Mediterranean cyclones, and a very thin line of winter rain makes possible a narrow southward extension of the farming zone. Also anomalous are the three "gulfs of drought" where the rain-shadow effect behind the mountains is particularly marked. The most severe is the long finger of desert extending up the Palestinian rift valley north of the Dead Sea, which itself has only about 50 mm. (2 in.) of rain a year. The second is the area of deficient rainfall east of the Anti-Lebanon Mountains, and the third penetrates the Beqaʿa region, between the Lebanon and Anti-Lebanon, from the north.

"Wine to gladden the heart of man, and oil to make his face shine, and bread to strengthen man's heart" (Ps. 104:15) are the three staple products of the eastern Mediterranean shorelands, and the Israelites, indeed, did not colonize any area in which all three could not be grown together. Cereals, for making bread, are the most widespread, the preferred grain being wheat, barley being important in the areas of marginal rainfall. Wild wheat and barley are native to the Middle East, especially in the plateau regions between 600 and 900 m. (2,000 and

3,000 ft.), the home also of the wild sheep and goats. Though cereals were grown both on the coast plain and in the clearings in the forest, the major granaries were on the plateau: the Hamath and Aleppo steppes in northern Syria, and Bashan west of the Jebel Druze. On the south and east they merged into the pastoral steppe and desert.

The olive will not easily ripen outside the true Mediterranean climate; prolonged or severe frost is harmful, but because it grows slowly it can endure long periods of drought. It is almost confined to the coast plain and the seaward side of the highlands to about 900 m. (3,000 ft.), usually coming to an end once the ridge of the coastal range has been passed. There are, however, three exceptions: the plain of Antioch and the adjacent plateau region; the irrigated oasis of Damascus; and the higher hill country of Gilead, which has a more or less Mediterranean type of climate. Olives will grow along the eastern plateau edge more readily than was believed a few years ago, as far as the southern end of the Dead Sea. They were grown here in Roman times, and the present trend is to restore this marginal cultivation.

Vines are a hillside crop, grown in all mountain areas. The long taproot enables them to resist both severe winter cold and prolonged summer drought, though the heavy summer dew on the mountains greatly helps the swelling of the grapes. Of the three staples, vines need the greatest care, and Isaiah 5:1–7 gives a vivid picture of the work of a vineyard. They must be carefully pruned, and in summer protected against wild animals, driven desperate for food and moisture by the summer drought (Song of Sol. 2:15). Farming families, in fact, often move out into tents in the vineyards in summer to protect the precious crop.

Fruit was also important in the mountains. The thick shade and delicate fruit of the fig, grown near springs and in wadis, made it a symbol of

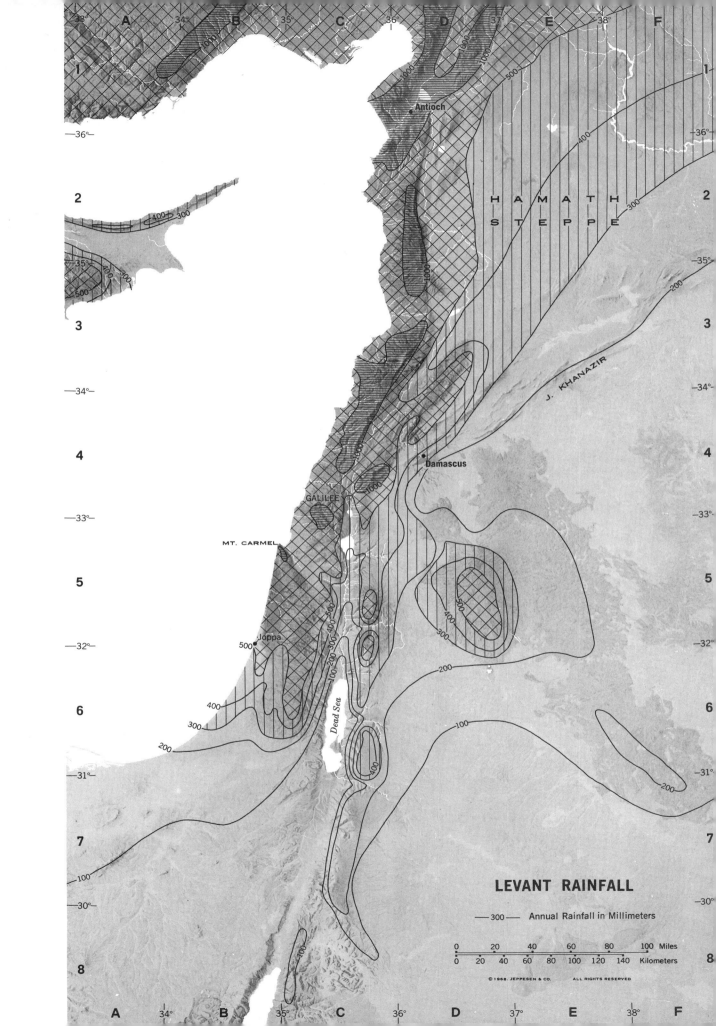

LEVANT RAINFALL

——— 300 ——— Annual Rainfall in Millimeters

| 0 | 20 | 40 | 60 | 80 | 100 Miles |
| 0 | 20 | 40 | 60 | 80 | 100 | 120 | 140 | Kilometers |

HAMATH
STEPPE

J. KHANAZIR

Antioch

Damascus

GALILEE

MT. CARMEL

Joppa

Dead Sea

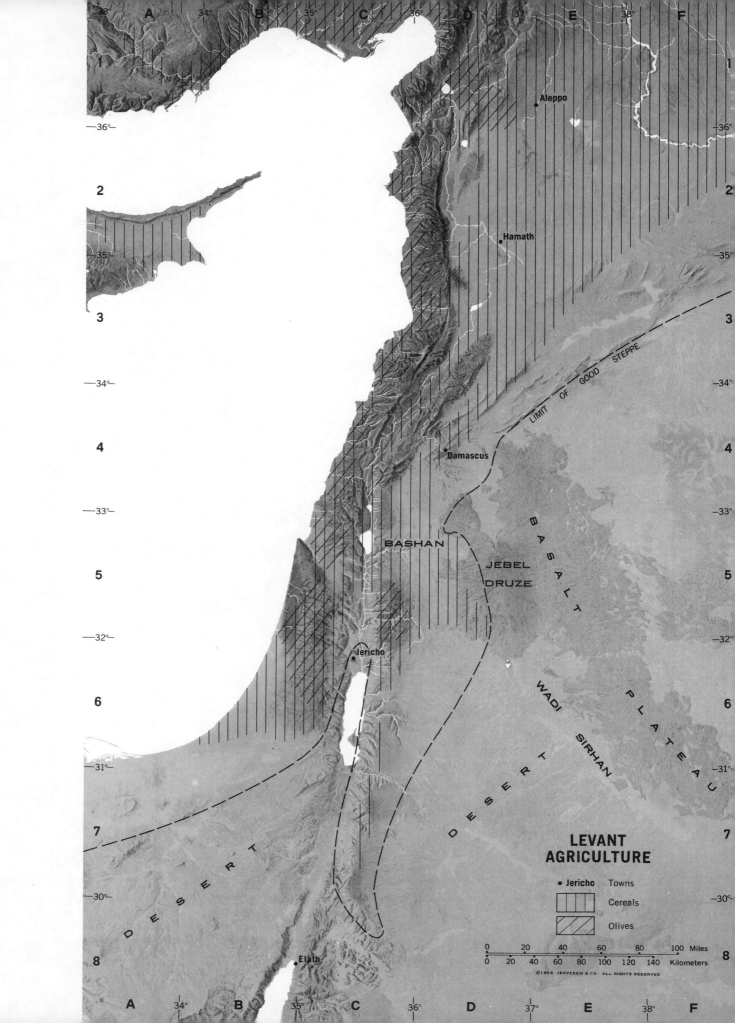

LEVANT
AGRICULTURE

- Jericho  Towns

Cereals

Olives

| 0 | 20 | | 40 | | 60 | | 80 | | 100 Miles |
|---|----|---|----|---|----|---|----|---|---------|
| 0 | 20 | 40 | 60 | 80 | 100 | 120 | 140 | | Kilometers |

pleasure, and on the coast carobs, or locust beans, were also an important shade and fruit tree. Grapes, figs, and carobs were all valuable for their sugar, of which the only other source, until the more developed farming of the Hellenistic period, was wild honey from the rocks (I Sam. 14:26–27). Walnuts, almonds, and pomegranates were other important fruits, and at Jericho and at Elath on the Red Sea dates were grown. Vegetables included the cucumbers, melons, leeks, onions, and garlic (Num. 11:5), which the Israelites remembered from Egypt, and which they also grew in Palestine. Others were peas, beans, lentils, and lettuce.

With the variations of the rainfall from year to year, the frontier between the desert and the sown shifted backwards and forwards. This was also partly dependent upon the power of the central government, for a strong administration with an effective army and police held back the bedouin, but when these were lacking the desert people moved in upon the cultivated land. There was also a persistent though fluctuating drift from the desert to the sown, and a tendency for the pastoralists in the border zone to become less nomadic, and finally to settle down altogether. Nelson Glueck has argued that the settlement of the Trans-

Jordan plateau had extended gaps, settlement occuring in the Patriarchal period (c. 2100–1900 B.C.), during Iron Age I and II (thirteenth to sixth century B.C.), and again after about 300 B.C. In the intervening period he claims that it was the home of nomadic bedouin. Whether these interruptions of settlement are in any way connected with fluctuations of the climate in this marginal region is still disputed, Glueck himself arguing strongly to the contrary. However, not all Palestinian archaeologists accept these gaps, and Kathleen Kenyon has recently questioned whether western Trans-Jordan was occupied during the Middle Bronze Age.[1]

[1] Kathleen M. Kenyon, *Amorites and Canaanites* Oxford University Press, 1966), p. 64.

# CLIMATIC TYPES OF THE MIDDLE EAST
## Map 9

There are three commonly used methods of classifying types of climate. The one used here is that first devised in 1918 by Wladimir Köppen of Graz in Austria, with some modifications. By this system there are five major divisions: **A. Tropical rainy climates; B. Dry climates** in which evaporation is greater than precipitation; **C. Warm temperate rainy climates; D. Cold climates,** with snow rather than rain in winter; **E. Polar climates.** Small letters are used to indicate variations within these major regions. **a.** hot summers; **b.** cool summers; **f.** rain throughout the year;

**h.** hot desert or steppe regions; **k.** cool desert or steppe; **s.** dry summers; **w.** dry winters; **x.** spring maximum of rainfall. A prime following a letter (e.g., h') indicates a modification of this type. In the Middle East we may distinguish the following:

**Aw. Tropical Savanna.** Hot, wet climate with rain in summer and a distinct dry winter season, in which the coolest month has an average temperature above 18° C. (64.5° F.). The natural vegetation of this type of climate is tropical grassland with scattered trees. It is marginal to the Middle East, and found only in the Upper Nile and India.

**BWhs. Sahara-Arabian Climate** (tropical deserts with summer drought) found in the greater part of the Sahara and the plateau of Arabia. The average annual temperature is over 18° C. (64.5° F.), and temperatures well over 38° C. (100° F.) often occur. There are great ranges of temperature, both daily

and annual. Such rain as there is comes during the winter months.

**BWhw. Tropical Deserts with Winter Drought.** These are found on the coasts of the southern Red Sea, the Gulf of Aden, and the lower Indus Valley, where the occasional rain occurs in the summer months rather than in winter. Since evaporation is greater in summer, this means that the rain is less effective in providing moisture for plant growth.

**BWh'x. Deserts of the Persian Plateau.** These are subtropical deserts, where the average temperature for the year is above 18° C. (64.5° F.), and with the sparse rainfall concentrated in the months of April and May. Plant growth is interrupted in winter by the cold, the temperature of the coldest month averaging around 2.5° C. (36° F.).

**BWk. Middle Latitude Deserts of the Aral Sea Region.** Here the average annual temperature is under 18° C.

(64.5° F.) and the winters are severe, with at least one month with an average temperature below freezing. The hottest month has an average of about 27°C. (80° F.).

**BShs. Syrian Steppe Climate** (subtropical semiarid steppe with winter maximum of rain). This forms a belt to the north of the tropical deserts in north Africa and Arabia, and also occurs in the northeastern section of the west Arabian highlands, and the mountains of Oman.

**BShw. Tropical Semiarid Steppe with Summer Maximum of Rain.** This is found in the central Sudan region and the southwestern part of the Arabian plateau. In the Indus Valley region, it surrounds the tropical desert.

**BShx. BSh′x. Semiarid Steppes of the Persian Plateau.** These have a quite distinct spring maximum of rainfall in March and April. The lower portion of the plateau in the south has about 10° C. (50° F.) in the coolest month, but the northern section has about 2.5° C. (36° F.).

**BSk. Middle Latitude Steppes of Turkestan and Anatolia.** The temperatures are similar to those of the Middle Latitude deserts, but there is about 200 to 300 mm. of rain a year (8–12 in.). Anatolia has no dry month, but a winter and spring maximum of rain; Turkestan has a marked summer drought, with winter rainfall and a maximum in March. A somewhat similar climate occurs in the Kuban plateau north of the Caucasus Mountains.

**Csa. Mediterranean Climate.** C-type climates in general have an average temperature during the hottest month above 10°C. (50° F.), and below 18° C. (64.5° F.) in the coldest month. The coldest month, however, is above −3° C. (26.5° F.), which coincides roughly with the southward limit of frozen ground. The climate of the coastal regions of the eastern Mediterranean has a marked winter maximum

of rain, though toward the north (e.g., in Turkey) there is no absolutely dry month. The summers are hot, with an average temperature during the hottest month of more than 22° C. (71.5° F.).

**Csa′. Western Anatolian Highlands.** Technically, these fall into Csa category, but a distinction needs to be drawn, since the winters are less mild than on the coasts, and the summers, though hot, have cool nights. The rainfall regime is similar to that of the coast. The necessity of making this distinction is shown by the fact that the olive, the characteristic Mediterranean plant, does not normally grow here.

**Cfa. Black Sea Coast Climate.** This has a temperature regime similar to that of the Mediterranean coast, but has rain throughout the year with a tendency to an autumn maximum. Also found on the south shore of the Caspian.

**Cfb. Thracian Mountain Climate.** This has rain throughout the year and cool summers. It is marginal to the Middle East, and on this map found only on the extreme northwest.

**Cxa. East-Central Anatolia.** There is a marked spring maximum of rainfall and hot summers, with, however, a considerable daily range. This is a transitional region, since there tends to be one month with an average temperature of slightly below freezing. An outlier of this type is found in northeastern Iraq, where, however, the winter temperatures are rather higher.

**Cxa–b. Zagros Climate.** This distinction is made because the highlands fall into the Cxb type with cool summers, and the valleys into the Cxa. The higher parts, in fact, should be classed as Dxb. Also in the Caucasus region.

**Cwa–b. Abyssinian Climate** with summer rainfall and hot summers. The highlands of southwest Arabia fall into this type also. Once again, the valleys are considerably warmer than the highlands.

**Df. Tadjik Mountain Climate.** D climates differ from C climates in that the average temperature for the coldest month is below −3° C. (26.5° F.), and sometimes very much below. The warmest month, however, is over 10° C. (50° F.). Precipitation in winter is in the form of snow. In the Middle East, D climates are confined to the high mountain regions. The Df climate is humid, and marginal to the region, being found only in the mountains of the far northeast.

**Dxa–b. Urartu Climate.** This is a mountain climate, characterized by cold winters with cool summers on the highlands, but hot summers in the valleys. Precipitation comes mainly during the winter months in the form of snow, but with a very distinct maximum in March and April, when there are torrential storms of rain. Also found on the Elburz Mountains.

**Dxb. Afghanistan Mountain Climate.** The greater height of these mountains over a wide area makes it necessary to distinguish this from the Urartu type. Though the lower-lying valleys have hot summers, the cool summer areas predominate.

**Dwa–b. Cold, Monsoonal Climate.** This is marginal to the Middle East, and is found on the southward-facing slopes of the Pamir region, where the summer monsoon produces a summer maximum of rain, though there is also a slight amount of rain or snow in winter. The lower areas would really be Cwa–b.

**ET. Tundra Climate.** The average temperature for the warmest month is below 10° C. (50° F.) but above freezing. There is a very prolonged winter period with average temperatures well below freezing. The growing priod in summer is very brief. In the Middle East this type of climate is confined to the highest mountain regions, notably in the Pamirs, the Caucasus, and the highest parts of the Urartu region and the Elburz.

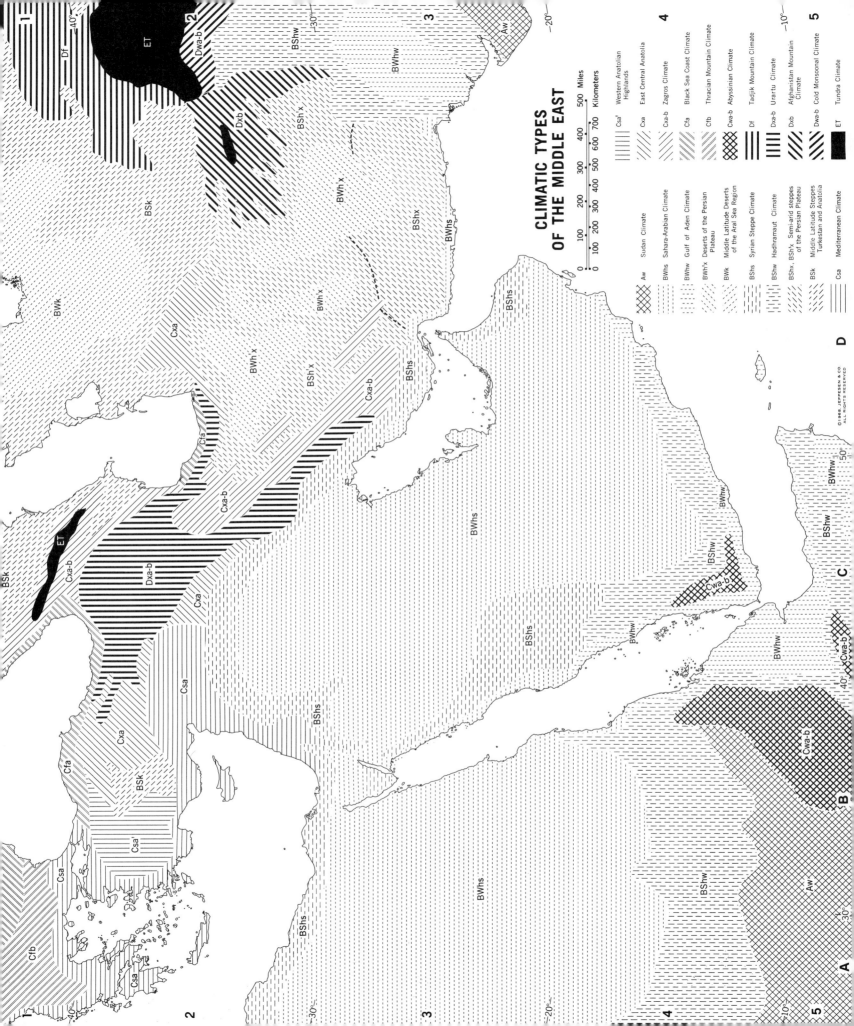

## CLIMATIC TYPES
## OF THE MIDDLE EAST

| | | | | |
|---|---|---|---|---|
| Csa' | Western Anatolian Highlands | | Aw | Sudan Climate |
| Cxa | East Central Anatolia | | BWhs | Sahara-Arabian Climate |
| Cxa-b | Zagros Climate | | BWhw | Gulf of Aden Climate |
| Cfa | Black Sea Coast Climate | | BWh'x | Deserts of the Persian Plateau |
| Cfb | Thracian Mountain Climate | | BWk | Middle Latitude Deserts of the Aral Sea Region |
| Cwa-b | Abyssinian Climate | | BShs | Syrian Steppe Climate |
| Df | Tadjik Mountain Climate | | BShw | Hadramaut Climate |
| Dxa-b | Urartu Climate | | BSh'x | BSh'x Semi-arid steppes of the Persian Plateau |
| Dxb | Afghanistan Mountain Climate | | BSk | Middle Latitude Steppes Turkestan and Anatolia |
| Dwa-b | Cold Monsoonal Climate | | Csa | Mediterranean Climate |
| ET | Tundra Climate | | | |

500 Miles

100   200   300   400   500   600   700   Kilometers

100   200   300   400   500

# Map 10

# VEGETATION REGIONS OF THE MIDDLE EAST

Any attempt to map the vegetation of the ancient Middle East is a hazardous and indeed an impossible task. For very wide areas the evidence is seriously lacking. Consequently, this map is essentially a map of existing vegetation, and it must be used with caution, since the vegetation cover of the Middle East has been changing, more or less continuously, since prehistoric times. By 2000 B.C., just before the beginning of the "biblical period," it is probable that the areas marked on this map as desert had already acquired this character. The areas of semidesert which border them must also, then as now, have carried only a sparse vegetation, though even in these areas there is some evidence of woodland on the higher elevations. That mountains were much more thickly forested in those days than they are now is beyond question, and it is certain that the regions marked on this map as having "open forest" were then fairly densely covered, and the regions marked as "dense forest" must have had a continuous forest cover, instead of the intermittent patches of thick forest which is what one sees in such regions today. Where such mountainous regions bordered the sea, an almost impenetrable forest came right down to the shore, a condition which persisted in parts of Turkey until relatively recent times. Similarly,

Mediterranean *maquis* regions were then forested.

The chief question concerns those regions marked as "steppe." This is an extremely general term, and in the preparation of the base maps for this atlas it was discovered that the various sources used the word with startling looseness, so that a very wide area indeed of the Middle East was described by someone or another as "steppe," ranging all the way from semidesert to partially wooded country. The term has been confined here to those regions which carry a fairly good grass cover during the growing season, however barren they may appear in the drier months, but where there are no trees except along some of the water courses. These are usually more or less level regions, with marginal rainfall, where agriculture is possible, at least by dry-farming methods, without irrigation. It seems probable that we must still think of them in ancient times as grassland, and indeed the home of the wild wheat and barley from which agriculture developed. Nevertheless, one must postulate more woodland then than now. We have definite evidence that the hills which in places diversify the Syrian steppe were once wooded, even to the extent of impeding movement, and the steppes of the Anatolian and Persian plateaus probably had in those days quite a fair amount of open woodland. In general, the level steppe-land was an area of easy movement where neither forest nor desert obstructed progress. Man has, however, an insatiable desire for timber, both for building and for firewood, and in the steppe, because of its easy accessibility, his depredations must have begun long before the biblical period. The Assyrian homeland was in this region, and we know from Assyrian records how deeply they penetrated into the mountain fastnessess to get for building purposes the good timber that was not available nearer at hand.

**1. Salt Flats and Salt Marsh.** This is the

most desolate of all desert regions, and true salt deserts are completely uninhabited. The largest area (and the only one shown on this map) is the Dasht-i-Kavir in Persia, but even here it is far from continuous. Patches of salt desert may also be found in other desert regions.

**2. Erg.** Known as **rig** in Iran and Afghanistan, this runs the previous region close for lack of hospitality. It is the sand-dune type of desert which most people associate with the word "desert," and has almost no vegetation.

**3. Hamada** or stony desert. Here, especially at the bottom of wadis, where water tends to collect, some thorny vegetation exists, and pasture for camels is possible.

**4. Semidesert—Plains Type.** This is transitional from near-desert to poor steppe. Plants are adapted to dry or salty conditions, thorny bushes (e.g. tamarisk), being important. Vegetation is thickest in the wadi bottoms and on the northern and western sides of hills. The incense-producing shrubs of southern Arabia and the neighboring regions of Africa belong to this type.

**5. Thorny, deciduous thicket.** A semidesert type of vegetation, characteristic of the Horn of Africa and marked by cactuslike plants and acacias.

**6. High Plateau Semidesert.** This is similar to 4 above, but plant growth is interrupted by winter cold as well as by summer drought. The main growing period is therefore very brief, in March and April.

**7. Plains Steppe.** Grassland, with sage and thyme bushes, and occasional trees beside the streams, especially carob, juniper, and terebinth. More than half the plants of the steppe disappear in the dry summer months.

**8. High Plateau Steppe.** Similar to 7 but

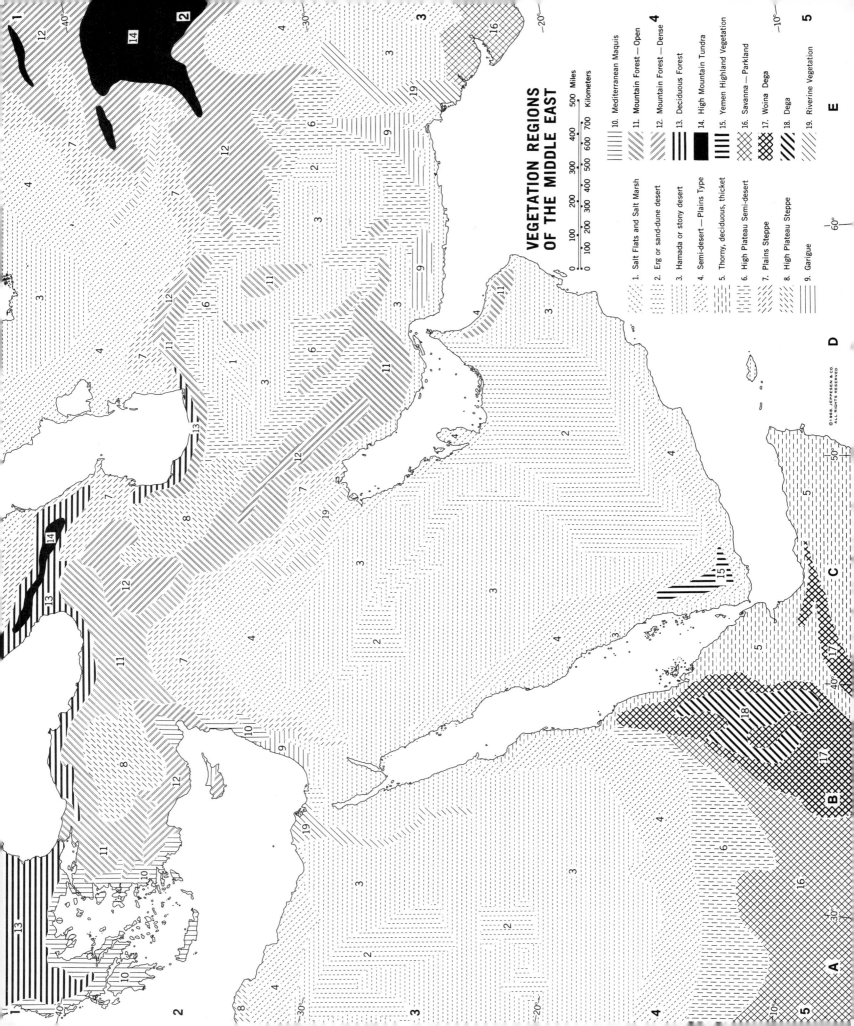

## VEGETATION REGIONS
## OF THE MIDDLE EAST

|  |  |  |  |
|---|---|---|---|
| 1. | Salt Flats and Salt Marsh | 10. | Mediterranean Maquis |
| 2. | Erg or sand-dune desert | 11. | Mountain Forest — Open |
| 3. | Hamada or stony desert | 12. | Mountain Forest — Dense |
| 4. | Semi-desert — Plains Type | 13. | Deciduous Forest |
| 5. | Thorny, deciduous, thicket | 14. | High Mountain Tundra |
| 6. | High Plateau Semi-desert | 15. | Yemen Highland Vegetation |
| 7. | Plains Steppe | 16. | Savanna — Parkland |
| 8. | High Plateau Steppe | 17. | Woina Dega |
| 9. | Garigue | 18. | Dega |
|  |  | 19. | Riverine Vegetation |

Miles 0 100 200 300 400 500
Kilometers 0 100 200 300 400 500 600 700

with the same limited growing period as in 6.

**9. Garique.** The poorer type of Mediterranean vegetation, with an incomplete covering of low, often thorny bushes. Gorse, broom, thyme, and asphodel are common. Probably this area had only a thin, scrubby forest cover in ancient times.

**10. Mediterranean Maquis.** There is very little true *maquis* in the Middle East, but rather a kind of rich *garique*, including kermes oak, wild olive, and carob bushes. It is gay· with tulips, narcissus, anemones, anchusa, and cyclamen in spring. Once thickly forested, today it forms in the richer regions an impenetrable thicket.

**11. Mountain Forest—Open.** Very much of this today is grassland, with only scattered clumps of trees, including evergreen holm oak and Aleppo pines.

**12. Mountain Forest—Dense.** Today this is only moderately dense, with wide open areas. Includes Aleppo pine, valonia oak, fir, juniper, and some cedar,

with umbrella pines on sandy soils in the Mediterranean region.

**13. Deciduous Forest.** In the true Middle East this is found only on the Black Sea and south Caspian coasts, but outside it in the Balkan mountains. The Caspian area has oak, maple, alder, hazel, chestnut, and hawthorn, while the Black Sea region has oak, hazel, walnut, hornbeam, with a dense undergrowth, and very widespread rhododendron and azalea.

**14. High Mountain Tundra.** Alpine pastures begin about 2,700 m. (9,000 ft.), but it is heathland rather than the lush grass of Switzerland. Tundra conditions develop at about 3,000 m. (10,000 ft.).

**15. Yemen Highland Vegetation.** A scrub composed of cactuslike euphorbias, tamarisk, and acacia, though many of the Yemen mountains today are extraordinarily barren. Information is lacking about the extent to which they may have been forested in ancient times.

**16. Savanna—Parkland.** During the wet summer in the Sudan there is a luxuriant growth of tall grass, as high as or even higher than a man. This dies

down in the drier months. Acacia and mimosa bushes persist during the drought, and there are scattered, thorny trees, which develop a characteristic umbrella shape as a protection against the wind.

**17. Woina Dega.** This is the name given to the highlands of Abyssinia between about 1,500 and 2,400 m. (5,000 and 8,000 ft.), where forest or rich savanna conditions prevail, with the juniper as an important tree. This is the most thickly inhabited portion of the Abyssinian highlands.

**18. Dega.** This is an almost Alpine type of mountain grassland, rich and lush, which characterizes the high plateau regions of Abyssinia above 2,400 m. (8,000 ft.).

**19. Riverine Vegetation.** A thick jungle of tamarisk and reeds, with much marsh, is characteristic of the strips of land flooded by the great rivers. Today, very much of this is under intense cultivation. Date palms are important in Mesopotamia and Egypt. Southern Mesopotamia still has a very large area of untamed marshland.

*Map 11*

# LAND USE IN THE MIDDLE EAST

**1. Virtually Uninhabited Desert.** These areas comprise the salt flats and *ergs*, or sand deserts, shown as 1 and 2 on Map 10. These regions can be and are crossed occasionally by small groups of nomads, but the extreme paucity of vegetation means that they do not provide pasture for any sizeable herd.

**2. Pastoralism—Camel Predominant.** These are the areas of true desert, with pure camel herds being found in the central areas, some sheep and goats beginning to be introduced on the margins. It is normally considered that the Arabian camel was not tamed until

after 1500 B.C.—though this is now disputed (see p. 19)—and consequently these regions of Arabia and the Sahara must have had a reduced use before that date. However, it must not be assumed that they were uninhabited. Game was reasonably plentiful, even in the desert, and hunting communities must have existed. Moreover, before the taming of the camel it is probable that sheep and goats were pastured much farther out into the desert than they are now, even though it would have been a hazardous business. Unfortunately, archaeological information for the Sahara is very scanty and for Arabia nonexistent.

# LAND USE
## IN THE MIDDLE EAST

Miles  
0   100   200   300   400   500  
0   100   200   300   400   500   600   700   Kilometers

1. Virtually Uninhabited Desert
2. Pastoralism — Camel Predominant
2a. Persian Deserts
2b. Bactrian Camel Region
3. Pastoralism — Mixed Camel and Sheep
3a. Pastoralism — Sheep and Goats
4. Pastoralism and Agriculture
5. Pastoralism — Cattle
6. Mountain Farming and Transhumance
7. Mediterranean — Olive Cultivation
8. Piedmont Oasis Regions

9. Terraced Mountains of Lebanon and South-West Arabia
10. Ferghana Basin and Cyrus Valley
11. Riverine Cultivation
    (a) The Nile Valley
    (b) Mesopotamia
    (c) The Indus Valley
12. Abyssinian Plateau (Dega) — Cattle Pastoralism
13. The Abyssinian "Woina Dega"
14. The Pamirs
15. Dense Temperate Forest — Limited Agriculture

**2a. Persian Deserts.** A certain distinction must be drawn, because, although the camel became a very important element in the Persian herds and sometimes overwhelmingly so, the Indo-Europeans had brought with them the horse and cattle, and cattle were an element in the marginal herds here.

**2b. Bactrian Camel Region.** The Bactrian, or two-humped, camel has a very thick winter coat, which enables it to endure the much colder winters of the Russian deserts. There is some evidence that it may have been tamed rather earlier than the Arabian camel, perhaps about 2000 B.C.

**3. Pastoralism—Mixed Camel and Sheep.** This characterizes the borders of Region 2, and especially in the north Arabian region and the central Sudan. These mixed herds are despised by the *sharif* (noblemen), the true camel herders of central Arabia, but are important because they mean a greater diversity of products. Goats usually form part of the herd also. The inclusion of sheep greatly lessens the mobility of the herd, since they die by droves if they are overdriven in the heat (Gen. 33:13).

**3a. Pastoralism—Sheep and Goats.** These are semidesert regions very similar to 3. However, the camel is of only minor importance. Sheep almost completely predominate in the semidesert regions of the Indus Valley, and tend to do so also east of the Euphrates. In central Anatolia the same is true. However, in the past, when men were dependent upon animals for transport, the camel was much used both in Anatolia and Mesopotamia, and indeed throughout the steppe regions.

**4. Pastoralism and Agriculture.** With increasing rainfall, cereals begin to be important—wheat in the better-watered regions, and barley in the hotter and drier sections. Nevertheless, this is a transitional region, whose frontier fluctuates with the vagaries of the rainfall.

The frontier against the camel herds of the desert also fluctuates, but for political reasons. In times of political security, the shepherds from the villages take their flocks of sheep and goats far into the desert. It is also a region where there is a fairly continuous settling of the nomads, as they pass from the stage of roughly cultivating a patch of land which they visit only twice a year, to a situation of true mixed farming.

**5. Pastoralism—Cattle.** The true cattle herders belong outside the Middle East proper, in the southern Sudan.

**6. Mountain Farming and Transhumance.** Very much of the Middle East belongs to this type, and transhumance, or vertical nomadism, may be said to characterize every mountain region, as the herdsmen move between the winter pastures in the valley to the summer pastures on the mountains. In the Zagros, sheep, goats, and camels are all involved in this movement. The valleys are often lush, and wheat and barley are grown, together with vines and such fruits as almonds, plums, mulberries, apples, and so on.

**7. Mediterranean—Olive Cultivation.** Olives are not absolutely confined to the Mediterranean coastlands. There are olive yards in the Damascus oasis, in scattered patches on the Jordanian plateau, and—very surprisingly—in the valley of the Safid Rud which flows out into the Caspian near Resht. Nevertheless, olives are the Mediterranean product *par excellence,* unbroken olive groves being characteristic of the alluvial plains. Wheat and vines are also important in the olive regions, especially on the hills.

**8. Piedmont Oasis Regions.** These are regions at the foot of the mountains of intense cultivation of cereals and fruit wherever there is water from the mountains, but of long streches of pastoral country, mainly sheep and cattle, between the oases.

**9. Terraced Mountains of Lebanon and Southwest Arabia.** Terraced farming is practiced in a number of mountain districts in the Middle East, but nowhere is it done with such skill and so extensively as on the seaward slopes of the Lebanon mountains or in the Yemen, where one may sometimes see as many as a thousand terraces one above the other. This highly developed terracing is a result of the great shortage of level land for agriculture, and it is not surprising that both regions instigated widespread trading organizations, and "exported men." It is not known when the terracing was first started, but it must have been well advanced by New Testament times. There is evidence for Nabatean terracing at Beidha, and in southern Palestine.

**10. Ferghana Basin and Cyrus Valley.** These are both somewhat marginal to the true Middle East, but they deserve mention. Each is a wide valley with high mountains on either side, where there is ample water for irrigation purposes. They are a kind of joint riverine and piedmont oasis region, growing cereals, vines, and temperate fruits.

**11. Riverine Cultivation.** Although on the map these look very similar, each must be distinguished from the others.

a. The Nile Valley is narrow, except in the Delta region, and the chief crops were emmer wheat, barley, flax for linen, castor oil, sesame, and saffron (both also for their oil), lettuce, and the celebrated cucumbers, melons, leeks, onions, and garlic (Num. 11:5).

b. In Mesopotamia, barley was more important than wheat, and the leeks, onions, and garlic so common in Egypt were a relatively late introduction. Oil was produced from sesame, and linen from flax. Completely dominating everything else, however, in the Tigris and Euphrates delta was the date palm, here far more intensively grown than anywhere else (Plate XI).

c. In the Indus Valley, millet was the

most important grain, though wheat and barley were also grown. Melons and peas and beans were produced, and possibly rice, though this is uncertain. There may perhaps have been some date palms, and quite certainly cotton was cultivated here, earlier than anywhere else in the world. The elephant, horse, ass, zebu, camel, and humpless cattle were all tamed by the Harappā civilization.

**12. Abyssinian Plateau (Dega)—Cattle Pastoralism.** The rich grasslands of the high plateaus of Abyssinia are especially suited to the rearing of cattle, though agriculture was also practiced in the ancient state of Aksum.

**13. The Abyssinian Woina Dega.** Because of its constant warmth, heavy summer rains, and fertile volcanic soil, this region can produce a great variety of crops, including cereals, vegetables, and fruits, and sometimes more than one crop a year on the same soil. Very little, however, is known about the conditions of the Abyssinian mountains in the biblical period.

**14. The Pamirs.** This towering mountain region exhibits today an almost complete lack of forest cover, and very little cultivation, which is confined to the valley bottoms and is dependent upon irrigation. However, there is an abundance of pasture on the vast, windswept plateaus. Millet is grown to about 1,950 m. (c. 6,500 ft.) and barley to about 2,450 m. (c. 8,200 ft.).

# SOME EFFECTS
## OF THE
# MIDDLE EASTERN
# CLIMATE

## Chapter Three

If one of the marks of "Middle Easternness" is the extreme constriction of the land available for settlement (see page 18), another is the extraordinary diversity of the environment, a diversity that extends even into the desert wastes. There is a great range of environmental situations from the dense and tangled Colchian and Hyrcanian forests, which clothe the seaward slopes of the eastern Pontic and the Elburz Mountains, to the almost incredible desolation of the Rubaʿ el-Khali or the Dasht-i-Lut, and different regions are sharply separated from each other, either by the physical barriers of steep mountainside and hill or by the sudden climatic changes. All this is in large measure the result of the marginal character of Middle Eastern rainfall, for under such conditions, as we have already seen, there is a remarkable difference between the amount of rain that falls on the windward and the leeward slopes. It is almost impossible to overemphasize this, for even a slight increase in height is often sufficient to trigger the much-needed rain, but on the other side the burning heat of the sun, coming "like a bridegroom out of his chamber, and rejoicing as a giant to run his course" (Ps. 19:5), parches every slope exposed to its rays. The northern and western slopes of even so minor a hillock as an archaeological tell are always greener than those to the east and the south. Moreover, differences in the underlying rock assume unusual importance, the rainfall that might be just sufficient with one type of soil becoming suddenly inadequate when the boundaries of that soil are passed. Thus the ridge of even a very low and unimpressive line of hills, or the edge of an outcrop of inhospitable chalk may mark, discreetly but emphatically, the vital frontier between the Desert and the Sown.

The climate is also the source of those forces of erosion and deposition which have created the visible physical landscape out of the underlying structural elements. Of the three main groups, water, wind, and ice, we are concerned only with the first two. Glacial erosion has admittedly taken place in the highest parts of the Caucasus, the Elburz, and the volcanic peaks of eastern Turkey, and glaciers still exist in each of these three regions today (e.g., the Sarchal glacier, 4 km. or 2.5 mi. long, in the Elburz, and the Hendevade glacier on the slopes of the Çilo Dağ, 4,168 m. (13,680 ft.) near Hakkari in eastern Turkey), and even more extensively in the high Pamirs and Karakorams, but the Pamirs, Karakorams, and Caucasus are all outside the true Middle East, and the other regions are extremely limited in extent.

Erosion and deposition by water can be divided into the work of seas and the work of rain and rivers. Since the nature of the Middle Eastern coasts is discussed on pp. 70–72 in relation to Map 12, we need here consider only land forms of the second type. Naturally, these are dominant in regions of heavier rainfall, but flash floods also erode the deserts, and much of the present desert landscape seems to be the result of river action in that period before 8000 B.C. when, it is believed, the rainfall was heavier than it is now.[1] Flash floods are, in fact, a frequent feature of Middle Eastern climates, because of the general tendency already noticed for the rain to be concentrated into brief periods of torrential downpours. The drier the region, the greater the tendency for the valleys to take the form of *wadis,* with dry stream beds in which water flows only after rain,[2] but even elsewhere dry valleys are common, because of the erratic rainfall, and because so much of the rock in the Middle East is porous limestone or sandstone. Even valleys with permanent streams have few tributary valleys. Consequently, though surface soil erosion is heavy in all deforested areas, actual rock erosion tends to be restricted to the valley bottoms, where the rivers are confined between steep or precipitous slopes. In the Middle East it is dangerous to use a physical map uncritically for plotting natural routes, for very often, as in western Judah, the tracks follow the rocky highlands between the valleys rather than the valleys themselves. Thus, none of the major river courses of the Levant is a natural routeway, though more than one of them has been so described by an unwary author.

In the Zagros, the deep valleys which divide the high mountain ridges from each other are connected by relatively few, but very narrow, transverse gorges, or *tangs,* whose origin has been much disputed, and which may have developed in a variety of ways.[3] They have towering, clifflike sides, and look as if the long mountain ridge has been slashed by a gigantic knife (Plate 18). Because there is little alternative, these valleys do provide, it is true, the means of communication, but only with great difficulty. Thus, the River Kashan below Khorramabad, followed by the Susa-Ecbatana road, runs through an almost continuous gorge for 128 km. (80 mi.), deeply incised even in the intervening valleys. Above Khorramabad there is no

river valley for the road to follow, until it turns north at Borujerd, and it must climb tortuously over one ridge after another. The road from Susa to Persepolis was even more difficult, for here there is in the higher, central ridges a succession of tremendous hogbacks, each with a level, only slightly serrated, skyline, and no transverse valleys. They may be crossed only by climbing the steep and winding tracks which lead to the high passes, or *kotals,* on their very summits.

This erratic and defective erosion of the high mountain regions explains the isolation of so many of the mountain valleys from one another, and the fact that often such valleys have no drainage outlet to the sea, or even to the interior plateaus. The isolation is illustrated by the fact that many of the rivers acquire different names as they pass from one valley to another. The major lakes of Anatolia and the Urartu region are usually basins of inland drainage (though Lake Sevan, which drains into the Araxes, is not); in the Urartu mountain knot, inland drainage is often the result of blockage of the valleys by volcanic outflows. Farther west, in the "Lake District" of southwest Turkey, it is caused also by the extreme porosity of the limestone, and here there are a multitude of minor basins, or *polijen,* where the limestone has been dissolved by rainwater (Plate 2).

On the plateaus, whether within or beyond the

[1] B. W. Sparks, *Geomorphology* (London: Longmans, 1960), pp. 253–54; C. Voute and E. J. Wedman, "The Quaternary Climate as a Morphological Agent in Iraq," in *Changes of Climate: Proceedings of the Rome Symposium Organized by UNESCO and the World Meteorological Organization* (Paris: UNESCO, 1963), p. 400; S. K. Seth, "A Review of Evidence Concerning Changes of Climate in India During the Protohistorical and Historical Periods," in *Changes of Climate,* pp. 443–52. At the same symposium R. J. Braidwood in his paper "Summary of Prehistoric Investigations in Kurdistan in Relation to Climatic Change" (*Changes in Climate,* pp. 251–53) and Hans Bobek in "Nature and Implications of Quaternary Climate Changes in Iran" (*Changes of Climate,* pp. 403–10) argued against the concept of a Pluvial Period. See also Hans Bobek, *Features and Formation of the Great Kawir and Masileh* (Arid Zone Research Centre, University of Tehran, 1959), pp. 49–58, and K. W. Butzer, "Deserts in the Past," *Arid Lands: A Geographical Appraisal,* ed. E. S. Hills (Paris: UNESCO, 1966), pp. 127–44.

[2] The use of the word *wadi* is somewhat confusing in Middle Eastern geography, because its meaning in geographical circles differs from its original meaning in Arabic. For the physical geographer it is a technical term for a dry valley in desert or semidesert regions, which carries water only during a rare flash flood. But in Arabic *wādī* means a valley of any kind, whether it has a permanent stream in it or no. Thus, the valley of the Yarmuq, which does have a permanent stream, is Wadi el-Yermuq, and the broad, shallow depression on the borders of the modern Jordan and Saudi Arabia is known as Wadi Sirhan. Confusion arises for the student, because on maps of Arabic-speaking countries the name *wadi* often occurs to designate valleys which are not wadis in the technical sense at all.

[3] T. M. Oberlander, "The Origin of the Zagros Defiles," in *The Land of Iran,* ed. W. B. Fisher, "Cambridge History of Iran," vol. 1 (Cambridge: The University Press, 1968), pp. 195–211.

mountains, the same excessive steepness of the slopes prevails, hindering communication and dividing one region from another. The interior of Anatolia has only one area of extensive level land, the Konya Plain, draining into the salty Tuz Gölü (Plate 4), and elsewhere is much interrupted by mountains and hills, many of them volcanic. The Persian plateau is more of a true intermontane plateau in that it has a much larger extent of level, or more or less level, land. It is composed, however, of many desert basins of varying sizes, or kavirs, separated from each other by ridges, which may be relatively low but may also be prominent tectonic structures, including folded hills, volcanic ridges, and uplifted blocks, rising perhaps from 600 to 900 m. (2,000 to 3,000 ft.), or occasionally more, above the plateau. These almost always have precipitous slopes, though at their foot there is likely to be a more gentle glacis of gravel.

In the plateau regions of the Levant, and in Arabia and northeast Africa, where the aridity increases southwards, the wadis are deeply incised trenches, bordered by high cliffs, but with relatively level floors (Plate 9). The Jordan Valley is both tectonic and erosional. The main valley, with its steep scarp slopes on either side, 1,200–1,500 m. (4,000–5,000 ft.) high, is the result of rifting, but in the center the river has carved a secondary trench, along which it meanders in a dense jungle of tamarisk, the Zor, once the home of a variety of wild animals, and still of wild boar. The edges of this secondary trough are steep and difficult badlands, known as the Qattara (Plate 28).

Where, usually because of faulting, the plateau has been considerably dissected, as in southern Jordan and the adjacent parts of Saudi Arabia, the residual fragments stand up like islands from the level, often sand-covered floor (Plate XVI), and one finds the mesa and butte formations characteristic of parts of the southwestern United States, for example at Monument Valley. Of particular importance are the anqāb (singular, naqb), or plateau edges, where the ground suddenly breaks away in a gigantic step to the lower land, as much as 1,200 m. (4,000 ft.) below. This formidable precipice may wind for many miles across the countryside, as does Jebel Tuweiq in central Arabia, presenting an obstacle impossible to circumvent to those who would approach it from below.

Deserts are popularly thought of as being monotonously flat, but this is a misapprehension, for they are a fascinating combination of vertical and horizontal forms, resulting from the combined activity of wind and water. In conditions of extreme drought, prolonged exposure to burning sun, and rapid changes of temperature at the beginning and end of the day, the surface of the rock tends to break into countless fragments, ranging in size from boulders to particles of sand. It is possible that isolation is somewhat less important in causing such weathering than was previously supposed, but it is clear that it is still a major cause.[4] Rapidly rising currents of air form above the hot land, and the wind picks up the lighter material in local dust devils, more extensive dust storms, or blinding sandstorms, when, in the vivid phrase of Gertrude Bell, "the wind bore down upon us and the parched earth rose up and enveloped us."[5] All this lighter material is swept into the sky, and the stony plateau is left exhausted and desolate. The result is a destructional plain, or hamada, which may be an expanse of bare rock or may be covered with "gibbers," millions of pebbles and boulders as far as the eye can see. Over very wide areas these are not large, and sometimes a gibber plain provides no great obstacle, but where the rock is volcanic basalt, the landscape is known as harrah, which is either continuous rough basalt, or else carpeted with an impenetrable jungle of large black boulders, and in any case well-nigh impossible to cross (Plate IV).

From time to time, a rainstorm assists in carrying the material. Desert storms, though rare and strictly limited in extent, are often torrential, and staggering amounts of eroded material can be carried in suspension until the flood subsides, though usually only for short distances. The wide mud flats, qaʿa or sebkha, are constructional plains, created by deposition, and are as level as a billiard table, any irregularity in the landscape having been submerged, but the slightest precipitation makes them as slippery as glass and impossible for camels. Even in the drought of summer they may be treacherous, for the muddy water is often just below the surface, and the crust less than an inch or even half an inch thick. This seems to be especially prevalent in the Iranian deserts, where the kavir formations appear to represent a unique type of desert land-

---

[4] E. S. Hills, C. D. Ollier, and C. R. Twidale, "Geomorphology," in Arid Lands: A Geographical Appraisal, ed. E. S. Hills (Paris: UNESCO, 1966), pp. 59–60.
[5] Gertrude Lowthian Bell, Amurath to Amurath (London: Heinemann, 1911), p. 173.

scape. Bobek distinguishes in every *kavir* a "wet zone," drying out round the edges to a salt zone, and finally the *zardeh*, or yellowish dry soils.[6] Sometimes there is in the center a *namak*, or salt lake. Scharlau speaks of two types of *kavir*, fed respectively by direct rainfall or by underground seepage, the *kavirs* of the north and west being moister than those of the southeast.[7]

When the loose material is transported by wind, it is driven against rock surfaces, and undermines them at the bottom, since the heaviest material is carried close to the ground. This again produces steep cliffs, with piles of fallen boulders at their feet and "mushroom rocks" projecting from the desert floor in fantastic shapes, or *yardangs*, sharp ridges parallel to the direction of the wind. Some of the most impressive, and indeed startling, examples of wind erosion occur near Shahdad in the Dasht-i-Lut of Iran, in the *kalut* landscape, with its "boulevards" extending over 95 km. (60 mi.), and the *shahr-i-lut*, or "desert towns," where sand blast has carved the rocks into the appearance of cities with buildings several stories in height.[8] In central Arabia the Dahna' consists of a series of concentric cuestas (i.e., hills or ridges with one broad and gentle slope, and one steep slope), where the scarp slope, because of the nature of desert erosion, stands up in ferocious cliffs. The intervening valleys are choked with sand.

Lastly, there are sand deserts, or *erg*. These are found mainly in the Sahara, and in Arabia, where the smaller Nefūd in the north and the much larger Ruba' el-Khali in the south are both sand deserts. They are joined by the long sandy valleys of the Dahna'. However, smaller areas of *erg* are common elsewhere, in northern Sinai (Plate XIV), and on the Persian plateau, where they are known as *rig*, or *reg*, and seem to form at the southern end of a *kavir* basin. The largest area of *rig* in Iran is in the extreme southeast of the Dasht-i-Lut, and extends for about 215 km. (135 mi.).[9]

It is possible to distinguish a variety of types of sand desert:

**(a) Zibār,** or slightly rolling sandy country, which may extend over considerable distances, but where differences of altitude are usually less than 30 m. (100 ft.). Cressey speaks of much of the region south of Dhahran in eastern Arabia as being of this type.[10]

**(b) Barchans,** or crescentic sand dunes. They are formed where there is a fairly regular wind from one direction, and tend to be best developed where there is only a moderate amount of sand covering the bedrock, across which the dunes march gradually before the wind. *Barchans* have a maximum height of about 30 m. (100 ft.), and a maximum width and length of slightly over 400 m. (1,200 ft.). The windward slope is gentle and fairly solid, with the interior of the crescent on the lee side, which is steep and soft. Where the wind changes direction regularly every year, it is said that the *barchans* are regularly reversed.

**(c) Sand seas,** or vast expanses of sand, with a very complex pattern resulting from frequent shifting of the wind. The lee slopes are steep, and more or less crescentic, and face in every direction. This type is very widespread in all major sand desert regions, especially in areas of very plentiful sand.

**(d) 'Urūq, or Suyūf,** i.e., "veins" or "swords." These are long narrow sand dunes, or lines of sand dunes, sometimes of enormous length, as much as 160 km. (100 mi.) being reported in parts of the Ruba' el-Khali.[11] These dunes are higher than *barchans*, 60 to 90 m. (200 to 300 ft.) being common in the Ruba' el-Khali and the Sahara, and twice this being reported from Iran.[12] They may be very complex, and attain a width of 600 to 900 m. (2,000 to 3,000 ft.), and between them there are long avenues, which form passages through the *erg*, the rela-

---

[6] Hans Bobek, *Features and Formation of the Great Kawir and Masileh*, pp. 16, 22.

[7] K. Scharlau, "Geomorphology," *The Land of Iran*, p. 191.

[8] W. B. Fisher, "Physical Geography," *The Land of Iran*, pp. 97–98; K. Scharlau, *op. cit.*, p. 192.

[9] W. B. Fisher, *op. cit.*, pp. 98–99.

[10] George B. Cressey, *Crossroads: Land and Life in Southwest Asia* (New York; Lippincott, 1960), pp. 86–91.

[11] Cressey, *op. cit.*, p. 87.

[12] B. W. Sparks, *op. cit.*, p. 249. W. B. Fisher, however, denies that dunes of great height are found in Iran (*op. cit*, p. 93).

tive shallowness of the sand permitting the digging of wells to reach the underground water.

**(e) Sand mountains,** or pyramid dunes, which so far are reported only from Arabia.[13] They usually stand upon a smooth *sebkha* base, and attain heights of as much as 300 m. (1,000 ft.) in the Ruba' el-Khali, though they are found also in the Nefūd and Dahnaʾ.

**(f) Sand sheets.** In striking contrast to the varied landscape of the dunes are the regions, sometimes covering thousands of square kilometers, of almost absolutely level sand. The origin of these surprisingly smooth surfaces has not been fully explained. A vast area of this type of desert occurs on the present southern border of Egypt.

The essential cultural difference between *erg* and *hamada* is that movement is almost prevented in the *erg,* though not entirely so, and settlement there is impossible in normal circumstances. Contrary to popular belief, areas of dune sand do not appear to move over any distance through the centuries, though there is a fair amount of local shifting, and blown sand from the dunes frequently blocks wells and water channels. Though high winds have been reported, they do not seem to be a common feature of the *erg,* though they may be more frequent in sand-sheet regions. When they occur in dune country, the sand streams off the tops of the dunes like blown spume in a gale at sea, and dunes have been described by travelers as "smoking" in the wind.

The variety of the environment is reflected in a quite extraordinary cultural mosaic. Basically, there are three types of society in the Middle East: pastoral, agricultural, and commercial, all beginning in an embryonic form about 8000 B.C. It is impossible to state at what period complete differentiation occurred. Certainly, by 3000 B.C. the development of the great riverine civilization of the Nile, Mesopotamia, and the Indus mark a clear separation between the irrigated agricultural land and the arid wastes on either side.

On the rain-fed lands, the separation out into pure nomadism and settled farming perhaps waited until the taming of the camel between 1500 and 1200 B.C., though it may have come earlier on the Russian steppes, where E. D. Phillips speaks of the Tripolye culture of southern Russia, with its mixed farming, being broken up about 2000 B.C. by pastoral immigrants who had already tamed the horse and camel and knew the use of wheeled carts, all of which was necessary to a developed nomadism.[14] Phillips rightly insists that "the nomads are of special interest to us because their way of life was an alternative to civilization, not a mere absence of it,"[15] and we must give up forever the earlier view that nomadism was merely an intervening stage between food collecting and developed agriculture. The essence of pastoral nomadism is that animals are interposed between man and the inhospitable earth. The animals are sent far and wide in search of pasture, and men then live from the animals, deriving the bare necessities of life—food, clothing, shelter—from the materials which they provide.

The separation of the nomadic pastoralist from the settled farmer should not be exaggerated, for the two are very often dependent upon each other. Yet, in one sense, the division is almost absolute. The desert requires mobility, for those who are not free to move will surely die; and cultivation of the soil requires stability, and that men cherish forever the land which they have inherited. Upon this simple and primary fact rests the whole ceaseless struggle between the Desert and the Sown.

Desert society is itself far from simple, because the desert environment is complex. In Arabia, the desert Arabs distinguish among the *Sharif* ("noblemen"), who are camel owners living in tents all the year around; the *'Arab Dār* ("house Arabs"), who are tent dwellers but live for part of the year in simple houses; the *Huqraʾ* ("despised folk"), who are seminomadic villagers, from time to time bringing their flocks to the desert edges; and finally the *Hadhari,* who are true cul-

---

[13] Cressey, *op. cit.,* pp. 88–91.

[14] E. D. Phillips, *The Royal Hordes: Nomad Peoples of the Steppes* (Thames and Hudson, London, 1965), pp. 24–25. R. Walz, "Neue Untersuchungen zum Domestikationsproblem der altweltichen Cameliden," *Zeitschrift der Deutschen Morgenländischen Gesellschaft,* 104, 1954, 45–87, see pp. 78–80, 66–68. B. Brenties, "Das Kamel im Alten Orient," *Klio,* 38, 1960, pp. 33–48, and *Die Haustierwerdung im Orient: Ein Archäologischer Beitrag zur Zoologie* (Wittenberg/Stuttgart, 1965), pp. 54–57. I am grateful to Père de Vaux for calling my attention to the works in German, which I had not seen.

[15] Phillips, *op. cit.,* p. 10.

tivators tied to the *hādhir,* or agricultural land. Roughly speaking, these reflect a transition from the extreme aridity of the interior of Arabia to the slightly better watered zones on the edges. But the variety of the desert is infinitely greater than this, and Tricart and Cailleux indeed forbid us to speak of zones at all, so complex is the environmental pattern.[16] It is this diversity rather than simplicity which impresses itself upon the mind of all those who call the desert their home, and travelers in Arabia have insisted upon the ability of the bedouin to distinguish minutely between one part of the desert and another.

Another type of nomadism is found in mountain regions. This is transhumance, the regular movement of flocks and herds from the lowland winter pastures to summer pastures higher up the slopes. In the high mountain areas the rich meadows above the treeline are, of course, deep in snow and inaccessible all winter, but in the Middle East there is transhumance even where the mountains are not high enough to be snow-covered, for everywhere greater elevation means that grass endures longer in the period of drought. There used to be, for example, a transhumant movement of camels from the Dead Sea trough in winter up onto the plateau country in summer, and though camel breeding has declined, this still continues with sheep and goats.

Irrigation societies, on the other hand, tie the farmer to the land absolutely and develop also a high degree of social organization, for there must be a generally accepted system of distributing the water and this system must be maintained day by day. These riverine societies are again far more diverse than is obvious to the casual observer, being not only markedly different from one another, but also individually of so complex a pattern that unification within each society is a major political problem. In Egypt the difference between "the two lands" of the lotus and the papyrus was recognized from the days of the Old Kingdom, and within each land there was a variety of centers with conflicting interests. This was reflected in the multiplicity of the ancient Egyptian gods, and led to a collapse of order whenever the royal scepter passed into the hands of weaklings. The function of the Pharaoh was to unite in his own person the two lands, and this function is no less necessary today. Indeed, one finds at present a striking re-establishment of the ancient pattern.

The differences between the Nile Valley and Mesopotamia have been so often insisted upon, by Henri Frankfort and others,[17] that we need do no more than glance at them here. Yet they are of the first importance. Mesopotamia lies to the north, and Egypt to the south of 30° N.; the two flood systems are utterly different, Mesopotamia being inundated at that very season in the year when the Nile is at its lowest. The floods of the Nile are steady and predictable; those of the Tigris tumultuous and erratic. Within Mesopotamia also there is divergence. Ancient Assyria to the north depended upon rain-fed agriculture, but Babylonia in the south was the date civilization *par excellence.* Still today 80 percent of the world's dates are grown in southern Iraq, and though to the uninstructed tourist there may be a rather deadly monotony about the endless palm groves, the sameness is apparent rather than real. There are at present 345 different kinds of date palms, and of this variety the farmer is well aware.

Also dependent upon irrigation, but quite distinct from these vast riverine systems, are the oases. These include the desert oases of the Sahara and central Arabia, but also, strung out along the foot of the great mountain ranges, the piedmont oases, utilizing the water that has come down from the higher elevations. These are true oases in that there is insufficient rain for agriculture, so that the irrigated area is surrounded by barren and unproductive land, but on one side at least tower the mountains, which herald a new and more verdant world. They stand, therefore, at the junction of two very different natural regions.

Upon these piedmont oases have depended the great trade routes of the Middle East, for here the caravans can pick their way between the twin obstacles of the mountains and the desert. The famous Silk Road to China, the plateau route to India, the Royal Road to Sardis, the Incense Route from southern Arabia, and the Trunk Road across the Levant Bridge from Mesopotamia

---

[16] Tricart and A. Cailleux, *Le Modèle des Régions Sèches* (Paris: Centre de Documentation Universitaire, n.d.), vol. 1, p. 62.

[17] See, for example, H. and H. A. Frankfort, John A. Wilson, and Thorkild Jacobson, *Before Philosophy: the Intellectual Adventure of Ancient Man* (Baltimore: Penguin Books, 1949), and Henri Frankfort, *The Birth of Civilization in the Near East* (Garden City, N.Y.: Doubleday, 1956).

to Egypt—these were all of them piedmont roads. Many of the great caravan cities, such as Damascus, Iconium, Isfahan, Kerman, Merv, Bukkhara, and Samarkand, were piedmont oases, though this is less true in Anatolia, where the absence of desert conditions means an absence of oases. Erzurum and Sebaste (Sivas), for instance, are not oases.

These oases were connected with some form of tentative and embryonic trade from the very beginnings of human settlement. Jericho at the foot of the Judean hills, and Çatal Hüyük at the edge of the Konya Plain, both reveal, more than eight thousand years ago, a startlingly complex social organization, and a high degree of architectural skill, and they seem to have been in communication with each other, though they were fifteen hundred miles apart. Even at this far distant date obsidian, bitumen, shells, salt, and other natural products moved between the Red Sea and Jericho, between Jericho and the Anatolian plateau, and between the Anatolian plateau and Mesopotamia, though it is probably wrong to call this actual "trade." It has even been suggested that long before the taming of the camel there was already regular communication with southern Arabia, with small caravans of asses moving slowly from oasis to oasis along the foot of the west Arabian mountains. Proof of this, however, must await the extension of archaeological research to Saudi Arabia.

Irrigation societies, it should be noticed, are all climatically exotic, in that they exist only by reason of a climatic situation other than that of their own immediate area. They are therefore strictly limited in extent, and often politically insecure, for the farthest point reached by the irrigation canal is the end of the society. Oasis communities are often rich and cultured, and famous for their artistic and technical skills, but they cannot easily exercise political control over the surrounding peoples, with whom they are entirely out of sympathy, and they continue to exist in that political isolation to which their exotic character condemns them. To this day, this is the basic reason for the endemic political chaos of Syria. Damascus is politically the key to the entire Levant, but it can never provide an effective government for the diverse regions of the country, whose interests are ever at variance with those of the capital, and its role, therefore, as an imperial center was never more than temporary, as has been that of every oasis city. This has also been the persistent problem of the unification of Iran, where very nearly

every city of importance is an oasis.

There is, of course, another type of agriculture which is rain-fed. "The land which you are entering to take possession of it," Moses is reported to have told the Hebrews, "is not like the land of Egypt, from which you have come, where you sowed your seed and watered it with your foot, like a garden of vegetables; but the land which you are going over to possess is a land of hills and valleys, which drinks water by the rain from heaven." (Deut. 11:10–11.) In all such areas the dominant agricultural factor is the rain in the immediate vicinity, and there is no sudden boundary. Rather there is a gradation, first into steppe and then into desert, and this gradation alters from year to year. Thus, from 1957 to 1960 there was serious drought in Palestine, and in Jerusalem the total rainfall was more than halved. In all marginal regions such a deficit is disastrous and may bring about the collapse of the agricultural system; the farmers take refuge elsewhere, and the surrounding bedouin have little alternative but to advance on the deserted fields.[18]

Precariousness, indeed, is everywhere the dread companion of rain-fed agriculture in the Middle East, and especially toward the south and inward from the seacoast. Over very large areas it is impossible to exaggerate the sense of desperate insecurity which accompanies the farmer upon his rounds, for quite unlike the man who toils to maintain the irrigation channels, the cultivator here has absolutely nothing that he can do to procure the fertility of the ground. Almost the whole of Canaanite religion was built around this desperate anxiety, this passionate longing for a fertile earth, upon which, as they saw it, all existence and all meaningful life depended. In the Old Testament the battle between Yahwism and the worship of the Baalim was a debate upon these questions: "Can anyone understand the spreading of the clouds?" and, in the savage but at the same time welcome violence of the thunderstorm, when "from its chamber comes the whirlwind," is it possible to know "whether for correction, or for his land, or for love, he causes it to happen"? (Job 36:29; 37:9,13).

These three major types of society—pastoral, agricultural, and commercial—each so varied within itself, develop sharply different understandings of the world, different mores, and different religious ideas. What in general the desert world calls "good," the agricultural world calls "bad," and that which is "bad" in the desert

---

[18] D. H. K. Amiran, "Effects of Climatic Change in an Arid Environment on Land-Use Patterns," *Changes of Climate*, pp. 339–440.

is "good" in the settled communities. For the nomad a strong central government is a threat, and complete liberty of movement an absolute necessity; clearly defined boundaries are anathema, and the arts of war a virtue, for the desert tribe must of necessity protect itself. However, the pattern of desert warfare developed in such a manner as not to harm the society, and in the traditional Arabian fighting, and in the *ghazu* or desert raiding, very few people were actually killed.

Among farming communities, however, a strong central government is a necessity, "a king is an advantage to a land with cultivated fields" (Eccles. 5:9), and sharply defined boundaries a symbol of security, so that it becomes the greatest sin to move one's neighbor's landmark. When the government is weak, "caravans ceased, and travelers kept to the byways. The peasantry ceased in Israel" (Judg. 5:6–7). War is evil, for it takes the farmer away from his fields, and the fury of the invader can destroy in one day the patient cultivation of a lifetime.

Neither group could understand the other. To the nomad it is incredible that anyone should be so confined—confined to a little house, confined to his fields, and so confined by orchards, olive yards, and forest that men can never see the horizon. But to the farmer the desert is the "great and terrible wilderness," and he cannot comprehend how anyone can manage, much less desire, to live in a land where no rain is. For either the nomad or the farmer, life in the other environment would not be life at all; it would lack all that constitutes life in his terms.

The commercial society has no less its own mores and its own understanding of the world. It springs in large part from the perpetual inability of an agricultural community over vast sections of the Middle East to provide enough food for its own people, either for reasons of difficult terrain, or because of the constant shortage of water. Such communities must "export men," taking every unproductive person from the fields and sending him out to earn his living abroad. In the agricultural thinking it is the prodigal son who takes all that he has and goes into a far country (Luke 15:13), while the true son remains at home; but in a commercial community it is the function of every son to go out into the world; wealth becomes both a goal and a sign of virtue and divine favor. In such a society it is the wicked and slothful servant who buries his master's money in the ground, and does not make it earn more money (Matt. 25:14–30).

That it is possible to illustrate the mores of both the

agricultural and the commercial societies from parables in the Gospels demonstrates how in the Middle East the different societies impinge upon each other. Yet always it is the confrontation of opposites, the very virtues which form the pillars of one society being the evils which undermine the other. Even the arid peninsula of Arabia was never exclusively nomadic. Mecca, where Muhammad was born, was entirely a banking and trading city, where it was said that he who was not a merchant was nothing; and Medina, to which he fled, was the center of a group of agricultural oases.

It was not the bedouin who were responsible for the great trading caravans, and the merchants must be sharply distinguished from them. Certainly the merchants used the desert means of transport, and had to take a *rafiq*, or guide, from each tribe through whose territory they passed, and to this extent they were dependent upon them. Yet the two were enemies, deeply suspicious of each other, and the merchants had to pay heavily to avoid being the victims of the *ghazus*, which, as we have seen, were a necessary part of the bedouin pattern of behavior. The sturdy individualism of the merchants offended bedouin traditions, where all the emphasis was upon corporate responsibility, and Muhammad's early criticism of the new banking city of Mecca was of its neglect of the fatherless and the widow, for whom the desert system made a place.

No less opposed, and yet interdependent, were the merchants and the farmers. The international trade routes depended, it is true, upon the piedmont oases for food and water, but at the entrance and exit of every city heavy taxes had to be paid. Indeed, one of the wonders of this transcontinental trade is that it should ever have been profitable, so threatened was it by natural hazards along the road and oppressed by desert raiders and the rapacity of the city dwellers, but profitable it undoubtedly was.

"Coming up from the wilderness, like a column of smoke, perfumed with myrrh and frankincense, with all the fragrant powders of the merchant" (Song of Sol. 3:6), the caravan brought not only luxuries, but new ideas, new concepts, and new religions. The wealth of the merchants, their luxury, the unsettling new ideas, the manner in which they encouraged young men to leave their father's house and go out on their own—all these things shocked and disturbed the conservative farmers of the Middle East. They were suspicious of the rich, of the sharp practices by which they fleeced the unwary, of the idleness of their womenfolk, and they feared the rich man's power; they feared what would happen to them if they got into his clutches, that they would be unable to pay their debts in time of famine, and be forced to sell their children into slavery, or lose forever the inheritance of their fathers. Usury was abhorrent to the farmer, who would never profit from his neighbor's distress, but to the merchant usury was interest and entirely respectable.

Everywhere these different social systems interacted upon each other, threatening and criticizing. The great trade routes ran hither and thither across the land areas, and to and fro along the narrow seas. But no less do the Desert and the Sown constantly meet. Jerusalem itself stands poised between the two, for the western slopes of Judea are cultivated and the eastern slopes desolate. In Persia the two types of society seem for centuries to have been about equally divided—though the proportions varied markedly from time to time—and it is not impossible that the persistent dualism of Iranian thought springs from this endless struggle in which neither could gain the mastery and in which it became necessary to develop a concept of society which allowed for conflict.

Even within the different societies there were sharp, almost rigid, divisions. The Iranians distinguish between the *garmsir* or hot lands of the oases, the *sardsir* or cool areas for grain, and the *sarhadd* or cold region above the grain limit. The oases themselves are divided: there are the hot oases of the southeast where dates are grown, the fringe oases of more moderate heat, where there is a precarious date culture and today citrus, and the apples, pears, and soft fruit of the northern oases.

The ancient Hebrews never colonized any region where they could not grow together the three staples of wheat, olives, and grapes, and whenever one of these became impossible, as on the broad coastal plain or the wide expanses of the eastern plateau, their territory ceased, though they did press southward into the Negeb. "Their gods," said the Syrians with some justice, "are gods of the hills" (I Kings 20:23). Moreover, the ancient tribal divisions were primarily territorial and related to different agricultural systems, for though in all Israel the three staples were grown together, in Judah the vine predominated, in Ephraim the olive, and in Manasseh wheat.[19]

The same cause in part lies behind the very ancient and remarkably persistent attachment of Susiana to the Iranian plateau, from which it is divided by a whole series of mighty mountain ranges, instead of to the nearby Mesopotamian delta, which from a purely physical map would appear to be far more sensible. When one goes to Susa one grasps the reason: here there are no date palms, whereas in neighboring Babylon they are numbered by millions.

It is difficult for modern visitors from the west to grasp the strength of these divisions, for there is often no apparent physical reason to account for them. Rather it is the different rhythm of life, different seasons of seedtime and harvest, occasioning different times for the festivals and different rituals, even where similar crops are grown. The systems never mesh, because the temporal patterns are different. Again and again one finds that apparently insuperable barriers of mountain and gorge have been transcended, while invisible frontiers of soil and climate have proved impassable.

[19] For a fuller discussion of this, see Denis Baly, *Geographical Companion to the Bible* (New York: McGraw-Hill, 1963), chap. 3.

# Maps IV–VI

The second group of colored maps and photographs deal with the great belt of towering mountains and high plateaus which occupy the northern third of the biblical world. They come together in the tremendous Urartu Mountain Knot[1] in the center, and divide on either side round the intermontane plateaus of Persia and Anatolia.

**Map IV. The Persian Plateau.** This is an immense, uplifted region 900–1,200 m. (3,000–4,000 ft.) above sea level, surrounded by very much higher mountains and divided into two unequal parts by the Khurasan ranges, which run from north to south across the center of this map. In the north the Elburz Mountains curve around the

[1] This is the area known to most geographers as the "Armenian Mountain Region." The term "Urartu" is used in this atlas to avoid possible political misunderstanding.

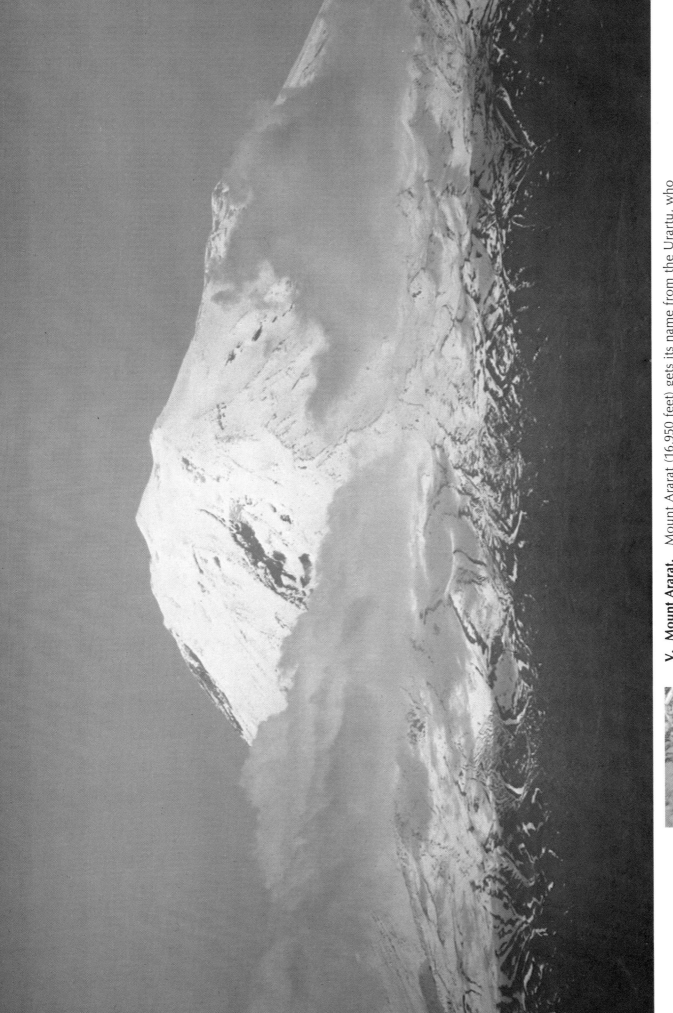

**V. Mount Ararat.** Mount Ararat (16,950 feet) gets its name from the Urartu, who established an important kingdom in the high mountain region around Lake Van in eastern Turkey in the first half of the first millennium B.C. It is an extinct volcano and in Mesopotamian mythology was associated with the abode of the gods.

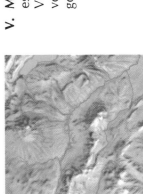

**VI. The River Halys.** Known today as the Kızıl Irmak, the Halys flows in a tremendous semicircle, which in ancient times formed a protective moat for the inner Hittite region. The picture gives a good impression of the Anatolian plateau in late spring. By the end of the summer the hills will be completely brown.

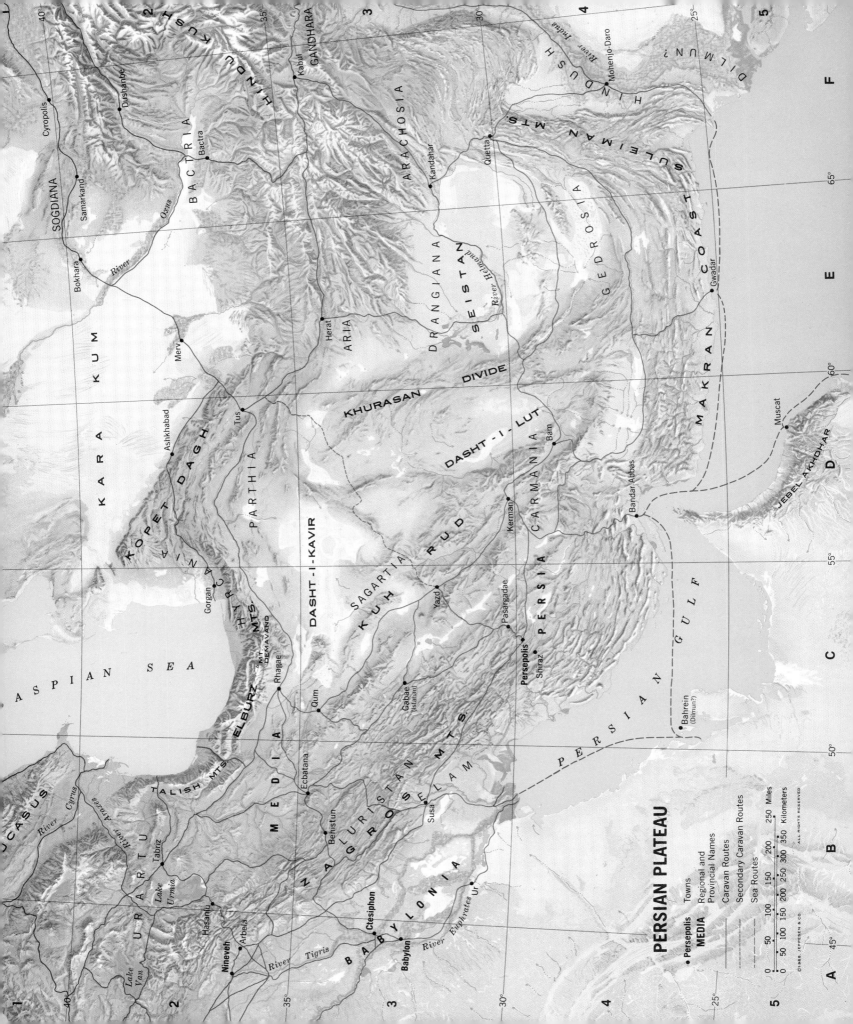

## PERSIAN PLATEAU

• Persepolis    Towns
MEDIA    Regional and
     Provincial Names
     Caravan Routes
— — —   Secondary Caravan Routes
- - - - -   Sea Routes

| | | | | | |
|---|---|---|---|---|---|
| 0 | 50 | 100 | 150 | 200 | 250 Miles |
| 0 | 50 100 | 150 200 | 250 | 300 350 | Kilometers |

©1968, JEPPESEN & CO.
ALL RIGHTS RESERVED

CASPIAN SEA

PERSIAN GULF

SOGDIANA
HINDU KUSH
GANDHARA
BACTRIA
ARACHOSIA
SULEIMAN MTS.
HINDUSH
DILMUN?
KARA KUM
DRANGIANA
SEISTAN
GEDROSIA
KOPET DAGH
PARTHIA
KHURASAN DIVIDE
DASHT-I-LUT
MAKRAN COAST
HYRCANIA
ELBURZ MTS.
DASHT-I-KAVIR
SAGARTIA
KUH RUD
CARMANIA
JEBEL AKHDHAR
TALISH MTS.
MEDIA
ZAGROS MTS.
LURISTAN MTS.
ELAM
PERSIA
BABYLONIA
CAUCASUS
URARTU

Cyropolis
Dushanbe
Samarkand
Bactra
Bokhara
Kabul
Quetta
Kandahar
Mohenjo-Daro
Gwadar
Merv
Herat
ARIA
Ashkhabad
Tus
River Helmand
Bam
River Indus
Muscat
Gorgan
Rhagae
Qum
Kerman
Bandar Abbas
MT. DEMAVAND
Yazd
Pasargadae
Gabae (Isfahan)
Persepolis
Shiraz
Bahrein (Dilmun?)
Ecbatana
Behistun
Susa
Tabriz
Hasanlu
Nineveh
Arbela
Ctesiphon
Babylon
Lake Van
Lake Urmia
River Araxes
River Cyrus
River Tigris
River Euphrates
River Oxus
Ur

## ANATOLIA AND THE AEGEAN

Major Trade Routes
Other Routes
Sea Routes

• Sardis   Towns
LYDIA   Regional Names

Miles  0  25  50  75  100  125  150
Kilometers  0  25  50  75  100 125 150 175 200

**BLACK SEA**

**AEGEAN SEA**

**MEDITERRANEAN SEA**

THRACE

RHODOPE MTS.

MACEDONIA

SAMOTHRACE

PONTIC MTS.

BITHYNIA

HATTI

CAPPADOCIA

KUE

PHRYGIA

LYDIA

PISIDIA

GALATIA

CYPRUS

CRETE

R. Danube
R. Struma
R. Vardar
R. Kelkit
R. Halys
R. Sangarius
R. Hermus
R. Maeander

Tuz Gölü

Beroea
Thessalonika
Apollonia
Amphipolis
Neapolis
Philippi
Delphi
Thebes
Athens
Cenchreae
Corinth
Mycenae
Sparta

Troas
Adramyttium
Mytilene
Pergamum
Thyatira
Sardis
Smyrna
Ephesus
Miletus
Halicarnassus
Cos
Samos
Patmos
Chios
Delos
Santorin
Rhodes
Cauda
Knossos
Fair Havens

Byzantium
Chalcedon
Nicomedia
Nicea
Prusa
Doryleum
Gordium
Ancyra
Pazarlı
Hattusas
Alaca
Alişar
Sebaste (Sivas)
Sinope
Amisus (Samsun)
Kanish
Caesarea
Archelais
Catal Hüyük
Iconium
Lystra
Derbe
Antioch
Apamea
Philadelphia
Hierapolis
Laodicea
Colossae
Attalia
Perga
Patara
Myra
Seleucia
Tarsus
Mersin
Issus
Karatepe
CILICIAN GATES
Antioch
Seleucia
Laodicea
Ugarit
Kadesh
Hamath
Halab

Salamis
Citium
Paphos

# URARTU MOUNTAIN REGION

- ● Asshur — Towns
- **URARTU** — Regional Names
-  —— Important Routes
-  — — Sea Routes

| 0 | 25 | 50 | 75 | 100 | 125 | 150 Miles |
| 0 | 25 | 50 | 75 | 100 | 125 | 150 | 175 | 200 Kilometers |

CASPIAN SEA

BLACK SEA

DAGHESTAN MOUNTAINS

TRANS-CAUCASIAN DEPRESSION

CAUCASUS

SARMATIANS

MT. ELBRUZ 18,480

MT. SAVALAN 15,784

TALISH MTS.

River Safid

Enzali (Bandar Pahlevi)

MEDIA

Ecbatana

Behistun

River Cyrus

River Araxes

River Araxes

Lake Sevan

Karmir Blur

Tiflis

MT. ALAGEZ 13,435

MT. ARARAT 16,945

Kars

Tabriz

Lake Urmia

Rezaiyeh

Selmas

U R A R T U

Tuspa (Van)

Hosap

Lake Van

MT. SUPHAN 14,547

Nineveh

Asshur

ZAGROS MOUNTAINS

River Tigris

ASSYRIA

BINGÖL MTS.

Erzurum

River Çoruh

TATOS MTS.

Trapezus (Trabzon)

Cerasus (Giresun)

Amisus (Samsun)

River Kelkit

AZZI-HAYASA

Altıntepe

River Karasu

River Murat

MUNZUR MTS.

ISUWA

MALATYA MTS.

Malatya

Sebaste (Sivas)

River Halys

HATTI

Kanish

Amida (Diyarbakir)

R. Tigris

Nisibis

MITANNI

Gozan

Tel Brak

JEBEL SINJAR

River Euphrates

River Euphrates

Euphrates

Haran

Edessa (Urfa)

Biredik

Hadatu

Carchemish

Sakçagözü

Karatepe

Alalakh

Halab

Hamath

TAURUS MTS.

AMANUS MTS.

**VII. Shepherd in the Zagros Mountains.** Almost everywhere in the high mountain regions the people practice transhumance. That is to say, they move their flocks from the lower pastures in winter to the high alpine pastures in summer.

**VIII. Piedmont oasis in Iran.** This is Mahan in southeastern Iran, a good example of a rich oasis formed at the foot of the high mountains which surround the interior desert plateau of Persia.

**IX. The River Euphrates.** This picture shows the river where it leaves the high mountains of Anatolia to enter the Mesopotamian plain. The white cliffs carved out by the river characterize its course in the section between the mountains and the delta of southern Iraq.

southern end of the Caspian Sea, the volcanic cone of Demavand (5,601 m. or 18,376 ft.) being the highest mountain in the Middle East (Plate 14). East of the Caspian the Elburz are joined by the Kopet Dagh, which are lower, but still in places surpass 3,000 m. (10,000 ft.). At the eastern end of the Kopet Dagh an important depression provides an easy route from the plateau to Merv in the northern plains. Farther east still are the huge ranges of the Hindu Kush, where the average height is greater than the Elburz, and very large areas are well over 3,000 m. (10,000 ft.), although no peak surpasses Demavand.

The Zagros Mountains leave the Urartu region south of Lake Urmia, and pursue a southeastward direction through Luristan into the ancient province of Persia (now Fars). Then they swing more directly eastward along the Makran coast until they make a dramatic swing northward in the Suleiman Mountains, which coalesce with the Hindu Kush in the Pamir Mountain Knot. The Zagros are much broader than the Elburz, and they reach their greatest height in Luristan, where some peaks are over 4,200 m. (14,000 ft.). Parallel to the Zagros, on the desert side of the mountains, is the high volcanic ridge of the Kuh Rud, reaching in places over 3,600 m. (12,000 ft.). In southeastern Arabia the Jebel Akhdhar ranges of Oman are an outlier of the Zagros system.

Within the encircling mountains there are a number of separate basin areas:

(a) The central Zagros basins, extending from Ecbatana through Isfahan, and a number of smaller basins, into Carmania, only 360 m. (1,200 ft.) above sea level.

(b) The narrow line of connected basins from Qum through Yazd to Kerman, between the Zagros and the Kuh Rud.

(c) The complex western plateau basins of the Dasht-i-Kavir (the Great Salt Desert) and the Dasht-i-Lut (the Great Sand Desert).

(d) The eastern plateau basins, of which the most important are Drangi-ana (Seistan), into which flows the River Helmand, and Gedrosia (modern Baluchistan).

This gigantic intermontane desert lacks a common center and a common way of life, and its history has been a struggle between unification and division, with the center of power passing from one oasis to another, the most important concentrations of population being in the west and northwest. Of the whole vast area, less than 10 percent is cultivated, because of a lack of water on the plateau and a lack of level land in the better-watered mountain regions. In ancient times the plateau population seems to have been roughly equally divided between settled people and nomads (a situation unique in the Middle East, though, as has been said, the ratio varied from time to time), and this may help to explain the persistent dualism of Persian thought, and the understanding of the world as involved in a continual struggle between two powers.

**Map V. Anatolia and the Aegean.** The mountain ranges of Central Europe curve around the solid block of the Rhodope Mountains, and run out into the sea in southern Greece, reappearing in the border ranges of the Anatolian plateau, the Pontic Mountains in the north, and the Taurus in the south. Earthquakes of disastrous proportions occur frequently in both Persia and Anatolia, especially along the Iznik-Erzurum fault in the Pontic mountain region (from Nicaea, or Iznik, in the west to Erzurum in the east, which is shown in Map VI) and on the northern edges of the Persian plateau. During the reign of Tiberius, a severe earthquake shattered the Pergamum-Sardis region, and the generosity of the Emperor to the stricken cities seems to have been one reason for the highly developed cult of the deified emperor, which is so strongly attacked in the Letters to the Seven Churches (Rev. 2:1 to 3:22).

The coasts of the Black Sea and the Mediterranean, though well watered, are narrow and rocky, and often the mountains rise straight out of the sea. Communication by ship rather than by land was the rule. In the north a down-faulted valley leads inland from Amisus towards Hattusas, the ancient Hittite capital. On the south coast, the only areas of level land are the small triangle behind Attalia (Antalya) and Perga, and the flat plain of Kue (Cilicia), which has been built up from sediment brought down from the mountains. Only in the west do valleys lead down from the plateau to the sea, notably the Maeander and the Hermus, but even here the slopes are much broken by fault scarps, and were once thickly forested, and so communication with the interior is seldom easy. The rich olive groves and vineyards turn their back on the land and face the sea, so that this became part of the Greek world, and the Aegean Sea a Greek lake. Saint Paul, it has been said, in all his travels was seldom out of sight of olive groves, and only when he penetrated to Antioch in Pisidia and Iconium did he really go beyond them.

The interior plateau, centered on the shallow salt lake of Tuz Gölü, is relatively dry (though nowhere desert) and thinly peopled, and the main cities cling around its edges. In the south at Çatal Hüyük is the largest Neolithic city known. Iconium, nearby, was an important town throughout biblical times. In the southeast is Caesarea (Kayseri), the capital of Cappadocia under the Romans, and close to it the ruins of Kanish (Kültepe), where from the nineteenth century B.C. there was an important colony of Assyrian merchants and metalworkers. On the north side of the plateau is Hattusas (Plate 31), the capital of the Hatti, or Hittites, who at the time of the Exodus had developed a powerful and coherent state behind the protection of the River Halys (Plate VI), which curved like a moat around their kingdom. This was the first Anatolian empire, and it came to blows with the Egyptian empire, notably at Kadesh on the border between the two.

The Hittite power was succeeded by that of the Phrygians, who swept into Anatolia from Thrace at the beginning of the first millennium B.C. The Phrygian capital was at Gordion on the River Sangarius, and their authority extended over the whole of the interior plateau.

## Map VI. The Urartu Mountain Region.

Structurally, this is highly complicated, for here the southwest-northeast direction of the mountains of eastern Turkey (e.g., the Taurus and Munzur ranges, the Tatos ranges on the Black Sea, and to the south the Malatya ranges) meet and conflict with the dominant northwest-southeast direction of the Caucasus and Zagros Mountains. Where these great mountain systems come together, there has been tremendous volcanic activity, some of which is very recent. Some of the many tall volcanic cones are named on this map—e.g., Ararat, 5,165 m. (16,945 ft.); Suphan, 4,434 m. (14,547 ft.); Savalan, 4,707 m. (15,784 ft.); and Alagez, 4,090 m. (13,435 ft.). The general level is above 2,000 m. (6,500 ft.), though the valleys may be somewhat lower and large areas exceed 3,000 m. (10,000 ft.). Today, though important forested districts remain, much of the region is alpine grassland.

Although mountainous, this is only partly a region of great mountain ranges, and much of it is high plateau country, created by the vast basalt outflows and interrupted by mountains. The deep purple or black color of this rock makes the countryside somewhat somber, but the wild flowers are glorious in late May and June. For several months in winter the whole region is deeply covered in snow.

The heart of the region is occupied by three large lakes: Sevan, 1,902 m. (6,320 ft.) above sea level, in modern Soviet Armenia; Van 1,720 m. (5,640 ft.) in Turkey; and Urmia, 1,297 m. 4,900 ft.) in Iran. All are surrounded by high volcanic mountains, and the last two have no outlet to the sea, so that they are salt lakes. Lake Urmia is much shallower than the other two and is gradually filling up, and indeed the Shahi peninsula was until recently a volcanic island. Urmia alone has much level land and marsh around its shores.

Beyond the mountains north of Lake Sevan is the Trans-Caucasian depression, where there is fairly easy communication between the Black Sea and the Caspian. The central route junction is at Tiflis, on the River Cyrus, which drains most of this depression into the Caspian. Farther north again is the terrific wall of the Caucasus, the highest mountain ranges in Europe. Mount Elbruz, in the west, is 5,633 m. (18,480 ft.) above sea level.

Although two of the lake basins themselves are regions of inland drainage, three important rivers rise in these mountains, and curve around the lakes to reach the sea. One is the Araxes (modern Aras or Araks), rising near Erzurum, and later joining the Cyrus, to enter the Caspian in a broad delta. Second is the Euphrates with two main sources, the Karasu, also rising near Erzurum, and the Murat not far from the foot of Mount Ararat. These flow westward, but then join and turn south to enter the Mesopotamian region at Birecik (Plate IX). Third, the headwaters of the Tigris rise on the southern slopes of the Malatya Mountains. They collect first in the basin of Amida (Diyarbakır), and then break through the low frontal range of the Zagros into the Mesopotamian plateau region. Other important, though smaller, river systems are the Safid Rud, curving round the Talish Mountains, and the Çoruh, which encloses the Tatos ranges on the Black Sea coast.

Despite the great difficulty of the terrain and the severity of the winter climate, this high mountain region has long been an important crossroads. Roads came around and across the Caucasus, up the Araxes Valley, and through the town of Kars; and from the Persian plateau in the east through Tabriz and Erzurum. To the west they led (a) along the fault valley of the Kelkit, (b) down the Karasu, and then to Sebaste on the Halys, and (c) along the Murat toward Kanish. From Erzurum, also, a road led over the mountains to the sea at Trapezus. The routes to the south followed in general the Euphrates, but tended to avoid the more difficult Tigris Valley.

There was constant pressure from the northern steppeland tribes around the Caspian, and the composition of the highland peoples was constantly changing. Movement along the great routes began well over 8,000 years ago, and two pieces of obsidian from Lake Van have been found at Beidha, near Petra, in a level dated c. 6600 B.C.[2] During the Old Testament monarchy Lake Van was the center of the important kingdom of Urartu (hence the name Ararat), and later this same region became the core of the great Armenian kingdom of New Testament days. The Hurrians, who formed the preponderant element of the Mitanni kingdom about 1500 B.C. and who also infiltrated widely into other parts of the Middle East, were probably related to the Urartians in this region. The Hurrians have been equated by some with the biblical Horites, but this is now questioned.[3]

The Urartu Mountains exercised great influence on Middle Eastern religious symbolism, for here, amid these towering volcanic peaks, was believed to be the abode of the gods "in the far north." The story of Noah's Ark coming to rest on Ararat (Plate V) expresses, in terms of Israelite religion, the ancient Mesopotamian belief that the order of the world emanated from this nuclear region. The Israelites translated this into the statement that here Yahweh, the almighty God of History, began the re-establishment of order and meaning in the world after the chaos and disorder of the Flood (Gen. 8:1–19).

[2] Diana Kirkbride, "Five Seasons at the Pre-Pottery Neolithic Village of Beidha in Jordan," *Palestine Exploration Quarterly*, Jan.-June 1966, p. 47. Also a personal communication.
[3] R. de Vaux, *Revue Biblique*, vol. 74, 1967, pp. 481–503.

2. The central Taurus Mountains. *A large part of the mountains of southern Turkey is rugged limestone country, partly covered with forest, but today also partly deforested. The level depression shown in the picture is known to geographers as a polje, and is caused by dissolution and collapse of the soluble limestone. The soil is washed down into these, and they are valuable both for cultivation and pasture.*

3. Southern coast of Turkey. *This photograph, taken about fifty miles east of Perga, shows how the towering mountains rise straight out of the sea, forming a precipitous and difficult coast. Cultivation is possible only in the small triangular deltas of the mountain streams. In ancient days the mountains would have been fairly thickly forested, and communication along the coast would normally have been possible only by sea.*

4. The Tuz Gölü. *The driest part of the Anatolian plateau is the small area of very level land east of Iconium (modern Konya). Here the rainfall averages about 12 inches a year, but there is no outlet to the sea, and so it drains into the broad, shallow salt lake known today as Tuz Gölü.*

5. Cappadocia. *East of Tuz Gölü lies an extraordinary region of soft volcanic deposits known as tufa, which have been cut into fantastic shapes by erosion. The "dwellers in Cappadocia" are reported to have been among the hearers of Peter's first sermon, and also among the recipients of the First Epistle of Peter (Acts 2:9; I Peter 1:1). This region is famous today for the medieval churches carved out of the rock.*

6. The gates of the Levant. *The black medieval castle of Toprakale is built on the Misis Dağ, where an outflow of hard basalt blocks the passage along the Cilician plain. Here invading armies and merchant caravans were confined to a very narrow gap, and just south of here, at Issus, the Persian army tried to block the advance of Alexander in 333 B.C. and suffered a smashing defeat.*

7. Spring floods in the high mountains. *The heaviest rain in the high Urartu mountains comes in spring, and coincides with the melting of the winter snow. This photograph was taken in mid-May 1967, when much damage was done to roads and bridges, and here turbulent, muddy water was swirling down what would normally be a dry valley. The bridge, evidently damaged in some earlier flood, was built by the Seljuk Turks just south of Tabriz in the thirteenth century A.D.*

8. A desert wadi. *This photograph was taken in northern Sinai, but would be typical also of much of Arabia and eastern Egypt. The tilted limestone strata, with a relatively smooth dip-slope but precipitous scarps, are characteristic, as is also the dry, level floor, with a single spina christi tree molded into an umbrella shape by the powerful winds.*

9. The mountains of Sinai. *In the south of the Sinai peninsula the very ancient granites and schists of the great Arabian platform, which underlies the later rocks, are exposed. Here the landforms are more rounded, but there are also fewer gentle slopes, and the general appearance is of a wild and stormy sea. The rocks are dark brown or dark red in color.*

10. Rain in the desert. *A picture taken in the north Arabian desert of east Jordan to show the effect of an exceptionally wet winter. A large shallow lake has formed in a depression where normally there would be a broad mud flat, and already the desert was beginning to be wonderfully clothed with green.*

11. Desert village in Iran. *Almost all the vast interior plateau of Iran is desert, shut off from the rain by the high mountains which surround it. However, at the foot of the mountains are the piedmont oases, collecting the water which has fallen on the higher elevations. Here is a tiny example, showing the carefully tended orchard, the adobe houses built without the use of wood, the neat adobe walls to prevent the animals straying, and the remains of the towers which once were necessary for defense.*

12. Lake Van. *The high mountain country between the Anatolian plateau and the Persian plateau has three important lake basins, separated from each other by towering volcanic mountains: Van in Turkey, Sevan in the U. S. S. R., and Urmia (or Rezaiyeh) in Iran. Lake Van, shown here, lies 5,640 feet above sea level. and was the center of the important Urartu kingdom during much of the Old Testament period.*

13. Eastern Turkey. *An enormous part of the east of what is now Turkey is a tumbled mountainous region, well over 1,800 m. (6,000 ft.) above sea level, and built of black volcanic basalt. Thickly covered with snow in winter, it has many permanent streams. Today it is mainly mountain grassland, with magnificent sheets of wild flowers in spring, but in ancient times it carried a great deal of forest.*

14. Mount Demavand. *The highest peak in the Middle East is the superb volcanic cone of Demavand in the Elburz Mountains south of the Caspian Sea (18,376 ft.). In the foreground is the black basalt which has flowed out from the now extinct volcano.*

15. The Zagros near Ecbatana. *The mountain ranges which surround the plateaus of Anatolia and Persia are built of intensely folded rocks. Here, in the region east of Hamadan (the ancient Ecbatana) the sandstone strata are almost perpendicular. The narrow layers of harder sandstone form knifelike ridges.*

16. Naqsh-I-Rustam. *In other parts, especially towards the interior of the plateau, the folding has been much gentler, as here near Persepolis. To the left, in the cliffs at the foot of the long dip-slope, are the tombs of the Persian kings.*

17. Living water. Very nearly throughout the Middle East water is life, and no one ever forgets this. Nowhere is this more apparent than in the Persian world, where to this day people love water and cherish it with a joy and affection that is more openly manifest than in any other Middle Eastern culture. This is the ancient sacred spring gushing out of the gigantic limestone precipice at Behistun on which is carved the famous inscription of Darius.

18. The Mesopotamian wall. *The border ranges of the Zagros towards the south and west, overlooking the Mesopotamian lowlands, are long anticlines, or upfolded ridges of rock, in which the narrow gorges, or tangs, are like gashes cut by a knife. The road from Susa to Persepolis had to cross a whole series of parallel ranges of this kind, in some of which there were no passes. This photograph is taken near Suleimaniyeh, east of Kirkuk in Iraq.*

19. Where the fire is not quenched. *At certain points along the vast Zagros ranges the oil in the rock oozes out, in some places producing the "eternal fires" which the Zoroastrians regarded as sacred. An interesting story connected with an outflow of naphtha of this kind is found in II Maccabees 2:19–36. This photograph was taken at Baba Gurgur near Kirkuk.*

20. The Fayyum Basin. *West of the Nile in northern Egypt there is a depression, about 150 feet below sea level, which is fed by an overflow channel from the river. From very early times this has been an important oasis and center of date cultivation, though related to the culture of the Nile rather than that of the desert.*

21. The Nile: the first cataract. *At six points in its course the Nile crosses barriers of hard granite, where the river breaks into a series of small falls and rapids which are a serious hindrance to navigation. They are numbered from the direction of Egypt, that is to say as one goes up the Nile, and the first cataract at Aswan marked the ancient boundary of Egypt proper, though the empire was subsequently pushed southwards to the second, and even the third cataract. The appearance of the Nile at Aswan has been greatly changed by the building of the dams.*

22. "The rod of an almond tree." *Over large areas of the Levant, Iraq, and Iran, the almond is the first of the fruit trees to burst into blossom, and so the flowering of the almond is an exciting time. The ancient Hebrews called it the "wakeful tree," and hence the play on words in Jeremiah 1:11–12. Almond orchards in spring are a mass of snowy white blossom. This photograph was taken in a valley in the Zagros mountains of western Iran.*

23. A sacred grove. *The northern stretch of the Syrian coast, between Tripoli and Latakia, has until recent years remained very isolated, by reason of the difficult forested mountains lying immediately behind it. Very ancient religious traditions have been preserved, and each village has its sacred grove, as it had in the days of the Canaanites.*

24. Mount Hermon in winter. During the winter months the parallel ranges of the Lebanon and Anti-Lebanon are thickly covered with snow, and the crossing of the Lebanon is often especially difficult. This photograph is taken looking south, with Mount Hermon on the left. The valley of the Hasbani, one of the tributaries of the Jordan, is in the center, and to the right of it a parallel range called Jebel Bir ed-Dahr. To the right, and free from snow, is the lower-lying Litani valley. The manner in which the hills come together in the south of the Beqa'a is clearly shown.

25. The cedars of Lebanon. *Only a few stands of the famous cedars of Lebanon still remain, and this is a photograph of a group in the southern part of the country. In the foreground may be seen the enormous trunks of the mature trees, and the background younger trees which have managed to seed themselves. In the ancient world Lebanon was famous not only for the great cedars but also for Mediterranean cypress and other large trees.*

26. The forests of Gilead. *The uplifted section of the plateau edge north of Rabboth Ammon (modern Amman) still carries much woodland of pine and Mediterranean oak. At one time very much of the hills west of the Jordan had this wooded appearance.*

27. The Dead Sea. *Here we see "walled up in her tomb for ever, the dead and damned Gomorrah." Such was Kinglake's description of this great salt lake, shut in between high cliffs, 1,274 feet below the level of the sea. The desperate barrenness of the cliffs on either side is clearly shown. The view is that of Moses from "the Pisgah," i.e., from the edge of the eastern plateau looking towards the Judean hills. On the far right of the horizon in this picture is Jerusalem, and on the far left is Hebron.*

28. The Jordan at Adam. *The central section of the Jordan valley, with the river meandering in a trough, the Zor, between the desolate badlands of the Qattara. The collapse of these soft cliffs in time of flood has, more than once in history, dammed the Jordan and temporarily stopped its flow. In the distance are the highlands of Gilead, with on the right the valley of the Jabbok, as it comes down to join the Jordan.*

29. The deserts of Midian. An aerial photograph of the dissected plateau country in the extreme south of Jordan, showing the mountainous islands of rock, sometimes over 1,500 m. (5,000 ft.) in height, rising out of a sea of sand. The long straight wadis caused by river erosion in the Pluvial Period along parallel geological faults are clearly shown. The Wadi Ram, which was an important caravan route to the north, runs diagonally across the center of the photograph, which was taken looking towards the southwest.

# THE NATURAL REGIONS OF THE MIDDLE EAST

## Chapter Four

The numbers of the sections in this chapter correspond to the numbers of the regions shown on Map 12.

## 1. COASTAL REGIONS

The Middle Eastern countries have a very extensive coastline on what are often known as the "Five Seas" (Mediterranean, Black Sea, Caspian, Persian Gulf, and Red Sea), but only two coastal areas are open to the ocean, the south Arabian coast and the Makran coast of Iran and Pakistan. All other coasts are on inland seas with restricted or nonexistent tides. Therefore, severe coastal erosion by wave pounding and tidal scour is rare, and there are almost no towering perpendicular cliffs, even though the mountains often plunge steeply into the sea.[1] The absence of tidal scour also means that the rivers tend to form deltas, dropping their sediment where they enter the sea. The formation of these deltas has been greatly hastened by deforestation in the mountains, and the resultant increase in soil erosion. This increase in delta formation can be traced on the coasts of Turkey to about the beginning of the first millennium B.C.

Marine deposition is dependent upon the local currents, which in the Mediterranean, Black Sea, and Caspian tend to flow in an anticlockwise direction. Ports are therefore sited on the edge of the deltas toward the head of the current, where there is less danger of silting. Deposition tends to be on the other side, notably the deposition of Nilotic sediment on the Palestinian coast south of Mount Carmel, which serves to deflect the current, and of Mesopotamian sediment on the western side of the Persian Gulf. Since these are the only two large river systems within the Middle East proper, such flat depositional coasts are the exception rather than the rule, and deposition elsewhere is of purely local significance.

The typical Middle Eastern coast is rocky, with a very narrow coast plain, and the mountains normally rise very steeply behind it, sometimes directly out of the sea. They are, furthermore, in general *concordant coasts*, in which the coast parallels the direction of the coastal mountains. In north and south Turkey, the south Caspian region, the Makran coast, and the greater part of the Oman coast, the fold mountains run parallel to the coast, and in the Red Sea and southern Arabia the coasts follow the fault lines. Such concordant coasts have few major harbors, though often a large number of little ones, and usually very difficult communications with the interior. The only important areas of *discordant coast*, where the folds are at right angles to the coast, are the southern coast of Greece, the Aegean coast of Turkey, the northern corner of the Levant, and the northern tip of Oman. Such regions normally have larger areas of protected water, and very much easier communication with the interior along the valleys between the mountain ranges. However, with the exception of the small area of northern Oman, the discordant coasts of the Middle East are all in regions of heavier rainfall, with consequently heavy silting at the mouths of the rivers. Ephesus, Miletus, Priene, and Tarsus were all ports in New Testament times but are now inland. Smyrna (Izmir) has been able to preserve its harbor because it

---

[1] A notable exception is the cliffs of Rūs el-Jibāl (see p. 76), where their cause is largely structural.

70

is not at the mouth of a river. (Compare also the port of Athens at the Piraeus.) Moreover, the heavier rainfall meant that in the past communication with the interior was hindered by forest.

The effect of all this is that coastal areas in the Middle East normally form regions apart, isolated from the interior, and also isolated from each other by stretches where there is no coast plain at all. They may be subdivided as follows:

**1 A. The Black Sea Coast of Turkey** *(Plate II)*. This is narrow, at times almost nonexistent, and backed by high mountains on the south. The climate is noticeably cooler than that of any other coastal area in the Middle East, and there is regularly snow in winter, Amisus (Samsun) averaging about ten days of snow a year. Rain occurs every month of the year, with a tendency to an autumn maximum and a spring minimum. Thick forest clothes both the coast and the mountain slopes, and land communications are very restricted. Three subregions are clearly recognizable: (a) the coast west of the promontory of Sinope (Sinop), with over 1,000 mm. (40 in.) of rain a year, and very difficult communications with the interior; (b) the coast east of Sinope round Amisus, which is in a rain shadow with about 750 mm. (30 in.), but has more level land and relatively easy access to the Anatolian plateau. This is the only olive-growing section of this coast. (c) The eastern section, with phenomenally heavy rain and especially dense forests, Rize having 2,441 mm. (97.6 in.) of rain a year on the average. Trapezus (Trabzon) was the end of an important caravan route to Persia.

**1 B. The Caspian Coast.** The rainfall regime is similar to that of 1A, though totals surpass 2,000 mm. (80 in.) only on the mountains. Sediment from the mountains has built up a narrow coast plain, bordered by blackish sandy beaches, for the river gravels are rich in mineral deposits. The dense Hyrcanian forest makes communication difficult, but this coast was used in ancient times as a routeway. Today, a variety of domestic architecture indicates the relative isolation of one section from another. (a) The valley of the River Cyrus (Kura), between the Caucasus and the Urartu mountains, is in a very marked rain shadow, and has less than 400 mm. (16 in.) of rain, and the coast itself is semidesert. Properly speaking, this should be a separate region, and would be so designated if it were not marginal to the area. (b) The central section of Mazarderan around Resht has the heaviest rains. Behind Resht, the valley of

the Safid Rud permits easy communication with the interior plateau. (c) The Gorgan coast, where the rainfall declines with surprising suddenness at the southeastern corner of the Caspian, Gorgan having only 500 mm. (20 in.), and the eastern shore of the sea being almost immediately desert. Between the Elburz and the Kopet Dagh a difficult, but possible, route led up to the plateau.

**1 C. The Sea of Marmora.** A small and structurally complicated region, important mainly for its communications, both from the Black Sea to the Aegean and from Europe to Asia Minor. The Greeks penetrated by sea to establish colonies on the Black Sea coast, and more than one movement of nomadic peoples came round the Black Sea and into Anatolia across the Bosporus. Both the Bosporus and the Dardanelles are part of a drowned river system, the Bosporus averaging about a mile wide (700 yards at its narrowest), and the Dardanelles about 3 miles. Troy guarded the western entrance to the Dardanelles. Although there is rain all the year, the climate shows the beginning of the Mediterranean regime, the average total being 600 to 750 mm. (24 to 30 in.) and the driest months being July and August. Because of the regular flow of cool water from the Black Sea to the Aegean, temperatures are similar to those of the Black Sea coast, though snow is more frequent because the body of water is much smaller, and the moderating influence is therefore less.

**1 D. The Aegean Coast of Greece.** Greece lies outside the true Middle East, and so both this and the next region are marginal. The eastern half of Greece is characterized by more frequent basins within the limestone mountains, and in these the Greek city-states developed. The climate is drier than that of the west coast, Athens having 375 mm. (15 in.) of rain a year, with a winter maximum and dry summer. The coast is rocky, but the Aegean islands, which are really tops of drowned mountain ranges, make communication with the Asian coast easy.

**1 E. The West Coast of Greece.** This receives a heavier rainfall, of over 500 mm. (20 in.), but is less thickly peopled. The sandstone mountain ranges run parallel to the coast, and level land for settlement is rare.

**1 F. Ionia.** Here the mountains run out into the sea, and though in general the coast is rocky, there are frequent level stretches built by deposition from the mountains. The climate is Mediterranean with a marked concentration of rain during the winter months. No month is absolutely dry, but less than 25 mm. (1 in.) falls during the two-month period of June and July. The total averages around 750 mm. (30 in.), though Smyrna (Izmir), being slightly protected, has 690 mm. (27.6 in.). Winters are warmer and summers hotter than on the Black Sea coast, and snow is very rare. This is olive and grape country, the vines being grown on hillsides and the olives mainly in the plains, and the Greeks developed here a number of great cities, such as Pergamum, Smyrna, Ephesus, Miletus, Priene, and Didyma. The coast plain is narrow, backed by forests and steep slopes though not high mountains, and the greatest concentration of settlement was between the mouths of the Hermus (Gediz) and the Maeander (Büyük Menderes), with Pergamum as an outlier in the smaller Bakir valley to the north. The increased deforestation after about 500 B.C. led to severe soil erosion, and the majority of the Greek harbors (except Smyrna, which is not on a river) are today several miles inland.

**1 G. Pamphylia.** In general, the southern coast of Anatolia is so mountainous that it is better included in the next category. However, in the triangle formed behind Attalia, where the folds are aligned in an acute angle, there is a fertile though small and hilly plain, with an annual rainfall of about 1,000 mm. (40 in.) and hot and humid summers, but very little rain in July and August. Once again excellent olive country, it was thickly settled by the Greeks, and was in close communication both with the island of Cyprus, from which Paul and Barnabas came to Perga on the first missionary journey (Acts 13:13), and with the interior plateau, by means of two rather difficult roads across the mountains.

**1 H. Cilician Plain.** A considerable mass of sediment pouring down from the surrounding mountains has built up a flat alluvial plain around the base of a line of low northeast-southwest hills, partly limestone and partly volcanic, known today as the Misis Dag (Plate 6). The rainfall varies from about 600 to 1,000 mm. (24 to 40 in.), and though the coastal areas are swamp, the interior is a sea of olives. Known to the ancient Egyptians as "the place where one turns round," this little plain was the Kue of the Old Testament and eastern Cilicia in the New Testament period. Almost all traffic from the Anatolian plateau to the Levant was funneled through here, coming down by the Cilician Gates (Plate 43) to Tarsus, which at that time could be reached from the sea. Another road led up into the highlands of the northeast. Movement was severely channeled by the marshes, the mountains on every side, and the central obstacle of the Misis Dag. Solomon imported horses by this route for re-export to Egypt (I Kings 10:28–29), and here, at the battle of Issus (333 B.C.), Alexander inflicted a smashing defeat on the Persian armies.

**1 J. The Tihama.** The Red Sea is divided from the Gulf of Aden by a shallow sill extending across the Bab el-Mandeb, so that the deep waters on either side are unrelated, creating special conditions within the Red Sea trough. No rivers enter the Red Sea, since a desert climate prevails for almost the entire length, and the high evaporation has resulted in unusually high salinity. The heat, combined as it is with high humidity, is exhausting, though slightly moderated by a sea breeze in the afternoon, and at most points the average temperature, even in January, is over 21° C. (70° F.). For the greater part of its length, the narrow coast plain is desolate and barren beyond description, and was known to early travelers as the home of fish eaters and pirates. Coral reefs along the coast make navigation difficult. Only in the southern section, where the monsoonal rains of summer on the bordering mountains send water down the valleys during part of the year, is any cultivation normally possible.

**1 K. The South Arabian Coast.** Here again the average monthly temperature never falls below 21° C. (70° F.), and the annual rainfall is less than 100 mm. (4 in.). The northeastern and southwestern sections appear to have the driest climate. During the seven months from April through September, the southwestern monsoon predominates, but since it blows parallel to the coast it brings almost no rain. From October to March it is replaced by the northeast monsoon, and from early times these winds were used by sailors for the passage to and from India. The Bay of Salalah is the part of the coast most affected by the summer monsoon, and here rain is concentrated in the summer months with, apparently, heavy rain on the mountains immediately behind. Because of this summer moisture, this is the one section of the Arabian coast where the coconut palm replaces the date.[2] From Salalah southwestwards this was the "incense coast," and still today incense from the interior plateau is exported from Salalah and Mukalla to India.

---

[2] Peveril Meigs, *Geography of Coastal Deserts* (Paris: UNESCO, 1966), p. 59.

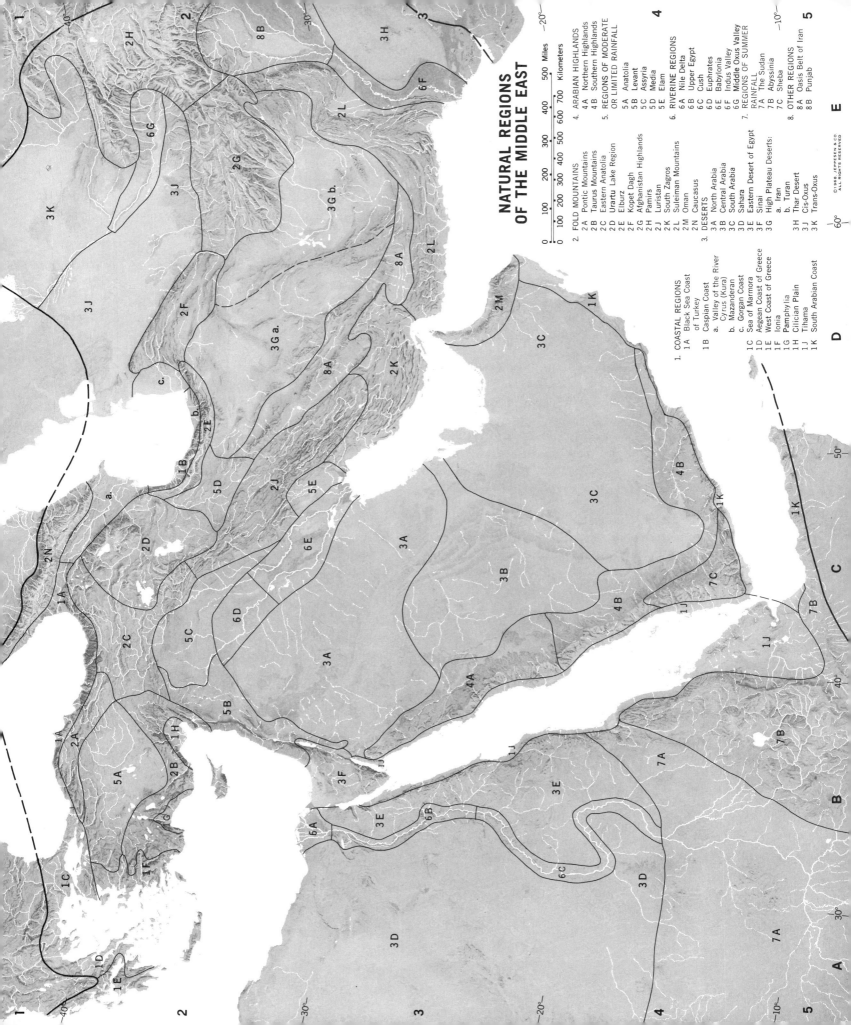

# NATURAL REGIONS
# OF THE MIDDLE EAST

Scale: 0 100 200 300 400 500 600 700 Kilometers
0 100 200 300 400 500 Miles

1. **COASTAL REGIONS**
   1A Black Sea Coast of Turkey
   1B Caspian Coast
      a. Valley of the River Cyrus (Kura)
      b. Mazanderan
      c. Gorgan Coast
   1C Sea of Marmora
   1D Aegean Coast of Greece
   1E West Coast of Greece
   1F Ionia
   1G Pamphylia
   1H Cilician Plain
   1J Tihama
   1K South Arabian Coast

2. **FOLD MOUNTAINS**
   2A Pontic Mountains
   2B Taurus Mountains
   2C Eastern Anatolia
   2D Urartu Lake Region
   2E Elburz
   2F Kopet Dagh
   2G Afghanistan Highlands
   2H Pamirs
   2J Luristan
   2K South Zagros
   2L Suleiman Mountains
   2M Oman
   2N Caucasus

3. **DESERTS**
   3A North Arabia
   3B Central Arabia
   3C South Arabia
   3D Sahara
   3E Eastern Desert of Egypt
   3F Sinai
   3G High Plateau Deserts:
      a. Iran
      b. Turan
   3H Thar Desert
   3J Cis-Oxus
   3K Trans-Oxus

4. **ARABIAN HIGHLANDS**
   4A Northern Highlands
   4B Southern Highlands

5. **REGIONS OF MODERATE OR LIMITED RAINFALL**
   5A Anatolia
   5B Levant
   5C Assyria
   5D Media
   5E Elam

6. **RIVERINE REGIONS**
   6A Nile Delta
   6B Upper Egypt
   6C Cush
   6D Euphrates
   6E Babylonia
   6F Indus Valley
   6G Middle Oxus Valley

7. **REGIONS OF SUMMER RAINFALL**
   7A The Sudan
   7B Abyssinia
   7C Sheba

8. **OTHER REGIONS**
   8A Oasis Belt of Iran
   8B Punjab

## 2. THE FOLD MOUNTAINS

These require a separate category, because they are in general much higher than the other mountain regions, with the exception of the volcanic mountains of Abyssinia and southwestern Arabia. Unlike block mountains, fold mountains form long parallel ranges, with the level land confined to the valleys rather than to high tablelands. Movement is always easier parallel to the folds than in a transverse direction, and the valleys are often isolated from each other.

**2 A. The Pontic Mountains.** There are two ranges parallel to the coast and divided by an interior fault valley. Forests in ancient times were thick, but there was always a marked difference between the intensely forested slopes immediately overlooking the Black Sea and the drier interior ranges. The western forests are deciduous, but in the higher, and very much wetter, eastern section coniferous forests are found. Here, behind Rize, the seaward slopes have a dense jungle vegetation: ". . . such a forest as I have never seen. The species were familiar—sweet chestnut, walnut, alder, beech, hornbeam and spruce—but all were giants. They hung over the gorges, and were so large that each tree remained a distinct sylvan personality three thousand feet above. From their branches trailed liana-like growths. Even laurel and box grew high as houses."[3]
Rhododendron and azalea are common, and it is from the yellow azalea that is made the intoxicating honey of which Xenophon speaks. Except only where the mountains are lower in the center behind Amisus (Samsun), communication across the mountains is excessively difficult, for the rivers occupy deep, impenetrable gorges.

**2 B. The Taurus Mountains** (Plates 2, 3). These differ from the much faulted northern mountains in that they are true fold mountains. Only in the east, where they are highest, do they run parallel to the coast. Their forests are mainly Mediterranean evergreen or coniferous and, though certainly thick in ancient times, never had much undergrowth because of the drier summer and the porous limestone. In the west, the folds are arranged in a huge inverted V, enclosing the narrow triangular plain of Pamphylia (region 1G). In the interior

these form the "Lake District" of Turkey, but farther south, on either side of Pamphylia, they plunge in steep wooded cliffs into the sea (Plate 3). The true Taurus are the high snow-covered ranges in the east behind the Cilician plain, and are divided from the western ranges by the valley of the Gök Su, the easiest route from the plateau to the south, reaching the sea at Silifke, the ancient Seleucia.

**2 C. Eastern Anatolia.** A line drawn from Trapezus (Trabzon) through Sebaste (Sivas) and Caesarea (Kayseri) to Cape Anamur, the southernmost promontory opposite Cyprus, more or less divides the lower central plateau of Anatolia from that higher eastern region where most of the land is over 1,500 m. (5,000 ft.). Sebastea and Caesarea, important caravan cities at the junction of the two zones, stood on the northeast-southwest road which runs parallel to the Upper Halys (Kızıl Irmak) at the edge of the highlands. In general, the valleys tend to run from northeast to southwest, and so the movement of the ancient nomadic tribes from central Asia was in this direction towards the northern Levant, as well as eastwards, by the Kelkit or Halys valleys, into the central Anatolian basin. Melid or Melitene (the modern Malatya) holds a position within a few miles of the Upper Euphrates, where a narrow valley leads southwards, over the Reşadiye Pass, and then down to Antioch in the southwest.

**2 D. The Urartu Lake Region** (Plate 13). This is discussed in relation to Map VI (page 52). Very extensive tracts are above 2,000 m. (6,500 ft.), and the more elevated portions exceed 3,000 m. (10,000 ft.). Even in the lower parts there are only 125 frost-free days, and Karaköse (height 1,650 m. or 5,000 ft.) close to Mount Ararat has four months with an average temperature below freezing, extremes of -43° C. (-45° F.) having been recorded in both December and January. The lakes exercise a moderating effect. Thus Van, at the same height as Karaköse, has only three months below freezing, and the lowest recorded temperature there is -26.5° C. (-17.5° F.). Both Van and Urmia are too salty for fish, though fishing is important in the river mouths (Plate 12).

**2 E. The Elburz.** With these must be included the Talish Mountains to the west. Together they form a narrow

---

[3] Robin Fedden, "Giant Forests above Black Sea Mists," The Times (London), August 30, 1963, p. 9.

crescent about 1,100 km. (700 mi.) long, but only 110 km. (70 mi.) wide, curving round the southern end of the Caspian Sea. The structure is very complex, but in general there are two parallel ranges, divided by a narrow, down-faulted trough, the northern range being the true Elburz. This presents a tremendous, densely forested wall to the north, rising almost straight out of the sea, which is a few feet below sea-level, to heights of well over 3,300 m. (10,000 ft.), some peaks exceeding 4,500 m. (15,000 ft.). The southern ranges are lower, rather simpler in structure, and drier, especially on the southern slopes. Precipitation (both rain and snow) well in excess of 2,000 mm. (80 in.) falls on the high northern Elburz. The main communications between the plateau and the coast are round the eastern and western ends of the true Elburz, the interior valleys being often difficult of access, though plentifully supplied with water. Here, in medieval times, was the home of the Assassins.

**2 F. The Kopet Dagh.** This is a continuation of the line of the Caucasus, cutting across the Elburz almost at right angles. The two ranges, though decidedly lower than the Elburz, both exceed 3,300 m. (10,000 ft.) in places, but the interior valley, though partially wooded, is broad and more open, forming an important routeway controlled by Tuz[4] at the southeastern end. The western mountains have about 1,000 mm. (40 in.) of rain a year, but in the Kuh-e-Binalud overlooking Tuz it is already less. The interior valley is much drier, with about 400 mm. (16 in.) at the northeastern end, and 200 mm. (8 in.) or less at the southeastern end. Here the rain falls during the winter months, with a tendency to a March-April maximum, but in the northwest it is very erratic. Rain, though heavier in winter, may fall in any month, but the distribution varies enormously. The mountains are now largely barren, but they must have carried good woodland at one time, mainly juniper.[5]

**2 G. The Afghanistan Highlands.** These are the Hindu Kush system, which is an offshoot of the Pamirs. They form a remote, little penetrated region, where no pass is lower than 3,000 m. (10,000 ft.). The higher mountains are snow-covered throughout the year, but the narrow rocky valleys are intensely cultivated wherever possible. Transhumance is practiced almost everywhere, for the summer pastures are rich and the lowlands very dry in summer. Kabul stands at a vitally important crossroads, where the direct but very difficult route from Herat to the Khyber Pass is joined by the road from Kandahar in the southwest, and another from Bactra and the valley of the Oxus over the narrowest section of the Hindu Kush.

**2 H. The Pamirs.** These mountains are outside the Middle East. The greater part is over 3,000 m. (10,000 ft.), and many peaks exceed 6,000 m. (20,000 ft.). Even so, an important route led to Sinkiang (Chinese Turkestan) from the Indus Valley in the south, and it was by this route that Buddhism was brought to China.

**2 J. Luristan.** Although this name properly belongs to one section, it may be extended to include all the broad central Zagros region, whose high parallel ranges often exceed 3,000 m. (10,000 ft.). The remote interior valleys grow wheat, barley, and temperate fruits. A great deal of transhumance is practiced. Luristan is chiefly famous archaeologically for its magnificent bronzes, whose date has been much disputed. Some scholars have dated the earliest bronzes around 2250 B.C., but the majority would place them later than this. Some believe that they were developed by the Kassites after they had been driven back from Mesopotamia, and that the best work should be dated about 1000 B.C., while others attribute the bulk of them to the Cimmerians, who, it has been suggested, moved into Luristan about 750 B.C. Others again argue for an extended development, lasting perhaps from the sixteenth to the seventh century B.C.[6] The home today of fiercely independent tribes who resist government control, it was no less so in ancient times, and they were a constant threat to the civilizations of the Mesopotamian lowlands. Recent evidence, however, is beginning to suggest that there have been periods when nomadism was less important, and that the first half of the first millenium B.C., for instance, may have been a time when there were numerous settlements in this area.[7]

---

[4] The present town of Meshed, a city sacred to Shia$^c$ Muslims, is several miles from the older site.

[5] Hans Bobek, "Vegetation," in *The Land of Iran*, ed. W. B. Fisher, *Cambridge History of Iran*, vol. 1 (Cambridge: The University Press, 1968), pp. 286–87.

[6] E. Porada, *The Art of Ancient Iran* (New York: Crown Publishers, 1965), pp. 75–89.

[7] Henrik Thrane, "Tepe Guran and the Luristan Bronzes," *Archaeology*, vol. 23, no. 1 (Jan. 1970), pp. 26–35.

**2 K. South Zagros (or Makran Ranges).** These must be distinguished from the previous region because of the increasing drought which results from the generally lower elevation and the greater distance eastward. A moderate rainfall occurs only on the mountains, and the interior valleys and coastal areas are desert.

**2 L. Suleiman Mountains.** Climatically, these are a continuation of the southern Zagros, with slight winter rain on the higher elevations, but otherwise very widespread desert conditions. Only in the central knot, near Quetta, are there peaks higher than 3,000 m. (10,000 ft.), and here the Bolan Pass to the southeast and the Zhob River to the northeast provide relatively easy routes across the mountains. The absence of forest makes these mountains less of an obstacle than many other ranges, and though the passes are not easy, there are said to be about 350 tracks across the mountains usable by camels.

**2 M. Mountains of Oman.** These are an outlier of the folded ranges, and similar in their climate to the southern Zagros. They are extremely rocky, and in the northern section, known as Rūs el-Jibāl, often drop sheer into the sea, one section of cliff being over 270 m. (900 ft.) in height.[8] The highest sector is Jebel el-Akhdhar in the center, where Jebel Kawi is 2,970 m. (9,900 ft.), and here the interior valleys and bordering piedmont regions have a large number of oases, with dates at the lower levels and vines in the highlands. The coastal lowlands near Muscat, known as the Batina, have continuous date groves for about 135 km. (80 miles).

**2 N. The Caucasus.** The highest mountains in Europe, these form the outer limit of the Middle East between the Black Sea and the Caspian.

## 3. THE DESERTS

Here it is possible to indicate only certain broad divisions which would certainly have to be elaborated if space permitted a more detailed survey. The criterion has been the 200-mm. (8-in.) line, which is normally taken as being, very roughly, the limit of rain-fed agri-

culture, 100 mm. (4 in.) marking roughly the boundary between semidesert and true desert.

**3 A. North Arabia.** This should be divided into the forbidding basalt plateau and highlands to the northwest, the sandy wastes of the Nefūd in the south, and the Wudian (or Widyan, i.e. "valleys") in the northeast. This last is a wide, rolling plateau, dissected by a large number of broad wadis, roughly parallel to each other, running northeastwards to the Mesopotamian trough. Movement in this section is relatively easy, and it contains a fairly large nomadic population. The important caravan oasis of Dumah (el-Jauf) lies where the tracks across the Wudian gather together to pass between the northernmost extension of the Nefūd and the southern limit of the basalt. There is a considerable underground water, even in the Nefūd, where the wadis have a surprising amount of desert shrubs and small animal life.

**3 B. Central Arabia.** This is the region known today as Najd, where a large number of deep wadis, fairly plentifully supplied with underground water, cross the peninsula from the granite plateau and the volcanic highlands with their enormous expanses of *harrah* in the west. The important caravan routes across the peninsula are hindered, and often deflected, by a series of high westward-facing precipices along the edge of the semicircular lines of hills, and by the treacherous sandy valleys of the Dahna, between them. The most formidable of the precipices is the western edge of Jebel Tuweiq, and the importance of Riyadh is that it is a large oasis controlling from the eastern side the major gap in this scarp. The other oasis towns lie in the northern half of this region.

**3 C. Southern Arabia.** Most of this is occupied by the dread Ruba' el-Khali. The Gulf coast of Arabia is the only large stretch of lowland coast in the Middle East. The climate is hot and humid, with monthly average temperatures below 10° C. (50° F.) only in December and January, and about 75 mm. (3 in.) of rain falls each year. There is a fair amount of scrub vegetation, and some important oases. It was noted for pearlfishing in ancient times.

**3 D. The Sahara.** Lying west of the Nile, this must be classed as beyond the limits we have drawn for the

[8] Meigs, *op, cit.* p. 52.

Middle East. Very large areas are sand desert, but the line of oases roughly parallel to the Nile should be noticed.

**3 E. The Eastern Desert of Egypt.** This is a long and narrow spine of fairly low, very rocky mountains, surpassing 2,000 m. (6,600 ft.) only in the extreme south, on the edges of the Abyssinian highlands. At its nearest point the Nile is only 135 km. (85 mi.) from the sea. The wadis are not lacking in springs, and the mountains can be crossed at many places, but there was little inducement to do so because of the excessive barrenness of the Red Sea coast. The two main routes across it were from Thebes and Syene (Aswan) to the ports of Myos Hormos and Berenike respectively.

**3 F. Sinai** (Plate 9). This triangular peninsula reaches its greatest height in the granite peak of Jebel Katarina (2,637 m. or 8,651 ft.), close to Jebel Musa, the traditional site of Mount Sinai. The northern half of the peninsula is a broad wasteland of limestone and chalk hills, known as el-Tih. The southern mountains were important in ancient days for their turquoise and to some extent for copper. This whole region falls into the semidesert category, for every winter there is some rain and on the southern heights snow is not uncommon.

**3 G. High Plateau Deserts.** The deserts of the Persian plateau are divided by the Khurasan range into the western Iran basin and the eastern Seistan basin. The Iran basin slopes from about 1,200 m. (4,000 ft.) in the northwest to less than 450 m. (1,500 ft.) in the southeast, and it is also divided into two major basins, the Dasht-i-Kavir in the north, and the long Dasht-i-Lut in the south, though each is actually a highly complex system of smaller basins or *kavirs*. Between the two is a line of low volcanic and limestone hills, the Kuh Duren, which makes possible a transdesert caravan route from Tuz (or today Meshed) southwestward to Yazd.

The Seistan basin is as yet very little known. The River Helmand, and three semipermanent streams, bring the melting snows of the Afghanistan mountains down to the Lake Hamun basin, where already in the Persian empire there was a complicated irrigation system and a relatively large population. This was apparently considerably expanded by the Parthians.

All travelers describe the low-lying basins of Dasht-i-Lut and Seistan as almost unbelievably desolate, bitterly cold in winter and unbearably hot in summer, when the dreaded *bad-i-sad-o-bist ruz,* or "wind of 120 days," blows relentlessly day after day, through most of the period from May to October, in a perpetual dust storm. A force of 135 km.p.h. (80 m.p.h.) is not uncommon, and 190 km.p.h. (120 m.p.h.) has been recorded!

**3 H. The Thar Desert.** Once again, this is really outside our region. Some authorities claim that it had rather more rain and still carried scrub woodland perhaps even as late as the time of Alexander.[9]

**3 J. Cis-Oxus.** If it were not that it lies north of the mountain belt and is therefore marginal, this varied region should properly be subdivided. In the north is the true desert area, known as the Kara Kum, or Black Sands, merging in the south into dry steppe, with around 200 mm. (8 in.) of rain at the foot of the mountains. There are, however, broad expanses of sand desert right up to the mountains. The important oasis area of Merv is fed by the waters of the Murghab, and a road led up this valley to the important route center of Herat in the broad gap between the Kopet Dagh and the beginning of the Hindu Kush.

**3 K. Trans-Oxus.** The Oxus was the effective frontier of the great empires centered on the Persian plateau, and the region between the Oxus and the Jaxartes an unruly frontier zone which they sought to command. The sand desert to the northwest is here known as the Kyzyl Kum, or Red Sands, and the important Silk Road followed the oasis cities at the foot of the mountains. Both this region and the previous one are exposed to the cold air from Siberia, and everywhere has at least one month with an average temperature below freezing.

## 4. THE ARABIAN HIGHLANDS

Structurally, these are the uplifted edge of the Arabian plateau, formed either of the exposed granite platform

[9] S. K. Seth, "A Review of Evidence Concerning Changes of Climate in India During the Protohistorical and Historical Periods," in *Changes of Climate: Proceedings of the Rome Symposium Organized by UNESCO and the World Meteorological Organization* (Paris: UNESCO, 1963), p. 447.

of Arabia, or recent basalt which has erupted through the cracks. The average rainfall on these mountains is anyone's guess, since statistics do not exist, but it is sufficient to supply the wells all along their eastern edge used by the yearly caravans. The dividing line is the gap in the mountains in the latitude of Mecca.

**4 A. Northern Highlands.** These are lower, and exceed 1,500 m. (5,000 ft.) only in a few areas. There are two lines of highlands, an eastern volcanic one with vast stretches of *harrah,* and a western granite line. The more important routes followed the valley between them, though they spread out in the north. This region is known today as Hijaz, and receives all its rain during the winter months. Occasionally this can be very heavy, and in 1968-69 the Ka'abah at Mecca was flooded to a depth of 3 m. (10 ft.).

**4 B. Southern Highlands.** The mountains of 'Asir, south of Mecca, form a high rim usually over 2,000 m. (6,600 ft.) in height, and are so inaccessible that parts of them are said not to have become Muslim until the eighteenth century. When they receive their rain is a problem. Much surely comes from the Mediterranean cyclones of winter, but we do not as yet have sufficient evidence to say how far north the summer rains of southwest Arabia extend. Quite possibly it is for some considerable distance, since the western edge of 'Asir is a dramatic and towering scarp.

To the southeast is the plateau of Dhofar and the Hadhramaut, the incense-producing district of Arabia. Dhofar is the name applied to the plateau behind Salalah, which is said to have quite heavy summer rains and prolonged periods of thick mist from the summer monsoon.[10] Opinions differ as to whether the other parts of the plateau have most of their rain in summer or winter. Rainfall does not appear to be great, and probably may occur in either season, though northeast of Dhofar it seems concentrated in winter. The most striking feature of the Hadhramaut plateau is the extraordinary, deep, and cliff-walled valley which cleaves it from one side to another. It has been important from very early times, both as a routeway, and because of the fertility of its upper reaches where a large number of oases are gathered round the main center at Shibam. In the heyday of the incense trade, this was an extremely wealthy region.

# 5. REGIONS OF MODERATE RAINFALL

These are regions of relatively level land, with sufficient rainfall for agriculture, though irrigation is practiced wherever possible since the rainfall is always precarious and often completely lacking during the summer months. None of the regions is entirely agricultural; pastoralism always played an important part, and at certain periods of history nomadic herdsmen took over large areas where at other times there were cultivated fields.

**5 A. Anatolia.** The lower parts of the Anatolian basin are about 900 m. (3,000 ft.) above sea level, but the surface is far from level. Uplifted blocks and volcanic outflows occur at many points, with no very clearly defined pattern, and there are a number of separate basins divided by higher land. Wheat and barley are very extensively grown on the floors of the sediment-filled basins, and vines on the hillsides. The basin east of Iconium (Konya) is the driest section, and this is more suited to transhumant pastoralism, which is very widely practiced all over the plateau. More than half of the plateau is drained into the Black Sea by rivers which cut back to capture the drainage of the interior, especially the Sangarius and Halys (Plate VI).

**5 B. The Levant.** This is discussed in relation to Maps XI, 2, 3, 7, and 8, and also in detail in the next chapter.

**5 C. Assyria** (*Plate X*). This is a wide expanse of generally level country, interrupted in places by lines of low hills running parallel to the mountains. It is given over to the growing of wheat and barley, though sheep are also very important, and by nature supports a population of merely moderate density. The enormous cities of the Assyrian kings were an entirely artificial creation which collapsed with the end of the empire. The agricultural villages, however, remained prosperous.[11] Where the average rainfall is less than 300 mm. (12 in.), cultivation is very patchy, and the settled population was concentrated north of this line. This whole area was probably always steppe rather than woodland, though in the earliest days near the foot of the mountains there may have been trees which were very soon cut down. In the *Anabasis,* Xenophon speaks of this region as being completely devoid of trees.

---

[10] Meigs, *op. cit.,* p. 59.

[11] David Oates, *Studies in the Ancient History of Northern Iraq* (London: Oxford University Press, 1966), p. 52.

**5 D. Media.** This is a highland region of broad parallel valleys and wide basins more than 1,500 m. (5,000 ft.) above sea level, and divided by high mountains surpassing 3,000 m. (10,000 ft.). Ecbatana is in a synclinal basin, dominated by the great granite mass of Alvand (3,511 m. or 11,514 ft.). It has occasionally been suggested that tin was produced there in ancient times, but there is some doubt about this. Rainfall is precarious, averaging about 400 mm. (16 in.) in the valleys, or sometimes less, but there is plentiful water from the high mountains for irrigation. Much of the winter precipitation is in the form of snow, even in the valleys. Pastoralism and agriculture are about equally divided (Plates VII, 22).

**5 E. Elam.** Known today as Khuzistan, this corner of the Mesopotamian trough has between 200 and 400 mm. (8 to 16 in.) of rain, though the amounts vary greatly from year to year and the distribution is wildly erratic. Sometimes, as much as a third of the rain for a year may fall in tremendous storms over three or four days, and these days may occur in any of the five months of November through March. Considerable recourse is therefore made to irrigation, using especially the Karkheh and Karun, which enter the plain from the north. Elam is divided from the Sumerian and Babylonian cities by wide areas of marsh into which the Karkheh empties its waters. Communication between the two was constant, but at least from about 3500 B.C. there was also frequent intercourse with the plateau, despite the formidable mountain barrier. The chief city was Susa, which the Persian kings made one of their capitals.

## 6. RIVERINE REGIONS

The flood plains of all these rivers must originally have been thick and tangled jungle and the haunt of wild beasts, and therefore they did not provide the homes of the first settled peoples. Nevertheless, they did become the scene of the first civilizations, starting about 3000 B.C. in the Nile Valley and Lower Mesopotamia and possibly a little later in the Indus Valley, because the effective use of water and indeed permanent settlement on the river banks at all demanded control of the floods, which itself required a complex social organization and the invention of some form of written means of communication. Trade was also facilitated by means of the river itself.

**6 A. Nile Delta.** The land of Egypt is discussed in relation to Map X (p. 116), and so here it is necessary only to emphasize the differences between the three major sections of the Nile Valley. The delta, like all deltas, is broad and flat, but in ancient times probably still contained a large amount of marshland. From the earliest times of which we have record, it was recognized as quite different from the enclosed valley above Memphis.

**6 B. Upper Egypt.** This extended from Memphis to the First Cataract at Syene. Here, between the high containing cliffs, the cultivated area on each side of the river was continuous, though in ancient times the farmer could grow crops only in winter after the flood had subsided.

**6 C. Cush.** Above the First Cataract (Plate 21), the valley narrows and the cliffs often approach the river, so that cultivation becomes intermittent. The distance from Thebes, the interruption of navigation by the First Cataract, and separation of the patches of cultivated fields from one another, all served to mark this as not part of Egypt proper, even though the Egyptians pushed their frontier to the Second Cataract, and during the empire well beyond it. The limit of Egyptian expansion was the difficult Fourth Cataract, at the lower end of which stood Napata, the Ethiopian capital. In 591 B.C., the Egyptians besieged and apparently destroyed Napata, and the capital was moved up the Nile to Meroe.[12] The surrounding country is here not desert but steppe, and the grasslands between the Nile and the Atbara were known as the Island of Meroe. Meroe became an important center for the production of iron, whose use came late to the Upper Nile Valley, and for the training of elephants, which were exported to Egypt and Rome. A fascinating feature of its culture is its evidently close relations with India and Persia by means of the sea route around southern Arabia. The Ethiopian eunuch of Acts 8:26–40 seems to have come from here, for he was "a minister of Candace, the queen of the Ethiopians," and the name Candace we now know to have been the title of the queen in the Meroitic kingdom.

[12] Information about the kingdom of Meroe is difficult to obtain, and I am indebted for the material in this paragraph to a valuable recent study by P. L. Shinnie, *Meroe: A Civilization of the Sudan* (London: Thames and Hudson, 1967).

**6 D. The Middle Euphrates.** The waters of the Euphrates have always been of more value for irrigation than the turbulent floods of the Tigris, and the long stretch where the river flows southeastwards across the broad Syrian plateau forms a quite distinct region with a character of its own. It has also cut a trough between steep cliffs, though lower than those which border the Nile (Plate IX). It flows through steppeland and semidesert, and is exposed to attack from the numerous pastoral tribesmen against whom the riverine peoples have little defense. Cultivation is not continuous, and from the mountains to the beginning of the delta few large cities have ever developed, and none has exerted political power for more than a brief period. It is essentially a region of villages and small towns.

**6 E. Babylonia.** This is discussed in relation to Map VII (p. 82).

**6 F. The Indus Valley.** Whether the Harappā civilization developed independently or whether it was prompted by infiltration from Sumer is still a matter of dispute. It extended up the river for about 1,600 km. (1,000 mi.), and is remarkable for its uniformity over this enormous distance, bricks of the same size and shape being used throughout the whole region. Remains of the same civilization have been found to the east, in the Ganges River basin of India. There was later regular communication between the Indus Valley and Lower Mesopotamia both by land and by sea, and some scholars have argued that this was Dilmun, which was both a real place with which the Sumerians traded and also the Sumerian paradise, "a holy, pure, clean, and radiant land, where there is neither sickness nor death . . . with fresh, sweet water and grain-abounding fields."[13] The civilization apparently was brought to an end by the Aryan invasions from the Persian plateau about 1500 B.C.

**6 G. The Middle Oxus.** This did not have the dense population of the Nile, Lower Mesopotamia, or the Indus, and we have as yet few remains of an indigenous civilization in antiquity. Nevertheless, the Oxus moves steadily into the desert, and along its banks there developed a culture which can properly be called riverine, though this did not extend all the way to the Aral Sea, which the river entered through a swampy marshland. The Upper Oxus is closely surrounded by mountains, and receives many tributaries. Here, between the river and the Hindu Kush, was the district of Bactria. The whole region was of great importance from very early times because of the caravan routes which crossed it, both from north to south, following the edges of the mountains, and from east to west, down the river from the Pamirs.

## 7. REGIONS OF SUMMER RAINFALL

These include the mountains of Abyssinia and neighboring parts of the African tableland, and the highlands of Sheba in southwestern Arabia. The first two are both marginal to the Middle East.

**7 A. The Sudan.** This is part of the broad grassland plateau that stretches all the way across Africa at this latitude. The rainfall increases and the grassland turns to forest toward the south, and in the biblical period the forest probably extended farther north than it does now. During the summer months the southern part of this region is a vast expanse of swamp, where the masses of floating vegetation on the rivers, known as *sudd,* prevented all penetration in this direction. The kingdom of Meroe extended as far south along the Nile as the junction of the Blue and White Niles.

**7 B. The Abyssinian Mountains.** The largely volcanic mountains are at their highest on the east, where they often exceed 3,000 m. (10,000 ft.), rising in a tremendous series of scarps from the Rift Valley. They slope more gently to the west, and hence most of the drainage is toward the Nile. The heavy summer rains, over 2,000 mm. (80 in.) on the mountains, are the cause of the Nile floods, which bring down the rich silt to Egypt. This region began to achieve importance with the rise of the kingdom of Aksum in the northern part of the highlands, probably as a result of immigrants from southwest Arabia, sometime in the fifth century B.C. Later, the Roman emperors developed friendly relations with Aksum as part of their policy of controlling the sea routes through the Red Sea to India and the Far East.

---

[13] S. N. Kramer, "Dilmun: A Quest for Paradise," *Antiquity,* vol. 37, no. 146 (June 1963), pp. 111–15. The real Dilmun is now known to be Bahrein, though the paradise description seems more applicable to the Harappā culture.

**7 C. Sheba.** This area is discussed in relation to Map IX (pp. 83–84).

## 8. OTHER REGIONS

Two regions do not really fit into any of the above categories.

**8 A. The Oasis Belt of Persia.** Climatically, this is a desert or semidesert region, with usually less than 200 mm. (8 in.) of rainfall, but it requires to be treated as a separate region because of the double line of oases running around the western and southern edges of the Persian plateau. Although they become more widely separated as one proceeds eastward, they made possible one of the major lines of communication between India and the Fertile Crescent. Already by 4000 B.C.

copper was being exported to Mesopotamia from Tal-i-Iblis some 80 km. (50 mi.) southwest of Kerman.[14]

**8 B. The Punjab.** This might reasonably have been included in the previous category, since it receives its rain from the summer monsoon—as much as 1,250 mm. (50 in.) on the mountains and 750 mm. (30 in.) or less on the lowlands. However, its remoteness and very different history suggest that it might fittingly be treated separately. The "five rivers" which give it its name are the headwaters of the Indus, and are considerably used for irrigation, though their value for transport is limited. The rainfall is heaviest in the east, since the monsoon approaches up the Ganges Valley. The significance of this region for the biblical world is that it lies at the foot of the passes from the mountains on the west, and receives, therefore, all the invasions from that direction. Together with the lower Indus Valley, it constituted the "India" of the ancient world.

[14]Joseph R. Caldwell, "Pottery and Cultural History on the Iranian Plateau," *Journal of Near Eastern Studies,* vol. 27, no. 3 (July 1968), p. 179.

# Maps VII–IX

"The Arab Island" is a name that is given today to all the vast Arabian peninsula lying south and west of the mountains. It includes the Levant, which is illustrated in the next series of maps, the broad lowlands of Mesopotamia, and great plateaus of Arabia. Except only on its edges, this enormous area is desert.

**Map VII. Mesopotamia.** The twin rivers of the Tigris and Euphrates occupy a wide trough between the solid block of Arabia and the high mountain ranges. Like the Nile, the Euphrates after the Khabur receives no further tributaries, and indeed continually loses water because of evaporation and irrigation, but the Tigris is supplied with water from the mountains even as far as its mouth. The two rivers join finally in the extreme south, and the combined stream is known today as the Shatt el-Arab. The Mesopotamian flood system differs from that of the Nile, for the two rivers flood in March and April, the very season when the Nile is lowest. The melting snow and thunderstorms can pour sudden and disastrous floods into the Tigris in spring (Plate 7); in Mesopotamia the rivers have to be tamed before they can be used, and the irrigation system depends upon a high degree of cooperation among all the users of the water.

The delta is much larger than in Egypt and begins at Tutul on the Euphrates and Samarra on the Tigris.[1] South of this was Babylonia, Babylon itself standing on one of the branches of the Euphrates, just south of the "waist" where the two rivers approach each other. An immense area of the southern delta is marshland, the home today of the "Marsh Arabs," and much also seems to have gone out of cultivation because of excessive salinization of the land, which was clearly a problem from an early date (Plate XII).

The earliest civilization was that of Sumer, around such towns as Ur, Erech, Larsa, and Eridu, centering on the more manageable Euphrates, though Lagash was on a branch of the Tigris. The position of the coastline at this early date is a matter of dispute, but probably it was not far from its present position, for under the weight of the sediment the trough is slowly sinking at a rate which roughly compensates for the building up of the delta by the rivers.

Although the earliest civilization developed around the lower Euphrates, the Tigris in New Testament times became the main artery of Mesopotamia—as it still is today—partly because it is more easily navigable except in the flood season, and partly also because it was by that time more central to the main concentrations of population. These are naturally along the two rivers, but also along the tributaries of the Tigris, notably the Diyala, and in the oases at the foot of the mountains. The Euphrates was the route between Mesopotamia and the Levant, often known in biblical literature simply as "the River."

The heartland of Assyria was on the central Tigris, where it is joined by the Greater and Lesser Zab rivers. Here just sufficient rain falls for agriculture, and there is easy communication with the outside world up the rivers into the mountains and along the foothills westward to the Mediterranean. It is not surprising that Assyria established the first "world empire," for only on the northeast does it have clearly defined physical limits and there is constant temptation to expand along the trade routes.

Upper Mesopotamia, between the central sections of the two rivers, is known today as the Jezireh, or the Island. It is a broad, rolling plateau, interrupted by lines of hills parallel to the mountains—for example, Jebel Sinjar. In the center is a long depression,

[1] Samarra is not a town of the biblical period but was built by the Abbasids in the ninth century A.D. It is shown here for purposes of reference.

**X. The Assyrian homeland.** Khorsabad, the site of Dur Sarrukin, the capital city built by Sargon II, the Assyrian king who finally destroyed Samaria and the Israelite kingdom. The picture shows the rolling Assyrian plain at the foot of the high Zagros mountains and gives a good idea of a *tell*, i.e. the mound formed by the collapse of successive layers of an ancient Middle Eastern city.

**XI. Date palms near Babylon.**  Babylonia was in the delta region of the two rivers, where irrigation is absolutely necessary, whereas Assyria was centered on the piedmont plains in the north, where rain-fed agriculture is possible. There are today more than 18,000,000 date palms, of 350 different varieties, lining the two rivers in the Mesopotamian delta. Throughout history this has been the center of the world's date production.

**XII. The curse of Babylon.** Without irrigation from the rivers there could be no cultivation in the Mesopotamian delta, but the intense evaporation during the hot summer months causes the irrigated fields to become in the course of time encrusted with salt, amidst which all vegetation withers. This appears to have been the cause of the decline of more than one powerful city-state in the ancient history of this region.

# MESOPOTAMIA

● Asshur   Towns
ASSYRIA   Regional Names
————————   Important Routes
————————   Sea Routes

0   25   50   75   100   125   150   Miles
0   25  50  75  100 125 150 175 200   Kilometers

CASPIAN SEA

ELBURZ MTS.

TALISH MTS.

Road to Samarkand

Rhagae

MEDIA

Ecbatana

Bisutun

ZAGROS MOUNTAINS

GUTIANS

KASSITES

PERSIA

Masjid-Suleiman

ELAM

Susa

Choga Zambil

Karun River

Shatt el - Arab

PERSIAN GULF

URARTU

Turushpa (Van)
Lake Van

Amida

Edessa

Haran

Carchemish

Halab

Hamath

To Damascus

Tadmor

Nisibis

Chagar Bazar

Gozan

Tel Brak

MITANNI

JEBEL SINJAR

Sinjar

Rimah

Tel Afar

Dur Sharrukin

Nineveh

Calah

Arba-Ilu

Hassuna

Hatra

ASSYRIA

JEZIREH

Wadi Tharthar

Tigris River

Lake Urmia

Jarmo

Nuzi

Zab (Greater Zab)

Zab (Lesser Zab)

J. HAMRIN

(Samarra)

Diyala

River

Eshnunna

Tutub

Ctesiphon

Jemdet Nasr

Babylon

Kish

Borsippa

Dur Kurigalzu

Sippar

Palukat

Hit

Tigris River

Nippur

BABYLONIA

Euphrates River

Lagash

Erech

Larsa

Ur

Ubaid

Eridu

River Khabur

Dura Europos

Mari

Euphrates River

SYRIAN DESERT

WADIAN DESERT

NEFUD

ARABIAN DESERT

To Sheba

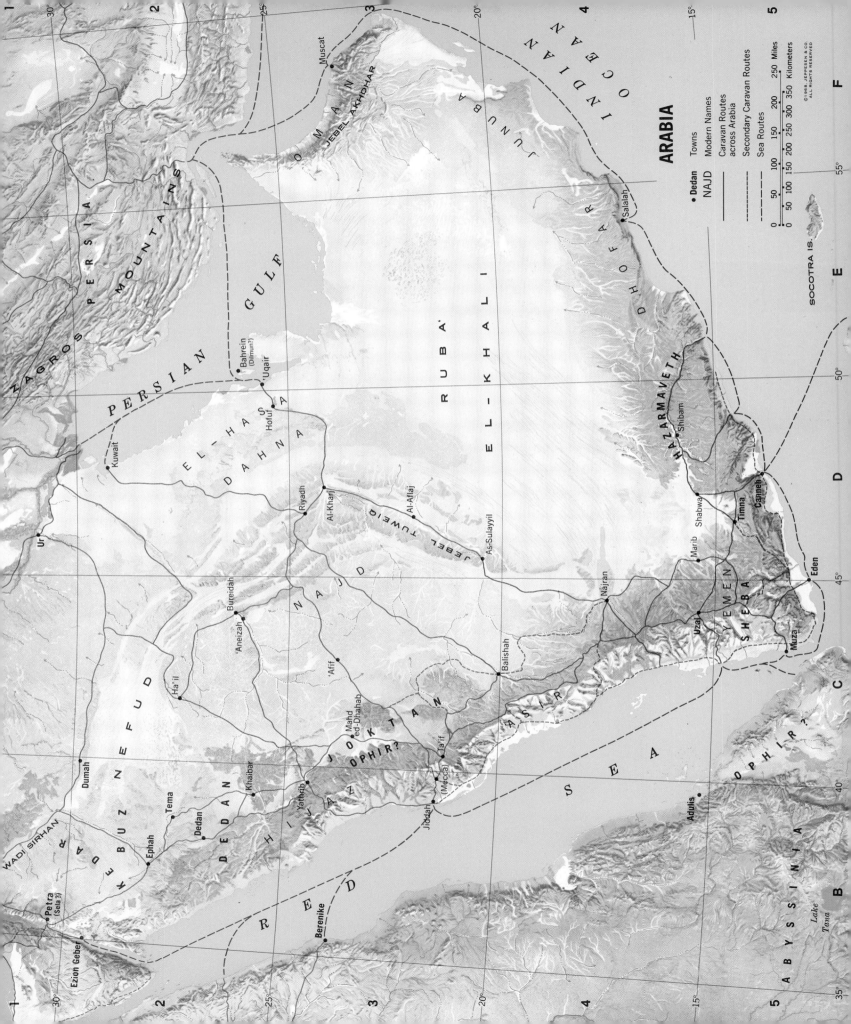

ARABIA

Towns: • Dedan
Modern Names: NAJD
Caravan Routes across Arabia
Secondary Caravan Routes
Sea Routes

250 Miles
0   50  100  150  200
0  50 100 150 200 250 300 350 Kilometers

©1968, JEPPESEN & CO.
ALL RIGHTS RESERVED

SOCOTRA IS.

INDIAN OCEAN

ZAGROS MOUNTAINS
PERSIA

PERSIAN GULF

Muscat
OMAN
JEBEL AKHDAR

Bahrein (Dilmun?)
Uqair
EL-HASA
Hofuf
DAHNA

Kuwait

Ur

Riyadh
Al-Kharj
NAJD
JEBEL TUWEIQ
Al-Aflaj
As-Sulayyil
RUBA' EL-KHALI

DHOFAR
Salalah

Bureidah
'Aneizah

Ha'il
KEBUZ NEFUD
'Afif

Dumah
WADI SIRHAN
KEDAR
Tema
Ephah
Dedan
Khaibar
DEDAN
HIJAZ
Yathrib

Mahd ed-Dhahab
JOKTAN
OPHIR?
Ta'if
(Mecca)

Balishah
ASIR

Najran

HAZARMAVETH
Shibam
Shabwa
Marib
Timna
Canneh
YEMEN
SHEBA
Uzal
Eden
Muza

Petra (Sela?)
Ezion Geber
RED SEA
Berenike
Jiddah

Adulis
ABYSSINIA
Lake Tana
OPHIR?

SOUTHWEST ARABIA

- • Marib    Towns
- **SHEBA**    Regional Names
- —————— Caravan Routes
- – – – – – Secondary Caravan Routes
- — – — – Sea Routes

| 0 | 25 | 50 | 75 | 100 | 125 | 150 Miles |

| 0 | 25 | 50 | 75 | 100 | 125 | 150 | 175 | 200 Kilometers |

©1968. JEPPESEN & CO.

ALL RIGHTS RESERVED

**1** **2** **3** **4** **5** **6** **7**

A 40° B 42° C 44° D 46° E 48° F

22°

20°

18°

16°

14°

12°

10°

R E D  S E A

T I H A M A

A S I R

RUBA'  EL

KHALI

(Mecca)
Jiddah
Ta'if

Bisha

Abha

Zahran
Najran

Qizan

Sa'da

Ma'in

MINAEANS

Amran

JEBEL NUQUM

Sana'

**Marib**

RAMLAT
SABATEIN

HAZARMAVETH

Tarim
Shibam

Shabwa

Massawa
(Adulis)

TIHAMA

SHEBA

QATABAN

Manakha

Hudeida

Beit el-Faqih

Dhamar

Beihan

**Timnah**

Mukalla

Yarim

O P H I R ?

P U N T ?

Qatabah

Ta'iz

**Muza**

Assab

Bab el-Mandeb

Eden

**Canneh**

A B Y S S I N I A

M E L U H H A ?

Djibouti

GULF  OF  ADEN

P U N T ?

**XIII. Fire altars near Persepolis.** An important feature of the Zoroastrian religion of the Persian Empire was the care of the sacred fire on altars such as these. The photograph was taken in April, just before the onslaught of a torrential thunderstorm such as is apt to mark the spring transitional season of the high plateaus.

**XIV. The great and terrible wilderness.** Sand dunes in the Sinai peninsula along the traditional route of the Exodus. Much vaster sand deserts of this type are to be found in the Sahara and in southern Arabia. Most of Sinai is actually rock desert.

Wadi Tharthar, which in earlier times was a routeway through the steppe, and today is used to receive the excess floodwater from the Tigris. Because it collects the water from the desert wadis, it attracts the bedouin, and here the Parthians built the town of Hatra, as a means of controlling the nomads. The northern Jezireh, in the foothills, forms a wide embayment in the mountains, and was at one time the center of the Mitanni kingdom.

Far to the southeast is another embayment, that of Elam or Susiana, watered by the Karun and its tributaries. This was related both to the plain and the mountains. The Mesopotamian influence is demonstrated by the great ziggurat of Choga Zambil, but it was also closely associated with the plateau, as it is today, despite the difficulties of communication.

**Map VIII. Arabia.** About 2,000 km. long and 1,050 km. broad (1,250 by 650 mi.), this is a gigantic platform of very hard and ancient rock, exposed in the west and covered in the east by later sediments. It is tilted from the southwest down toward the northeast, and is bounded by long geological faults, which have produced very straight coasts with usually only minor and inferior harbors. To this rectangular platform have been added the folded mountains of Oman in the southeast. In the west, great outflows of volcanic basalt form serious obstacles to movement, the main areas of this *harrah* being (i) the high mountain region of Sheba in the extreme southwest; (ii) the central region of the western plateau edge; and (iii) the extreme northwest, east of the long depression known as Wadi Sirhan (Plate IV).

Except along the coasts, which are rainless but very humid, Arabia has a climate of excessive dryness, mitigated only in those mountainous regions which are high enough to receive some fugitive rain. In the interior are two large regions of sandy, nearly absolute desert: the smaller Nefūd in the north,

and the much vaster Ruba' el-Khali in the south, which only now is being adequately explored, as prospectors search its wide, empty spaces for oil. Both these regions are avoided by the caravan routes. They are joined in the east by narrow parallel lines of sand desert, known as the Dahna', which divides the coastal region of el-Hasa from the central Arabian region of Najd.

Najd contains the major oases of central Arabia, which form a kind of rough crescent from Riyadh and el-Kharj through Bureidah and 'Aneizah to Ha'il. These are fed by water percolating along the wadis underground from the west. The other major oases are either at the foot of the western mountains (e.g., Najran, Balishah, Yathrib or Medina, and Khaibar) or close to the low-lying east coast. The western mountains themselves must be divided into two main sections, the Hijaz north of Mecca, and 'Asir to the south.

Mecca is not a true oasis and has a deficient water supply. Throughout biblical times there was no city there, and the town was built not long before the time of Muhammad. Formerly, it had been a sacred camping area for the caravans. Jiddah was from early times an important port because here there is a break in the mountains. North of the Meccan area, the Incense Road passed through Yathrib (the modern Medina), Khaibar, and Dedan, to Petra (Sela), and thence to Gaza. In the south it divided at Najran, and a difficult though important route ran northeastwards through Riyadh to the Persian Gulf. It followed the high escarpment of Jebel Tuweiq, at the foot of which are wells, and cut through it from one side to another at as-Sulayyil. Other trans-Arabian routes followed the wadis across the peninsula from Yathrib and the Meccan region, Ha'il and Riyadh gaining importance from the fact that here one could cross the forbidding Dahna'. Another route skirted the northern edge of the Nefūd from lower Mesopotamia, and ran up

the Wadi Sirhan to Rabbah and Damascus. It should be noticed that away from the Nefūd and the Ruba' el-Khali the caravan routes are many and complex. One must not think of only a single track from Sheba to Petra.

**Map IX. Southwest Arabia.** Known to the classical world as Arabia Felix, as contrasted with the vast expanse of Arabia Deserta, this region was of great importance, since it held an absolute control of the fabulous trade in "gold and frankincense and myrrh," had close contacts with the rich highlands of Abyssinia, and even from an early date traded with India. Some think that in Abyssinia we must place Ophir, whence Solomon obtained his gold, the Land of Punt, to which Queen Hatshepsut of Egypt sent her celebrated expedition, and Meluhha, with which the Sumerians traded. However, these are speculations, and it is possible that Punt is farther south in East Africa, that Ophir is Mahad edh-Dhahab in the Hijaz. Meluhha must now most probably be identified with the lower Indus valley.

Both frankincense and myrrh are resins obtained from bushes in southern Arabia and the adjacent regions of Africa. The production areas overlapped, but the chief center for frankincense was the plateau east of Hazarmaveth (Hadhramaut), and the chief center for myrrh was Qataban round Beihan. This trade developed markedly after the introduction of the camel caravan toward the end of the second millennium B.C., and by Roman times had reached quite fantastic proportions, but we should probably place the first beginnings very much earlier, because even before the taming of the camel, ass-nomads may already have been moving regularly between northern and southern Arabia.

The southwest corner of Arabia is an uptilted section of the great plateau, whose height has been further increased by volcanic action. A series of gigantic steps, caused by faulting, leads up from the Red Sea coast (the Tihama) to the towering highlands (the Jibāl), which average about 3,000 m. (10,000 ft.) in height, the highest point being 3,760 m. (12,336 ft.) thirty miles south of Sanaʿ. All approaches are difficult and exhausting, and the interior is cut up by lava flows and complicated cross-faulting into highland valleys and basins, isolated from one another by steep and formidable ridges. Sanaʿ is in a valley 2,700 m. (7,200 ft.) above sea level, and to the east is Jebel Nuqūm, a high mountain ridge dividing the Jibāl from the sloping plateau, which descends gradually eastward toward the much lower Rubaʿ el-Khali. An arm of the Rubaʿ el-Khali extends southwards in Ramlat Sabatein (the "Sands of the Two Sabas"), dividing the majestic mountain region from the Hazarmaveth plateau, about 1,800 m. (6,000 ft.) high, though it reaches 3,350 m. (11,200 ft.) south of Shibam. Shibam and Tarim lie in a deep valley with precipitous sides that is the heart of the Hadhramaut.

The climate of this whole region is still a problem, since no records exist. The coast is excessively dry and has water only in the oases, but the Jibāl has apparently about 500–625 mm. (20–25 in.) in the valleys, and over 750 mm. (30 in.) on the mountains, mainly concentrated in the summer. Everywhere the water must be carefully husbanded, and the hillsides are intricately terraced. At Marib, a series of great dams was built in the eighth century B.C., and later expanded until the dams reached fifty feet in height and over a mile in length. They lasted for well over a thousand years, and their collapse in the late sixth century A.D. sent a thrill of horror throughout Arabia. The Yemenis today are all town dwellers or farmers, and there are almost no true nomads in the country.

Southwest Arabia first enters biblical history with the visit of the Queen of Sheba to King Solomon (I Kings 10:1–13), evidently a trade mission to investigate the power of this new rival at the northern end of the trade route. The kingdom of Sheba was gradually weakened during the third and second centuries B.C., and was replaced by the Minaean and Qataban kingdoms. In 24 B.C., Augustus Caesar sent Aelius Gallius on a disastrous expedition designed to bring this region under control. He managed to reach Marib, which he besieged for a week, but had to withdraw for lack of water.

The chief ports were Canneh, Eden (Aden), and Muza (near the modern Mocha). These served as entrepôts, collecting the myrrh and frankincense from outlying districts, and then dispatching it in bigger ships for the more distant journeys. For the great overland trade there were a number of collecting points, such as Shabwa, Beihan, and so on.

# THE NATURAL REGIONS OF THE LEVANT

## Chapter Five

The number of the sections in this chapter correspond to the numbers of the divisions shown on Map 13, covering an area the greater part of which, though not quite all, falls into the region marked on Map 12 as *5B. The Levant,* one of the five regions of moderate or limited rainfall. Yet within this area many subregions may be distinguished. That it is possible for one of the regions of the Middle East to be so subdivided is a measure of the complexity of the Middle Eastern environment, for one could make similar subdivisions of almost every other region. The primary factor determining the natural regions of the Levant is the fourfold division into the *coast plain,* the *western highlands,* the *central valley,* and the *eastern plateau,* though a distinction must be made in the last category between regions of highland and those of more level plateau. Beyond these four major zones, to the east and south is the desert, which is itself complex. Another category is provided by the transverse rift valleys, which cut across the western highlands. Finally there are certain special regions, most of which really lie outside the Levant proper.

## 1. COASTAL REGIONS

**1 a. The Cilician Plain.** This is the region marked 1H on Map 12, and is external to the Levant, where the rainfall deficiency and the lack of any major rivers flowing into the Mediterranean have resulted in a coast quite different from this flat, alluvial lowland.

**1 b. Arvad.** The name is taken from an island just off the coast, which throughout the biblical period was an important commercial center. In general, a narrow coast plain, hardly more than 8 to 16 km. (5 to 10 mi.) wide, divides the rocky Nuseiriyeh Mountains and the sea. It is nowhere absolutely flat, and is not especially fertile, being often chalky, and its most striking characteristic is its isolation. It is cut off from the interior by the Nuseiriyeh Mountains and the marshes of the Orontes, and isolated from the coastal areas to the north and south by the steep cliffs of the Amanus Mountains and the Lebanon, both of which interrupt the coast plain for a considerable distance. It is also divided in the center by a mass of basalt, on which stands today the medieval castle of Marqab, and consequently the three ports of the ancient world—Ugarit in the extreme north, the island of Arvad in the center, and Tripolis south of the marshes of the Nahr el-Kabir —were quite distinct units, with little stimulus to unification.

**1 c. Phoenicia.** South of Tripolis is a 24-km. (15 mi.) stretch of high limestone cliffs, but to the south the coast plain, though usually very narrow and occasionally interrupted, is more or less continuous. It is backed for the most part by high, and at one time thickly forested, mountains. The shore is rocky, with a large number of good anchorages for the small ships of ancient days, but cultivation in the plain is of necessity intermittent, and communication often easier by boat than by land. A number of separate harbors developed, dominated in course of time by Tyre, securely placed on an island in the center of the region. Previously, the chief city had been Sidon, some 40 km. (25 mi.) to the north, where the coast plain is wider and communications with the interior easier. Farther north still was Berytus, the modern Beirut, well sheltered behind the headland of Ras Beirut but very much shut in by the high Lebanon, and to the north again lay Gebal (Byblos), close to the modern Jebail. Berytus and Gebal were separated by the headland at the mouth of Nahr el-Kalb (the Dog River). Here in ancient times was an important defensive barrier, and many conquerors recorded their passage on the high limestone cliffs.

In the south the region must be extended beyond the headland of Carmel to the marshes of the Crocodile River, where this type of coast comes to an end, for in the days of the great empires these were evidently considered by the imperial powers to be the limit of the province of Phoenicia.

By the beginning of the biblical period this coast was under the influence of the Egyptians, who maintained a merchant colony at Gebal, but already by the Exodus Egyptian authority in the area had declined. The rise of Tyre as a major power dates from the tenth century B.C., and it became a byword for wealth and pride (Ezek. 27:1 to 28:19). The chief exports of this region were wood (cedar, pine, fir, and cypress), oil, wine, and the valuable Tyrian purple dye, made from shellfish.

**1 d. Sharon.** South of Mount Carmel the coast is clogged with sand brought by sea currents from the Nile, and the small rivers are choked and swampy. Sharon was, therefore, throughout Old Testament times, a region of forest and marsh with only a tiny population. By New Testament times, the draining of the marshes and the building of the port of Caesarea had brought it within the inhabited world.

**1 e. Philistia.** The increasing drought in the south changes the coastal forests into grassland, and permanent streams disappear. The great Trunk Road which in Sharon had hugged the highlands now swings westwards to the coast, though a little way inland to avoid the sand dunes. This was Philistine territory, a gently rolling lowland admirably suited to wheat and barley. Their five major cities were Gaza, Ashkelon, and Ashdod on the main trade route, and Gath and Ekron guarding the western border. The coast is everywhere sandy, and the harbors open roadsteads, very exposed to the Mediterranean storms. Gaza was both a seaport, exchanging the products of Arabia for those of Greece and Rome, and also a "desert port," where the cara-

vans for Egypt were formed (Acts 8:26), and so gave Philip an excellent opportunity to bring the Word to Gentiles from many distant lands.

**1 f. Sinai Coast.** This is a narrow stretch of semidesert and sand dunes, followed by the Trunk Road to Egypt, "the way of the land of the Philistines" (Exod. 13:17). There is underground water from the highlands of Sinai but very little rain, and the sandy deposits of the Nile current have been carried by the wind far inland. Kinglake, whose journey from Gaza to the Nile took nine days, describes the road as "sand, sand, sand, still sand, and only sand, and sand, and sand again."[1] He traveled with only a handful of men; the large caravans would normally take longer.

## 2. THE COASTAL HIGHLANDS

These are normally block mountains, with fairly level summits often broad enough to be a narrow plateau. Since they lie close to the sea, the western slopes were usually heavily wooded. The eastern slopes are always in a very marked rain shadow, and vegetation there must have been much more sparse.

**2 a. Amanus Mountains.** These run from southwest to northeast, and end abruptly on the southeastern side in a steep fault scarp. They are crossed in the south by a pass 600 m. (2,000 ft.) above sea level, but on either side are very much higher, reaching in the south 1,795 m. (5,889 ft.) in Kïzïl Dağ and 2,262 m. (7,421 ft.) in Miğir Dağ to the north. These thickly forested mountains formed an important barrier on the road from Cilicia to the south.

**2 b. Cassius Mountains.** Although rather lower than the Amanus, the well-wooded, volcanic pinnacle of Akra Dağ (Jebel Akra), the ancient Mons Cassius, 1,759 m. (5,771 ft.) above sea level, is the more striking headland, and in ancient times was accounted a sacred mountain.

**2 c. Nuseiriyeh Mountains.** Also called the Ansariyeh Mountains, these are really the beginning of the true western highlands, the Amanus and Cassius mountains being the structural continuation of Cyprus. They form a broad upfolded plateau with a more gentle western

[1] A W. Kinglake, *Eothen* (London: Longmans, 1935 edition), p. 156.

slope and a steep fault scarp overlooking the Orontes Valley. The western slope is cut by deep and narrow gorges, useless for communication, and the karstic limestone once carried dense forest. It was an isolated region, almost unapproachable and remote. One of the homes in medieval times of the dreaded Assassins, it is still the preserve of a religious minority, the Nuseiris, and immediately marked as different by the absence of minarets, and by the sacred groves beside every village (Plate 23), demonstrating the persistence in this mountain fastness of very ancient religious beliefs.

**2 d. The Lebanon Mountains.** These reach their greatest height in Qarnet es-Saoudah (3,088 m. or 10,131 ft.) in the north. Jebel Sannine, close to Beirut, is 2,628 m. (8,621 ft.), but in the south no point surpasses 2,000 m. Though very much higher, this region again has a precipitous scarp to the east, and a remarkably even sky-line with no sharp peaks. The western slopes are seamed with tremendous gorges, and penetration has always been difficult, making the Lebanon, like the Nuseiriyeh Mountains, a region of refuge for older cultures. The massive Cenomanian limestone is exposed at the lower levels, then the older reddish and yellow sandstone, and still higher the Jurassic limestone. Powerful springs develop at the junction of these last two, and there is in consequence a line of towns and villages about 1,400 m. (4,200 ft.) above sea level, though these cannot have come into existence until after the clearance of the forests. The small remnants of the cedar forests are found today only above the highest settlements (Plate 25), while on the sandstone grows the umbrella pine that one associates normally with the sandy coastal regions.

**2 e. The Sidonian Depression.** This little region has been scarcely noticed in accounts of the physical geography of the Levant, but it is important. Just north of Sidon, a line of weakness strikes inland almost due southeastwards, bringing to an abrupt end the high mountainous regions of the Lebanon and Anti-Lebanon. The western highlands now form a dissected plateau only about 600 to 800 m. (2,000 to 2,600 ft.) above sea level, and only at one point exceeding 900 m. (3,000 ft.). Since the altitude is lower and the region consists largely of the less attractive Eocene limestone and the Senonian chalk, the forests here must always have been more open. The significance of this region, therefore, is the ease with which it can be crossed from west to east, an important factor in the growth of Tyre and

Sidon. The valleys, especially that of the Litani, are all deeply incised and useless for communication, but three roads climb the limestone spurs between the valleys and join together near Abel-Beth-Maacah to cross the central Rift Valley between the mountains and the marshes of the Jordan.

**2 f. Galilee.** The land rises again south of Tyre, and Jebel Jarmaq in Upper Galilee reaches 1,208 m. (3,963 ft.). Thickly forested in the past though open moorland today, it was a frontier zone and region of refuge, clearly dividing the Phoenician and Israelite worlds. Lower Galilee, which begins with the esh-Shaghur fault scarp in the latitude of Acco (Acre), is a district of down-faulted basins divided by hills which nowhere exceed 600 m. (2,000 ft.).

**2 g. Samaria.** Although physically part of the western highlands, this is a basin structure in which the younger rocks have been preserved round Shechem in the center. The harder Eocene limestone is hilly, and in Ebal and Gerizim has been elevated by faulting to 928 and 881 m. respectively (3,044 and 2,890 ft.). Around this central core are the Senonian chalk valleys which opened Samaria to the invader. Because it was accessible and only thinly forested, this was the first part of the hill country to be fully settled, and at the time of the Israelite take-over was a Caananite stronghold, where strictly Yahwist ideas were never able completely to dominate the traditional mores.

The elevated basin of Samaria became the territory of Manasseh, but on the south the high dome of Cenomanian limestone was Ephraim, almost certainly originally a regional rather than a tribal name. Thickly forested and protected by steep cliffs, this was the first strategic nucleus of Israel, and the Ark was apparently kept at Shiloh, though the history of the Ark in the early period is very obscure. With settlement and the clearing of the forest, it became an important olive-producing district.

**2 h. Benjamin.** This is a small region, only about 16 km. (10 mi.) wide from north to south, but it must be distinguished from Ephraim to the north and Judah to the south. Structurally it belongs with Judah, for in the latitude of Bethel the ridge of Cenomanian limestone suddenly narrows, and thenceforward the Senonian chalk is exposed on either side. Here in Benjamin, two fault valleys lead up from the west and the east, and the highlands are some 120 m. (350 ft.) lower. This decrease in height means a noticeable lessening of the rainfall, and the forests of Ephraim give place to more open woodland. Benjamin was therefore a saddle between the two better defended regions to the north and south, and an important zone of movement between east and west.

**2 i. Judah.** Here the level of the plateau rises again to slightly over 1,000 m. (3,300 ft.) close to Hebron, which was the heart of Judah. This region, and the two adjacent ones, **2 j. the Shephelah** and **2 k. Jeshimon,** are discussed in relation to Map 20 (pp. 112–114).

**2 l. Kyrenia.** The island of Cyprus is structurally an outlier of the Amanus and Cassius, and consists of an interior lowland between two mountain ranges. The Kyrenia range in the north is a long narrow limestone spine with precipitous slopes on both sides, about 900 m. (3,000 ft.) at its highest and extending a long finger eastwards in the Karpass peninsula. More heavily wooded on the northern than the southern slopes, it forms an important climate barrier.

**2 m. Troodos.** The Troodos block is formed of a mass of volcanic material which has forced its way through the limestone to a height of 1,951 m. (6,400 ft.) in Mount Olympus, which is snow-covered throughout the winter. There is still a considerable amount of residual forest, which must have been dense in ancient times. The important ancient copper mines were mainly in this region.

## 3. THE INTERIOR RIFT VALLEYS

These are inland depressions, shut in by steep fault scarps, which sometimes exceed 1,000 m. (3,300 ft.) in height, with much reduced rainfall and prolonged, very hot summers. The regions differ markedly from one another, and communication along them is seldom as easy as one might expect from the physical map.

**3 a. Antioch.** The alignment of the Amanus and Cassius ranges is northeast to southwest, parallel to that of the Taurus Mountains, and the central valley runs out to the Mediterranean. The rain shadow is therefore less marked, and the annual rainfall is rather over 1,000 mm. (40 in.). The valley is narrow, blocked in the north by basalt, and an open plain has developed only where

there is a transverse depression. This was at one time the territory of Alalakh, and later dominated by the magnificent city of Antioch (Antakya), one of the earliest centers of Christianity. The Orontes, curving round Mons Cassius, enters from the southeast, and is joined here by the Karasu, but the outlet to the sea is very narrow, and the plain is swampy and easily flooded. The forests, marshes, and surrounding mountains all strictly limited movement and gave this region a numinous quality which is reflected in its ancient reputation for sanctity. Mons Cassius itself to the southwest, the strong springs and dense vegetation of Daphne, close to Antioch, and the cave of Sanpier, which Christian tradition later named as the first church, are all examples of this.

**3 b. The Ghab.** The section of the central rift immediately east of the Nuseiriyeh Mountains is blocked in the north, near the present town of Jisr esh-Shaghur, by an outflow of basalt, and the waters of the Orontes turned this whole valley into a marsh. This was an added reason for the isolation of the Nuseiriyeh Mountains and the north Syrian coast.

**3 c. The Entry of Hamath.** The north-south valley of the Ghab is brought to an end by an outcrop of Cenomanian limestone, and by a great basalt outflow. The central valley is completely interrupted, and the Orontes curves far to the east, past Emesa and Hamath (Homs and Hama) to avoid these obstacles. Farther south, the uplifted valley between the Lebanon and Anti-Lebanon is entered from the north by a funnel-shaped slope rising from about 500 m. (1,650 ft.) to 700 m. (2,300 ft.), drained by the Upper Orontes and composed largely of infertile gravels. Settlements here are few, and it was always a frontier zone. Scholars now identify "the entering in of Hamath," or Lebo-Hamath, with a definite place, Lebweh, but the possibility that it was a regional name cannot be excluded. In any case, Lebweh marks the extreme southern end of this region.

**3 d. Coele-Syria.** This is discussed in relation to Map 15. Not all of it is fertile, much being either gravel or limestone ridges, and the best agricultural land is beside the Litani, which rises near Baalbek, 1,002 m. (3,287 ft.) above sea level. Toward the south, the Litani runs in a narrow gorge, which then makes a sharp right-angled turn to the west, and the little plain of Ijon (*el-marj* of Marjayoun, or Plain of Springs) forms a separate, very fertile little subregion.

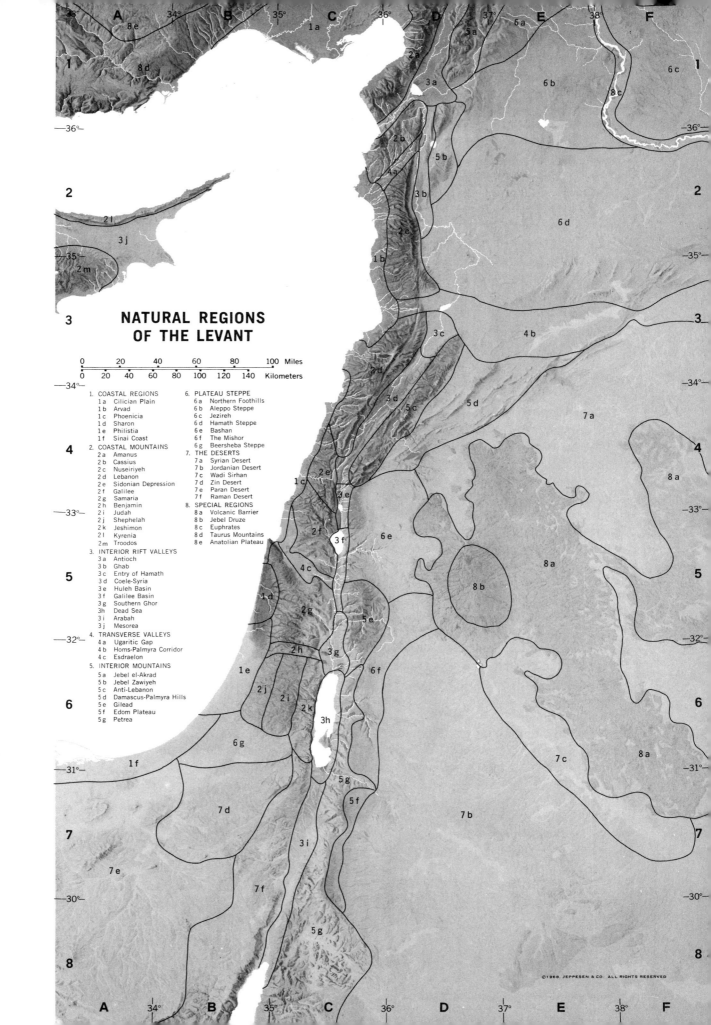

# NATURAL REGIONS
# OF THE LEVANT

0   20   40   60   80   100 Miles
0  20  40  60  80  100  120  140 Kilometers

1. COASTAL REGIONS
 1 a  Cilician Plain
 1 b  Arvad
 1 c  Phoenicia
 1 d  Sharon
 1 e  Philistia
 1 f  Sinai Coast
2. COASTAL MOUNTAINS
 2 a  Amanus
 2 b  Cassius
 2 c  Nuseiriyeh
 2 d  Lebanon
 2 e  Sidonian Depression
 2 f  Galilee
 2 g  Samaria
 2 h  Benjamin
 2 i  Judah
 2 j  Shephelah
 2 k  Jeshimon
 2 l  Kyrenia
 2 m  Troodos
3. INTERIOR RIFT VALLEYS
 3 a  Antioch
 3 b  Ghab
 3 c  Entry of Hamath
 3 d  Coele-Syria
 3 e  Huleh Basin
 3 f  Galilee Basin
 3 g  Southern Ghor
 3 h  Dead Sea
 3 i  Arabah
 3 j  Mesorea
4. TRANSVERSE VALLEYS
 4 a  Ugaritic Gap
 4 b  Homs-Palmyra Corridor
 4 c  Esdraelon
5. INTERIOR MOUNTAINS
 5 a  Jebel el-Akrad
 5 b  Jebel Zawiyeh
 5 c  Anti-Lebanon
 5 d  Damascus-Palmyra Hills
 5 e  Gilead
 5 f  Edom Plateau
 5 g  Petrea

6. PLATEAU STEPPE
 6 a  Northern Foothills
 6 b  Aleppo Steppe
 6 c  Jezireh
 6 d  Hamath Steppe
 6 e  Bashan
 6 f  The Mishor
 6 g  Beersheba Steppe
7. THE DESERTS
 7 a  Syrian Desert
 7 b  Jordanian Desert
 7 c  Wadi Sirhan
 7 d  Zin Desert
 7 e  Paran Desert
 7 f  Raman Desert
8. SPECIAL REGIONS
 8 a  Volcanic Barrier
 8 b  Jebel Druze
 8 c  Euphrates
 8 d  Taurus Mountains
 8 e  Anatolian Plateau

**3 e. The Huleh Basin.** A clearly defined fault line running eastwards from Tyre causes the central valley to drop suddenly from 500 m. (1,650 ft.) to 100 m. (330 ft.). The Hasbani and Bureighit enter from the north, and a number of strong springs, notably at Dan and Caesarea Philippi, mark the fault scarp. The basin is blocked at the southern end by a great dam of basalt, behind which the shallow Lake Huleh was formed, and in biblical days the whole area to the north was impenetrable marsh. Travelers hugged the western highlands, or crossed over at the head of the basin where remoteness, waterfalls, and strong springs made Abel, Dan, and Paneas (Caesarea Philippi) into famous cult centers.

**3 f. The Galilee Basin.** This extends from the basalt dam which the Jordan cleaves in a narrow, rocky gorge to the "waist," where the highlands come close together south of Bethshan. The Lake of Galilee has been formed behind another, but this time small, sill of basalt, and there are some hot springs by its shores and in the lower Yarmuq Valley. Though very important in the New Testament, the lake is hardly mentioned in the Old, and seems to have lain outside the Israelite homeland, the rough basalt by which it is surrounded being unsuited to Israelite farming. Farther south the important stronghold of Bethshan guarded the entrance to the Valley of Jezreel on the west.

**3 g. The Southern Ghor.** The Ghor is the Arabic name for the Rift Valley, and here, south of the "waist," the rain shadow is so pronounced that desert conditions prevail. There are important oases, of which the most noted is Jericho, and frequent springs at the foot of the eastern slopes, which face the rain-bearing winds. The Jordan is imprisoned in a narrow, marshy, and forested trough between desolate badlands and, despite its smallness, has comprised historically a major obstacle. At the northeastern corner of the Dead Sea a hinge fault has cut back into the plateau to form the Plains of Moab.

**3 h. The Dead Sea** (*Plate 27*). The Dead Sea, 396 m. (1,274 ft.) below the level of the Mediterranean, and about as much as that again at its deepest point, is the saltiest body of water in the world. It is shut in by high cliffs, but on the west the limestone scarp permits a narrow passage along its foot, while in the east the sandstone precipices north of the Lisan peninsula rise directly out of the water. Apart from the Jordan, rivers enter the Dead Sea only from the east, by narrow, impassable gorges, but along the western shore there is a line of springs, which were of great importance since the average rainfall is only 50 mm. (2 in.). The community of Qumran lived at the northern end of this western shore, and Engedi stands in the center, where a road comes down from Hebron. In the south is the remarkable salt mountain of Jebel Usdum. The Lisan peninsula, and the Sebkha plain south of the Dead Sea, are both areas of badland similar to the cliffs which border the Jordan farther north. The southern basin is very shallow and may, perhaps, cover the ill-fated Cities of the Plain. At some periods in history it has been possible to ford the sea opposite the Lisan, and this passage was guarded in New Testament days by the great fortress of Masada.

**3 i. The Arabah.** From the Dead Sea to the Red Sea is about 160 km. (100 mi.), and so this region is distinctly larger than any of the others. It is given unity by its desert character, but physically it is divided into two sections by the ridge of Jebel Risheh in the center where the valley floor is 200 m. (660 ft.) above sea level. The importance of the Arabah was twofold. It provided a route to the Red Sea, and it contained the valuable copper mines which were a bone of contention between Judah and Edom.

**3 j. The Mesorea.** Although the central plain of Cyprus is open to the sea at both ends, the rainfall is usually under 400 mm. (16 in.) or even less than 300 mm. (12 in.), and the summers exceptionally hot. There are wide expanses of semidesert, mesa-type landscape, and on the cultivated fields barley is as important as wheat. Sheep and goats are very numerous. At the eastern end stood Salamis (Plate 49), which was visited by Paul and Barnabas on the first missionary journey (Acts 13:4). Although they are reported to have "gone through the whole island" (13:6), it seems more probable that they merely went through the towns of the better watered southern coast to Paphos.

## 4. TRANSVERSE VALLEYS

At certain points, rifting in the western highlands has created lowland corridors which are of primary importance for communication with the coast. To the three listed here we might add the lower Orontes valley (region 3a above), but this is structurally parallel to the alignment of the mountains and is therefore more properly classed as an "interior valley."

**4 a. The Ugaritic Gap.** Between the Cassius Mountains and the Nuseiriyeh range, a series of small curved faults has created a narrow passage reaching the sea near Laodicea (Lattaqieh), south of the headland of Ras Shamrah, where the more ancient port of Ugarit had stood. A road led inland by this valley to Jisr esh-Shaghur, across the Orontes marshes by the basalt dam, and thence to Aleppo.

**4 b. Homs-Palmyra Corridor.** This remarkable depression though not profound is of great length, and extends all the way to Mari on the Euphrates, where the river suddenly changes direction. Its western end is blocked by a great basalt outflow, but a coastal stream, the Nahr el-Kabir, has cut back into this so that the road across it only just touches 400 m. (1,200 ft.).

**4 c. Esdraelon.** This nowhere exceeds 90 m. (300 ft.) above sea level. It is broadest in the center, where it is dominated by the isolated hill of Mount Tabor, and very nearly closed in the northwest, where the little river Kishon edges its way between the hills of Lower Galilee and the steep scarp of Mount Carmel. In consequence, the plain tended to be marshy, though it produced wonderful crops of wheat in spring. The Valley of Jezreel, 5 km. (3 mi.) wide, connects the central section with the Jordan Valley, here about 250 m. (820 ft.) below sea level.

## 5. THE INTERIOR HIGHLANDS

Sometimes these are true mountains and sometimes merely the abrupt edge to the plateau. The one feature they have in common is that they present a steep barrier toward the west, and channel all transverse movement into a few clearly defined passages.

**5 a. Jebel el-Akrād.** This continues the line of the Cassius Mountains beyond the Antioch plain. It is largely volcanic, similar to the Cassius and Troodos regions, and in the north exceeds 1,400 m. (4,600 ft.) in height. Thickly forested in the past and still partially wooded today, it deflects all movement from the north either down the valley of the Karasu toward Antioch or around to the east toward Aleppo.

**5 b. Jebel Zawiyeh.** Here the western edge of the plateau is at its least impressive, only about 750 m. (2,500 ft.) above sea level, and 500 m. (1,500 ft.) above the marshes of the Ghab. It is much broken by faults, and in the north encloses another very marshy downfaulted basin parallel to the Ghab. The eastern slope is very gradual, and this region could almost be considered part of the plateau were it not for its isolation, since it is bypassed by the great caravan routes from Aleppo to Hamath.

**5 c. The Anti-Lebanon.** This is discussed in relation to Map 15. The highest point in the northern section is 2,629 m. (8,625 ft.), and Mount Hermon, south of the cleft of the River Abana, is 2,814 m. (9,232 ft.). The Anti-Lebanon are much less disturbed by faulting than the Lebanon, and have only a few springs, except at the lower levels. The barren, karstic highlands are largely uninhabited, except by transhumant shepherds, and wild bears still today haunt the remoter slopes.

**5 d. Damascus-Palmyra Hills.** These simple anticlinal ridges fan out northwards from Damascus. Once wooded, they are today barren, though the northwestern slopes carry grass in the spring and the valleys have a moderate pasture of small desert shrubs. This is a region of nomads, and permanent settlement is confined to the few places where there is water .

**5 e. Gilead.** Southeast of the Lake of Galilee the continuation of the Judean upwarp has elevated the edge of the plateau to 1,247 m. (4,179 ft.) at its highest point. The rock is mainly the valuable Cenomanian limestone, but in the center the River Jabbok has exposed the underlying Nubian sandstone. Precipitation, sometimes in the form of snow, is usually in excess of 750 mm. (30 in.); frequent westward-flowing streams have cut deep valleys in the scarp slope, and there is still today much scattered forest of pine and Mediterranean oak (Plate 26). This is the only part of the eastern plateau ever effectively brought under Israelite control, because it is the only region sufficiently similar to the Palestinian hills to enable them to practice the way of life familiar to them, based on the cultivation together of olives, wheat, and vines.

**5 f. Edom Plateau.** This is a very narrow zone, some 100 km. (65 mi.) long. Most of it is above 1,500 m. (5,000 ft.), and it touches 1,734 m. (5,688 ft.) just north of Petra. The King's Highway follows the high plateau edge, but the settlements are usually somewhat below this to the west, where faulting has created springs in the limestone scarp. The scarp slope is extraordinarily steep, but on the east the land drops very regularly and moderately rapidly to about 1,200 m. (4,000 ft.), where it levels off. The decrease in rainfall on the east is very sudden, but the plateau edge and the higher parts of the scarp slope receive sufficient rain for there to have been a good forest cover right up to the beginning of this century. Even today there is scrub woodland on the higher parts of the scarp.

**5 g. Petrea.** These are the wild, desolate, and fantastically carved sandstone slopes of the plateau escarpment. The region extends as a fairly narrow belt from the northern end of the Dead Sea to south of Petra, but suddenly widens in the south. It therefore includes the dissected plateau region of the Wadi Ram (Plate 29), and might very well be carried farther east to include Jebel Tubeiq in southeastern Jordan, though on Map 13 this has been treated as part of the desert region of 7b. It also includes the granite Mountains of Midian, though structurally these ought to be counted as a separate region. In wetter regions the Nubian sandstone forms fairly gentle slopes, but here, where there is little rain, it stands up in almost perpendicular dark red cliffs, everywhere much fractured by faulting, and with long deep gorges cutting back into the plateau edge. In the center, a group of faults splaying out like a fan has cut a wide embayment in the plateau, and divides Edom into a clearly defined northern and southern section. At the foot of this embayment are the famous copper mines of Punon. Farther south, still another group of faults have created the valleys in which the city of Petra is carved. Much of this region is so unpenetrated by man that leopards and ibex still exist.

# 6. THE PLATEAU STEPPES

These lie behind the plateau edge, and are regions where there is generally good pasture for sheep and goats, grading into grain fields in the better watered west. However, ineffective government control or possibly extended periods of drought may allow the nomads to take over much of the settled land, because here there is only a fluctuating frontier between the desert and the sown.

**6 a. The Northern Foothills.** This region lies north of the present Syrian-Turkish border, and therefore strictly speaking outside the Levant. It is well watered, and has a line of important towns, such as Birecik on the Euphrates, Edessa (Urfa), and Carrhae (Harran, the Haran of the Old Testament).

**6 b. The Aleppo Steppe.** This is broad plateau country, crisscrossed by tracks from the Euphrates to the west. It carries good grass in winter and spring, but has a number of basins of *sebkha* or salt marsh.

**6 c. The Jezireh.** This is essentially a continuation of the last region east of the Euphrates, but it is better drained. As in the previous region, the settlements are all in the northern half, and the southern part is pastoral.

**6 d. The Hamath Steppe.** The sudden curve eastwards of the Euphrates means that there are fewer east-west routes, which tend to concentrate where the river comes closest to the sea, and in any case are hindered here by the northward-draining wadis. Movement, in fact, is largely from north to south, especially in the settled western portion. In the north there are again a number of ill-drained areas of *sebkha,* but in the south the land rises to over 1,200 m. (4,000 ft.) in the hills overlooking the Homs-Palmyra corridor. These mark the end of the good steppeland.

These three regions are almost totally devoid of trees, and seem always to have been grassland, except only where they are crossed by hills.

**6 e. Bashan.** The good steppe is interrupted by the penetration of the desert to the foot of the Anti-Lebanon, and is resumed only when this great climatic barrier comes to an end. South of this, the platform extends across the canyon of the Yarmuq to the beginning of the Gilead highlands, and is largely covered with fertile volcanic soil. It was an important grain-producing and cattle region (Ps. 22:12), but without defense against the invading armies because it is so level.

**6 f. The Mishor.** This is the name given in the Old Testament to the generally level plateau country south of Gilead, translated in the King James Version as "plain," but usually in the Revised Standard Version as "tableland" (e.g., Josh. 13:9, 16). Since it is farther south than Bashan, it is drier and pastoral farming tends to take the place of grain, though the sheep are kept by settled as well as nomadic herdsmen. Sheep and wool were the most important product of Moab (II Kings 3:4).

**6 g. The Beersheba Steppe.** This is the only steppeland region west of the central rift. Composed of gently rolling slopes, facing westward, and therefore receiving the benefit of the rain-bearing winds and of heavy dew in summer, it is essentially a borderland region which has moved into and out of cultivation at various periods in history. When the modern Israelis speak of reclaiming the Negev, this is essentially the region that they mean.

# 7. THE DESERTS

The deserts of the Levant are all "tame" deserts, where there is every year a certain amount of rain (Plate 10), but it is unpredictable and irregular. Occasionally, in a good year, grass grows far out to the east and the plateau is carpeted with flowers, but then years may go by in which there are only scattered storms and the herdsmen must wander far afield in search of the pasture.

**7 a. The Syrian Desert.** This lies between Jebel esh-Sharqi and the Palmyra-Homs corridor to the north, and the basalt regions of the south and west. In the northeast it drains by parallel wadis into the Palmyra-Homs corridor and the Euphrates, but farther south the corridor is limited by a long escarpment, which is especially formidable in Tarag el-Aalab south of Palmyra. Beyond this escarpment is a remarkably level tableland with very indeterminate drainage, where pastoral nomadism is the only possible way of life. Because it is so far north, this is far from being absolute desert, and the nomadic population is relatively large.

**7 b. The Jordanian Desert.** This is a large triangle east of the present Hejaz railroad. Although in general moderately level plateau country, it is highest in the center just west of Bayir. Here it surpasses 1,000 m. (3,300 ft.). Drainage is outward from this central highland. To the south the wadis congregate in the depression of al-Jafr, to the northwest they are directed towards the scarp streams, and in the east, the largest section of all, they

run in parallel lines northeastwards toward the long depression of the Wadi Sirhan. This eastern section is known as Ardh es-Suwān (the Flint Country), and desert travelers tend to avoid it, since the millions of sharp flints cut the soft feet of the camels. Bayir was an important Nabatean center in New Testament times for the control of the desert.

**7 c. Wadi Sirhan.** This shallow depression at the foot of the basalt barrier, more than 240 km. (150 mi.) in length, receives water from the basalt to the east, and from the wadis of Ardh es-Suwān. Though there is much treacherous *sebkha*, it provided a relatively easy route from Dumah in the southeast to the oasis of al-Azraq in the northwest, between the difficult flint plateau on one side and the even more impenetrable volcanic highlands on the other. From both al-Azraq and Dumah, desert tracks splay out in a number of directions.

**7 d. Wilderness of Zin.** The western highlands continue as low hills southwestwards from the southern end of the Dead Sea, and divide the southern desert of Palestine into two very distinct regions. The westward facing slopes are gentle, with wide wadis divided by broad uplands. The wadis can be cultivated, but only if the greatest care is taken to conserve water, and they have often passed out of use, except for the rough and ready farming of the seminomadic tribesmen. The art of cultivating this poor steppeland was brought to its greatest heights between about 100 B.C. and A.D. 100 by the Nabateans, for whom the importance of controlling the trade routes made the maintenance of settlements in the desert economically worthwhile.

**7 e. The Wilderness of Paran.** This is the northern part of region 3F on Map 12 (Sinai). Although it is crossed by the track known as the Way to Shur, it is unattractive and desolate country, largely composed of chalk and poor limestone. Cultivation is here at an end even in the wadis.

**7 f. The Raman Desert.** The eastern slopes of southern Palestine, overlooking the Wadi Arabah, are wild and forbidding. Sometimes the great bare folds of rock plunge downwards in a tremendous monocline, as in the Ascent of the Akrabbim, and sometimes they break away in precipices and *anqab* (see p. 44). In either case they present a severe obstacle to those who would reach the coast from the east. The easiest route is in the center, where the Wadi Murra cuts back through the hills, and the road never has to climb higher than 450 m. (1,500 ft.), but another leads directly up the Ascent of the Akrabbim toward Beersheba, and a third, which was the most important in Roman times, entered the great cauldron known as the Wadi Raman (or Maktesh Raman) from the east, and was then forced to climb the precipitous western wall. These cauldrons are a curious feature of this region. They seem to have been formed by the collapsing of the center of an upfold to produce a deep, elongated basin completely surrounded by cliffs.

## 8. SPECIAL REGIONS

**8 a. The Volcanic Barrier.** This is a vast expanse of basalt with low volcanic peaks, averaging about 500 m. (1,600 ft.) above the Sirhan Depression, and (except in the Jebel Druze, which is to be considered separately) rising to about 1,000 m. (3,300 ft.) above sea level. It is an excessively rough and barren region, and much is a mad jumble of huge boulders. Occasionally, there are depressions in which sediment has collected, its yellow color being in striking contrast to the purplish black of the basalt (Plate IV). It is high enough to receive some rain, and though the basalt is impervious, it has been so fractured that in many places the water sinks into the rock, to be paid out in the wells of the Wadi Sirhan. More than 100 km. wide (65 mi.) and 320 km. in length (220 mi.), it is one of the most effective obstacles to movement in the whole Levant, and all the desert traffic is channeled around it.

**8 b. The Jebel Druze.** The highest part of the great mass of basalt is toward the northern end, and here many points exceed 1,700 m. (5,650 ft.) and Tell Rhineh just touches 1,800 m. (5,905 ft.), the word *tell* being used both here and in Bashan to indicate small volcanic cones. The Jebel Druze does not have the towering volcanic peaks that one finds in Turkey and Iran, but is instead an enormous hump of black basalt, fairly level on top, and rising steeply 1,300 m. (4,300 ft.) above the general level of the plateau. Rainfall is heavy here, certainly exceeding 500 mm. (20 in.) and probably more than 750 mm. (30 in.) on the highest parts. During winter the summit is covered with snow for at least two months. This increased precipitation and the fertility of the volcanic soil have encouraged settlement at the lower levels, where there are a number of towns and villages—for example, Kenath (Qanawat) and Salecah (Salkhad). Agriculture is difficult, for the tiny fields are almost incredibly stony, but vines are an important crop. It was famous among the Israelites for its forests, and Mount Bashan was often equated with Carmel and Lebanon (for instance, Isa. 33:9; Ezek. 27:5–6). Still today much of it is covered with a tangle of thorny bushes, very difficult to penetrate. This, coupled with the extraordinary difficulty of the terrain, made it an important region of refuge (Jer. 22:20), and so it remains today, for it is the home of the fiercely independent Druzes, whom no government in Damascus has truly managed to control.

The regions shown on the map as 8d., The Taurus Mountains, and 8e., The Anatolian Plateau, have already been discussed in the previous chapter. So has 8c., The Euphrates, which is only a small section of the region designated there as the Middle Euphrates. Here it has only just left the mountains, and the valley is narrow and still enclosed between high white cliffs (Plate IX). Almost exactly on the present Syrian-Turkish border stands the tell marking the site of Carchemish, where in 609 B.C. the Assyrians were so decisively defeated (II Chron. 35:20).

## Map 14

# THE LEVANT COAST: STRATEGIC FACTORS

This map shows why the Levant was such an important battleground in the ancient world. To the southwest lay the great kingdom of Egypt. To the northwest, in the early biblical period, was the powerful Hittite kingdom on the plateau of Anatolia. During the period of the Israelite monarchy, the chief power was Assyria in northern Mesopotamia, but in the sixth century B.C. the role of Assyria was taken over by Babylon, in southern Mesopotamia. In 539 B.C., Babylon was overthrown by Cyrus, King of Persia, and the Persian empire lasted for almost exactly two hundred years. It fell because a new conqueror made his way across Anatolia, Alexander of Macedon. Throughout this long period, and during the subsequent struggle between the Ptolemies and the Seleucid Kingdom to the north and east, there was a continual power struggle between the rulers of the Nile Valley and these kingdoms—between, that is to say, north and south at first, and then east and west.

From the Palestinian point of view it came to the same thing, for even Babylon, the most southerly of the eastern powers, could not come directly at her, since on the east the entire Palestinian area, as far north as Damascus, was protected, not only by the desert but even more potently by the great barrier of black basalt. Under desert conditions this is a savage rock, sharp and destructive to the feet of camels, a confused jumble of boulders, with no valleys for direction or passage, and over very wide areas completely without water. The desert extended even further to the north, being bounded by the Palmyra hills.

To the west lay the sea, but also another obstacle, that of forest, marsh, and crag. The great fold mountains of the Taurus and Zagros formed a continuous barrier around the north of what is now the country of Syria, though for the most part it is too far north to be shown on this map, and a long tongue of high mountain country stretched southward along the coast as far as the southern limit of Upper Galilee. Sheer height and even great steepness were not in themselves major obstacles, though obviously armies preferred if possible the easier lowland routes. However, the characteristic rock of these mountains was limestone (see Map 3), and notably the Cenomanian limestone, which stands up in great precipices and cliffs. The valleys of this type of country are deep and sinister gorges, and very often it was not the valleys but the rock areas between them which provided the easier routes, especially in Palestine, where the forests were not quite so thick.

All the coastal ranges were forested in biblical times, though more so on their western than on their eastern slopes, and thick forest, especially in rocky mountains, could be as difficult for an army as the brutal and desolate basalt of the desert. Where the forests were more open, of course the difficulties were less, but a rich Mediterranean *maquis,* with its dense tangle of thorny bushes often higher than a man, could be no less of a hindrance, and even a moderate slope, as in the central Carmel area, could block all military passage if it were covered with forest or thicket. Hence the importance of the Senonian chalk valleys in Palestine, as at Megiddo, for these were smooth and carried little or no forest cover.

Finally, an excess of water can hinder movement as effectively as the total lack of it, and marshes baffled even the most skillful of ancient armies. Permanent marsh existed in the coastal areas of the Cilician plain, in the lower Orontes Valley (both in the Ghab and less extensively near Antioch), above Lake Huleh, and in the plain of Sharon. All these areas had to be skirted. Ancient roads, it must be remembered, were no more than rough tracks, often of great width, and no effective network of made roads existed till New Testament times. Consequently, temporary marsh conditions could block passage along these tracks, sometimes for prolonged periods. In regions where

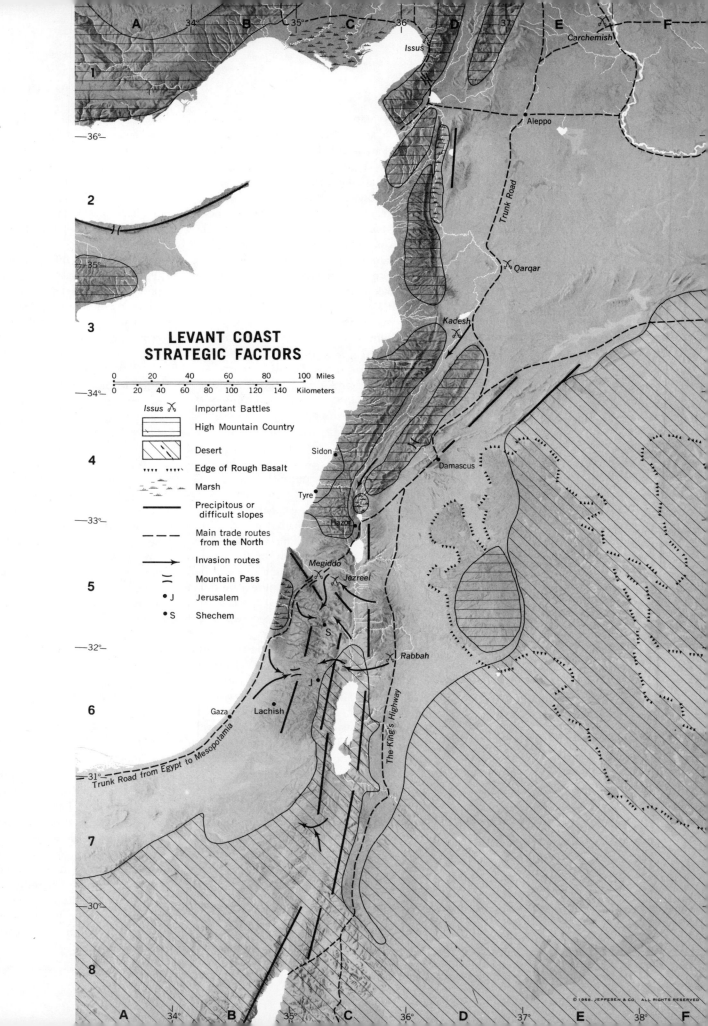

# LEVANT COAST
# STRATEGIC FACTORS

| | 0 | 20 | 40 | 60 | 80 | 100 Miles |
|---|---|---|---|---|---|---|
| 0 | 20 | 40 | 60 | 80 | 100 | 120 | 140 | Kilometers |

*Issus* ⚔    Important Battles

High Mountain Country

Desert

▼▼▼▼ ▼▼▼▼    Edge of Rough Basalt

Marsh

Precipitous or difficult slopes

Main trade routes from the North

→ Invasion routes

‿ Mountain Pass

• J    Jerusalem

• S    Shechem

Carchemish

Issus

Aleppo

Trunk Road

Qarqar

Kadesh

Sidon

Damascus

Tyre

Hazor

Megiddo

Jezreel

S

Rabbah

The King's Highway

J

Gaza

Lachish

Trunk Road from Egypt to Mesopotamia

rainfall is intermittent or severely limited, as over the whole of the Levant, drainage is apt to be defective, since the temporary streams have not carved a sufficient passage through the obstacles along their path. As a result, all low-lying areas, and especially the enclosed fault basins that are so common in the Levant, rapidly become flooded and marshy after heavy rain, and these conditions may last from one storm to the next, so that a small plain, which can be crossed in any direction in summer, is impassable throughout the winter unless there are long dry periods. This was the importance of Megiddo, that it controlled not only the chalk valley across Carmel but also a narrow basalt causeway across the marshy plain of Esdraelon.

In general, of course, soldiers and merchants followed the same routes, where there was level land and water to facilitate the movement of large bodies of men and animals. The great trade routes were, therefore, the invasion routes. However, the necessities of circumventing opposition, or bringing under subjection a mountain people who threatened the trade route from its flank, caused the military commanders to look for alternatives. Thus the long valley between the Lebanon and Anti-Lebanon was not an important commercial route, because it was forested, rocky, and blocked at both ends. However, it was passable, and was occasionally used by an army wishing to circumvent Damascus. Similarly, there is another narrow chalk valley crossing the Carmel ridge near Jokneam (see Map 27, where it is marked by the road crossing Carmel to Dora), which was sometimes used as an alternative to the direct route to the stronghold of Megiddo.

Judah was singularly well protected (see Map 20), but the northern kingdom of Israel was open to invasion from every side except the south, where it was protected by the forested limestone highlands of Ephraim. Elsewhere, chalk valleys or narrow fault valleys led directly to the heart of Manasseh. This led to Israel's expansion at the expense of the less powerful tribes around it until the kingdom controlled all the danger points, including the Valley of Jezreel and the highlands of Gilead to the east. This meant, however, that Israel now lay athwart the great Trunk Road from Egypt to Damascus and the north and east, which opened for it the rich possibilities of international trade but exposed it at the same time to the military adventures of the great powers, across whose path it lay. Its position, in fact, was not unlike that of Belgium in the history of Western Europe.

Both Israel and Judah were threatened with pressure from the small kingdoms and the desert dwellers on the eastern plateau. Again, the major threat was to the northern part of the country, since a fairly easy route led down from Gilead across the Jordan to Bethshan at the entrance to the Valley of Jezreel, and another led up the Wadi Fariʿa in the center of the country. The lower Jordan flowed through a thorny jungle of tamarisk in a narrow trough bordered by badlands, and was an effective obstacle. But it could be crossed near Jericho, and from here a possible route led up into Judah, which the Hebrews remembered as having been taken by themselves in the time of Joshua.

# LEBANON—ANTI-LEBANON

## THE KEY TO THE LEVANT

*Map 15*

Roughly in the middle of the long stretch from Anatolia to Egypt the land has been thrust upward, in a complicated pattern of faulting and folding, to a height far exceeding that found elsewhere in the Levant. This mountainous region dominates the Levant not only physically but politically, and a proper understanding of this region gives the key to a great deal of the historical development of the whole area.

Both the Lebanon Mountains in the west and the Anti-Lebanon Mountains in the east surpass 2,700 m. (9,000 ft.). The Anti-Lebanon are cut by the valley of the River Abana (the modern Barada), but the Lebanon Mountains have no proper passes, and all routes across them are forced to surmount the crest. Even the central rift valley, which in Palestine is below sea level, is here elevated 900 m. (3,000 ft.) above the level of the Mediterranean. Superficially, the central valley appears to continue that of the Jordan, but strictly speaking it does not, for this region has a north-northeast—south-southwest alignment, the north-south line of the Jordan rift appearing to come to an end at Ras Beirut, the headland which protects the harbor of Berytus. The meeting of the two systems is complex, and this has blocked the southern entrance to the valley. A line of weakness cuts back eastward near Tyre, and is responsible for the sudden drop in the level of the land near Abel, Dan, and Paneas, where the true Palestinian rift begins. With this is connected also the sudden right-angled turn by which the River Litani cleaves its way in a narrow gorge across the mountains to the sea. To the east, Mount Hermon towers majestically above Paneas (Caesarea Philippi of the Gospels) and then drops precipitously to the plateau of Bashan.

The folds of the Anti-Lebanon develop fanwise toward the north in a series of lower hills opening out to the northeast; Jebel Shamali ("the northern hills"), Jebel Dua', and Jebel esh-Sharqi ("the eastern hills"). At right angles to this northeast-southwest direction other faulting has developed, and this can be seen from the valleys immediately behind Damascus. Enormous outflows of basalt have erupted upwards through the cracks in the plateau, and now extend southwestward from Damascus far into the Arabian desert. The most northerly extension of them forms the desolate regions known as el-Leja (the Trachonitis of the New Testament) and es-Safa. Farther south are the volcanic highlands of the Jebel Druze.

The mountains receive heavy rains, especially on the seaward side, and are white with snow throughout the winter (Plate 24), the routes across them, except the low-lying Abana Valley, remaining for long impassable. Some snow remains in protected crevices even in summer. The eastern slopes and the interior valley are, of course, in a rain shadow. Thus Beirut (Berytus) on the coast has 850 mm. (34 in.) a year; Bsharreh, near the most famous group of the few remaining cedars of Lebanon high up on the western slopes of the Lebanon Mountains, has 1,000 mm. (40 in.); Zahle, at the eastern foot of the Lebanon, has 685 mm. (27.5 in.); Baalbek, across on the eastern side of the interior valley, has 410 mm. (16.4 in.); and Damascus, at the eastern foot of the Anti-Lebanon Mountains, has only 215 mm. (8.6 in.). The desert here sweeps very close to the foot of the mountains.

This difficult mountain region seriously interrupts communication not only from west to east but also from north to south. The mountains themselves are rocky and precipitous, and in ancient times were heavily forested, especially on the limestone and on the seaward slopes. Then the contrasts in vegetation were much greater than they are now, for forest clothed both the mountains and the central valley, and even the eastern hills were wooded, though more thinly. The open semi-desert of the plateau was consequently the more striking. The westward-flowing streams on the Lebanon are sunk in

## LEBANON—ANTI-LEBANON:
## THE KEY TO THE LEVANT

• Sidon  Towns
**SYRIA**  Regional Names
──────  Major Routes
- - - - - -  Other Routes
— — — —  Sea Routes

30 Miles
Kilometers

Tadmor
(Palmyra)

JEBEL BILA

HOMS - PALMYRA GAP

GRAHS - ESH

J. DUA

JEBEL SHAMAL

Hazarenan

Zedad

En-Nebk

Dumeir

ES - SAFA

Emesa
(Homs)
Avva

Lake of Homs

R. Orom

Riblah

Kadesh

Lebo-Hamath

ANTI - LEBANON

MOUNT
AMANA

Helbon

Damascus

L E B A N O N

Baalbek

J. ZEBDANI

R. Abana

S Y R I A

Kenath

EL - LEJA

Bosor

Raphon

B A S H A N

Karnaim
Ashtaroth

Golan
Hippos

Bsharreh

COELE SYRIA MOUNTAINS

Zahle

MOUNT
HERMON

Caesarea Philippi
(Paneas)

Baalgad

Tripolis

Byblos
(Gebal)

Berytus

L E B A N O N

Ijon

Abel
Dan

BRIDGE OF
JACOB'S DAUGHTERS

Lake
Huleh

Hazor

Lake
of
Galilee

Migdal

GALILEE

Meron

Kedesh

R. Litani

Sidon

Tyre

Arvad

30. Palmyra: the temple of Bel. *This shows the monumental entrance to the sanctuary, dedicated to the three gods Bel, Iarhibol, and Aglibol, in A.D. 32. Pliny tells us that this rich oasis tried to maintain a neutral position between Parthia and Rome, but by the New Testament period it had become tributary to the Roman Empire.*

deep and precipitous gorges, in part created by the multiplicity of geological faults which are shown on Map 24, and often hinder, rather than assist, communication. The coast plain almost completely disappears, and the coast is rocky and broken by abrupt, cliff-rimmed headlands. For this reason, communication was easier here by sea than by land, for there are many safe anchorages in the rocky inlets. This was Phoenicia, a region rich in fine lumber but lacking in level land for agriculture, which had to be coaxed out of the steep mountain sides. Throughout history it has turned its back on the plateaus to the east and looked westward, and in Old Testament times the Phoenicians, from their great center at Tyre, developed the first maritime empire, sending the adventurous "ships of Tarshish" far out into the unknown waters of the west.

The interior valley does not provide the easy corridor for communication that might appear from a map. The southern end is closed by the tumbled hills where the two fault systems meet, and the northern end by rough basalt country. Here in the northern valley was a marked "gulf of drought" (see Map 7). The center of the valley is also far from level and constantly interrupted by sharp ridges, the foothills of the Anti-Lebanon. This valley, though apparently more easily connected with the east by the Abana Valley, was in ancient times almost always associated with Phoenicia, despite the gigantic barrier that separates it from the coast. This is because its agricultural way of life is more akin to the restricted cultivation of the coastland than to the pastoralism of the broad steppes east of Damascus.

All major land routes were therefore deflected eastward around the mountains to the arid, but open and relatively level, plateau, where they followed the spring line at the foot of the hills. Easily supreme was Damascus, the oldest continuously inhabited city in the world, a place where men must settle if there are any men at all. Endowed with a magnificent water supply from the mountains, it receives all the routes of the plateau, which are directed to this center by the configuration of the long lines of hills and the obstacles of the impassable basalt. He who would command the Levant must always control Damascus, which is the hub of the entire area.

Yet those who control Damascus find it far from easy to command the Levant, and despite continual efforts Syria has never been the center of an effective and extensive empire, even the Ummayad rule lasting less than a century. This is because Damascus stands alone, isolated in her splendor. Beyond the limits of her rich oasis there are no people to furnish her with armies, and the nearest centers of population are all sufficiently remote so that, though she may compel them to submit for a while, it is never long before they manage to revolt.

In the north, extending eastwards from the bay near Tripolis, by the Lake of Homs, to beyond Tadmor (Palmyra), is the broad depression of the Homs-Palmyra gap. It continues to the Euphrates near Mari, and forms the southernmost of the routes which curve around the north of the Arabian desert. It also marks an important division between the good steppeland of the kingdom of Hamath in the north and the poor steppe and desert of Syria to the south. There is a clear cultural division here even today, and in ancient times this separation between two ways of life was recognized as a political division. The people of Israel, who often dreamed of bringing Syria under their control, saw it as the limit of the imperial adventures to the north, and as such it appears in Numbers 34:7–9 and Ezekiel 47:15–17. Unfortunately, not all the towns can be identified (e.g., Ziphron, Hethlon, Berothah, Sibraim), but the mention of such frontier posts as Zedad and Hazarenan makes this clear.

# Map 16

# PALESTINE IN THE PATRIARCHAL PERIOD

There is no other period in biblical history of which we can say at the same time that we know both so much and so little as of the period of the Patriarchs. The first quarter of the second millennium B.C. is one on which a flood of light has been thrown by archaeological research. Middle Bronze Age tombs excavated at Jericho, with their contents remarkably preserved (it seems by the intrusion of volcanic gases), have given us a vivid picture of the household furniture, clothes, and food of the period. Recent exploration of the Negeb, the southern desert of Palestine, has revealed how extensively it was covered with farming villages, which practiced, probably, a mixed economy of agriculture and pastoralism. Thousands upon thousands of texts from Mari (over 20,-000 from this site alone), Cappadocia, Babylon, Alalakh, and Nuzi, as well as the Execration Texts from Egypt, have helped us to understand the social and legal customs of the time. What still remains extraordinarily unclear, however, is the nature of the events described in Genesis, chapters 12–50, and the character of the Patriarchs themselves. Scholars have conjectured that Abraham was "a soldier of fortune," "a merchant-prince," or "a priest-king," to name only three suggestions. A "merchant-prince" seems to make him too grand, and a "soldier of fortune" too unruly—perhaps we should think of him as the sheikh of a pastoral tribe, involved in the incessant commerce of the Levant, and fully capable of a *ghazu,* or raid, if necessary.

There is little reason now to doubt the existence of Abraham and Jacob, even though the association of Abraham with the south and Jacob with the center of the country suggests that we have here two parallel memories of origins from different regions, which have later become merged as part of the common heritage of Israel. If, as seems possible, the story of the four kings against five in Genesis, chapter 14, is from a foreign source, and almost certainly a very early one (possibly northern Mesopotamian), then we have a unique foreign reference to Abraham, which presents him, however, as quite a different kind of person from the rest of the stories. It has been suggested that the story reflects the penetration of the Palestinian area by merchant adventurers from Mesopotamia, seeking the copper of the Arabah. In any case, the route followed by the invaders is perfectly clear: southwards, through Ashteroth-Karnaim along the King's Highway on the edge of the Trans-Jordanian plateau, until they were worsted by the people who lived at the southern end of the Dead Sea. Abraham is represented as a "Hebrew," apparently one of the *habiru,* or an enemy of society, who pursued them north of Damascus, and then on his return through Cis-Jordan was met by Melchizedek, who seems to have been a priest-king of Salem, the later Jerusalem.

The tradition of Abraham's connection with Ur in southern Mesopotamia is rather doubtful, though not impossible, but there can be no question of his connection with the northern Jezireh, the land between the rivers at the foot of the Zagros. The tradition of movement on the part of the Patriarchs to and from Palestine and northern Syria, and even as far south as Egypt, has suggested to some scholars a connection with trade, though others see no necessity for this. The picture is one of an essentially pastoral society, and this would fit in well with a date about 1900 B.C. for Abraham. Previously to this, in the last quarter of the third millennium, a new group of people had apparently moved into Palestine, who are in some way related to the movements of Asiatics who had entered Egypt at the beginning of the First Intermediate Period and the Western Semites who disrupted the civilization of Mesopotamia. These are the people whom the Bible calls the Amorites, and who at the time of the conquest are spoken of as being in Trans-Jordan. They were pastoralists, and over very much of Palestine at this time we see an almost complete takeover of the sown by the shepherds. However, at the beginning of the Middle Bronze Age (c. 1900 B.C.) a more sophisticated people, the biblical "Canaanites," having close ties with the coastal towns of Phoenicia, entered Palestine, and established a town culture which not only persisted to the time of the Israelite conquest, but was also extraordinarily widespread.[1] The free movement of the Patriarchal period from the north to the south of the Levant seems to reflect the unity of the culture in this period.

There is no mention of any Egyptian control of Palestine in the Genesis stories, and so they must concern a time earlier than the rise of the Egyptian empire. The "Hittites" of Genesis, chapter 23, seem to have little or no connection with the Hittite empire of Anatolia. Furthermore, if the going down into Egypt is in some way related to the Hyksos movement into the Delta, then an early date for Abra-

---

[1] This is the argument put forward by Kathleen M. Kenyon in *Amorites and Canaanites* (Oxford University Press, 1966). See especially ch. III. It is not, however, universally accepted.

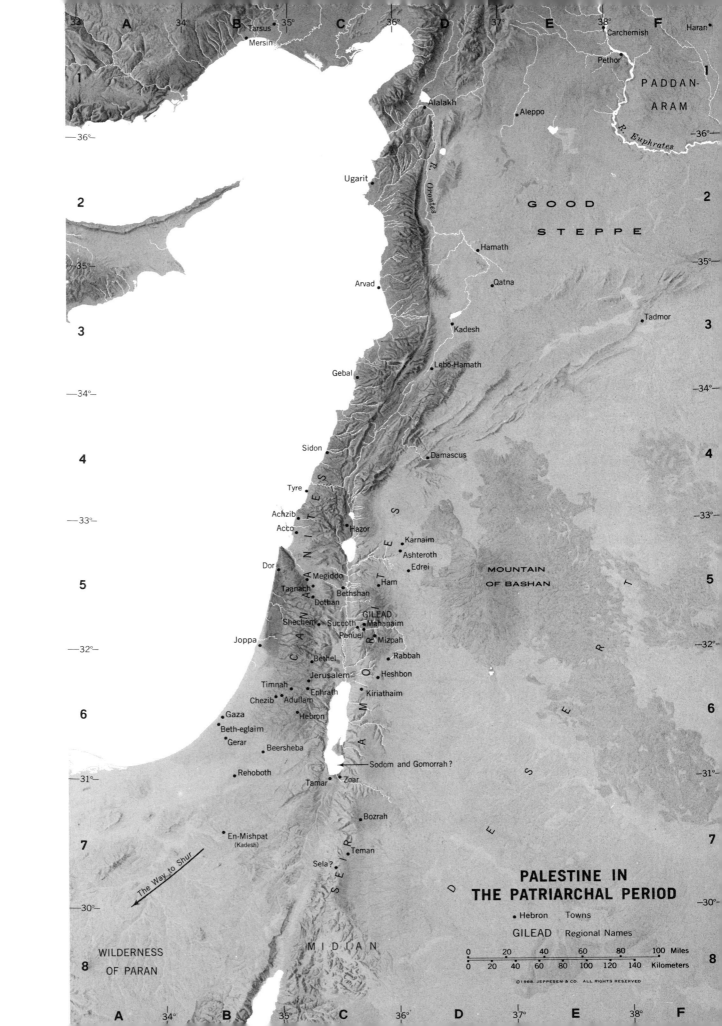

PALESTINE IN
THE PATRIARCHAL PERIOD

● Hebron    Towns

GILEAD    Regional Names

ham seems probable. We seem to have a picture in Genesis which partakes both of the pastoralism of the Amorites and also the universal order of the Middle Bronze, but before its strongly urban character had had time to make itself felt.

The story of the destruction of the Cities of the Plain (Sodom, Gomorrah, Admah, and Zeboiim) in Genesis 18:16 to 19:29 poses a problem for the mapmaker, for they have never been traced. Scholarly opinion has, in fact, swung full circle from completely rejecting the story in the early years of this century to confidently accepting once more its essential truth today. Arguments have been advanced for these cities being under either the northern or the southern end of the Dead Sea. It seems prob-

able that we should accept the southern hypothesis, and place them somewhere in the very shallow basin south of the Lisan peninsula. It is true that aerial photography, and other methods of research, have failed to produce any sign of them, but it seems reasonable to assume that there was an earthquake which lowered the surface of the land by faulting. A volcanic eruption seems very much less likely, because, though the Dead Sea has been known to throw up blocks of asphalt, which float on the surface (it was known to the Romans as Lacus Asphaltitis), there is only one known small basalt intrusion in the valley itself, all the others being on the Trans-Jordanian plateau.

Mount Moriah, the scene of Abraham's attempted sacrifice of Isaac (Gen-

esis, chapter 22), must surely be looked for somewhere in the Wilderness of Paran, rather than at the traditional site in Jerusalem, an identification which is impossible. Likewise, Hagar's flight into the desert, on the Way to Shur, was southward and Beer-lahai-roi somewhere not far from En-Mishpat (that is, Kadesh Barnea at 'Ain Qudeirat). Shur was the line of frontier fortresses which bordered Egypt.

The strange story of the slaughter of the men of Shechem for their treatment of Dinah in Genesis, chapter 34, seems to reflect the struggle and subsequent failure of the tribes of Simeon and Levi to gain land in central Palestine, and is part of the evidence for the probability that not all the Israelites went down into Egypt.

*Map 17*

# THE MIDDLE EAST BEFORE THE EXODUS

The Exodus was, comparatively speaking, a modern event in the long history of the Middle East. The Israelite takeover of the Palestinian hill country must be dated round about 1250 B.C., that is to say, a little over three thousand years ago. But a small stone-walled shrine, the most ancient building in the world of which we have any trace, already existed at Jericho by about 7800 B.C., almost ten thousand years ago,[1] and eight hundred years later there stood a strongly defended city, surrounded by a city wall more than 12 feet high and 6 feet wide, and by a rock-cut moat, 27 feet wide and 9 feet deep. There was also a great stone tower, with an interior staircase, which still stands to a height of 30 feet.[2] Thus, by the time of the Exodus, when the Hebrews first became a nation, the country they were to inhabit had already had a history of settlement, of agriculture, trade, and pastoralism, and the necessity of defense against the in-

vader, for something like six thousand years, twice as long as has elapsed since that time. The amazing succession of planned and well-defended cities covering an area of 32 acres, at Çatal Hüyük in southern Anatolia, were built between 6500 and 5700 B.C., and presuppose a history of settlement as long as that of Palestine. Probably, settlement in the foothills of the Zagros is of similar antiquity.

By about 3500 B.C., two thousand years before the Exodus, the building of elaborate cities in Sumer in southern Mesopotamia was already far advanced, and from the same date comes the first known example of picture writing, on a small limestone tablet found at Kish. Civilization in Egypt is almost comparable in date, though probably slightly later.

The Sumerians may well have been native to Mesopotamia, though some scholars have suggested that they came, as did so many of their successors,

[1] Kathleen M. Kenyon, *Archaeology in the Holy Land* (New York: Praeger, 1960), pp. 41–42.
[2] *Ibid.*, pp. 43–44.

THE MIDDLE EAST
BEFORE THE EXODUS

- Kadesh  Towns
KEDAR  Regional Names

50 0 50 100 150 200 250 Miles
50 0 100 150 200 250 300 350 Kilometers

©1966 JEPPESEN & CO.  ALL RIGHTS RESERVED

CASPIAN SEA

PERSIAN GULF

MEDITERRANEAN SEA

RED SEA

URARTU

HATTI

KIZZUWATNA

TAURUS Mts.

KITTIM

HURRIAN

MITANNI

ASSYRIA

MEDIA

GUTIUM

AKKAD

BABYLONIA

SUMER

ELAM

KEDAR

MIDIAN

ARABIA

EGYPT

NUBIA

Lake Van

Lake Urmia

Ecbatana

Susa

Eshnunna

Sippar

Babylon

Borsippa

Nippur

Isin

Erech

Lagash

Larsa

Ur

Eridu

Nineveh

Calah

Asshur

Nuzi

R. Tigris

Sinjar

Tel Brak

Tel Halaf

Haran

R. Euphrates

Mari

Tadmor

Dumah

Tema

Dedan

Carchemish

Halab

Hamath

Kadesh

Damascus

Alalakh

Ugarit

Arvad

Gebal

Sidon

Tyre

Acco

Dor

Joppa

Gaza

Beersheba

Megiddo

Shechem

Jericho

Jerusalem

Hebron

Avaris

On

Memphis

Ikhetaton

Abydos

Thebes

Syene

R. Nile

Alaca

Hattusas

Ankuwa

Kanish

from the mountains to the east, or perhaps the steppes farther afield to the north and west. North of Sumer, in the Mesopotamian "waist," where the two rivers come close together, a Semitic people known as the Akkadians were settled by the middle of the third millennium B.C. They established an empire which lasted over a hundred years (c. 2360–2180 B.C.), but was destroyed by the onslaught of the wild Gutians from the Zagros Mountains, and of a second wave of Semitic-speaking peoples from the west, the later Babylonians, an event which paved the way in course of time for the Sumerian renaissance under the Third Dynasty of Ur around 2000 B.C.

The third millennium in Egypt saw the unification of "the Two Lands," the Delta and Upper Egypt, the glories of the Old Kingdom (2700–2200 B.C.), and the collapse of the First Intermediate Period (2200–2050 B.C.). The Fourth Dynasty (2650–2500) was the period when the great pyramids were built, though they had forerunners in the Third Dynasty. The southern frontier was at Syene, at the First Cataract, whence trading and military expeditions pushed southwards into Nubia. About 2300 Herkhuf, the first known explorer, made four journeys to well beyond the Second Cataract. In Palestine and Syria, the Pharaohs of the Old Kingdom exercised an intermittent command over the trade routes, and had at Gebal (Byblos) an important merchant colony.

In Asia Minor the long history of the city of Troy begins about 3000 B.C., and lasts until the destruction of the city toward the end of the twelfth century B.C. An impressive culture had already developed within the bend of the Halys River (the later Hittite homeland), as illustrated by the royal tombs at Alaca Hüyük (c. 2500–2300 B.C.); and at Kanish, near the modern Kayseri, an important city, trading with Syria, Cilicia, and Mesopotamia existed around 2200 B.C.

The second millennium B.C. saw the collapse of the power of Ur and the rise of Elam in the Zagros piedmont region. From about 1800 to 1530 B.C. is the period of the First Dynasty of Babylon (Hammurabi, 1728–1686), and roughly contemporary, is the brief but very impressive power of Mari on the middle Euphrates (c. 1750–1700). Mari was a great city, with far-flung trade relations, but its power was overthrown by the rival state of Assyria to the northeast.

Order and unity were restored in Egypt with the establishment of the Middle Kingdom (2050–1800 B.C.) under the Twelfth Dynasty, whose first Pharaoh may possibly have been a Nubian. The frontier was pushed southwards to the Second Cataract, near the present Egyptian-Sudanese frontier, and Egyptian power was felt both farther up the Nile and in the Levant. During this period also Kanish grew in size and importance, and became the home of a large colony of Assyrian merchants, whose records on clay tablets have been found.

The second quarter of the second millennium witnessed a convulsive movement of peoples in the Middle East, with resounding results. The best known of these is the penetration and occupation of the Nile Delta by the Hyksos, the period of the "great humiliation" of Egypt, when Hyksos control extended south of Memphis, and the southern frontier was pushed back, at any rate for a time, as far as Syene. The origins of the Hyksos are very obscure, but they seem to have been a largely Semitic people, who undoubtedly had their capital at Avaris in Lower Egypt. It was apparently in their wake that a group of Asiatics, with whom we must associate the Joseph stories, moved into the edge of the Delta.

About the same time, we have the movement of the Hurrians, from the high mountain knob district (the later territory of Urartu) into all parts of the Fertile Crescent. By 1500 they were the overwhelming majority at Alalakh on the Orontes, and Nuzi in the Zagros foothills (from which town also thousands of clay tablets have been recovered). At the same time there arose the Old Hittite kingdom within the Halys bend, and Babylon collapsed before the onslaught of the Kassites from the Zagros Mountains.

Around the middle of the second millennium a new pattern began to emerge. The Kassites were established in Babylon, where they held power for four hundred years, but in Egypt a native ruler, Ahmose I, drove the Hyksos out of Egypt, and re-established the unity of the Nile. The Egyptians were determined that they should not be so humiliated again, and they extended the boundaries of their empire far beyond the earlier limits, both in Nubia and in the Levant. Here, however, they came in conflict with the new Hittite empire, which was pressing southward, commercially and militarily. Rameses II records, at Karnak near Thebes, Abu Simbel, and elsewhere, a great battle at Kadesh on the Orontes in the fifth year of his long reign (1290–1224). It was apparently indecisive, but the Hittite-Egyptian frontier zone seems to have been established along roughly the Homs-Palmyra depression, which was for each of them the limit of effective control. About 1500 B.C. Indo-European nobles established the kingdom of Mitanni in the predominantly Hurrian region of northern Mesopotamia, and it pressed for a time on the Egyptian empire, supporting the ruler of Kadesh against Thutmose III in 1468 B.C. However, Mitanni succumbed to the rising power of Assyria under Asshur-uballit (1354–1318).

*Map 18*

# THE EXODUS

It seems extremely likely, at any rate at present, that the problem of the route of the Exodus will never be solved. Indeed, it is a problem which becomes more, and not less, complicated. Not only are we really quite in the dark about the actual site of Mount Sinai, but we have to ask serious questions about what we mean when we speak both of the Exodus and of the Conquest. There is a great argument about which tribes went down to Egypt, the most commonly accepted theory being that they included the Joseph tribes (Ephraim and Manasseh) and the Leah tribes (Reuben, Simeon, Levi, and Judah), since there is evidence for the use of some of the tribal names (e.g., Asher) in Palestine before the time of the Exodus. However, there is strong probability that most, if not in fact all, of the tribal names were originally regional names, and were not used in a tribal sense before the occupation of Canaan. The archaeological evidence is extremely complex. For instance, the destruction of many Palestinian cities about this time is not in itself evidence of actual conquest, but only of destruction by some means. Two of the most important sites mentioned in the initial stages of the conquest, Jericho and Ai, have revealed no evidence at all of any destruction at this time—Jericho because there is no evidence of any occupation in this period, and we must assume at best a small settlement whose traces have been completely eroded; and Ai because it had clearly been deserted a thousand years earlier. Some believe that an account of the destruction of Bethel was transferred to the nearby ruins of Ai. Scholars who still accept the idea of an actual conquest recognize that it cannot have been simple, and must have consisted of at least two waves, and probably more, of marauding bedouin and others, extending over more than a century.

The core of the story is quite certainly the experience of those people who left Egypt proper, and problems of "the route of the Exodus" concern the journeyings of these people, but others must have joined them, who themselves had never been in the Nile Valley but who "became Hebrews," and identified themselves with the experience. Palestine at this period was part of the Egyptian empire, and the reign of Rameses II (1290–1224), the Pharaoh of the Oppression, represents a culmination of Egyptian imperialism, and a clamping down on any attempt to question the absolute, and in principle changeless, system of the Nile. The overassertion of the system shown in the inscriptions, and the extraordinary multiplication of statues of the Pharaoh (Plate 33), reflect this. Small groups of social misfits, both from Palestine and from Egypt proper, broke with this bondage, and fled to those wastelands where the Egyptian writ did not run and where the Egyptian "gods" had no power. "Out of Egypt," though unquestionably based upon the historical experience of those who had left Egypt quite literally, may well have come to be something more than a purely geographical concept, and to represent a rejection, and therefore a movement out of, the Egyptian system and Egyptian society. This taking to the wilderness of "everyone who was discontented and everyone who was in distress" is a constantly repeated feature of Palestinian history.

The connection between "the Hebrews" and the *habiru* (a word used apparently for a variety of people who were viewed as enemies of society) is much disputed, but it seems a reasonable interpretation. In the Bible "Hebrews" is consistently used by foreigners, and is not the manner in which the Israelites speak of themselves. Kadesh Barnea was apparently an important gathering center for such people who in course of time moved back to settle in Canaan, especially in the hill country. This takeover of the forested hill country by these subversive elements involved conflicts with those who were already there, but one must probably see the destruction of the cities as only partly the work of outsiders, and very much as also brought about by restless elements who had taken to the wilderness locally, and even occasionally by dissatisfied groups within the cities themselves. Recent excavations in the region of Bethel and Ai suggest the infiltration here of elements from Anatolia.[1] All these people would have been *habiru* in terms of the established society.

That some overwhelming and never-to-be-forgotten experience took place at the holy mountain, variously called Sinai and Horeb, is beyond question, but the traditional identification with Jebel Musa in what we now call the peninsula of Sinai is a late one. When Mount Zion in Jerusalem became for Judah the "holy mountain" *par excellence*, memories of where the holy mountain of the Exodus experience actually was became vague. At one time there may have been a pilgrimage to it, on which the stopping places may be listed in reverse in Numbers 33:41–49, but the pilgrimage to Jerusalem took its place, and it was probably increasingly discouraged by those who wished to keep the Israelite worship pure from alien influences. Elijah's journey to Horeb (I Kings 19) is the last evidence we have that it was thought of as a sacred center. What does seem abundantly clear (though like everything else, it is not accepted by all) is that the experience at the holy mountain reflects memories of a volcanic eruption, and there are no volcanoes

in the Sinai peninsula. However, there does exist in north Arabia a mountain called Jebel Harab, not far from the northern end of the great outflow of volcanic basalt known as Harrat er-Rahah, where the volcano of Jebel el-Badr was active in historic times. The bedouin regard it as sacred, because they have an ancient tradition of a destructive eruption, and they do not let their flocks approach it (cf. Exod. 19:23). It is very tempting to place Mount Horeb or Sinai in this region.

Nevertheless, it must be admitted that many scholars still hold to the traditional identification with Jebel Musa and consequently tentative identifications of other places mentioned in the story have been made in relation to this fixed point. Some of these are shown on the map. It follows, however, that if we were to accept the north Arabian theory, the Exodus sites would have to be looked for over there, but we know too little of this region to make more than guesses. The north Arabian Sinai would fit in much better with the position of Midian, which is certainly related to the mountainous area in Saudi Arabia, at the northern end of the Red Sea, known today as Madyan.

That some of the Hebrews came from the Delta region and that their experience formed the core of the subsequent account is little to be doubted. Pithom, Raamses (= Avaris or Tanis), Baal-Zephon, Migdol, and possibly Succoth can be identified with reasonable cer-

tainty. Also at the end of the story such places as Tophel, Dibon, Heshbon, and Madeba are beyond question, since they have almost the same names today. Punon is surely Feinan, where the ancient copper mines were, and it was apparently here that Moses made the bronze serpent (Num. 21:4–9).

Kadesh Barnea is generally accepted as being at ʿAin Qudeirat, which would make it a very suitable gathering site for those who took to the wilderness from both Egypt and Palestine. There is a good water supply here. This identification has, however, not been unquestioned.

The term translated "the Red Sea" (Yam Suph) should be "the Reed Sea" and be identified with the marshy country somewhere near where the Suez Canal now is.

Mount Nebo, where Moses is said to have viewed the Promised Land (Deut. 32:49), is normally identified with a definite place, Siyaghah, and this traditional site is the one marked in this atlas. Nevertheless, it is probable that the expression "Mount Nebo" is the equivalent of the Arabic expression *nabwah* (or *nabawah*), which means "a height." Mount Nebo would therefore be a general term, and in the biblical account would mean that Moses was brought to the high edge of the eastern plateau, where the precipitous slopes plunge dramatically down to the Rift Valley and the Dead Sea.

[1] From a lecture given by Professor Jay Callaway at the annual meeting of the Society of Biblical Literature, Toronto, Nov. 17–19, 1969. Quoted by permission of Dr. Callaway.

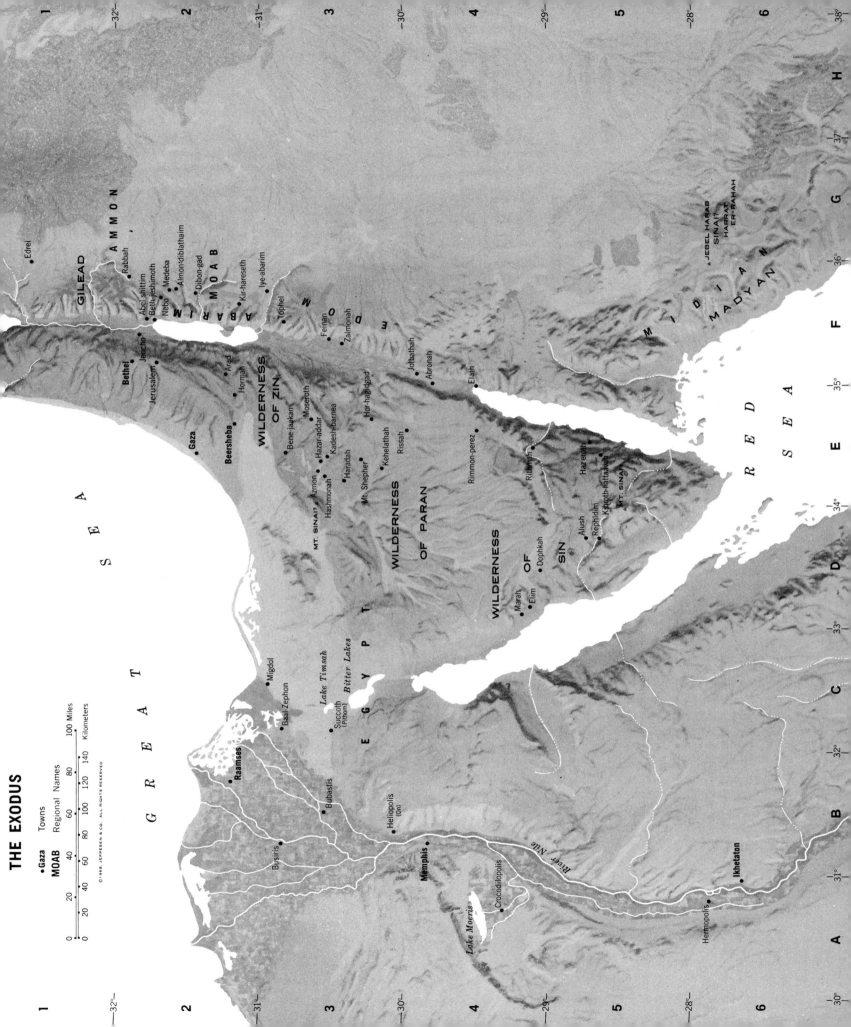

# THE EXODUS

- Gaza  Towns
- MOAB  Regional Names

0 20 40 60 80 100 Miles
0 20 40 60 80 100 120 140 Kilometers

GREAT SEA

Edrei

GILEAD

AMMON

Rabbah

Abel-shittim
Beth-jeshimoth
Nebo  Medeba
Almon-diblathaim
Dibon-gad

MOAB

Jericho
Bethel
Jerusalem

ABARIM

Kir-hareseth
Iye-abarim

Tophel

M O A B

Feinan
Zalmonah

E D O M

Arad
Hornah

WILDERNESS OF ZIN

Beersheba

Gaza

Bene-jaakan
Hazar-addar
Kadesh-barnea
Haradah

MT. SINAI?  Azmon
Hashmonah
Mt. Shepher

Hor-hagidgad

Jotbathah
Abronah

Elath

Kehelathah
Rissah

WILDERNESS OF PARAN

Rimmon-perez

WILDERNESS OF SIN

Rithmah

Hazeroth

Kibroth-hattaavah
MT. SINAI

Alush
Rephidim

Dophkah

Marah
Elim

EGYPT

Migdol

Baal-Zephon

Lake Timsah

Bitter Lakes

Succoth
(Pithom)

Raamses

Bubastis

Heliopolis
(On)

Busiris

Memphis

Crocodilopolis

Lake Moeris

River Nile

Hermopolis

Ikhetaton

RED SEA

R E D   S E A

MIDIAN

MADYAN

JEBEL HARAB
SINAI?
HARRAT
ER-RAHAH

# JOSHUA TO THE DEATH OF SAUL

Map 19

The period from about 1250 to about 1000 B.C. is a time when the land of Canaan was greatly in dispute. The book of Joshua records a straightforward conquest of the country, first in the south and then in the north, and then its partition among the twelve tribes, and the next book, the book of Judges, gives an account of a series of crises, usually invasions, which were successfully resisted under the leadership of charismatic personalities, known as "judges." Once more, all this seems to be the simplifying and telescoping of memories of a complex situation, in which the events cannot now be arranged in neat chronological order.

There was for all this period no clearly recognized, primary authority, and three groups struggled for the supremacy: the Canaanites, who belonged to the already existing city-states; the "Hebrews" or Israelites, who were establishing themselves amid the forests and woodlands of the hill country, admirably suited to a kind of guerrilla warfare, and where they could not easily be attacked; and finally the Philistines, who had moved into the southern coastal region about 1200 B.C., overcoming the cities and occupying the same sites, but not apparently building new cities of their own. They were a part of the great movement of "Sea Peoples," who were at this time moving from the north into the whole of the eastern Mediterranean region with quite catastrophic results upon the existing civilizations.

The Israelites at this time were probably a more or less amorphous mass of people from various parts of the country, all of whom, for reasons of their own, were in revolt against the established order, which was, in any case, at that time collapsing, and in its collapse producing exactly this discontent. A fairly small group of outsiders, who had had the experience at the holy mountain, provided out of that experience the new concept of both the true society and its God, which was the impetus to action and the principle of cohesion. Many Palestinians would have

joined them. Slowly these people established themselves in the hills, forming as they did so a loose confederation of twelve units, with a center of pilgrimage at Shiloh, in the high, well-protected, limestone hill country of Ephraim, where the sacred Ark was kept. Little by little they groped toward unity, based upon covenant with one another and with their God, but because of their passion for liberty they also resisted it, and it is evident that never until the time of Saul did all twelve tribes unite to resist an enemy.

Chapter 1 of Judges reveals that the takeover was much slower and less complete than the book of Joshua would suggest, for the Hebrews had only bronze weapons, except what they might be able to capture from their enemies, and certainly did not know how to make iron, a new technique which was jealously guarded by the more advanced Philistines and Canaanites (I Sam. 13:19–22). The accounts in Joshua and Judges suggest that settlement was easier in the less populated highlands of Ephraim and Judah and the southern steppe round Beersheba, but that it was resisted in the more strongly Canaanite center and north, as well as east of the Jordan, where the small kingdoms of Ammon, Moab, and Edom had already begun to take hold.

The strange and shadowy figure of Cushan-rishathaim in Judges 3:7–11 may not have been an actual historical character. The name is apparently invented. Apart from this, the enemies are all local, Sisera and Jabin from the north, and Ammon and Moab from the east. From farther east still came also the Midianites in the time of Gideon, the first example we have of the long-distance raiding made possible by the taming of the camel. The story also reflects the persistent distrust and rivalry between the west and east banks of the Jordan (Judg. 8:4–21; see also Judg. 12:1–6). The story of Abimelech in Judges, chapter 9, reflects the difficulty of establishing the new concept of

# JOSHUA TO THE DEATH OF SAUL

● Hebron  Towns
AMALEKITES  Regional Names

Miles 0 5 10 15 20 25 30 35 40
Kilometers 0 5 10 15 20 25 30 35 40 45 50 55

© 1968. JEPPESEN & CO. ALL RIGHTS RESERVED

Sidon

Damascus

Baalgad
Ijon
Ahlab
*R. Litani*
Tyre
Abel
Dan

Misrephoth-maim
Kedesh

Achzib

Hazor
Beth-anath  Merom
Acco  Rehob
Achshaph  Chinnereth
Aphek  Cabul
Nahalol  Migdol  Karnaim
Rimmon  Madon  Golan
Bethlehem  Ashteroth
Harosheth  *R. Yarmuk*
Shimron
Jokneam  Endor  Edrei
Dor  Shunem  Ramoth-gilead
Megiddo  Jezreel
Taanach  Kamon
Engannim  Tob
Ibleam  Salecah
Dothan  Beth-shan
Hepher ?  Abel-meholah
Thebez  Jabesh-gilead
Tirzah  Tabbath
Zarethan
Shechem  Succoth
Pirathon  Arumah  *R. Jabbok*
Baal-shalishah  Penuel  Mahanaim
Aphek  Tappuah  Adam
Gath-rimmon  Lebonah  Ataroth
Joppa  Eben-ezer  Mizpah
Beth-dagon  Ramathaim-zophim  Shiloh  Jogbehah
Timnath-serah  Ophrah  Betonim
Lower  Bethel  Naarah  Beth-nimrah  Rabbah
Beth-horon  Beeroth  Ai
Gezer  Beth-Horon  Gilgal ?
Jabneel  Mizpah  Michmash  Abel-Keramim
Aijalon  Gibeon  Jericho  Gilgal ?
Kiriath-Jearim  Gibeah  Shittim  Elealeh
Ekron  Timnah  Zorah  Jerusalem  Heshbon  Bezer
Ashdod  Beth-meon
Beth-shemesh  Zanoah  Bethlehem  Beth-jeshimoth
Libnah  Azekah  Medeba
Ashkelon  Adullam  Kiriathaim  Beth-meon
Keilah  Tekoa  Zereth-shahar
Mareshah  Beth-zur  Kedemoth
Gaza  Eglon  Lachish  DEAD SEA  Dibon
Hebron  Engedi  *R. Arnon*  Aroer
Gath  Debir  Ziph
Gerar  Ziklag  Carmel
Anab  Maon  Madmen
Jattir  Ar
Arad
Beersheba  Kir-Hareseth
Hormah

PHILISTINES

AMALEKITES

Ziph  Zoar
Tamar  *R. Zered*
Tophel

M I D I A N I T E S

covenant, and of a society without a king, in an area where the Canaanites predominated over the Israelites. The fact that there was at Shechem a temple of El-berith, or "the God of Covenant" (Judg. 9:46), which Abimelech destroyed, indicates something of this struggle.

The Philistines, however, were a far more difficult enemy, for they could not be dealt with by the technique of temporary unification of the tribes concerned under the leadership of a dynamic personality. They were themselves a vigorous people, and well organized under the leadership of the princes of their five cities (Gaza, Ashkelon, Ashdod, along the coast; Gath and Ekron on their land frontier). They expanded over the whole of the coast plain south of the Sharon forest and marshes, which at the time were wellnigh uninhabitable, and though they never settled any part of the hill country, they brought the Shephelah under their control, and pressed northward along the Trunk Road to include the Valley of Jezreel and the great stronghold of Bethshan under their authority. Their expansion forced the tribe of Dan to retreat from their infiltration of the coast plain, and trek to the most northerly part of the Jordan Valley

(Judg. 18), and the rough and savage stories of the Samson epic (Judg. 13–16) reveal the constant strife along the frontier zone between the Philistines and the people of the hills.

It became clear that a more permanent leader would have to be chosen, with authority to compel the obedience of all the tribes, though to the more conservative elements this choosing of a king was tantamount to going back to Egypt and rejection of all that the Exodus had meant. Saul was the first such king, chosen from the little tribe of Benjamin to prevent jealousy, and excavation at his stronghold at Gibeah just north of Jerusalem has shown that he was no more than the leader of a still very simple and bucolic society.

Nevertheless, the fact that the Israelites were uniting at all disturbed the Philistines, who struck northward into the hills of Benjamin up the Valley of Aijalon past Beth-horon to Michmash, along the one weak place in the defenses of Judah. Though the Israelites drove them back down the same valley (I Sam. 14), it is evident that they were hard pressed, and this is the explanation of the much misunderstood command to massacre all the Amalekites (I Sam. 15:3). Saul had dealt with the Ammonites, who might perchance

thrust at them from across the river up the Valley of Achor, and it was imperative that he eliminate the only other external danger, that of a stab in the back by raiders from the south along the Beersheba road. His failure to do so meant that their raids were still a danger when at last he was forced to a pitched battle with the Philistines on the slopes of Mount Gilboa on the southern side of the Valley of Jazreel, the same battleground in which Gideon had routed the Midianites (Judg. 7; I Sam. 29:1; 31:1–13). Saul, however, was defeated, and the whole Hebrew people were thrown into confusion, the adherents of Saul's family taking refuge east of the Jordan in Gilead, and the people of Judah rallying round David in the southern stronghold of Hebron.

David had earlier been forced into opposition to Saul, and like many others before and since, had taken to the wilderness, where he was joined by the malcontents and misfits of society (I Sam. 22:1–2). We find him thereafter, until the death of Saul, a wanderer in the Judean moat between the hill country and the Shephelah, in the region round Beersheba, and in the Wilderness of Jeshimon.

# THE TERRITORY OF JUDAH
## Map 20

The actual territory of Judah was extremely small. Beersheba marked the southern and Geba the northern frontier of the kingdom (II Kings 23:8), the direct distance between them being no more than 80 km. (50 mi.). From the western edge of the Judean plateau to the shores of the Dead Sea averages about 32 km. (20 mi.). This territory was, however, extremely well defended, and could be attacked only at certain points.

To the east there was the triple protection of the Dead Sea, the steep limestone cliffs which border it on the western shore, and the desolate waste of the dry Senonian chalk (the Wilderness of Judea, or Jeshimon). To the

west the defenses were also multiple, for here the rugged limestone plunges down in a great monocline, in which the winter streams have cut only narrow and difficult gorges. Beyond this was the unattractive Eocene limestone region of the Shephelah, covered with woods and thickets, though with important strongholds such as Libnah, Lachish, and Mareshah controlling the valleys. Between the Shephelah and the high plateau of Judah runs a narrow chalk valley, too small to be shown upon any but a large-scale map, but of major strategic importance, for it served as a moat to reinforce the western wall of Judah.

The Philistines and the people of Ju-

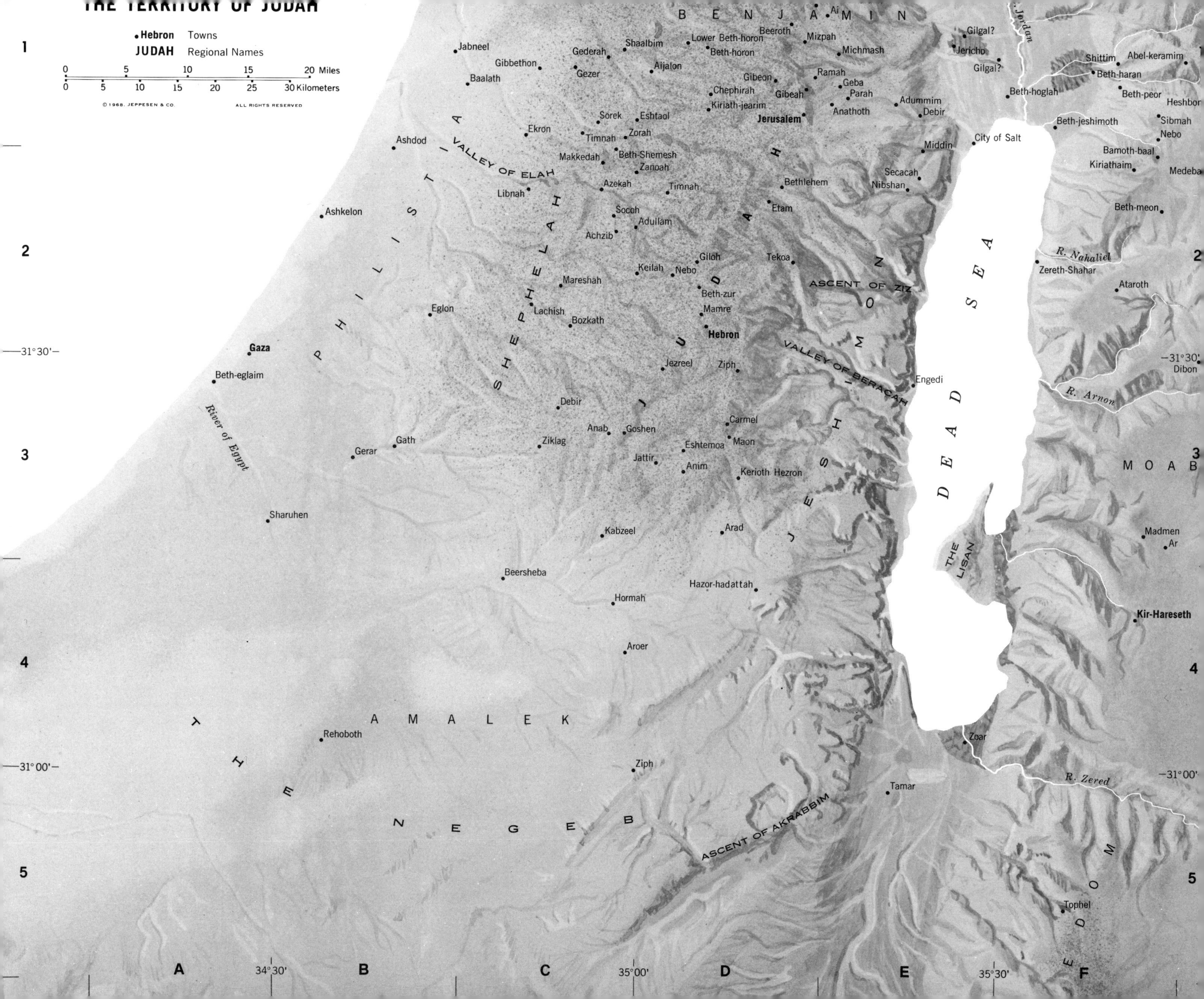

# THE TERRITORY OF JUDAH

THE TERRITORY OF JUDAH

**M O A B**

Dibon
Madmen
Ar
Kir-Haraseth

Heshbon
Medeba
Atroth
Ataroth
Beth-meon
Beth-peor
Nebo
Sibmah
Abel-keramim
Beth-haran
Kiriathaim
Bamoth-baal
Beth-jeshimoth
Shittim
Beth-hoglah

R. Nahaliel
Zereth-Shahar
R. Arnon
R. Zered

Tophel

Jordan
Gilgal?
Jericho
Gilgal?
City of Salt

**THE DEAD SEA**

THE LISAN

Zoar

Adummim
Middin
Debir
Secacah
Nibshan
Engedi
Tamar

Michmash
Mizpah
Geba
Parah
Anathoth
Ramah
Gibeah
Bethlehem
Etam
Tekoa

**Jerusalem**
Beeroth
Gibeon
Chephirah
Kiriath-jearim
Lower Beth-horon
Beth-horon

Carmel
Maon
Ziph
Jezreel
Goshen
Anab
Eshtemoa
Anim
Jattir
Keilah
Nebo
Beth-zur
Mamre
Giloh
**Hebron**
Ziph

Kerioth Hezron
Arad

Hazor-hadattah

Ajalon
Shaalbim
Gederah
Gezer
Ekron
Gibbethon
Baalath
Jabneel

Zorah
Eshtaol
Timnah
Sorek
Beth-shemesh
Zanoah
Azekah
Socoh
Adullam
Achzib
Makkedah
Lachish
Mareshah
Bozkath
Eglon

Kabzeel
Hormah
Aroer
Ziph
Beersheba
Rehoboth

Debir
Ziklag
Gath
Gerar

Ashdod
Ashkelon
Libnah

**Gaza**
Beth-eglaim
Sharuhen
River of Egypt

**P H I L I S T I A**
**B E N J A M I N**
ASCENT OF ZIZ
VALLEY OF BERACAH
VALLEY OF ELAH
**THE SHEPHELAH**
**THE NEGEB**
**THE AMALEK**
ASCENT OF AKRABBIM

31°30'
31°00'
31°30'
31°00'
34°30'
35°00'
35°30'

dah waged constant warfare across the Shephelah and this narrow moat, for possession of it meant defense against attack. The Shephelah itself carried only a small population, for it was infertile, but the valley was marked by a line of frontier towns, famous in the wars of Judah: Aijalon (Josh. 10:12), Beth-she-mesh (I Sam. 6:12), Adullam (I Sam. 22:1), Keilah (I Sam. 23:1–5), Debir (Josh 10:38–39). David killed Goliath in the Valley of Elah, which crosses the Shephelah between Socoh and Azekah, and farther north are Timnah, Sorek, Eshtaol, and Zorah, known for the exploits of Samson. Lachish, farther south in the Shephelah, was treated as an advanced frontier post by Judah, and for-

tified by Rehoboam (II Chron. 11:9). It was constantly under attack, and is reported as having been besieged in turn by Joshua (Josh. 10:31), Sennacherib (II Kings 18:3 ff.), and the Babylonians (Jer. 34:7), when Lachish and Azekah were the only fortified cities left to Judah.

Aijalon marked the entrance to a small down-faulted valley leading up into the hill country by way of the Ascent of Beth-horon. This was the Achilles' heel of the Judean defenses, for it provided the only easy route up into the highlands, and it was through this door that every invasion of Judah came. Gibbethon and Gezer, frontier towns of the northern kingdom against

the Philistines, stood out in the plain not far from its mouth.

Opposite the Valley of Aijalon, on the eastern side of the hill country, is the hinge fault which cuts back into the steep scarp north of Jericho. This is apparently the valley that is meant in the story of the attack on Ai (Josh. 7), and the area between these two valleys was a zone of passage across the highlands, and also the territory of the tribe of the Benjamin. The description of Benjamin's boundaries in Josh. 18:13–27 makes clear that it extended from Ophrah in the north to Jerusalem in the south, and that it included these two valleys of entry. After the division of the kingdom, Bethel marked the south-

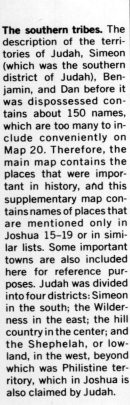

**The southern tribes.** The description of the territories of Judah, Simeon (which was the southern district of Judah), Benjamin, and Dan before it was dispossessed contains about 150 names, which are too many to include conveniently on Map 20. Therefore, the main map contains the places that were important in history, and this supplementary map contains names of places that are mentioned only in Joshua 15–19 or in similar lists. Some important towns are also included here for reference purposes. Judah was divided into four districts: Simeon in the south; the Wilderness in the east; the hill country in the center; and the Shephelah, or lowland, in the west, beyond which was Philistine territory, which in Joshua is also claimed by Judah.

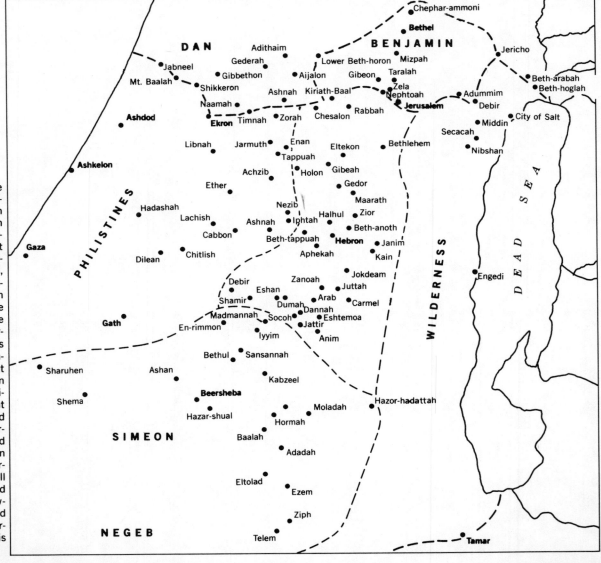

**XV. Dwellers in the clefts of the rocks.** Petra, the capital of the Nabatean kingdom in New Testament times, had earlier been the site of a settlement of the Edomites. The high sandstone cliffs were utilized for dwellings and places of worship as well as tombs. This was the northern emporium at the end of the great incense route from southern Arabia.

**XVI. The land of Midian.** Some of the most dramatic scenery in the Middle East is to be found in the dissected sandstone plateaus of southern Jordan and northern Arabia, where the rocks are cleft by tremendous geological faults and fretted by the desert sandstorms. The scale of the towering cliffs may be judged by the figure in the foreground. Through these awe-inspiring valleys came the lumbering caravans of the merchants of Sheba.

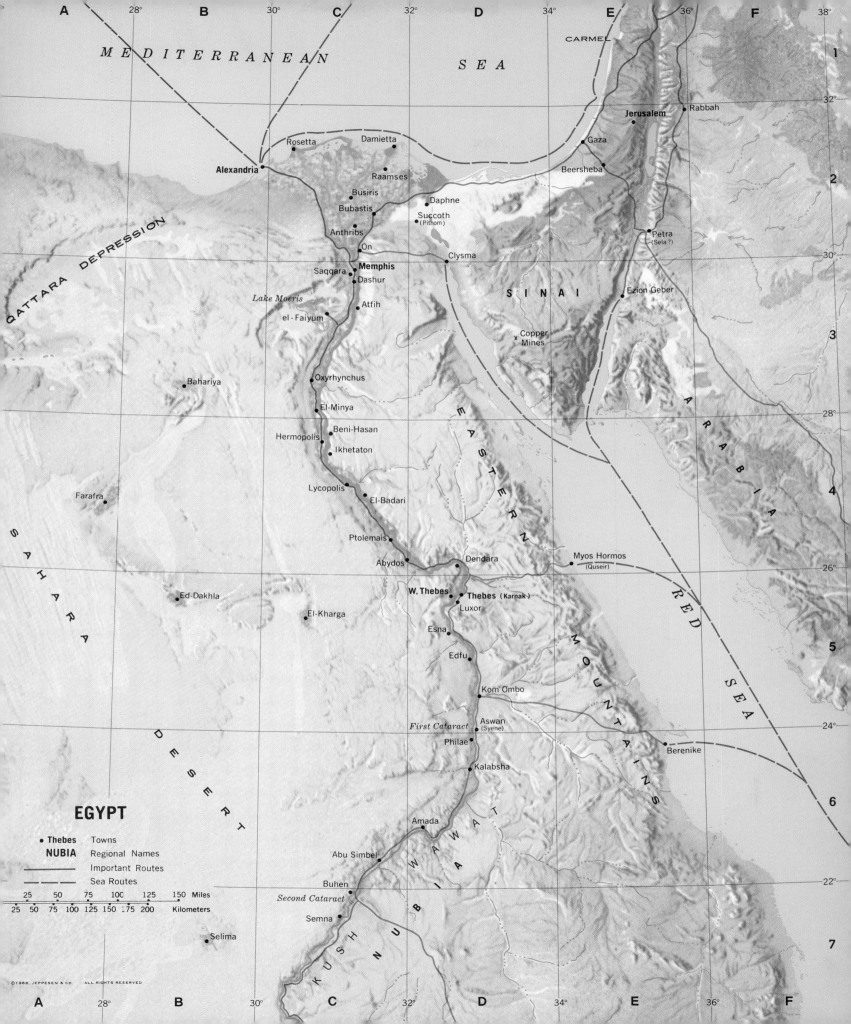

# EGYPT

- • Thebes   Towns
- **NUBIA**   Regional Names
- — — —   Important Routes
- — · · —   Sea Routes

| | | | | | | |
|---|---|---|---|---|---|---|
| 25 | 50 | 75 | 100 | 125 | 150 Miles | |
| 25 | 50 | 75 | 100 | 125 | 150 | 175 | 200 | Kilometers |

MEDITERRANEAN      SEA

CARMEL

QATTARA DEPRESSION

Rosetta
Damietta
Alexandria
Raamses
Busiris
Daphne
Bubastis
Succoth
(Pithom)
Anthribs
On
Saqqara
**Memphis**
Dashur
Clysma
*Lake Moeris*
Atfih
el - Faiyum
Bahariya
Oxyrhynchus
El-Minya
Beni-Hasan
Hermopolis
Ikhetaton
Farafra
Lycopolis
El-Badari
Ptolemais
Abydos
Dendara
Ed-Dakhla
Myos Hormos
(Quseir)
**W. Thebes**
**Thebes** ( Karnak )
El-Kharga
Luxor
Esna
Edfu
Kom Ombo
*First Cataract*
Aswan
(Syene)
Philae
Berenike
Kalabsha
Amada
Abu Simbel
Buhen
*Second Cataract*
Semna
Selima

Jerusalem
Rabbah
Gaza
Beersheba
Petra
(Sela ?)
Ezion Geber
SINAI
x Copper
Mines
EASTERN
MOUNTAINS
ARABIA
RED   SEA

SAHARA      DESERT

KUSH
NUBIA
WAWAT

©1968. JEPPESEN & CO.      ALL RIGHTS RESERVED

CILICIAN
GULF

MEDITERRANEAN

SEA

LEVANT COAST:
RELIEF AND VEGETATION

©1968 JEPPESEN & CO. ALL RIGHTS RESERVED

0    10    20    30    40    50    60 Miles
0  10  20  30  40  50  60  70  80 Kilometers

RED

SEA

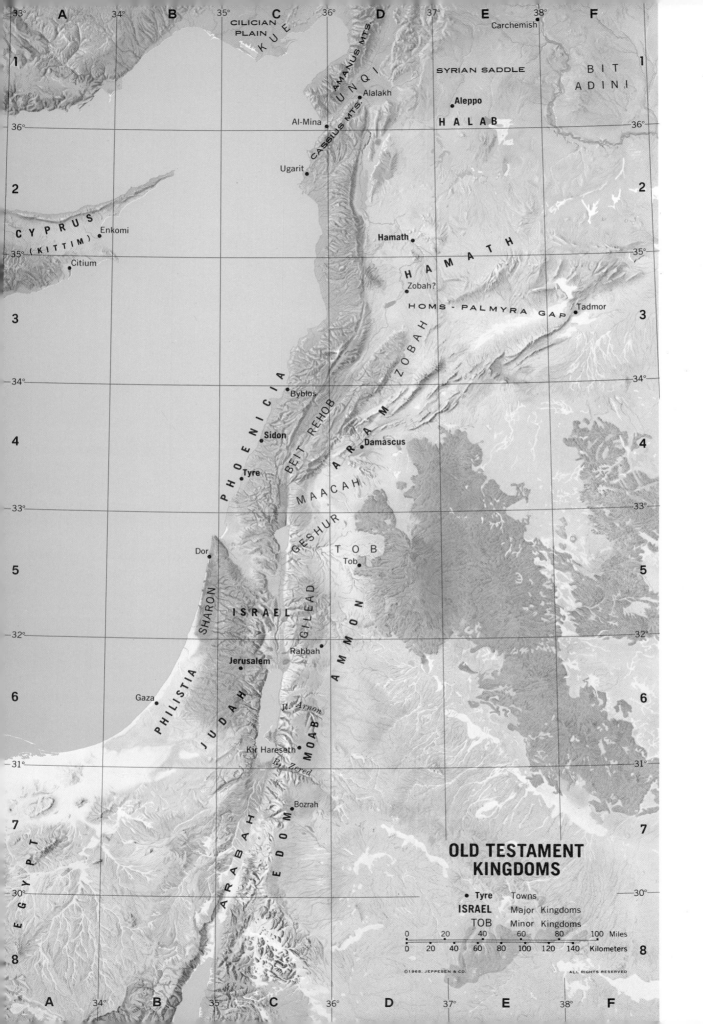

# OLD TESTAMENT KINGDOMS

- **Tyre**    Towns
- **ISRAEL**    Major Kingdoms
- **TOB**    Minor Kingdoms

Miles scale: 0, 20, 40, 60, 80, 100 Miles
Kilometers scale: 0, 20, 40, 60, 80, 100, 120, 140 Kilometers

Map labels:

CILICIAN PLAIN · KUE · AMANUS MTS. · UNQI · Alalakh · SYRIAN SADDLE · Carchemish · BIT ADINI · Al-Mina · CASSIUS MTS. · Aleppo · HALAB · Ugarit · Hamath · HAMATH · CYPRUS (KITTIM) · Enkomi · Citium · Zobah? · HOMS - PALMYRA GAP · Tadmor · ZOBAH · PHOENICIA · Byblos · BEIT REHOB · ARAM · Sidon · Damascus · Tyre · MAACAH · GESHUR · TOB · Tob · Dor · SHARON · ISRAEL · GILEAD · AMMON · Rabbah · Jerusalem · JUDAH · PHILISTIA · Gaza · R. Arnon · MOAB · Kir Hareseth · B. Zered · ARABAH · EDOM · Bozrah · EGYPT

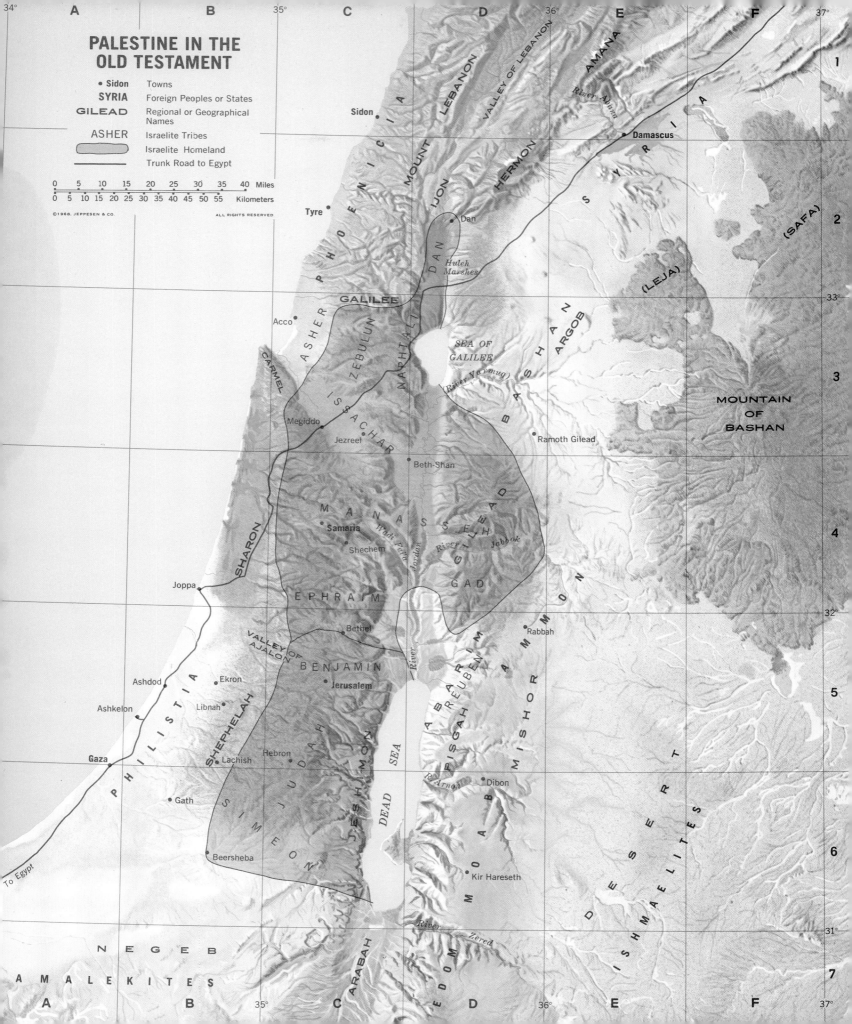

# PALESTINE IN THE OLD TESTAMENT

- Sidon      Towns
- **SYRIA**      Foreign Peoples or States
- **GILEAD**      Regional or Geographical Names
- ASHER      Israelite Tribes
-      Israelite Homeland
-      Trunk Road to Egypt

0   5   10   15   20   25   30   35   40 Miles
0   5   10   15   20   25   30   35   40   45   50   55 Kilometers

Sidon

Tyre

Acco

Megiddo

Jezreel

Beth-Shan

Samaria

Shechem

Joppa

Bethel

Ashdod

Ekron

Ashkelon

Libnah

Jerusalem

Gaza

Lachish

Hebron

Gath

Beersheba

Dan

Damascus

Ramoth Gilead

Rabbah

Dibon

Kir Hareseth

To Egypt

PHOENICIA

MOUNT LEBANON

VALLEY OF LEBANON

AMANA

River Abana

HERMON

SYRIA

(SAFA)

(LEJA)

IJON

DAN

Huleh Marshes

GALILEE

ASHER

ZEBULUN

NAPHTALI

CARMEL

ISSACHAR

SEA OF GALILEE

(River Yarmug)

BASHAN

ARGOB

MOUNTAIN OF BASHAN

MANASSEH

GILEAD

River Jabbok

Wadi Farah

Jordan

GAD

SHARON

EPHRAIM

VALLEY OF AJALON

BENJAMIN

River

AMMON

ABARIM

REUBEN

PISGAH

MISHOR

HERMON

PHILISTIA

SHEPHELAH

JUDAH

SIMEON

JESHIMON

DEAD SEA

R. Arnon

MOAB

DESERT

ISHMAELITES

ARABAH

EDOM

River Zered

NEGEB

AMALEKITES

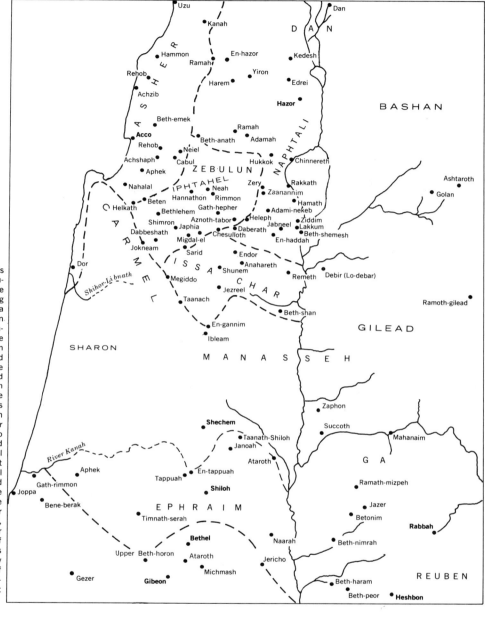

**The northern tribes.** This map shows the distribution of the land among the northern tribes according to the lists in Joshua 16–19. The information for this part of the country is much less complete than it is for the southern part. For Ephraim and Manasseh, only the boundaries are given, and hence the blank areas on the map. More names are given for the territories of the smaller northern tribes, but it is not clear how far these extended to the north. Asher and Naphtali are regional names for the sea coast and the northern hill country respectively, and probably only the extreme southern sections were really Israelite. Issachar was the valley of Jezreel, and Zebulon was Lower Galilee. The territory of Gad, east of the Jordan, is very vague. Reuben lay mainly to the south of this map, but all its territory soon became a part of Moab.

ern frontier of Israel, and Geba and Mizpah the northern frontier of Judah, with about five miles of a kind of no man's land between them. This frontier remained extraordinarily constant despite the frequent warfare between the two kingdoms. There is no apparent physical boundary here, but this much-used cross route marked a very definite division between two types of agriculture; the vine culture of the more open highlands of Judah, and the olive culture of the richer Cenomanian limestone dome of Ephraim.

The division of the kingdom left Judah with its capital, Jerusalem, dangerously exposed to attack, but at the same time so placed that its people could best profit from the trade which tended otherwise to bypass the Judean hills. The real center of Judah was at Hebron, where David's capital had been at first, and which seems to have resented the transfer of power farther north (II Sam. 15:10). This city stood at a crossroads, where a difficult but viable transverse route led over the hills from Lachish and Mareshah down

to the Dead Sea at Engedi, whence a road followed the shore southward to the Arabah.

The only other possibility of penetration into Judah was from the south, by the road which led up from Beersheba in the southern steppe to Goshen on the edge of the true Judean hills. To the south were the nomadic Amalekites, against whom Saul fought (I Sam. 15), and much later on the Idumeans, who were severely subdued by Judas Maccabeus, "because they kept lying in wait for Israel" (I Macc. 5:3).

# Maps X–XIV

# EGYPT AND THE LEVANT

The last series of colored maps and plates illustrate what are most commonly thought of as "Bible Lands," Egypt and the Levant.

**Map X. Egypt.** The land of Egypt is almost completely rainless, only the delta normally receiving a few showers in winter, and every drop of water which the people need for the maintenance of life itself enters the country from the south along the narrow channel of the Nile. There are no further tributaries, and thereafter water is steadily lost by evaporation and percolation into the soil. The floods come in summer as a result of torrential rains on the Abyssinian mountains, and are both gradual and prolonged. The river starts to rise slowly in late May and June, and reaches its maximum in September. The decline of the flood is slow, and extended until January, and the waters are at their lowest in early May.

The Nile flows in a narrow trough, bordered by cliffs, and usually no more than five miles wide. Before it enters Egypt proper it makes an enormous S-bend, and in this section it is interrupted by six cataracts, or stretches of rapids, where the river crosses ledges of hard granite. The modern country of Egypt has its southern frontier at the Second Cataract, but ancient Egypt started farther north at Syene (Aswan) on the First Cataract (Plate 21). South of Syene is Nubia; north of it was Egypt proper, where cultivation is continuous. Then as now, Egypt was divided into the long, narrow ribbon of Upper Egypt and the broad Delta in the north. The city of Cairo dates only from after the Muslim conquests, and the ancient city which guarded the junction of "the Two Lands" was Memphis, slightly to the south of Cairo. Upper Egypt was a thin line of towns, strung out like beads on a string, and dominated by Thebes; Lower Egypt is a large triangle, 250 km. (155 mi.) long from its beginning to the sea, and 215 km. (135 mi.) wide at its greatest extent. Like all deltas it was marshy, and it

was only gradually brought under control. The great port of Alexandria was founded by Alexander the Great in 332 B.C. on the site of an earlier and smaller port called Rhacotis, which had existed there from about 1500 B.C.

The Egyptian struggle to control Nubia began in the First Dynasty, about 3000 B.C., and an inscription near Buhen records an Egyptian victory at this date. Between 2735 and 2325 B.C. the first known explorer, Herkhuf, made four expeditions to Cush (northern Sudan). In the Twelfth Dynasty, just before the Hyksos invasion, Wawat, between the First and Second Cataracts, was firmly in Egyptian hands, and the frontier was at Semna, whence pressure could be brought on Cush. During the Hyksos period Egypt seems to have surrendered both the Delta to the Hyksos and Wawat to the Nubians, but in the imperial period which followed Egyptian power was pushed farther and farther southward, though there were frequent revolts. Buhen now became a great military center, and the frontier extended as far as Napata on the Fourth Cataract (see Map III). By the time of the Israelite monarchy, however, Egyptian strength had weakened, and Cush was a world power, with Napata rivaling Karnak as a center for the worship of Amon-Re. In 720 B.C., the Nubians succeeded in conquering Egypt itself, which then became part of a short-lived Nubian empire, with its capital at Napata. This was the position at the time of the Assyrian invasion of Judah (see Isa. 18:1–6, 19:1–15; 30:6–7; 31:1–3).

On either side of the Nile lie the deserts, on the west the Sahara, and on the east the mountains that border the Red Sea. Unlike Arabia, the Sahara contained no great hordes of nomads to threaten the settled peoples of the Nile (though nomadic peoples certainly lived there), and the separateness of the desert life is reflected in the names of two of the oases, ed-Dakhla (meaning "inner") and el-Kharga (meaning "outer").

**Map XI. The Levant Coast: Relief and Vegetation.** Once again this is a map without names over the land, but there is this difference: an attempt has been made to show the natural vegetation as it would have been in the days of the Israelite monarchy, when the hills were still considerably wooded and Sharon was forest and marshland. The manner in which the hills and the desert funnel all movement into ever more restricted lines in the south is very evident. Ancient Israel was imprisoned between those two regions of "disorder," the desert and the sea, and condemned to suffer forever devastation by the armies of the great imperial powers.

**Map XII. Old Testament Kingdoms.** The Israelite monarchy lasted nearly five hundred years, during which there was persistent pressure toward consolidation; the smaller kingdoms and city-states of the early period were, in course of time, swallowed up in the larger units. The southern coast plain was occupied in the fourteenth and thirteenth centuries B.C. by the Philistines, apparently with Egyptian support. They were part of the "sea peoples" who had attempted to invade Egypt during the reign of Merneptah (1224–1204), and again under Rameses III about 1175 B.C. On the hills farther east David established the united monarchy about 1000 B.C., but neither he nor Solomon overcame the constant internal tensions, and after Solomon's death the country split into two parts, Judah in the south and Israel in the north. East of the Jordan the three kingdoms of Ammon, Moab, and Edom remained during the entire period of the Israelite monarchy, though expanding and contracting according to the fortunes of war. Israel absorbed Gilead, and Ammon lay east of this on the plateau, though constantly trying to push up into the Gilead hills. Moab was on the plateau south of Gilead, on both sides of the Arnon gorge. Edom was confined south of the Zered, and sought to dominate the Arabah and, after the fall of Jerusalem, southern Palestine.

North of the Philistine plain lay the marshy, forested area of Sharon, but then the coast becomes narrow and rocky, and here in the ninth century B.C. the isolated port cities consolidated as the Phoenician kingdom under the leadership of Tyre and Sidon. The Phoenicians expanded westward to the Mediterranean coastlands and islands, establishing colonies at Citium and Enkomi in Cyprus, and moving steadily farther and farther afield. Far to the north was the small kingdom of Kue, from which Solomon imported horses to re-export them to Egypt (I Kings 10:28). Kue obtained them from the Anatolian plateau farther north. In the narrow valley between the Amanus and Cassius ranges stood at one time the city of Alalakh, which flourished from the eighteenth to the beginning of the twelfth century B.C., when it was suddenly destroyed. It seems to have had almost a monopoly in the valuable ivory trade from the elephants that existed in this region. Its port was el-Mina, later known as Poseidium, which was rebuilt after the destruction of Alalakh.

This is the Syrian saddle, where communication between the Mediterranean and the Euphrates is easiest because the river is here only 160 km. (100 mi.) from the sea and rainfall is plentiful. On the plateau were the powerful city-states of Calneh and Aleppo, and farther east on the Euphrates itself were Carchemish and Bit Adini (probably the Beth-Eden of Amos 1:5, and Eden in Ezek. 27:23). Farther south, the broad and level plateau was controlled by "Hamath the great" (Amos 6:2), whose territory came to an end in the south with the shallow depression of the Homs-Palmyra gap.

In the semidesert region behind the Anti-Lebanon was at one time a group of small states, Zobah in the north (perhaps at Nebk, or possibly Homs), Damascus, Maacah, Geshur, and Tob. In the central valley was Beth-Rehob. We meet these kingdoms in the early wars of David (II Sam. 8:3–12; 10:6–19). Later Zobah, Maacah, Geshur, and Tob were all absorbed into the powerful kingdom of Aram, with its capital at Damascus. Beth-Rehob, interestingly enough, became part of the Phoenician territory (see Map 15).

**Map XIII. Palestine in the Old Testament.** In the ancient Israelite territory south of the high mountains of the Lebanon and Anti-Lebanon, the four north-south zones (coast plain, western highlands, rift valley, eastern plateau) are clearly marked, but they are cut by the important lowland corridor from the Bay of Acco to Beth-shan, and the highland ridge of Mount Carmel, which breaks the coast plain. The nuclear Israelite area was the western highlands south of the corridor, forming three distinct sections: the arched plateau of Judah west of the Dead Sea, the domelike region of Ephraim north of this, and the more dissected basin of Manasseh between Ephraim and the corridor. Manasseh was less well protected than the other two, and extended its territory to include the corridor itself, which properly was the region of Issachar, and the hills of Gilead on the eastern plateau. Between Judah and Ephraim lay a transverse saddle, approached by valleys from both east and west. This was the territory of Benjamin.

The tribal districts north of the corridor were Asher on the coast, Zebulun in what later became Lower Galilee, and Naphtali on the eastern slopes overlooking the lake. Dan held a precarious position around the sources of the Jordan beyond the Huleh marshes. All these were exposed to attack from the north, and so lay outside the Israelite heartland. Another marginal region was the indeterminate district of Simeon in the south.

In the Rift Valley the Jordan flows through the marshes of the Huleh, a massive dam of volcanic basalt, the Lake of Galilee, and then increasingly desert country to the Dead Sea, 396 m. (1,290 ft.) below sea level (Plates 27, 28).

The eastern plateau was divided into four main sections, each characterized by a different way of life. In the north was the level agricultural plateau of Bashan, which became part of the kingdom of Syria, or Aram; and south of it was the forested hill country of Gilead (Plate 26). The tribe of Gad was somewhere in this region, but its territory is obscure, and "Gilead" and "Gad" may be alternative names for the same district. Reuben was the district just south of Gilead, but it was early swallowed up by Moab. Here the dissected heights overlooking the Jordan and the Dead Sea are known generally as the Abarim (Num. 27:12), though this is a very vague term, and the level plateau surface was the Mishor or tableland (Josh. 13:9). The actual edge of the plateau was called the Pisgah (Num. 21:20). South of the Zered the kingdom of Edom drew its livelihood from the caravan trade with southern Arabia. To the northeast, beyond Ammon, was the volcanic "Mountain of Bashan," known today as the Jebel Druze.

The four great canyons that cleave the plateau did not form regional boundaries, nor were they usually political frontiers, except for the Zered. Each kingdom tended to expand until it reached the limit of its accustomed way of life, and there its colonization ended. Likewise, within the territory of Israel, the tribal names were probably regional in origin, and represent subdivisions of the general Israelite way of life. Only Manasseh and Judah, for strategic reasons, extended any form of permanent control beyond these invisible limits.

**Map XIV. Palestine in the New Testament.** By the first century A.D. Palestine had greatly changed. Much of the forest had been cut down; everywhere was good husbandry, and careful control of the precarious water supply; in place of rough tracks a system of well-built roads covered the country; marshes were drained; large cities were built; and cultivation extended well out into the edges of the desert. Moreover, the role of the country was changed. Certainly it was still part of the great north-south Levant Bridge, but with the appearance of the Romans, it had become what it is once again today, a bridgehead of the west in the eastern world. The coast now took on new significance, and the center of power moved down from the mountains to the plain. Cae-

sarea became the Roman capital, and Ptolemais (the old Acco), Joppa, Ascalon, and Gaza, thriving ports. The transverse east-west roads now ceased to be merely connecting routes, and became instead major arteries of trade. A road ran inland from Ptolemais to the Lake of Galilee, and by this road fish from the lake, and wheat from Gaulanitis and Batanea (the earlier region of Bashan), were exported to the metropolis at Rome. Another important road ran southwestward from Gaza to Petra, the rock-cut capital of the Nabateans, far exceeding in size the ancient Edomite settlement (Plate XV). This was the great emporium for the trans-Arabian incense trade.

The Romans had the same difficulty in controlling Palestine that every western power has had, and they tried similar expedients. In the days of Herod the Great, they governed indirectly through a client king, but in time they became impatient with the endemic instability of the area and moved toward increasingly direct control. In the days of Jesus' ministry, they governed directly only a part of what had been Herod's kingdom, but by the second century they found themselves compelled to take the whole of the Levant under their rule.

*Map 21*

# THE IMPERIAL ADVENTURES

The whole history of the monarchy in ancient Israel and Judah lasted rather over four centuries, but it was a very checkered period. The first attempt at establishing unified control of the whole country, under Saul, ended in complete disaster, and in fact he never succeeded in controlling, partially and erratically, more than the hill country. In the latter part of the eighth century B.C., the Assyrian expansion and the destruction of Samaria meant the complete elimination of the northern kingdom of Israel, and after 734 B.C. Judah was a vassal state to Assyria, with only a brief stab at independent action under Josiah (640–609 B.C.), when the Assyrian control weakened. Therefore, the period of effective Israelite control of the land of Palestine, from the unification of the monarchy in the eighth year of David's reign (c. 992 B.C.) to the destruction of Samaria in 721 B.C. was only 271 years. Under David and Solomon the country was united, but after Solomon's death in 928 B.C.[1] the

[1] There is much dispute over this date. Others would suggest 931, 925, or 922 B.C.

ten northern tribes broke away from his successor, Rehoboam (I Kings 12), and thereafter until Samaria fell to the Assyrians there were two kingdoms, the more powerful Israel in the north, and Judah in the south.

David and Solomon initiated a policy which the stronger of their successors sought to imitate, of expansion for the purposes of controlling both the Trans-Jordanian plateau and the great Trunk Road. However, these imperial adventures never led to lasting hegemony. From the beginning of David's external conquests to the death of Solomon is only a quarter of a century; the empire of Omri and Ahab lasted only a third of that time (876–850 B.C.); and the third, and final, imperialist effort, under Jeroboam II of Israel and Uzziah of Judah, did not survive their deaths forty years later. Thus, the Israelite "empire," though it excited the imagination of the people and caused men to dream dreams of its restoration, was at best an ephemeral affair, and the three periods of expansion, which together total no more than a century and a half, mere interludes in Palestinian history. It is not surprising that this policy earned the scorn of the prophets (Amos 6:12; Jer. 6:20).

It was, however, a policy which the more vigorous rulers found almost forced upon them if they were to assure the security and well-being of the state. All the kingdoms of the Levant, except perhaps the broad steppelands in the north, suffered from a serious food deficiency if the population grew beyond a moderate density, as it tended to do in times of peace. Consequently, when a strong ruler gave his country the blessings of peace by repressing the depredations of his neighbors, he subjected it also to the dangers of famine, though, of course, no one foresaw this. An alternative source of wealth with which to purchase food came to be an absolute necessity, and throughout the Levant this was sought always by means of trade. But the great caravan routes

were notoriously insecure, and to ensure the smooth passage of the merchants military control of the roads was essential. Therefore, every Levantine kingdom, in times of its strength, sought to exercise this control, and this led them inevitably into constant conflict with one another.

The policy introduced by David was followed by his successors. There were throughout this period three states for whom trade was a primary necessity because of the extreme scarcity of agricultural land: Phoenicia, with precipitous mountains rising from a narrow coast plain; Damascus, within the strict limits of its admittedly rich oasis; and Edom, perched on the southern highlands, where only a tiny strip of land received enough rain for farming. Of the other states, the Philistines controlled the Trunk Road in the Palestinian coast plain, and Egypt lay at its southern extremity. Moab and Ammon on the eastern plateau were no immediate threat to Israel's trade with the north and south, although it is true that they lay athwart the King's Highway, and a complete control on the commercial routes of the southern Levant would mean control of these two kingdoms. Nevertheless, their own land hunger, since they were both steppe-land states, caused them to press in continually upon the frontiers of the Israelite homeland.

In this situation, the Israelite rulers had to decide with whom to fight and with whom to seek alliance. With neither Egypt nor Phoenicia did they have any necessary conflict, for their interests were separate. Phoenicia's trade was all by sea, and its expansion was always westwards, once it had brought the rocky coastal harbors under its control. Egypt, even though the days of its glory were over, was still too powerful a state for Israel to hope to oppose. Therefore, with Egypt and Phoenicia alliances were made, though at a price, for each was strong enough to impose terms. The whole of the plain of Asher to the south of the port of Dor passed

forever out of Israelite hands into the Phoenician realm (I Kings 9:11–13), and no attempt was made to control the Trunk Road south of Gaza, the desert "port" where the camel caravans were assembled. Moreover, they paid in gold for peace in this quarter, and for the military support which was not always forthcoming. The lumbering caravans, of which Isaiah speaks so scathingly, carrying "their riches on the backs of asses, and their treasures on the humps of camels, to a people that cannot profit them" (Isa. 30:6), were certainly not the first that had gone southward to this treacherous ally, who had been ready enough to give asylum to the enemies of Solomon (I Kings 11:14–22, 26–40).

In the case of Moab and Ammon, it was felt sufficient to reduce them to the status of vassals but to impose no further control. Naturally, they broke away from this dependent position as soon as they could (II Kings 3:4–5). However, Edom, Philistia, and Syria were another matter, for control of the major land trade routes meant controlling those territories through which they passed. David's policy was complete suppression of the Philistines, and direct military control of Syria and Edom (II Sam. 8:6, 14), though all reasserted their independence after the death of Solomon. Gath, it is true, was apparently never rebuilt, but the Israelite frontier post of Gibbethon was so strongly manned that twice the commander of Gibbethon was able to seize the throne (I Kings 15:27; 16:17). With Edom there was constant strife, as Jerusalem controlled the copper mines of the Arabah and the port of Ezion-Geber only in times of its greatest strength, and the savage bitterness which this strife engendered long outlasted the end of the kingdom of Judah (Ps. 137:7–9; Ezek. 35:1–15).

The situation with regard to Syria changed after the end of the United Monarchy. In the days of David the plateau east and southeast of the Anti-Lebanon Mountains was divided among

**Administrative districts of Solomon.** The numbers on the map indicate the twelve districts in the order in which they are listed in I Kings 4:7–19. The names of towns fortified by Solomon (I Kings 9:15–19) are in bold type. It is often assumed that Solomon's reason for instituting the administrative tax districts was to break up the old tribal loyalties. This, however, seems very dubious, since five of the districts are identified by the old tribal names without any further explanation (1. Ephraim, 8. Naphtali, 9. Asher, 10. Issachar, and 11. Benjamin). Probably it was to divide for administrative purposes the unwieldy territory acquired by Manasseh on both sides of the Jordan, and to treat as a special territory for purposes of defense the approach to the Ascent of Beth-horon, where Gezer and Lower Beth-horon were among the cities Solomon fortified. Judah seems to have been exempt from the tax, and this must have led to considerable bitterness and may have been one of the reasons for the revolt of the northern tribes after Solomon's death (I Kings 12:1–20).

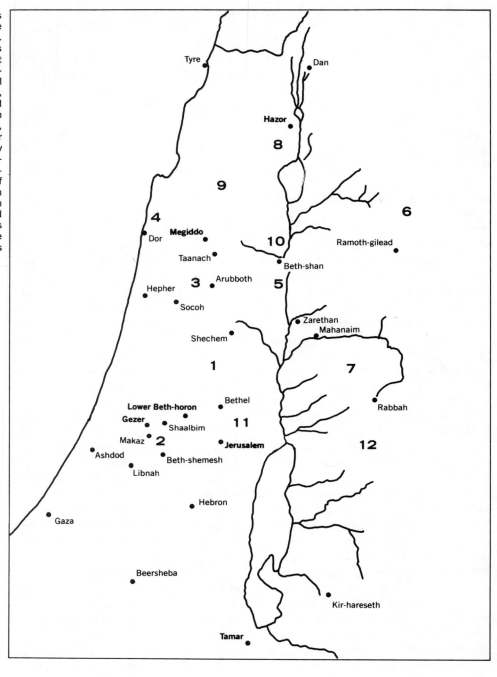

a number of minor kingdoms of which Damascus was the chief, and David, therefore, could seek to conquer and directly control them. But in the ninth century, by the time of Omri and Ahab, the strong kingdom of Aram had been established, with its center at Damascus, and the most that Ahab could hope for was that the ruler of Aram should permit an Israelite merchant colony with special privileges to be established in Damascus (I Kings 20:34). He was not able to maintain this, however, and he died trying to regain control of Ramoth-gilead, one of the Israelite frontier towns (I Kings 22). The records of Jeroboam II, it is true, claimed for him that he "recovered for Israel Damascus and Hamath, which had belonged to Judah" (II Kings 14:28), but Hamath was never part of the Israelite dominions, and the text may well be corrupt.

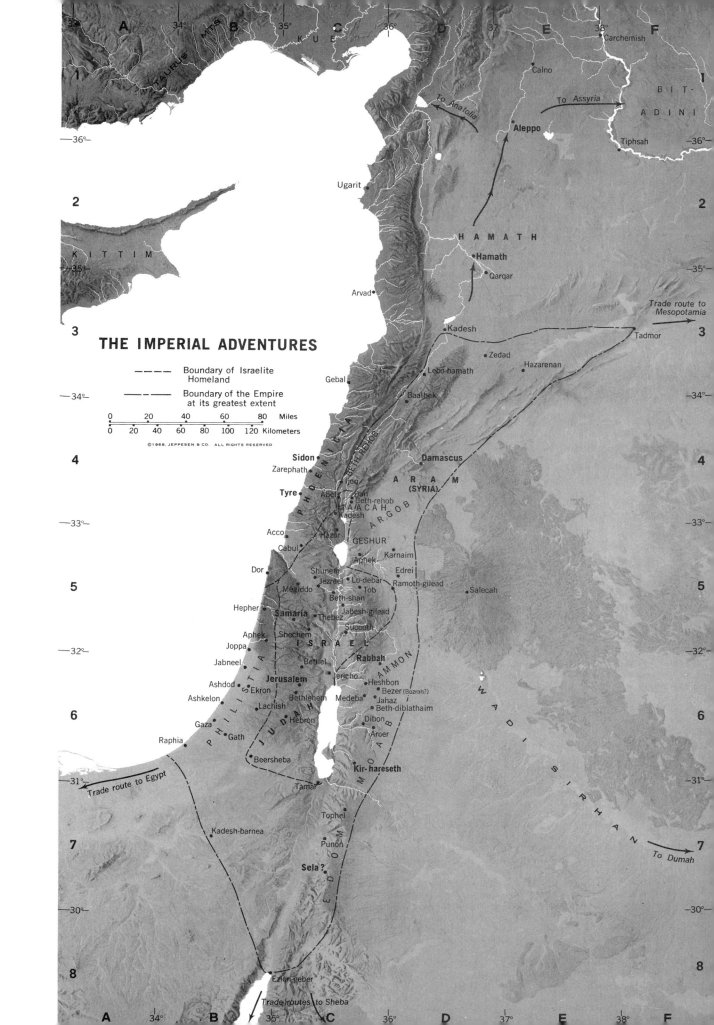

# THE IMPERIAL ADVENTURES

- – – – – –  Boundary of Israelite Homeland
- – · – · –  Boundary of the Empire at its greatest extent

| 0 | 20 | 40 | 60 | 80 | Miles |
| 0 | 20 | 40 | 60 | 80 | 100 | 120 | Kilometers |

©1968, JEPPESEN & CO.  ALL RIGHTS RESERVED

To Anatolia

To Assyria

Carchemish

Calno

BIT-ADINI

Tiphsah

Aleppo

HAMATH

Ugarit

Hamath

Qarqar

Arvad

Trade route to Mesopotamia

Kadesh

Zedad

Hazarenan

Tadmor

Gebal

Lebo-hamath

Baalbek

KITTIM

Sidon

Zarephath

Damascus

ARAM (SYRIA)

Tyre

Ijon

Abel

Dan

Beth-rehob

BETH-REHOB

PHOENICIA

MAACAH

Kadesh

ARGOB

Acco

Hazor

GESHUR

Cabul

Aphek

Karnaim

Dor

Shunem

Edrei

Jezreel

Lo-debar

Ramoth-gilead

Megiddo

Tob

Salecah

Beth-shan

Hepher

Jabesh-gilead

Samaria

Thebez

Succoth

Aphek

Shechem

ISRAEL

Joppa

Jabneel

Bethel

Rabbah

AMMON

Jericho

PHILISTIA

Jerusalem

Heshbon

Ashdod

Ekron

Bezer (Bozrah?)

Ashkelon

Bethlehem

Medeba

Jahaz

Lachish

Beth-diblathaim

JUDAH

Gaza

Hebron

Dibon

MOAB

Raphia

Gath

Aroer

WADI SIRHAN

Beersheba

Kir-hareseth

Trade route to Egypt

Tamar

Tophel

Kadesh-barnea

Punon

To Dumah

EDOM

Sela?

Ezion-geber

Trade routes to Sheba

*Map 22*

# THE ASSYRIAN EMPIRE

The eighth century B.C. witnessed an entirely new political phenomenon, the effort to create and maintain a world order and to establish a universal peace. The attempts of many Fertile Crescent states in the previous period to establish commercial empires had brought them all into constant conflict with one another. A futile and unproductive state of war had become endemic, and no less than two of the eighth-century prophets are said to have expressed the now urgent hope that "nation shall not lift up sword against nation, neither shall they learn war any more" (Isa. 2:1–4; Mica. 4:1–4). The prophecy may actually be later, but the instinct which attributed the theme to the eighth century is surely sound. One of the great contributions of Amos is his understanding that universal order must have the same basis as local or national order—i.e., covenant or agreement—and that therefore the universal God could be none other than Yahweh, the covenant God. In the sixth century this theme was magnificently developed in the poems of the great Prophet of the Exile (Isa. 40–55).

The first attempt to bring the "world" of those days, i.e. the Middle Eastern states, under one system was, not surprisingly, an *imposed* order, because this is always the simplest and most immediate means of establishing order in a chaotic situation. What is much less clear is why it should have been an Assyrian order. The Assyrian homeland is a small but complex region extending along the middle Tigris as far south as el-Fathah ("the Opening"), where the river cuts through the ridges of Jebel Hamrin. The lines of hills that run parallel to the Zagros, and the rivers by which the plain is crossed, give it a measure of protection, but there is no definite frontier. It is exposed to constant pressure from the tribes, both of the mountains to the north and east and the steppes to the west, and perhaps this is a clue to the recurrent and persistent Assyrian expansionism. Moreover, though the northern section is reasonably well watered, the south is increasingly dry. Asshur was a trading city rather than an agricultural center, and around 1900 B.C. we find merchant colonies from Asshur established at Kanish, Hattusas, and Alışar, in Anatolia. The concept that the king of Assyria was the ruler of the world is very ancient, and seems to be related to the Assyrian understanding of their god, Asshur, and a firmly ingrained concept in their thought. In any case, we find them constantly pressing southward into Babylonia, northward into the mountains, and westward to the Mediterranean, or Upper Sea, though in the early days with prolonged periods of weakness and regression.

Thus, during much of the second millennium B.C. Assyria was the vassal of the Mitanni, but after 1300 there is a resurgence of power, and a steady pressure on northern Syria and Phoenicia, with its valuable timber. Tiglath-Pileser I (1116–1078) claims to have crossed the Euphrates twenty-eight times, and he attacked Turushpa on Lake Van. During this period there was no attempt to move southwards in the Levant. The reign of Shalmaneser III (859–824) is another time of expansion. He was met at Qarqar on the Orontes in 853 by a coalition of the Levant states, in which Ahab of Israel played a prominent part. Assyrian records claim this battle as a victory, but it seems to have been something of a reverse, for there is little evidence that it was followed up. In 841 renewed confusion in the Levant enabled Shalmaneser to proceed farther. He besieged, but did not take, Damascus, and exacted tribute from the Phoenicians and Jehu, king of Israel.

The Assyrian empire took on a new character with the accession of Tiglath-Pileser III (745–727), who is called Pul in II Kings 15:19. He smashed the power of Urartu in the north (Plate 35), and he initiated the policy, which all his successors were to follow, of trying to bring the whole Middle East under Assyrian control. To the Palestinians, Assyria seemed like a relentless Jug-

# THE ASSYRIAN EMPIRE

Boundary of the Empire
at its greatest extent
in seventh century

• Asshur    Towns

SYRIA    Regional Names

Miles
0    50    100    150    200    250
0    50   100  150  200  250  300  350
Kilometers

*CASPIAN SEA*

*LOWER, OR*

*EASTERN, SEA*

*UPPER, OR WESTERN,*

*SEA*

RED SEA

LYDIA
Sepharad
(Sardis)

PHRYGIA
Gordium

GOMER

MESHECH

R. Holys

Usiana

TUBAL

Togarmah

MUSRI

Melid

KUE

TAURUS MTS.

HATTINA

HAVILAH

Samal

Carchemish    Haran

Calno
Arpad    Tiphsah
Aleppo

Hamath

Kadesh

Qarqar

Arvad

Gebal

PHOENICIA
Sidon
Tyre

Acco

Helbon

Damascus

SYRIA

Tadmor

Salecah

AMMON

ISRAEL
Samaria

Lachish
Jerusalem
Gaza

JUDAH

MOAB

EDOM

Ezion-geber

URARTU

MT. ARARAT

Lake Van

Turusha

NAIRI

Nisibis

MANNAI

Lake Urmia

Hasanlu

Gozan

Sinjar

Rimah

Tel Afar

MADAI

Ecbatana

Dur-Sharrukin
Nineveh
Calah  Arbela
Arrapkha

ASSYRIA

Asshur

R. Tigris

Tekritu

KHINDANU
Anat

SUKHU

Hit

Tirqa

R. Euphrates

BIT-ADINI

QIDRI

PEKOD

Der

Sippar

Cuthah

Babylon

Borsippa

BABYLONIA

Nippur

Erech

Larsa

Ur

CHALDEANS

ELAM

Shushan
(Susa)

Rhagae

ARABIA

Dumah

Ha'il

Tema

Dedan

Khaibar

Yathrib

Marea

Sais

On

Zoan

Bubastis

Pelusium

Migdol
Tahpanhes

Memphis

Hermopolis

Lycopolis

Abydos

EGYPT

R. Nile

Thebes

Syene

ETHIOPIA

gernaut, pressing farther and farther south. Damascus fell in 732, Samaria in 721, and Philistia in 711 (II Kings 16:9; 17:6; Isa. 14:28–32). Jerusalem had become a vassal in 734, and was besieged in 701 because its king, Hezekiah, was proving troublesome, but it was never completely eliminated as Samaria had been. In the seventh century, Esarhaddon (680–669) brought Egypt within the empire (Nah. 3:8–10).

By their own showing on the reliefs which adorn the royal palaces, the Assyrian methods of conquest were ruthless and savage, though not more so, it would seem, than the Pharaohs had claimed to be before them and the Romans were to prove later. Large-scale transfers of population were practiced, as in the case of Israel (II Kings 17:6–24). Brutality, alas, is often the means whereby imperial powers compel submission so that the subjects do not question the rightness of the system.

The Assyrian achievement was an extraordinary one, because there was no real precedent for it, and many of the features of their administration were to pass, almost unchanged, to the Persians, the Hellenistic monarchies, and even

Rome. Yet they never evolved a fully successful method of imperial government, partly because the smallness of their home base did not allow them to develop a standing army large enough to provide garrison troops. The conquered peoples were continually restive, for they did not relish a system imposed by force, and the death of every king was marked by revolts, the suppression of which was the first duty of his successor. In particular, Assyria never succeeded in bringing to heel the powerful and cultured region of Babylonia, which took the lead in organizing coalitions to overthrow Assyrian power. In one of these Hezekiah of Judah was involved (II Kings 20:12–19).

One gains from biblical records the impression that the subject peoples were "satellite communities," required to accept and put into practice the Assyrian understanding of the world, and establish in their temples the Assyrian gods alongside their own ((II Kings 16:10–18), but there is evidence that this did not necessarily apply everywhere, and recalcitrant Judah may have been something of an exception. Assy-

rian internal government does not seem to have been oppressive. The kings were not merely capricious oriental despots, and though the royal correspondence from Nineveh indicates that the government was by royal edict, the king had his official advisers whom, presumably, he consulted. His person was felt essential to the system, and every effort was made to protect him from untoward events. There is no evidence of terrorist methods obtaining in the gigantic cities which were built along the middle Tigris and which became a legend to later generations (Jonah 3:3). Indeed, there were laws which protected people against the power of the government.

The end of the Assyrian empire was swift and catastrophic. After the death of Asshurbanipal in 627 B.C., no strong ruler held the throne. Babylon became independent in 626, and in 614 Cyaxares, king of Media, captured Asshur. In 612, Nineveh fell to the Medes and Babylonians, and was utterly destroyed, to the delight of the subject peoples (Nah. 1–3). It was still in ruins when Xenophon led the Ten Thousand Greeks up the Tigris in 400 B.C.

# THE BABYLONIAN EMPIRE

## Map 23

The power of Babylon comes and goes in the history of Mesopotamia. We first hear of its greatness under Hammurabi (1792–1750), famous for his code of laws, though the increase of power must have begun slowly rather before his time. This first period of Babylonian supremacy lasted for about a century and a half, though increasingly weakened at the end by the inroads of the Kassites. It received the *coup de grâce* about 1600 B.C., when a Hittite invasion conquered the city and the Kassites took over full control. Thus began a prolonged period of obscurity, during which it was of only minor importance.

The return of strength was exceedingly slow, and may be said to begin with the conquest of Elam by Nebuchadnezzar I (1125–1103 B.C.), though there were frequent regressions. This whole period reflects the absence of any real center of power in the vast delta region of Mesopotamia, where a number of important cities jostled one another for leadership. However, with the rise to absolute control of the state of Assyria, especially after the accession of Tiglath-Pileser III in 744 B.C., the importance of Babylon's central position close to the Mesopotamian "waist" gradually became apparent. Trade from Arabia, the Persian plateau, the Per-

**THE BABYLONIAN EMPIRE**

- – – – Approximate northern limit
of the Babylonian Empire

● **Sidon** Towns

**MOAB** Regional Names

50     100     150     200     250 Miles

50 100 150 200 250 300 350 Kilometers

©1968 JEPPESEN & CO. ALL RIGHTS RESERVED

CASPIAN SEA

BLACK SEA

PERSIA

PERSIAN GULF

MEDIAN EMPIRE

URARTU

Lake Urmia

Lake Van

Rhagae

Ecbatana

Susa

ELAM

Nineveh

Arbela

Arrapkha

Asshur

R. Tigris

Nisibis

IZALLA

Haran

Carchemish

Balikhu

Khazazu

Arpad

Aleppo

Quramati

R. Euphrates

KHINDANU

Anat

SUKHU

Sallat

Sippar

Cutthah

Der

Babylon

Borsippa

Nippur

BABYLONIA

Erech

Ur

Tadmor

Hamath

Kadesh

Riblah

Damascus

Arvad

ARAM

AMMON

MOAB

EDOM

Gebal

Sidon

Tyre

Acco

Megiddo

Jerusalem

Lachish

Gaza

JUDAH

ARABIA

Ha'il

Dumah

Tema

Dedan

Khaibar

Yathrib

R. Halys

LYDIA

Sardis

Magnesia

IONIA

R. Maeander

CARIA

Rhodes

Byzantium

R. Sangarius

KUE

Tarsus

Kirshu

Pitusu

PIRINDU

Sallune

KITTIM

GREAT SEA

RED SEA

Pelusium

Migdol

Tahpanhes

Zoan

Bubastis

On

Memphis

Hermopolis

EGYPT

R. Nile

Lycopolis

Abydos

Thebes

Syene (Elephantine)

sian Gulf, and from the north brought it wealth, and it became the focus of resistance to Assyria, not only for southern Mesopotamia, but for the outlying provinces of the whole empire, with which Babylonian merchants were in constant contact (Isa. 39:1–8).

There was also another reason why this role should fall to Babylon rather than to any of the more remote southern cities, which were less certain that they did want to revolt, and that was the penetration of the delta by the Chaldeans. These seem to have been a nomadic people from Arabia, who moved into the southern delta in very much the same area as the later Muslims were to establish their first settlements when they invaded the country in the seventh century A.D. These newcomers on the one hand brought a great accession of military vigor to the delta peoples but at the same time threatened the security of the city dwellers because of the inroads they made on the cultivated land. Those cities, therefore, that were most exposed to the Chaldean onslaughts tended to look to the might of Assyria for protection. Babylon, however, welcomed them as providing the means whereby it could actively resist Assyrian control, and in course of time "Babylonian" and "Chaldean" became almost synonymous terms.

Though they made repeated attempts to throw off the Assyrian yoke, it was not until 626 B.C. that success crowned their efforts, and in that year Nabopolassar made himself king of an independent Babylon. Assyria was also weakened in the same year by the invasions of the savage Scythians from the high mountains of the Urartu region. Many scholars would date the call of Jeremiah at this time, and see the Scythians as the "foe from the north" of Jeremiah's earlier prophecies (Jer. 1:13–16; 4:5–7). Certainly, the increased weakness of Assyria made possible Josiah's assertion of Judean independence and his establishment in Judah (and even for a time in the north-

ern part of the country) of a purified worship of Yahweh, based upon the teachings of a group of reformers whose ideas, which had been worked out during the black period of Manasseh's reign (687–642), are embodied in the book of Deuteronomy. This total rejection of the Assyrian ideology would never have been tolerated for a moment by the earlier and more powerful rulers (II Kings 22:3—23:25).

The rapid collapse of Assyria before the attacks of both the Babylonians and the Medes aroused the fears of Egypt, to whom Assyria must have appealed as her vassal, which pledged to give support, and in 609 B.C. Pharaoh Necho marched northwards to throw his weight in against the rebels. Josiah unwisely opposed him at the pass of Megiddo, and was killed (II Kings 23:29–30), and for a brief time Egypt controlled Judah. However, in 605 B.C. Nebuchadnezzar II, at that time crown prince, utterly smashed the combined Assyrian and Egyptian forces at Carchemish on the Euphrates, and Babylon fell heir to most, though not all, of the vast Assyrian dominions.

It is true that Babylon had to fight to gain control of these lands and true also that her control lasted only a relatively short time, for after Nebuchadnezzar's death in 561 there were no great Babylonian rulers. This period was, nevertheless, decisive in the history of Judah, for the foolish Judean policy of rebellion whenever possible against the might of Babylon led at last to the destruction of the city of Jerusalem in 586 B.C., and the end of Judah as a separate state.

Though nothing can make this event anything but tragic for the people of Judah, and the exile to Babylon of all the leading people a desolate business, the Babylonians seem to have been something less than absolutely ruthless. The people were settled as a body in the Mesopotamian delta, not far from Babylon, and could continue to act and think as a recognizable community, which had not been possible for the

scattered exiles from the northern kingdom. Moreover, though the last king of Judah, Zedekiah, was blinded and taken in chains to Babylon, after having witnessed the execution of his sons in the Babylonian camp at Riblah on the Orontes (II Kings 25:6–7), his predecessor, Jehoiachin, who had been exiled to Babylon some time earlier, was not ill-treated, and Amel-Marduk (Evil-Merodach of the Bible, 561–559) took him out of prison and treated him as a royal dependent (II Kings 25:27–30), a fact which is confirmed by Babylonian records.

Amel-Marduk was driven from the throne, apparently by the power of the priests of Marduk, and Nergal-sharusur (Nergal-sharezer), who had played an active part in the siege of Jerusalem (Jer. 39:3,13), took his place. He restored the temples of Marduk at Babylon and Borsippa, but at his death power was seized by Nabonidus, who had been a high official under Nebuchadnezzar. Nabonidus neglected the worship of Marduk, and restored the temple of Sin, the moon god, at Harran (the homeland of Abraham), where his mother was high priestess, perhaps in an attempt to provide the decaying Babylonian empire with a unifying cult more acceptable to his Aramean and Arabian subjects.

Harder to explain, however, is his sojourn for ten years at Tema in northern Arabia, leaving his son, Belshazzar, as regent in Babylon (Dan. 5). He apparently built a new capital there, and subjugated the other oases as far south as Yathrib, planting in them colonies of his own subjects, possibly including the Jewish communities which survived there till the time of Muhammad. Some have argued that he wished to bolster the declining Babylonian economy by controlling the great trans-Arabian trade routes, but this would hardly require his permanent residence •there for ten years, particularly since it meant his prolonged absence from the New Year Festival at Babylon, at which the kingship was symbolically renewed. Nabonidus' own inscriptions[1] reflect his disgust at the failure of the Babylonians to accept this new religious order, and his removal to Tema must have been, in part at least, a deliberate withdrawal from their affairs. Although there was a partial reconciliation, he was afterwards bitterly reviled, and the disunity of Babylon opened its gates to Cyrus of Persia. It is probable that Nabonidus' retreat into the desert lies behind the strange story of the madness of Nebuchadnezzar in Daniel 4, having been transferred by tradition to the more famous name.

## Map 24

# THE PERSIAN EMPIRE

"Behold, I am doing a new thing" (Isa. 43:19). This often-repeated theme of the great prophet of the Exile reveals the impact upon the Fertile Crescent made by the conquests of Cyrus the Great, and the establishment of the Persian empire. Men had become used to the age-old struggle between Mesopotamia and the Nile Valley for domination of the Levant, but now suddenly, as it were from outside the world, a new and unsuspected power made itself master. The new empire extended from the Aegean to the Indus, and from the Oxus to the Nile, and commanded Arabia to the south. The way for this had been prepared by the Medes, whose rise to power in the northwest of the Persian plateau coincided with the weakening of Assyria and the renaissance of Babylon. In the toppling of Assyrian power the two were allies, but the increasing strength and expansion of the Medes frightened the Babylonians, who at some period built the "Median Wall" across the narrow waist of Mesopotamia to protect their homeland from attack from the north. In the west the Medes came in conflict with Lydia, and after the famous Battle of the Eclipse of the Sun in 585 B.C. the River Halys was made the boundary between the two. The Persians were settled in the region of the present Shiraz, and in the mid-sixth century, under Cyrus the Great, they exploded into power. Ecbatana, the Median capital, fell to him in 550 B.C., Sardis in 546, and Babylon in 539. He died in 530. The real architect of the empire, however, was Darius I, who seized the throne after the revolt of Gaumata in 522 had shaken the Persian world to its foundations, and the structure created by Darius was to last, though increasingly weakened toward the end, until it was overthrown by Alexander in 330 B.C. It was an extraordinary achievement. For the first time we see the problem of holding together the diverse worlds of the plateau and the plain, across the prodigious barrier of the Zagros Mountains, which much later was to haunt the Muslim world for centuries, and the problem of uniting the oases of the plateau itself. The Persian solution was to move the seat of government three times a year, in itself a logistic *tour de force*, from Susa in the winter to Persepolis in the spring, where at the great Nowruz festival the king received the delegates and their tribute from all over the empire, and then to Ecbatana in the cool uplands of Media in summer.

The enormous extent of the empire, of course, posed problems of its own, and these were dealt with by the divi-

---

[1] C. J. Gadd, "The Harran Inscriptions of Nabonidus," *Anatolian Studies,* vol. 8, p. 35 ff.

sion of the vast dominions into satrapies, or provinces, the satrap being granted considerable power. The title "King of Kings," which comes into prominence now and has persisted in Iran until today, was not in its origins an empty or inflated concept. The various centers of power were connected with the capital by post roads, which were now improved tracks though not always fully made roads. The system of couriers, derived originally from the Assyrians, by which the royal authority was speedily transmitted to any part of the empire, is famous (see Esther 3:12), and to it is related the Persian concept of angels, who now make their entrance into Jewish religious thought, and who were the divine messengers. Milton's well-known words best describe this parallel earthly and heavenly order,

> . . . his state
> Is kingly: thousands at his bidding speed,
> And post o'er land and ocean without rest. . . .
>
> *Sonnet xix, 11–13*

"The law of the Medes and the Persians, which cannot be revoked" (see Esther 1:19; Dan. 6:8,15) also caught the imagination of the subject peoples, for to many the principle of law that could not be changed at the whim of the ruler or by bribery was a new and impressive experience.

Directing all this, of course, was an ideology, or religious pattern of thought. Zoroaster's dates are traditionally given as 628–551 B.C., though these have been much questioned, and Zoroastrianism seems to have been a driving force behind the amazing Persian conquests, though it is uncertain how far the early rulers were true Zoroastrians. It may be significant that Zoroastrianism was dualistic, a concept which, as we have seen, may be re-

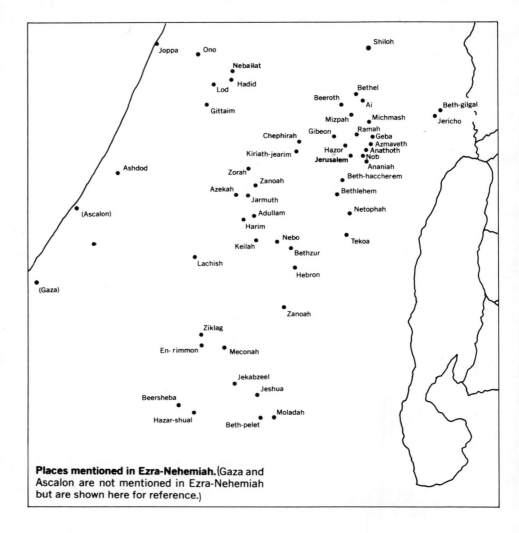

**Places mentioned in Ezra-Nehemiah.** (Gaza and Ascalon are not mentioned in Ezra-Nehemiah but are shown here for reference.)

lated to division of the Persian plateau between the desert and the sown, and therefore we have for the first time an ideology which saw conflict as a necessary part of society, and not something which must ruthlessly be suppressed. Evil, as exemplified by the enemies of society, "the followers of the lie," had to be fought and overcome, but conflict in itself was not necessarily bad. Indeed, it was part and parcel of the nature of things. This allowed the Persians to treat with much greater tol-

erance than others had done the alternative religious systems of their subjects. Cyrus' famous edict permitting the Jews to return and rebuild the temple at Jerusalem (Ezra 1:1–4) was not the only such order given.

The history of the return is excessively difficult to sort out, but it is clear that the territory of the restored Judah was merely a pocket handkerchief of a country in the wide imperial expanse. Yet it was restored, and that one fact outweighed all others.

# THE PERSIAN EMPIRE

• Babylon Towns
MEDIA Regional and Provincial Names
– – – – Limit of the Empire

Miles
Kilometers

© 1968. JEPPESEN & CO. ALL RIGHTS RESERVED

**Regions and Provinces:**
SCYTHIANS
SOGDIANA
BACTRIA
CHORASMIA
ARACHOSIA
HINDUSH
GEDROSIA (MAKA)
ARIA
PARTHIA
DRANGIANA
HYRCANIA
SAGARTIA
CARMANIA
PERSIS
MEDIA
SUSIANA
ATHURA
BABYLONIA
ARMENIA
MOSCHI
COMMAGENE
CAPPADOCIA
PHRYGIA
LYDIA
IONIA
PAMPHYLIA
CYPRUS
PHOENICIA
ARABIA
SHEBA
CUSH
EGYPT
THRACE
MACEDONIA

**Towns:**
River Jaxartes
Cyropolis
Bactra
Margiana
River Oxus
Artacoana
Tus
Zadrakarta
Damghan
Rhagae
Belistun
Ecbatana
Pasargadae
Yazd
Gabae
Kerman
Persepolis
Pura
Susa (Shushan)
Erech
Ur
Der
Babylon
Arrapkha
Arbela
Amida
Haran
Thapsacus
Tadmor
Aleppo
Hamath
Issus
Tarsus
Iconium
Gordium
Ancyra
Byzantium
Apollonia
Odessus
Doriscus
Mytilene
Delphi
Marathon
Corinth
Salamis
Athens
Sparta
Delos
RHODES
CRETE
Xanthus
Miletus
Ephesus
Sardis
Magnesia
Soli
Salamis
Citium
Gebal
Sidon
Tyre
Damascus
Samaria
Jerusalem
Gaza
Pelusium
Heliopolis
Memphis
Sais
Zoan
Hermopolis
Lycopolis
Abydos
Thebes
Syene (Yeb)
Siwa
Dedan
Tema
Ha'il
Dumah
Yathrib
Ta'if
Najran
Sana'
Muza
Shibam
Muscat
Gerrha
Phasis
Trapezus
Meletene
Sinope
Pattala

**Seas and Rivers:**
BLACK SEA
HYRCANIAN SEA
LOWER SEA
ERYTHRAEAN SEA
RED SEA
UPPER SEA
River Indus
River Jaxartes
River Oxus
R. Tigris
R. Euphrates
River Nile
R. Araxes
River Cyrus
R. Halys
R. Sangarius

## Map 25
# THE CONQUESTS OF ALEXANDER

It is impossible to overemphasize the cataclysmic effect upon Asia of the conquests of Alexander, who died at Babylon in June, 323 B.C. He had crossed the Dardanelles and taken Troy in the spring of 334, and had his first meeting with the Persian army at the River Granicus. He then moved south again to the heart of Ionia round Ephesus and Miletus, subsequently making the difficult journey around the coast to capture the other Greek-speaking coastal region of Pamphylia. There he turned north once more to secure the plateau, but made no attempt to cross the Pontic Mountains to the Black Sea coast, a fact which emphasizes the separateness of that region. From Ancyra he pressed southward with such speed as to surprise the Persians at the Cilician Gates, and capture Tarsus. He thrust forward into the northern Levant across the formidable series of mountain "gates," but had to turn back to meet Darius, the Persian king, who threatened his communications with the rear. The Battle of Issus (333 B.C.) in the southern Cilician plain was among the most dangerous of his whole career, and his victory there was one of the most decisive in the history of the world, for it confirmed his control of Asia Minor and opened the way to Mesopotamia.

He now stood at the turning point, where the roads to Africa, Asia, and Europe meet, and he chose first to secure the Mediterranean coastlands, which he did by a successful, though bitterly fought, siege of Tyre, and the submission of Egypt, where he founded Alexandria, destined to be one of the greatest cities in the world. He returned to Tyre, moved inland by the Sidonian depression, and followed the great Trunk Road through Damascus and Aleppo to the Euphrates, which he crossed at Thapsacus, advancing eastwards across the Jezireh to meet, and

soundly defeat, the Persians at the Battle of Gaugamela, not far from the ruins of Nineveh (331 B.C.). This laid the whole of the Mesopotamian plain before him, and Babylon and Susa opened their gates. From Susa, in a daring move, he crossed the Zagros in winter, and captured, with all its treasures, the royal palace at Persepolis. This was destroyed by fire, though whether by accident or on purpose will never be known.[1] From Persepolis he advanced upon the Median capital at Ecbatana, and then followed the "Golden Road" through Rhagae near Tehran to Shahrud, where he found the murdered Darius (330 B.C.).

However, there was still much fight left in the Persian empire. Alexander turned north to the Caspian, for he was always anxious to maintain contact with the ocean, and it was still at that time uncertain whether the Caspian was a vast lake or connected with the Mediterranean through the Black Sea. He then followed the central valley of the Kopet Dagh to the lowland corridor south of Merv, and turned south to Seistan, and thence up the Helmand through Kandahar to Kabul, founding at various points along this route a series of cities to ensure control of the eastern plateau.

He crossed the high ranges of the Hindu Kush with great difficulty in the spring of 329, and conquered Bactria, but the subduing of the region beyond the Oxus cost him a prolonged struggle, and it was not achieved until the summer of 328. He did not return to Kabul until 327. In this year he advanced down the Kabul River into the Punjab, which he conquered, but his troops, dismayed by fighting against elephants and weakened by the exhausting climate of the Indian monsoon, refused to proceed beyond the Beas, though Alexander himself seems to have believed that only a short advance

[1] W. W. Tarn adheres to the traditional theory that it was done on purpose (*Alexander the Great* [Beacon Press, 1956], p. 54), but R. Ghirshman argues that it was accidental (*Iran* [Penguin, 1954], pp. 213–214).

# THE CONQUESTS OF ALEXANDER

- Pella    Towns
- • Pella    Towns
- ⚔    Battle Sites
- ——    Overland Routes
- - - -    Sea Routes

500 Miles
100 200 300 400 500 600 700 Kilometers

INDIAN OCEAN

CASPIAN SEA

BLACK SEA

MEDITERRANEAN SEA

RED SEA

PERSIAN GULF

Pella
Thessalonika
Sestos
Troy
Grenicus
Athens
Dascylium
Sardis
Ephesus
Miletus
Halicarnassus
Xanthus
Ancyra
Gordium
Synnada
Side
Perga
Aspendos
Phaselis
L. Ascanius
Tyana
Tarsus
Soli
Antioch
Issus
Aleppo
Thapsacus
Orhai
Nisibis
Emesa
Damascus
Tripolis
Sidon
Tyre
Gaza
Pelusium
Memphis
Alexandria
(Mersa Matruh)
Ammon
Gaugamela
Arbela
Opis
Babylon
Ecbatana
Susa
(Ahwaz)
Charax
Rhagae
(Amol)
Zadracarta
(Shahrud)
(Bojnurd)
Gabae
Pasargadae
Persepolis
Artacoana
Alexandria Areion
Prophthasia
(Kandahar)
Alexandria
(Kabul)
Taxila
R. Beas
Drapsaka
Bactra
Marakanda
(Bokhara)
Alexandria Eschate
(Pasni)
(Gwadar)
Alexandria
Harmozia
(Bela)
Pattala

would bring him to the eastern ocean. At last the army turned back, but not by the road by which they had come. Characteristically, Alexander sought the ocean, and proceeded southwards down the Indus, at that time flowing east of its present course, to Patala.

Part of the troops were sent back by sea, under the leadership of Nearchus, while Alexander himself attempted to march parallel to them along the desolate Makran coast, in order to provide supplies. The desert proved too much for him, however, and he had to return to the piedmont oases of the plateau, and the two bodies of men, thus separated, were not reunited until Nearchus reached the strait of Hormuz, after both had had three months of desperate and venturesome journeying. Nearchus then took the ships up the Gulf, and Alexander came back to Babylon, where he died before he could explore the Arabian coasts, as he had hoped to do.

W. W. Tarn has said that Alexander "proclaimed for the first time the unity and brotherhood of mankind"[2] and conceived of a state in which people from many diverse races should dwell together in harmony. Others have seen him rather as a brilliant military adventurer who, after the battle of Gaugamela, began to behave more and more like the King of Kings. However this may be, the impact of his conquests is beyond question. The Greek world had burst in upon the Persian dominions at the height of its amazing philosophical and cultural achievements, Aristotle having been the tutor of Alexander. Asia was dazzled by the revelation of all that Greece had to offer, just as in the century between Napoleon and World I it was to be dazzled by the achievements of Western Europe. In the Hellenistic age, to be "modern" was to be "Greek," and many Jews seem to have accepted wholeheartedly

this new way of life. The Wisdom literature represents a prolonged attempt on the part of others to reconcile what out of their past experience they had always understood to be true with the undeniable new truths that this triumphant culture was forcing upon them. Others again found themselves quite unable to accept this new teaching, for it seemed to them to embody a dangerous assessment of man as "the measure of all things," as Protagoras had said about a century before Alexander. The Greek athletic contests shocked them, not merely because the athletes competed naked, but because of the blasphemous glorification of the perfect man, which, as far as they could see, the whole philosophy behind the games involved. There were those among them who were driven to retreat from the world, and others who in course of time were spurred to active revolt.

---

[2] Tarn, *op. cit.*, p. 147.

## Map 26

# PALESTINE BETWEEN THE TESTAMENTS

Some three and a half centuries elapsed from the death of Alexander the Great to the time of the ministry of Jesus, and during this period two events, about a hundred years apart, are of major importance to the biblical record: the beginning of the Maccabean revolt in 165 B.C., which led to the establishment of the last independent Jewish state; and, in 63 B.C., the takeover of power in Palestine by the Romans, who in due course recognized Herod the Great as a client king. The whole period is one in which the interplay of the complex Levantine geopolitical forces is well displayed.

After the death of Alexander in 323 B.C., his conquests were divided between his generals, and there ensued in the Palestinian area the familiar struggle between Egypt under the Ptolemies, and Mesopotamia under the Seleucids. The Seleucids had at first their capital at Babylon, whence they attempted to bring under their control the whole of the vast area from the Indus to the Aegean, but it is significant of the shift of political power to the Mediterranean that the capital was moved to Antioch on the Orontes, and the great port of Seleucia established at its mouth. The Indian dominions and eastern Persia were gradually lost, though close contacts were maintained with India, from which the Seleucid kings obtained elephants to equip their armies (I Macc. 3:34; 6:28–47). The value attached to these animals as a weapon of war is clear from the fact that in 302 B.C. considerable territory in Afghanistan was ceded to Chandragupta of India in exchange for five hundred elephants.

For more than a century, the Ptolemies and the Seleucids wrestled for the possession of the Levant coast, with Palestine for much of the time being under the rule of the former, until in 198 Antiochus III made himself master of the Levant. His vigorous military policy, in which he was assisted by the fugitive Carthaginian general, Hannibal, led, however, to conflict with Rome,

and by the Peace of Apamea (188 B.C.) he was forced to leave the Romans in control of all Anatolia north of the Taurus. Antioch was therefore left dangerously near his new frontier though fortunately protected by the Taurus and Amanus ranges. Nevertheless, it was necessary to hold Antioch if he was to assert his authority over the Levant, and the ports which were so essential to western trade. Central and eastern Persia now passed effectively out of Seleucid control, and when Antiochus IV (Antiochus Epiphanes) seized the throne in 175 B.C. he found himself master of an area extending only from Cilicia to the edge of the Persian desert, and forced to fight at two extremes, southwestward toward Egypt and eastward to protect his Persian frontier.

In Egypt he was checked in 168 by the power of Rome, with whom he wisely chose not to join battle, but on the east he was more successful for a time, though I Macc. 6:1–4 suggests that the eastern frontier was a constant problem. He is reported to have died at Tabae in Persia (possibly Gabae, the modern Isfahan) in 163.

Antiochus IV sought to unify and to modernize his empire by making it "western" (that is to say, Greek), very much as Kemal Atatürk in Turkey, or Reza Shah and his son, the present Shah, in Iran, have done in their respective countries, and like them he found himself opposed by the conservative religious leaders who saw the older way of life, which they greatly valued and which represented to them order, dignity, and decency, threatened with disruption. In Palestine, this struggle between liberal modernists and conservatives took an acute form, for though the Hellenizers had many Jewish adherents who could rightly claim that they were the supporters of cultural and technological progress as well as political order and unity against a die-hard parochialism, the conservatives saw at the root of the whole Greek system a dangerous, and indeed disastrous, glorification of man, and the forceful methods adopted by the impatient Antiochus gave them the status of patriots defending local liberty against absolutism.

The revolt started at Modein, on the northern edge of the Shephelah (I Macc. 2:1–28), and in traditional fashion the rebels took to the wilderness (2:29), and "became fugitives to escape their troubles" (2:43). Under their leader Judas Maccabaeus they fought a guerrilla warfare in which the old Judah strongholds became once more important. Twice they fought the Seleucid armies in the vital gateway of the Valley of Aijalon (3:13–26; 3:32–4:25), and then Lysias attempted the more difficult but more direct route up from Marisa (Mareshah) toward the fortress of Bethzur, not far from Hebron, which became with Jerusalem the key to the control of the hill country (4:26–35). The attack was repulsed, and Judas sought to close the other two approaches from the south and the east (5:1–8). He then set out to rescue and bring to Judea two somewhat surprising outlying groups of orthodox Jews, who appealed for help from the highlands of Gilead and Galilee. We do not know when these pockets of orthodoxy had been established, but possibly in some earlier Judean crisis people had fled to these two traditional regions of

refuge. The winning of control of the Judean plateau was a slow and hazardous business, and when the rebels ventured into the plain near Jamnia, where the Seleucid army had more room to maneuver, they were defeated (5:55–62), though Judas made at least one successful raid as far as Azotus (5:65–68). Judas was killed in battle in 160 B.C.

His successors, Jonathan and Simon, bit by bit extended the Maccabean authority by continued fighting, and by taking advantage of the endless struggles over the Seleucid succession. However, from the period of John Hyrcanus (134–104 B.C.) the Maccabean leaders became more and more Hellenized themselves. Even in the days of Judas they had entered into an alliance with Rome, and it was to Rome that the two rivals, Hyrcanus and Aristobulus, appealed for help when Pompey arrived in Syria. Hyrcanus had earlier bought the assistance of the Nabateans, and King Aretas was, in fact, besieging Jerusalem at this very time. Pompey's siege of the Temple and his massacre of 12,000 Jews marked the end of effective independence, and the inclusion of Palestine in the Roman Province of Syria.

After some twenty years of strife and confusion, Herod the Great emerged as the most powerful figure in the

country, and was recognized as such by the Romans in 40 B.C. In 30 B.C. he was confirmed as King of the Jews, ruling a territory which included all Palestine north of Beersheba, which was part of the Nabatean kingdom, except the free city of Ascalon, and Scythopolis (Bethshan), which was the only city west of the Jordan to be counted as part of the Decapolis. The old Phoenician territory along the coast as far south as Dora (Dor) was also excluded, but Herod built the new port of Caesarea immediately south of this (see Map 27), as well as developing and embellishing the cities of Jerusalem and Samaria (now to be called Sebaste after Caesar Augustus [Sebastos in Greek]; Plate 45). Caesarea provided a valuable center for his dominions, which extended across the Jordan in the north to include Gaulanitis, Trachonitis, Batanea, and Auranitis—i.e., the region formerly known as Bashan and the Jebel Druze (Map 27). He was a skillful though savage ruler, who made a serious attempt to bind Jewry intact into the triumphant Western system of Greek culture and Roman administration. He failed, because the forces of resistance were altogether too strong for him, and he died of a painful illness in 4 B.C., leaving a troubled and bitter inheritance to his sons.

# PALESTINE BETWEEN THE TESTAMENTS

• **Samaria** Towns
GALILEE Regional Names

0  5  10  15  20  25  30  35  40 Miles
0  5  10  15  20  25  30  35  40  45  50  55 Kilometers

Sidon

Damascus

Tyre

Kadesh

Seleucia

Hazor

Maked

Ptolemais

Baskama

Chaspho

Raphon

Dathema

Bosor

Arbela

GALILEE

Hippos

Gamala

Carnaim

Asochis

Alema

Beth-yerah

Gadara

Abila

Arbela

Dor

Ephron

Bosora

ARBATTA

Scythopolis

Narbata

Pella

SAMARIA

GILEAD

Samaria

Gerasa

Shechem

Apollonia

Capharsaba

Akrabatta

Pharathon

Alexandrium

Aphek

Tephon

Gadara

Joppa

Jazer

Rathamin

Ono

Philadelphia

Adida

Beerzeth

Aphairema

Lod

Modein

Bethel

Senaah

Araq el-Amir

Gazara

Beeroth

Jamnia

Mizpah

Michmash

Jericho

Emmaus

Adasa

Dok

Kedron

Capharsalama

Heshbon

Ekron

Jerusalem

Samaga

Azotus

Bethbasi

Qumran

Medeba

Ascalon

Beth-zechariah

Adullam

Tekoa

Dabaloth

Marisa

Beth-zaith

Callirhoe

Libba

PHILISTIA

Beth-zur

Machaerus

Gaza

Adoraim

Hebron

IDUMEA

Engedi

Ziklag

Gerar

Masada

Raphia

Kabzeel

Jeshua

Areopolis

Beersheba

Hormah

Charachmoba

NABATEANS

AKRABATTENE

*Map 27*

## NORTHERN PALESTINE IN THE NEW TESTAMENT

Right up to the time of the Exile, Palestine north of the Esdraelon corridor was of relatively minor importance. It was a largely wooded, frontier region, which was the first area to fall victim to any invader from the north, and Isaiah rightly said of it that "in the former time he brought into contempt the land of Zebulun and the land of Naphtali" (Isa. 9:1). In the latter time, however, it was "made glorious." In part, this was so because the firm extinction of the Levantine kingdoms eliminated also the blood-stained frontiers between them. From the time of the Persian empire onwards, despite the relentless regional consciousness which has persisted to the present day, the concept of political frontiers requiring military defense was gradually overcome in the Levant. In fact, one of the unhappy gifts of the Western powers since World War I has been to restore this tragic consciousness to them. Even more, however, the transformation sprang from the Hellenization of the Levant after the time of Alexander, and the establishment of much closer connections between the Palestinian area and the West. Recent excavations at Tel Anafa (Tel el-Akhdhar) in Upper Galilee have revealed that during the second and first centuries B.C. (i.e., in the Hellenistic rather than the Roman period) it was enriched by trade with both the East and the West. Persian lamps, fine pottery from Athens, and wine from Rhodes were among the imports. Galilee in this area became, and remained, involved in the rapidly developing, and intensely valuable, east-west trade. After the death of Herod the Great, Galilee together with Perea (the slopes of the Trans-Jordanian plateau) formed the awkwardly placed inheritance of Herod Antipas, who was, after all, no more than a client of Rome, and answerable for his administration to them. The importance of Galilee in the trans-Palestinia trade meant that here at least (Perea was different) he would not be allowed a free hand. Herod himself

sat lightly to the dictates of the Torah, and Galilee became strongly westernized. The people of Galilee, however, seem to have resented this stern assumption of power by the Romans, and the region became, and remained, a hotbed of revolt. It is surely not by accident that Jesus was by upbringing a Galilean, a member of a people who, though firmly Jewish, had political reasons to resent and dislike both Jerusalem and Rome. It is another example of the tendency of reform movements to develop, not in the center of a country, but on its borders, in a region where no culture or political system is completely accepted. He seems to have drawn at least some of his followers from among those who wished to overthrow the Roman power by force, though he insisted that deliverance was to come from the political defeat of neither Rome nor Jerusalem.

Roman efficiency in administration and road-building, and the insatiable Roman desire for imported food and luxuries to supply the populace at home, also contributed to the development of this northern region. The broad and reasonably well-watered plateau of Bashan (by this time known under the administrative titles of Gaulanitis, Batanea, and Auranitis) became one of the important granaries of the empire, and the Lake of Galilee provided a rich supply of fish, the towns around it being vigorously engaged in its export, and in the trade in wheat from the eastern plateau. Pliny and Josephus indeed refer to Magdala, the later form of the old Hebrew name Migdal, as "Taricheia," which is a Greek word meaning "pickling," from the salting of fish done there, to prepare it for export through Ptolemais.

The hills crowd closely upon the lake, and only near Gennesaret and at the southern extremity of the lake is there any level land along the shore. From Magdala, however, a narrow valley ("the Valley of the Robbers") leads up between towering cliffs onto the broken plateau country of southern

# NORTHERN PALESTINE
# IN THE NEW TESTAMENT

• **Hippos**  Towns
**GALILEE**  Regional Names
─────── Important Routes
─ ─ ─ ─ ─  Other Routes

0    5    10    15    20 Miles
0   5   10   15   20   25  Kilometers

MT. HERMON

ITURAEA
ABILENE

PHOENICIA

River Leontes

Sarepta

Tyre

LADDER OF TYRE

Ecdippa

Ptolemais

Dora

Caesarea

Apollonia

TRACHONITIS

BATANEA

Raphana

GAULANITIS

Caesarea Philippi

Abelane

Danos

River Jordan

Cadasa

Gischala

Meroth

Sepphoris

Chorazin

Capernaum

Bethsaida Julias

Gamala

Dion

Abila

Hippos

Gergesa ?

Gennesaret

Magdala

Tiberias

Hammath

Hammath Gader

Gadara

Philoteria

AURANITIS

DECAPOLIS

Yarmuq

River

Gerasa

River Jabbok

Pella

Amathus

Scythopolis

Aenon

Salim

Agrippina

Arbela

MT. TABOR

Nain

MT. MOREH

MT. GILBOA

Ginae

GALILEE

Baca

Saab

Chabulon

Cana

Sepphoris

Nazareth

Japha

Asochis

Jotapata

Besara

Hippeum

MOUNT CARMEL

SAMARIA

Nabata

Gitta

Yishub

Sebaste

Neapolis

MT. GERIZIM

Sychar

River Jordan

—33° 30'—

—33° 00'—

—32° 30'—

33° 00'

32° 30'

36° 00'

35° 30'

35° 00'

1   2   3

A   B   C   D

or Lower Galilee, whence one route crossed the plain of Asochis to Ptolemais, another went through Sepphoris by the Pass of Jokneam to Dora (Dor), and a third, the very ancient Trunk Road from Damascus, led around Mount Tabor across the Pass of Megiddo to the new Roman capital at Caesarea and the coast plain. Nazareth, it will be noticed, is not on any main road, but was close to Sepphoris, which was one of the largest towns in Roman Galilee and at one time the capital of the district, until it was replaced in A.D. 25 by Tiberias.

Galilee is divided very sharply by a huge fault scarp cutting right across Palestine just north of Ptolemais, and dividing the lower southern section from the much higher region of Upper Galilee to the north, where Jebel Jarmak, the highest peak in western Palestine, reaches 1,208 m. (3,963 ft.). Lower Galilee is a "shattered" region, much broken by down-faulted basins, which are badly drained and marshy in winter but grow rich crops of wheat after the winter floods are over. This has always been the most thickly populated part of Galilee. Upper Galilee, though today an open, windswept plateau, was for-

ested in ancient times and carried only a sparse population.

It is impossible to draw any kind of map of the journeys of Jesus and his disciples during the period of his ministry, for the evangelists are not concerned with this kind of information. Nevertheless, we gain the impression that although Capernaum seems to have been his center, he was constantly on the move. The great cities of Sepphoris and Tiberias he left, apparently, unvisited (at least we have no record of his ever having entered them), and though reference is made to his teaching in Capernaum, Chorazin, and Bethsaida (the home of three of his disciples), it seems clear from the mention of such places as Nain and Cana that much of his work was done in small towns and even villages. It is possible that he was unanxious to visit what were essentially pagan cities in Palestine itself (though we have no definite information on this point) but it is quite clear that he was not in the least averse to going into pagan territory. Both Luke and John record his visiting the Samaritan region, which to an orthodox Jew of the time would have been considered quite as bad as pagan. More-

over, it is evident that he crossed the lake, which at that time marked the boundary between the Jewish and the pagan world, the eastern shores being essentially Gentile territory, and he seems to have made at least one journey into the coastal regions of the old Phoenicia. Possibly, these excursions farther afield were for the purpose of the private teaching of his disciples away from the pressures to which he was evidently subject in Galilee itself. It seems evident that the famous visit to Caesarea Philippi, where he asked his disciples to say who he was, was deliberate, for the city was not only the capital of the Tetrarchy of Philip, who at that time governed the districts of Iturea and Trachonitis, but also a very ancient and celebrated pagan cult center. Unfortunately, it is not possible to say which was the "exceeding high mountain" of the Transfiguration. Traditionally it was Mount Tabor near Nazareth, but the slopes of Mount Hermon towering above Caesarea Philippi seem more likely from the close association of the two incidents in the Gospel accounts.

*Map 28*

# THE JOURNEYS OF ST. PAUL

It has been said by more than one commentator that the difference between the Old and the New Testaments is that under the old dispensation the unity of the world was expected to be achieved by the Gentiles coming to worship the Lord in Jerusalem, whereas after the Resurrection of Christ the Christians went out of Jerusalem to bring the news of the Lord to the world. There is much truth in this judgment, but it is only partially true, for the way had been prepared for Christian missionaries by the Jews who had gone before them. The Diaspora, it is true, was not the result of missionary effort; it had come into being partly because the situation in Palestine had frequently become so intolerable that the people had fled, and this was to become again one of the most effective stimuli to Christian expansion in the days of the primitive Church (Acts 8:1). Partly, also, men were attracted abroad by the greater financial opportunities, by the possibilities of becoming better acquainted with Greek philosophy, by the presence of already well-established Jewish communities, and so on. There were groups of Jewish people all over the inhabited world of that day, in Mesopotamia, Persia, Asia Minor, Arabia as far south as the Yemen, Egypt, and all around the Mediterranean, and, whatever had been the cause of their migration, these people had taken the Law with them. Nor were they silent about it, and the book of Acts makes it clear that "the God-fearers" (those people who attended the synagogue and were interested in Jewish teaching but had not become fully Jewish) were the people who often listened most readily to the Christian message.

The vivid stories in the book of Acts must not blind us to the fact that the account is highly selective, and any map based upon this account is bound to be somewhat misleading, for it is a map of the tremendous efforts made by one man, but not a map of the outward spread of Christianity from its first home in Judea. We do not have the evidence from which to construct such a map, and so must let that alone forever. Such evidence as we have, however, leads us to believe that the drive to such expansion did not come from Jerusalem, where the people were indeed suspicious of this kind of move, but from the community at Antioch, to which people from Judea had fled as the result of persecution (Acts 11:19).

The first journey (Acts 13–14) was of a tentative, exploratory character, and the results of it led to very widespread disputes (Acts 15), not only about who should be admitted to the Church, but also about how far afield it was desirable to go. This journey was directed, apparently, only to those relatively nearby areas where there were already known to be Jewish Christians, as in Cyprus (Acts 11:19), or where the inhabitants already had considerable contact either with Tarsus or with Antioch. This seems to explain the decision to go inland to Iconium, a major caravan city of the interior, when in subsequent journeys, for reasons that are quite unknown to us, it was evidently thought undesirable to continue with missionary efforts on the Anatolian plateau (Acts 16:6–7). One long-standing problem about this first journey seems now to have been resolved, for the site of Derbe must probably be placed at Devri Şehri, about 48 km. (30 mi.) east of the traditional site.[1]

The second journey, which began apparently with nothing more than a decision to revisit and strengthen the communities that had been established on the first journey (Acts 15:36), turned

---

[1] Michael Balance, "Derbe and Faustinopolis," *Anatolian Studies,* vol. 14 (1964), pp. 139–140. I am grateful to Dr. Michael Gough for calling my attention to this identification, of which I had previously been unaware. Devri Şehri is 4 km. (2½ mi.) south-southeast of Kerti Hüyük, an earlier claimant for the site of Derbe.

into a missionary journey of major significance. Paul, with his driving energy and dynamic vision, was now on his own and no longer restrained by the presence of more cautious and conservative colleagues, and he was already at Troas when he received the invitation to cross over into Macedonia. Whether the decision to leave the plateau and come down to the coast arose out of Paul's own conviction that these Greek-speaking cities were the most important to convince, and also those where he himself could most effectively bear witness because he was at home in this environment, we cannot, of course, know, but there is no doubt that his own journeys, except for return visits to the original Christian communities on the road around the southern edge of the plateau, were confined to the Aegean coasts. It was on this second journey, apparently, that he was joined by Luke, who may even have been the messenger inviting him to come over to Macedonia. At any rate, the journeys hereafter are recorded in much greater detail, and the "we" passages in Acts begin and end at Troas (Acts 16:10; 20:5). After Paul's visit to Athens, he spent eighteen months at Corinth, establishing there one of the most important of the early Christian churches.

The third journey brought him again from Antioch to his first converts on the plateau, and thence to Ephesus. By what route he reached that city we do not know, as the text merely speaks of "the upper country" (Acts 19:1). In this atlas, the route down the valley of the Maeander is suggested, which would bring him close to Miletus, and so along the coast northwards to Ephesus, but he may have come down the valley of the Hermus past Sardis, in which case he would have approached Ephesus from the north. Here he spent two and a quarter years (Acts 19:8–10), though in constant communication, it would seem, with the other Christian communities with which he was acquainted, for we must not imagine that the Pauline letters that are preserved today are necessarily all that he wrote. "The daily pressure upon me of my anxiety for all the churches" (II Cor. 11:28) suggests a far more voluminous correspondence, and a constant coming and going of messengers. Before returning to Jerusalem he paid what he clearly saw to be a farewell visit (Acts 20:25) to the communities he had established on the previous journey.

The final journey was as a prisoner, though clearly a privileged one, to Rome, to bring his appeal to the Emperor, and was made by ship. The celebrated account of his shipwreck, as told in Acts 27, has been questioned by some authorities, who believe the story to have been included from some conventional sea story, but there is really very little reason to doubt its authenticity. It is interesting geographically for illustrating the ancient methods of sea travel, by hugging as far as possible the coasts, the complete cessation of shipping during the winter, and the dangers involved in the tempestuous winds which can develop in the Mediterranean. This was evidently not Paul's first experience of shipwreck (II Cor. 11:25).

Luke speaks of the Maltese as "barbarians" ("natives," in the RSV, Acts 28:2), but means by this probably no more than that they were not conversant with Greek and spoke a language which he could not understand. They were people of Semitic descent, from one of the early Phoenician colonies. Even today the language spoken on Malta has close connections with Arabic because of the historic relations with North Africa.

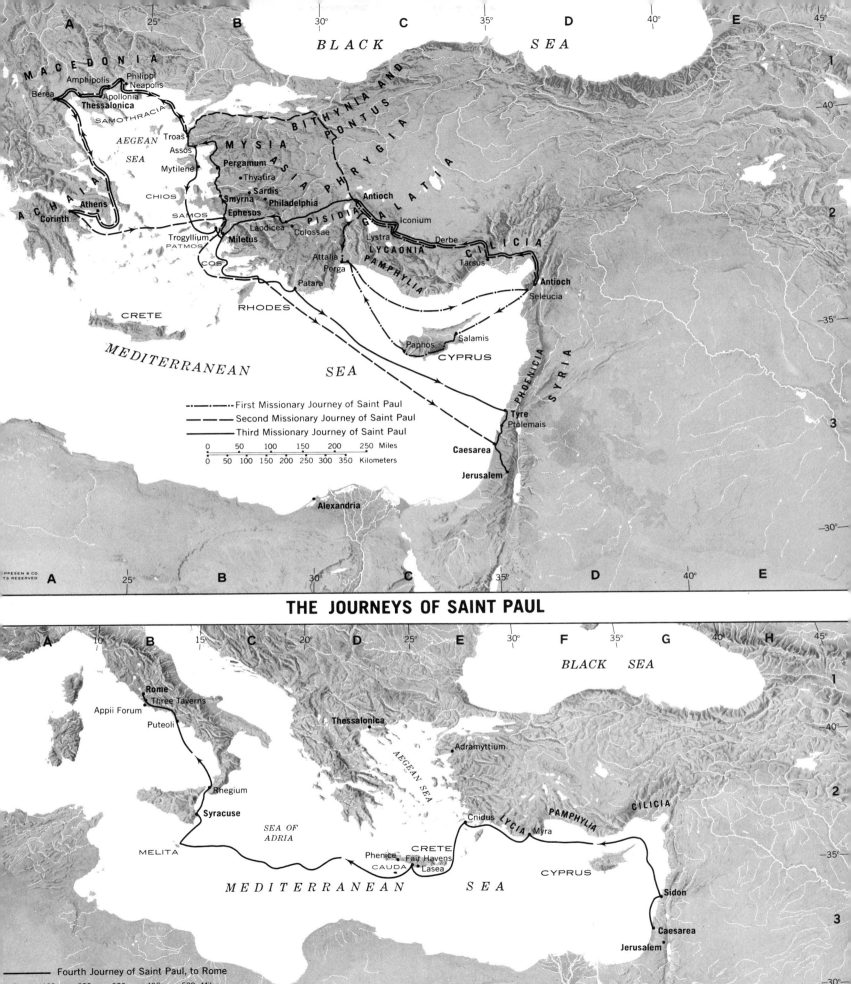

# THE JOURNEYS OF SAINT PAUL

**Top map labels:**

BLACK SEA

MACEDONIA
Amphipolis
Philippi
Neapolis
Berea
Apollonia
Thessalonica
SAMOTHRACIA
AEGEAN SEA
Troas
Assos
MYSIA
Mytilene
Pergamum
•Thyatira
ASIA
CHIOS
Smyrna
Sardis
Philadelphia
Ephesus
SAMOS
Laodicea
•Colossae
Trogyllium
Miletus
PATMOS
COS
PHRYGIA
BITHYNIA AND PONTUS
GALATIA
Antioch
Iconium
PISIDIA
Lystra
Derbe
LYCAONIA
CILICIA
Tarsus
PAMPHYLIA
Attalia
Perga
Patara
RHODES
Antioch
Seleucia
Salamis
Paphos
CYPRUS
PHOENICIA
SYRIA
Tyre
Ptolemais
Caesarea
Jerusalem
ACHAIA
Athens
Corinth
CRETE
MEDITERRANEAN SEA
Alexandria

—·—·— First Missionary Journey of Saint Paul
— — — Second Missionary Journey of Saint Paul
———— Third Missionary Journey of Saint Paul

0  50  100  150  200  250 Miles
0  50 100 150 200 250 300 350 Kilometers

**Bottom map labels:**

BLACK SEA

Rome
Three Taverns
Appii Forum
Puteoli
Thessalonica
Adramyttium
AEGEAN SEA
Rhegium
Syracuse
SEA OF ADRIA
MELITA
Phenice
CRETE
CAUDA
Fair Havens
Lasea
Cnidus
LYCIA
Myra
PAMPHYLIA
CILICIA
CYPRUS
MEDITERRANEAN SEA
Sidon
Caesarea
Jerusalem

———— Fourth Journey of Saint Paul, to Rome

0  100  200  300  400  500 Miles
0 100 200 300 400 500 600 700 Kilometers

31. The Hittites. *In the middle of the second millennium B.C., somewhat before the period of the Exodus, the Hittites established an empire centered at Hattusas northeast of Ankara in Anatolia. The Lion Gate, shown here, is an early example of a type of architecture (a gate guarded by lions or winged bulls) which was later so characteristic of Assyrian cities.*

32. Knossos. *In the Aegean region the island of Crete formed the center of a highly developed and artistic culture, with far-flung trade communications. This brilliant civilization collapsed suddenly as a result of the catastrophic explosion of the volcanic island of Santorin 70 miles north of Crete, about 1450 B.C. It is the greatest volcanic disaster of which we have knowledge, surpassing even the celebrated explosion of Krakatoa in the East Indies in A.D. 1883.*

33. Abu Simbel. *At the same period as the Hittite Empire in Anatolia the Egyptian rulers of the Eighteenth and Nineteenth Dynasties established an extensive empire, designed to prevent any repetition of the Hyksos disaster, when part of Egypt had passed under the hand of foreign invaders. Their frontiers were extended to the third cataract of the Nile and, in the northeast, as far as northern Syria, where they came in conflict with the Hittites. Rameses II, shown here on the great temple at Abu Simbel, fought a celebrated battle with the Hittites at Kadesh on the Orontes in 1285 B.C., where Thutmose II had earlier defeated them in 1470.*

34. Nubian prisoners. *A bas relief at Abu Simbel showing a pathetic group of Nubians roped together and at the mercy of the Pharaoh. A constant feature of Egyptian records is the demonstration of the triumph of the Pharaoh over the forces of disorder threatening the society from without, and the bringing of this disorderly element into abject submission.*

35. Assyrian expansion. Although there had been a preliminary period of Assyrian expansion in the second millennium, their greatest triumphs came in the two centuries between 884 and 669 B.C., when for the first time there was something approaching a "world order," with all Mesopotamia and the Levant, parts of Asia Minor, and even for a time Egypt, brought under one system. Evidence of their might is to be found in inscriptions on the citadel at Van (shown here), the center of the old kingdom of Urartu.

36. Babylon. For a brief period in the sixth century B.C. Babylon in the Mesopotamian delta made herself master of the great Assyrian empire, until she herself was overthrown by the Persians in 539 B.C. This celebrated statue of a lion killing a man, found near the Ishtar Gate at Babylon, is actually Hittite, and is apparently part of the loot from an expedition into that area by Nebuchadnezzar.

37. Persepolis. *With the overthrow of Babylon by Cyrus in 539 B.C. an entirely new situation was produced: an imperial system based on the great Persian plateau, which previously had been regarded by the peoples of the Fertile Crescent as lying "outside the world." However, to Darius I (522–486) belongs the honor of establishing on a sound basis the organization of the Persian Empire, centered on three capitals, Susa in the Mesopotamian plain, Ecbatana in Media, and Persepolis (shown here) in the Persian homeland near the present city of Shiraz.*

**38. Darius enthroned.** *Seated with great dignity upon his throne, Darius I receives a courtier, who covers his mouth as a token of respect (cf. Job 31:27, where Job speaks of the "mouth kissing the hand" in reverence to the sun).*

39. Persian and Median nobles at Persepolis. *On the great staircases leading to the audience hall shown in Plate 37 are carved reliefs representing the processions of the Spring Festival, when the whole empire united to celebrate the establishment of peace and order throughout the world. The Medes and Persians had positions of honor, and here a Mede is shown turning to speak to a Persian, who carries in his hand a sweet-smelling flower, just as men in Persia still do today.*

40. Syrians bringing rams to Persepolis. *The reliefs also show all the nations of the empire bringing their contributions to the maintenance of order and the support of the Persian imperial system. The whole atmosphere is one of peace and harmony, and demonstrates a concept of empire in striking contrast to the brutal suppression of foreigners portrayed in the Egyptian carving shown in Plate 34.*

41. The lions of Delos. *The seventh and sixth centuries B.C. also saw the rise of a civilization based upon the Aegean Sea, against which in due course the Persians were to come into head-on conflict, and which they were unable to subdue. Delos, amid the islands of the Cyclades, was before the triumph of Athens the center of an important confederation, and claimed to be the birthplace of Apollo. This is one of a line of stone lionesses erected there about 550 B.C.*

42. The empire of the seas. *Two rival powers struggled for supremacy in the Mediterranean: the Phoenicians, who founded the city of Carthage in Tunisia shortly before 800 B.C., and the Greeks, who established colonies in Sicily and southern Italy, and penetrated into the Black Sea. This picture shows part of a Greek ship carved on a rock at Lindos on the island of Rhodes, at the place where the sailors prayed before leaving for a journey, or gave thanks for their safe return.*

43. The Cilician Gates. *This narrow defile serves as a symbol of the dramatic conquests of Alexander, who boldly thrust his way by this route across the Taurus to capture Tarsus, and then to smash the Persian army at Issus in 333 B.C. The cataclysmic effect of his victories upon the history and the thought, life, and culture of the entire Middle East cannot possibly be exaggerated.*

44. The Decapolis. *One of the results of Alexander's conquests was the establishment east of the Jordan of a group of Greek cities, which later formed a confederation known as the Decapolis, frequently mentioned in the Gospels. The best preserved of these today is Gerasa (modern Jerash) north of Amman, and this photograph shows the great Temple of Artemis in that city.*

45. Samaria. *Mention of the Decapolis ushers us into the New Testament period, when the whole Mediterranean world was under the sway of Rome. The city of Samaria, once the capital of Omri and Ahab, was an important Palestinian center in this period, and this picture shows the remains of the great colonnaded street amidst the olive groves of the modern village.*

46. The Nabateans. *During the first century A.D. the Romans confined their rule to the coastlands of the Levant, and beyond the frontiers lay independent kingdoms. One of the wealthiest of these was that of the Nabateans, who controlled the fabulously valuable trans-Arabian trade from their rock-cut city of Petra, whose theater is shown here. Alarmed by the endemic insecurity of the Arabian desert, the emperor Trajan extended the frontiers much farther to the east, and in A.D. 106 overthrew the kingdom of the Nabateans.*

47. Hatra: the temple of Bel. *Between the Euphrates and the Tigris, in that broad debating ground between the Roman and the Parthian empires, stands Hatra, apparently a very ancient sacred area and camping ground of the nomadic tribes. A city was established here to facilitate the pacification of the desert. It is an extraordinary mixture of styles, and this facade, which is very characteristic of Hatra architecture, shows a combination of the Roman triumphal arch and the great iwan, or vast open arched hall, which we find later in the Sassanid capital in Ctesiphon near Baghdad, and in very nearly every major Persian mosque.*

48. Hatra: two heads. *A feature of architectural decoration at Hatra is series of heads, as it were emerging from the flat surface of the wall, and usually looking straight to the front. Both men and animals, especially the eagle, are represented. This frontal representation seems to derive from eastern influence.*

49. The expansion of Christianity (i). *The first place outside the area of Palestine and Syria which is recorded as having been the object of missionary endeavor is Cyprus (Acts 13:4). Paul and Barnabas went first to Salamis on the east coast, and today, close to Salamis, stands the old Greek monastery dedicated to Saint Barnabas.*

50. The expansion of Christianity (ii). *The first country to become entirely Christian was the Kingdom of Armenia in eastern Anatolia. In the center of this region, on the island of Aght'amar (Aktamar) on Lake Van, stands an eleventh-century Armenian church with superb carvings, mainly illustrating biblical stories. This represents Jonah being swallowed by a great fish.*

51. The triumph of monotheism (i). *The biblical accounts recognize two places as the primary centers for the worship of the One God: Sinai, where the Law was given, and Jerusalem, the site of the Temple, and the site also of the death and resurrection of Jesus. Both places today are revered by all three great monotheistic religions, Judaism, Christianity, and Islam. This picture shows the Muslim mosque which stands within the Christian monastery of Saint Catherine, on the traditional site of Mount Sinai.*

52. The triumph of monotheism (ii). *In Jerusalem today, on the site of the ancient Jewish temple, stands the wonderful Muslim mosque known as Haram ash-Sharif, or the Noble Sanctuary. In the center of the area is the Dome of the Rock, shown here, built over the old rock of sacrifice. The Crusaders converted it into a church, the Templum Domini. Part of the outside wall of the Haram ash-Sharif is the Western Wall (or "Wailing Wall"), the most sacred center in all Judaism.*

# Chapter Six

# JERUSALEM

Any attempt to describe the ancient form and extent of the city of Jerusalem must first reconstruct a physical landscape which has now virtually disappeared and is likely to vanish completely as building in the district goes on apace. The activity of man has brought many changes to the area in the immediate vicinity of the city, since for millennia he has quarried the hills to obtain building stone, cut down trees for firewood and for construction, and choked the valleys with his rubble. The visitor to Jerusalem today can see vivid evidence of this when he walks downhill to enter the Damascus Gate. To be sure, there must always have been a descending path to this gate, for it is situated in the central valley which itself drops rapidly toward the south, yet the needs of defense at all periods would have required that the gate dominate the terrain immediately in front of it. The fact that the present gate, dating from the Turkish period, does not do this is an indication of how much rubbish has accumulated in the last few centuries. Further, the sill of this gate is roughly level with the top of the central arch of the gate of Hadrian's day. In the last two millennia, therefore, the threshold of the gate has risen some 18 to 20 feet in an attempt to cope with the rise in level outside it; even so, the approach to the gate today is so steep that at a distance of perhaps a hundred yards, one can virtually see over the wall at this point.

Although suburbs have spread out in every direction over the last century, the walled "Old City" of Jerusalem still retains, essentially, the form established by the Roman Emperor Hadrian about A.D. 135. That city differed in some respects from its predecessor, the New Testament city, and the latter, in turn, was vastly different from the city which first came into David's hands a thousand years before.[1] (See Map 29.)

Jerusalem is a hill city, situated slightly to the southeast of the crest of the main hilly backbone of Palestine; it is therefore east of the watershed. At about 750 m. (2,500 ft.) above sea level, it occupies a forked tongue of land thrusting out from the central massif toward the south. It is separated from higher land to the east, including the Mount of Olives, by an eastern valley which is always deep but becomes narrower and has more precipitous sides as it runs southward. A few hundred yards above the point where this valley is joined by the two other major valleys from the north and west, the one ever-flowing spring in the neighborhood originally gushed from its western flank. This is the Old Testament spring of Gihon. Farther down the gorge, below the confluence with

---

[1] The bibliography on Jerusalem's topography is enormous. In the descriptions of the Jerusalem maps, all references to earlier excavations will be to J. Simons, *Jerusalem in the Old Testament* (Leiden: Brill, 1952), which is a compendium of facts and theories published in hundreds of books and journals, as well as a carefully reasoned study of the ancient city. For later information, references will be to the preliminary reports in the *Palestine Exploration Quarterly* on the recent excavations by the British School of Archaeology, the Royal Ontario Museum, and the Ecole Biblique et Archéologique de St. Etienne in Jerusalem. These excavations, and the interpretations of the director, Miss Kathleen M. Kenyon, have provided a wealth of new information, which is here gratefully acknowledged.

the other valleys, is a deep well—apparently supplied by the drainage of the eastern valley at a low level—called today "Job's Well." It may be the En-Rogel of Josh. 15:7, II Sam. 17:17, I Kings 1:9, and so on.

West of Jerusalem is another deep valley, which runs south parallel to the city walls and then turns sharply east to meet the eastern valley. A third, central valley virtually bisects the present city between the other two. Rising to the northwest, it enters the city near the present Damascus Gate and runs first southeasterly and then south. Toward its lower end it opens into a rather broad amphitheater before becoming constricted again and turning sharply east to join the eastern valley just north of where the western valley debouches. The central valley divides Jerusalem, therefore, into two parts—an eastern ridge and a western ridge.

The topographical picture is complicated by the existence of subsidiary and cross valleys. The northern part of the eastern ridge is cut by another valley running somewhat diagonally from northwest to southeast. Its line can be clearly seen at the north of the present city where it is marked by Herod's Gate; to the west of this gate is a high, rocky bulge which supports the present wall between Herod's Gate and the Damascus Gate. To the east, the original spur—now cut by a fosse—originally ran on to the north, and now bears the Palestine Archaeological Museum. The valley itself at its southern end contains the Pool of Beth-zatha (John 5:2), and then joins an important cross valley which almost completely severs the temple mount (now concealed beneath the great rectangular platform of the Haram or sacred area) to the south from the high land to the north (Bezetha of Josephus *War* V, 149, 151).* South of the temple mount, the eastern ridge narrows and reaches its waist about 200 meters south of the southern wall of the Haram. The recent excavations suggest that the constriction may be the result of a shallow bay running up from the eastern valley which may originally have delimited the south side of the "Ophel" ("swelling" or "bulge," II Chron. 33:14).[2] The eastern ridge therefore consists of three more or less distinct parts: Bezetha at the extreme north, the temple mount in the middle, and the southeast hill at the lower end.

The western ridge also has subsidiary features. It is divided into two parts—a northwest hill and a south-

west hill—by a cross valley which begins just east of the present Citadel and runs almost due east on the line of the present David Street to join the central valley. It is delimited on the north by a spur from the northwest hill; the north flank of this spur forms the southwest side of the central valley. At its root today stands the Church of the Holy Sepulcher. The main cross valley does not, however, completely sever the northwest from the southwest hill. They were joined by a neck of land which is now guarded by the Citadel at Jaffa Gate.

The southwest hill is irregular in form. To the east it runs out in a promontory delimited sharply on the east by the central valley and on the southeast by the "amphitheater" of that same valley which forms a deep but gradually sloping bay. To the south, the hill slopes down gradually until it drops off suddenly into the east-west stretch of the western valley.

The main topographic features of the city have their origins in the geological peculiarities of the district. Three types of rock succeed each other from west to east. First, the water-parting zone extending eastward to the western valley is composed of the hard and massive Cenomanian limestone, which normally carried a good forest cover, and breaks down into pockets of fertile *terra rossa,* preserved especially in hollows in the limestone. Then, between the western and eastern valleys—the area covered by the Old City—comes a rather narrow layer of Turonian limestone, which is somewhat softer and easier to quarry, and provides excellent building stone. Finally, to the east is the soft, infertile Senonian chalk, which tends to be eroded into a much more rounded and less dramatic landscape. This, of course, is the youngest of the three rocks, and lies on top of the other two, the Cenomanian being the oldest and exposed by erosion where the center of the upfold has been worn away. Consequently, in the east the valleys sooner or later cut down through the Senonian to reach first the Turonian and then the Cenomanian limestone. These two last form steeper and more precipitous slopes in the lower parts of the valleys.

In the immediate Jerusalem area, the valleys discussed above have tended to form at the junctions of the three rocks, as we have seen. The original city of Jerusalem, therefore, stood on a block of the Turonian limestone, and the availability of such good,

[2] This term is today sometimes applied by extension to the whole southeast hill.
* See footnote 5, p. 166, this volume.

easily worked building stone may have been one of the reasons for the choice of the site. The enormous underground quarries known as "Solomon's Quarries," which now lie under part of the Old City, are carved out of this rock.[3]

"As the mountains are round about Jerusalem, so the Lord is round about his people" (Ps. 125:2), and Jerusalem is in fact almost surrounded by a horseshoe of rather higher land, with a break only in the southeast, where the three valleys join together to form the Wadi an-Nar, which then tumbles down rapidly toward the Dead Sea. In particular, the high ridge formed by Mount Scopus and the Mount of Olives attracted the people of the city, for it stood between them and the rising sun, and in late apocalyptic writing we have the vision of the Mount of Olives being "split in two from east to west by a very wide valley" (Zech. 14:4). In Muslim tradition also it is associated with the Day of Judgment, and throughout the centuries devout Jews have wished to be buried on its slopes to await the coming of the Messiah. The Mount of Offense, which forms its southernmost extension, owes its name to the tradition that it was here that Solomon built high places for the foreign gods (I Kings 11:7).

Jerusalem is not really at a major crossroads, though roads approach it from all four sides, the main intersection of north-south and east-west routes lying about ten miles farther north. The road from Hebron to the north of the country lay somewhat to the west of the city, and the road from Jericho (Luke 10:30) crossed the eastern ridge by the saddle between Mount Scopus and the Mount of Olives. It was as Jesus crossed this ridge and saw the glory of the city and its temple laid out below him that he wept over Jerusalem (Luke 19:41–44). From the west a track, making use in part of the Valley of Sorek, climbed up from the coastal plain, but it was a decidedly more difficult route than the Ascent of Beth-horon farther north.

## Map 29
## THE SITE OF JERUSALEM

The main features of the geology and topography of the Jerusalem area are discussed in the text of Chapter Six. This map illustrates those features, but a word of caution must be given. The topographic rendering is based on the original rock contours of the city insofar as they are known; most of these depend on rock levels ascertained or proposed by the Ordnance Survey. Certainly, however, not enough data are at hand to be confident that the resulting picture is accurate in every respect. Furthermore, in nearly every site where the recent expedition reached bedrock, it was found that the rock had been quarried. The date at which the quarrying took place can be established from the levels of soil which seal the cuttings in each case. The fact of quarrying, however, suggests that existing absolute levels of bedrock recorded in Jerusalem may bear little relation to ancient levels in any particular case, although they can probably be trusted in the evidence they provide for the ancient major features of hills and valleys. A good example is the southeast hill itself. The heavy quarrying to which it was subjected during the reign of Herod the Great and later makes it virtually impossible to know what its vertical profile was originally, but that there was a hill here is indisputable.

The topographic map bears two overlays. The heavy dotted line marks the probable original limit of good woodland, as far as it can be determined from present climatic and geological evidence. It must be remembered that Jerusalem lay at the junction of the cultivable land and the wilderness,

[3] For a more detailed discussion of this, see M. Avnimelech, "Influence of Geological Conditions on the Development of Jerusalem," *Bulletin of the American Schools of Oriental Research*, no. 181 (Feb. 1966), pp. 23–31.

which starts abruptly to the east of the Mount of Olives. In such a marginal region, the difference between the greener western and the more barren eastern slopes would be very marked. Further, by the time David captured the city, much of the woodland in the immediate neighborhood would already have been cleared for agriculture, though we must imagine patches still remaining, especially toward the west. The relatively level plateau area on the northern side of the town would have been devoted to wheat; when ripe, it would have been threshed and, finally, winnowed on higher points where the powerful breeze from the west, which blows steadily during the summer afternoons, could separate the kernels from the chaff. The threshing floor of Araunah (II Sam. 24:18–25) was the flat top of what later became the temple hill. Olives, and possibly other fruit trees, would take the place of woodland on the western slopes, and vegetable gardens would occupy the narrow strip of alluvium along the valley bottoms.

The other overlay is a plan of today's "Old City" to provide orientation; at least a portion of this line is reproduced in all succeeding maps of the historical topography for the same reason. It will be immediately evident that this line excludes part of the southwest hill and all of the southeast hill. This fact has had definite advantages for the archaeologist. As the southeast hill was the site of the original Jerusalem, excavation has been possible there for the last century, and far more is known about the ancient wall system in this area than for anywhere else in Jerusalem. In the same way, it has been possible to trace the line of wall enclosing the southern end of the southwest hill and joining up with the defenses of the southeastern hill. But the archaeological evidence for that part of the site covered by the present city is almost nonexistent. Investigations beneath the houses, streets, and public buildings of any ancient city pose many problems. When

much of the city is occupied by shrines, churches, mosques, and holy places of many kinds, sacred to one or more of three great faiths, the problem is virtually insoluble. We must seize on those tidbits of evidence, often of uncertain value, which have turned up, often by accident, during the construction of buildings or new roads, the clearing or laying of sewers, and the repairs to walls and floors of major buildings.

Finally, a word should be said about nomenclature. The Bible preserves the names of only two of the main valleys of the city. The eastern valley is, by most scholars, identified with the biblical Kidron (Jer. 31:40; etc.). To the western valley the name Hinnom, or Valley of the Son (or Sons) of Hinnom (Josh. 15:8; 18:16; etc.), is usually applied. The central valley, called by Josephus* the Valley of the Cheesemakers (Tyropoeon), is usually considered to have left no ancient name in the Bible, a circumstance rather difficult to understand. The problem lies in the fact that for centuries Zion, the City of David, has traditionally been located on the southwest hill; as this city (see Bible texts above) was bounded by the Hinnom, the Hinnom would, therefore, be the western valley. But all archaeological evidence supports the view that the original city lay on the southeast hill and that no part of the southwest hill was walled before the Maccabean period. The logical conclusion is that the central valley is the biblical Hinnom and the Tyropoeon of Josephus. The maps that follow assume this identification.

## The Historical Topography of Jerusalem—General Considerations

The plans of Jerusalem that follow are based on available information—topographical, archaeological, and literary. The evidence, however, is by no means complete or conclusive, and all that can be claimed for the accuracy of the proposed wall lines of each period is some degree of probability. The reasons are not far to seek.

It has already been shown that too

much reliance cannot be placed on reported rock contours as representing the original topography. Archaeology, also, has not always provided conclusive evidence, for, although excavators have devoted much time to Jerusalem over the last century, it is only in the last few years that new techniques have allowed a close dating of the ancient remains found. Further, in most cases the archaeological evidence is restricted to small areas—many of them, fortunately, key areas—and the filling in of the gaps must depend on more indirect indications.

Such reservations are particularly cogent for the lines of walls and buildings on the temple hill. Herod the Great's massive construction program here, begun in 20–19 B.C., engulfed or obliterated almost every trace of earlier structures. His great platform exists today as the Haram ash-Sharif, or Noble Sanctuary, and bears the Dome of the Rock, the Aqsa Mosque, and other buildings. Excavation beneath, or even close to, this venerable area has always been forbidden, although the explorations and soundings of Sir Charles Warren a century ago have given us some idea of the underlying rock formation and contours.

The literary evidence—mainly the Bible—is, in itself, insufficient as a basis for reconstructing the ancient lines of the city at various periods. Even Josephus, although a prime source for the topography of Jerusalem in his own day (immediately before the conquest of the city by the Emperor Titus in A.D. 70), must be used with caution for the earlier periods. But no reconstruction which flies in the face of the contemporary literary evidence can be considered satisfactory.

Finally, there is room for interpretation of all three types of evidence, and every writer and cartographer must weigh that evidence for himself. The plans here produced are therefore not to be treated as final in detail but reflect what appears to be the simplest interpretation of the known facts and possibilities.

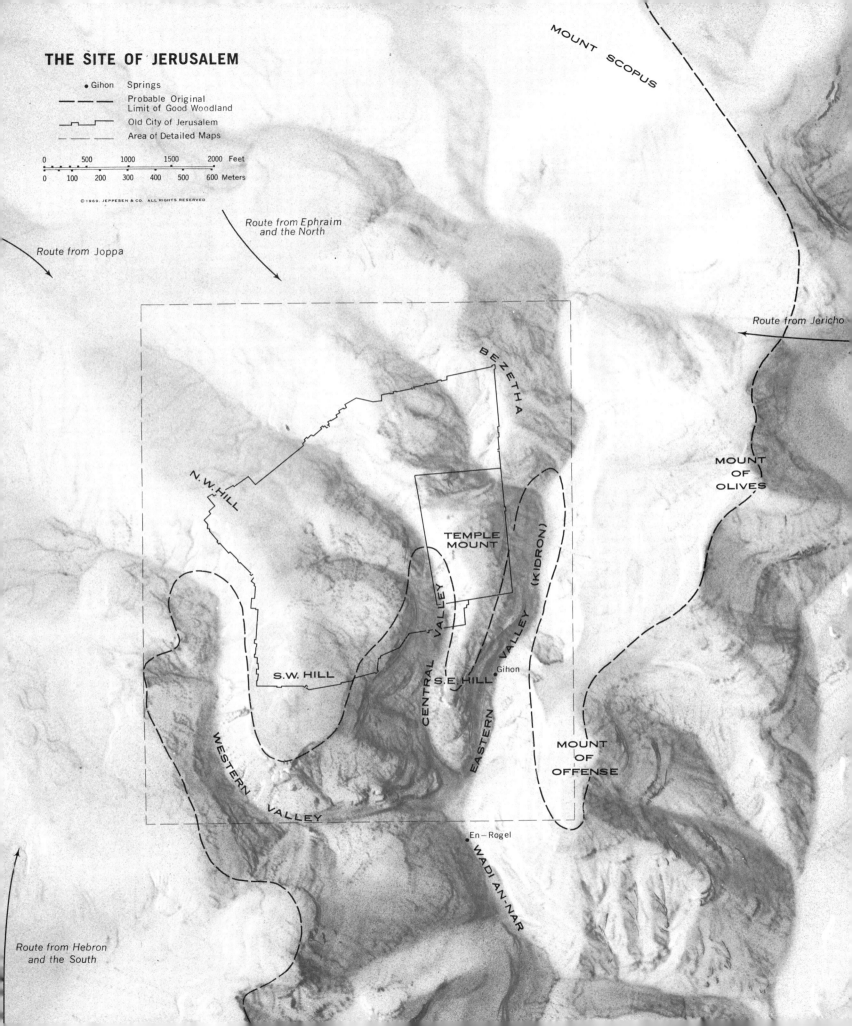

# THE SITE OF JERUSALEM

- •Gihon Springs
- Probable Original Limit of Good Woodland
- Old City of Jerusalem
- Area of Detailed Maps

0    500    1000    1500    2000 Feet
0  100  200  300  400  500  600 Meters

© 1969, JEPPESEN & CO. ALL RIGHTS RESERVED

MOUNT SCOPUS

Route from Ephraim
and the North

Route from Joppa

Route from Jericho

BEZETHA

MOUNT
OF
OLIVES

N.W. HILL

TEMPLE
MOUNT

CENTRAL VALLEY

(KIDRON)

S.W. HILL

S.E. HILL

•Gihon

EASTERN VALLEY

MOUNT
OF
OFFENSE

WESTERN VALLEY

•En–Rogel

WADI AN-NAR

Route from Hebron
and the South

*Map 30*

# CANAANITE JERUSALEM AND THE CITY OF DAVID

Jerusalem was first inhabited as a walled city about 1800 B.C. This pre-Jebusite city, like its successors for nearly a thousand years, occupied only the southeast hill. Its walls have been found low down on the eastern slope above the spring Gihon, and they presumably followed this low line all along the east side. On the west side of the hill, however, where there was no spring to protect, they appear to have run along just below the crest. The northern limit of the city is unknown, but there is no evidence that it extended beyond the later Jebusite wall (see below). Above the spring Gihon there was probably a water gate with out-thrust towers to protect and give access to this vital water supply, but the city itself, inside its walls, climbed up the steep slope. It was a small city; the comparatively level summit of the hill even today averages less than 75 m. (246 ft.) in breadth and is, at most, about 400 m. (1312 ft.) long—an area of about 7.5 acres. To this, however, must be added another 3 acres for the inhabited parts of the slopes on the east side, giving a total occupied area of about 10.5 acres.

The excavations have told us more about the Canaanite city, inhabited by the Jebusites, which was conquered by David about 1000 B.C. Their city wall followed the earlier course, but they introduced several improvements. On the east slope, above the spring, they constructed a series of terraces with heavy retaining and tie walls to hold the fill in place and consolidate the whole complex. On these artificial platforms they built houses, the several levels connected, no doubt, by stepped streets (at least this was true in the later Israelite period). The terraces appear to fill a rather localized hollow in the side of the hill which, on the north, extended no farther than the city wall, and on the south may have been bounded by a street leading down to the water gate (the north tower of which has probably been located). Understandably, such heavy constructions resting on a steep slope were unstable. Heavy rains, earth tremors, or sapping by enemies could so weaken them that they would tumble outward down the slope, not only ruining the houses built on them but breaching the city walls below. If, as has been proposed,[1] this system of terraces is the Millo or "filling" so often referred to in the Old Testament (II Sam. 5:9; I Kings 9:15; 11:27; II Chron. 32:5), we can well understand why the kings of Israel, from David on, had to repair and consolidate the Millo whenever they strengthened the defenses, or vice versa.

It is now possible, also, to identify the north wall of the Jebusite city. It is a massive structure, of huge irregular boulders, carefully plastered on its outer face. Only two courses of it remain, resting on bedrock, and it turns south at its eastern end.[2] Its position was dictated by two factors: it apparently crosses the narrowest part of the southeast ridge; and there are some indications that a small bay, running up to the crest from the Kidron, may have provided a natural fosse to the north of it. The wall, after its sharp turn to the south at its eastern end, appears to have run diagonally down the slope to join the line discovered above the north of the spring.[3] As the western wall ran along nearer the crest than the eastern wall, it is possible that there was a square corner where it joined the north wall.

As at other sites in Palestine, the

---

[1] Kathleen M. Kenyon, preliminary report of Jerusalem excavation, *Palestine Exploration Quarterly* (hereafter cited as *PEQ*), 1963, p. 14.

[2] *Ibid.*, p. 17.

[3] This wall would have run on the most strategic line—in this case an elevated tongue dividing the bay to the south (occupied by the terraces) from the assumed bay to the north.

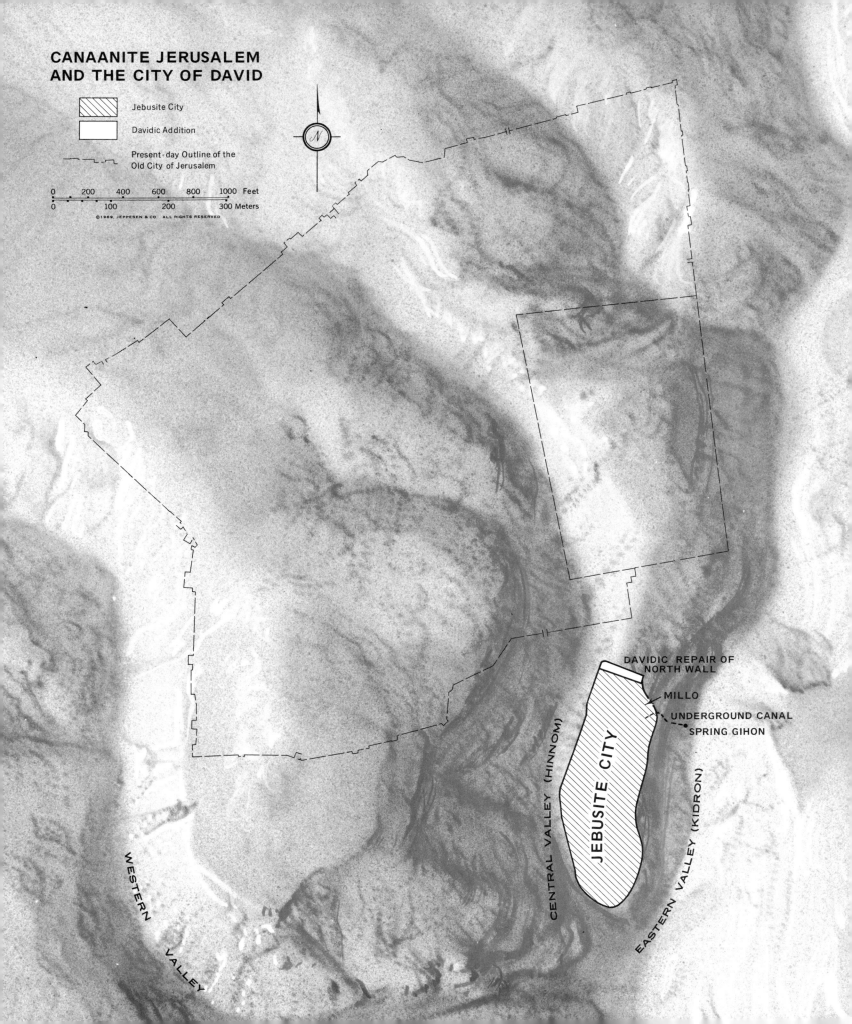

# CANAANITE JERUSALEM
# AND THE CITY OF DAVID

Jebusite City

Davidic Addition

Present-day Outline of the
Old City of Jerusalem

N

0   200   400   600   800   1000 Feet
0      100      200      300 Meters
©1969, JEPPESEN & CO.  ALL RIGHTS RESERVED

DAVIDIC REPAIR OF
NORTH WALL

MILLO

UNDERGROUND CANAL

SPRING GIHON

CENTRAL VALLEY (HINNOM)

JEBUSITE CITY

EASTERN VALLEY (KIDRON)

WESTERN VALLEY

Canaanite inhabitants of Jerusalem had guaranteed access to their water supply. A rock-cut tunnel was excavated to lead the waters of Gihon inward under the hill; a vertical shaft, approached from inside the city walls by a sloping gallery, allowed the besieged to drop buckets on ropes down into the water-filled tunnel and raise water, as needed, without fear of molestation.[4]

It is no wonder that this city, secure in its strong site, powerful defenses, and assured water supply, held out against the Israelites for centuries and that their taunts so angered David (II Sam. 5:6–8). But the city had an Achilles heel. Although the original entrance to the spring from the Kidron was probably masked, there had to be an overflow, and an attacker could find his way into the tunnel by following the course of the outflow to its source. The details are no longer clear to us, but there seems little doubt that it was by this tunnel that Joab made his way up

the hazardous ascent of the vertical shaft (nearly 50 feet high) and the sloping gallery and burst into the city behind the defenders' backs. Their consternation was probably the signal for a frontal attack on the walls by David's main force, the city fell, and Joab was suitably rewarded (II Sam. 5:6–8; I Chron. 11:4–6).

David made Jerusalem his capital, gave it the new name "City of David," and "built the city round about from the Millo inward" (II Sam. 5:9). A short stretch of wall parallel to and immediately adjacent to the east face of the old north Jebusite wall may perhaps be attributed to David. If so, and if the location of the Millo has been properly identified, we may interpret the text above to mean that, in general, David merely repaired the earlier walls but at the north end—from which his frontal attack may have come—he had to build a new wall. There is no indication, however, that this wall enclosed any major extension of the city to the north.

At the south end of the city, Weill discovered a postern gate and stairs,[5] which appear to be those referred to in Neh. 3:15; 12:37, and which preceded Nehemiah's restoration. Such a southern approach to the city is to be expected from earliest times, but there is no evidence on which a decision can be based as to whether the structure found by Weill is Jebusite or Davidic or belongs to some later period of the monarchy.

We are also told that David built a palace for himself (II Sam. 5:11). Where this was we do not know, but a "house of David" was known centuries later in the southern part of the city (Neh. 12:37). The Tombs of the Kings and the house of the Mighty Men (Neh. 3:16; I Chron. 11:10 ff.)—which may have been the barracks of David's chief military heroes—were also in this area; so too, probably, was the tent that sheltered the Ark.

---

[4] J. Simons, *Jerusalem in the Old Testament* (Leiden: Brill, 1952), pp. 165 ff.

[5] *Ibid.*, p. 92 ff.

David established the Israelite monarchy, but there was neither the time—because of his many wars—nor the immediate need for a larger and more ornate capital than that which he had inherited from the Jebusites. This task was left to Solomon.

As befitted his power and wealth, Solomon built a new quarter to the city to accommodate his palace and the temple. That this was on the hill north of the City of David there can be no doubt. The latest excavations have produced some evidence bearing on the lines of this extension. A few meters east of the east face of the old Jebusite north wall, and outside the fragment of wall attributed above to David, there is another wall. It is of casemate construction—that is, it is a double wall with cross-walls forming a chain of rectangular cells which could be used for storage or simply filled with rubble. It runs along the edge of an artificial rock scarp which would add to its strength.[1] Such walls are known from other cities in which Solomon carried out building operations (Hazor, Gezer, Megiddo). The course of this wall to the northeast is suggested by the discovery, at the point marked X on the plan, of a tower which, although slightly later than the time of Solomon, contains re-used stones which resemble, in size and dressing, the masonry of Omri's and Ahab's citadel at Samaria (the work of Phoenician workmen as was much of Solomon's construction). The suggestion is that Solomon's wall was close by and probably inside (i.e., west of) the tower.

The western wall of Solomon's extension to the north was slightly west of the old Jebusite/Davidic line,[2] clearly an attempt to widen the narrow waist of the southeast hill. Its continuation to the north may be roughly on the line of the salient in the present city wall south of the Haram enclosure, for indications are that an early—at least pre-Herodian—wall ran along this line.[3] A street of the Herodian period against the south wall of the Haram can only have led up to the Double Gate in that wall.[4] If so, the earlier, monarchic west wall probably ran east of the Double Gate.

The northern line of the new quarter on the temple hill is unknown, but the present plan assumes that it followed the southern side of the cross valley north of the platform on which the Dome of the Rock now stands. The eastern and western limits are even more hypothetical. If, as is here assumed, the clean break in the east wall of the present Haram some 32 m. (105 ft.) north of the southeast corner[5] represents the southernmost extension of the east wall of Zerubbabel's temple enclosure, and this, in turn, was merely a rebuilding of the Solomonic royal quarter, we must assume that the new quarter expanded outward to the east and west from the narrow waist by which it was attached to the old City of David. The overall width, as given in the plan, is predicated on the assumption that the temple of Solomon (and that of Herod) occupied the site of the Dome of the Rock.

There is no reason to believe that there were any major changes in the outer defense lines of the city in the two centuries that followed Solomon.

*Map 31*

## JERUSALEM UNDER SOLOMON AND THE LATER MONARCHY

[1] Kenyon, *PEQ*, 1963, pp. 18 ff., plate IX B; 1967, pp. 68–69.

[2] Kenyon, *PEQ*, 1966, p. 80.

[3] Kenyon, *PEQ*, 1968, p. 102.

[4] Kenyon, *PEQ*, 1962, pp. 88–89.

[5] This break (Simons, *op. cit.,* pp. 370–71 and fig. 50; Kenyon, *PEQ*, 1968, pp. 104–105 and plates XXXVII A, B) marks the point from which Herod the Great began the extension southward of his platform. The older masonry is thought to be Persian and so from the time of Zerubbabel.

After the political rupture that saw the withdrawal of the northern tribes to form their own kingdom, with its capital, eventually, at Samaria, it is probable that the tiny kingdom of Judah found little need for an enlargement of its chief city. There was frequent hostility between the two states, and, in one case, we are told that Jehoash of Israel destroyed "the wall of Jerusalem for four hundred cubits [about 200 m., or 656 ft.], from the Ephraim Gate to the Corner Gate" (II Kings 14:13; II Chron. 25:23). This must be the north wall because of the length involved, because of the reference to the Ephraim Gate, which must have led out to the north, and because such a destruction would make Jerusalem most vulnerable.

A far more serious threat appeared in the second half of the eighth century B.C.—the Assyrians. Especially after the destruction of Samaria in 722 B.C. and the incorporation of much of Palestine into the Assyrian empire, Jerusalem was on the front line. The defensive works of two kings are given in some detail. Hezekiah addressed himself to the water supply. He "closed the upper outlet of the waters of Gihon and directed them down to the west side of the city of David" (II Chron. 32:30). "He made the pool and the conduit and brought water into the city" (II Kings 20:20). Hezekiah's tunnel and the Pool of Siloam into which it empties today are both well known. The latter is a masonry structure open to the sky; it is also outside the line of Hezekiah's city walls! The original pool, however, may have been rock-cut and subterranean, accessible from within the walls but completely hidden from the enemy.[6] The "wall of the Pool of Shelah" (Neh. 3:15) was in this area, but there is nothing to indicate that it enclosed an open pool in the valley.

Hezekiah and Manasseh both concerned themselves with the city walls. Hezekiah "built up all the wall that was broken down, and raised towers upon it, and outside it he built another wall; and he strengthened the Millo in the city of David" (II Chron. 32:5). This new outer wall, from its association with the Millo and from what we know of his major hydraulic project at Gihon, was probably on the east side of the southeast hill. Manasseh's work was in the same area: he "built an outer wall for the city of David west of Gihon, in the valley, and for the entrance into the Fish Gate, and carried it round Ophel, and raised it to a very great height" (II Chron. 33:14). The construction of two new outer walls on the east side of the city within such a short period of time has received striking confirmation from the recent excavations. The old city wall above Gihon, in continuous use since about 1800 B.C., received its last rebuilding in the late eighth or early seventh century B.C. Later, outside this, a new wall was constructed, although not a stone of it has been found. Of a third wall, built inside the other two and 5.50 m. (18 ft.) thick, a long stretch remains. This wall underwent three collapses and rebuildings and was succeeded by the latest wall, built farther down the slope and now completely destroyed. This series of buildings and rebuildings all belong to the period extending from the late eighth century—when the Assyrian threat became ominous—to the destruction of Jerusalem by the Babylonians in 587 B.C. The third of these walls—the only one that has been traced for some distance—follows a new course. It runs more directly to the north and, when projected, is seen to enclose a whole new area—the Ophel—which other biblical passages (e.g., Neh. 3:26–27) indicate

was south of the temple area and in proximity to the east wall. Probably, in this part of the new wall, also, was the Water Gate (Neh. 3:26), from which a path presumably led down to the spring (possibly the forerunner of the present path from the north). As this wall fulfills the requirements of the literary evidence, this wall may be Manasseh's or a later one following the same line.

The statement that Manasseh's wall extended to "the entrance into the Fish Gate"—usually located in the north wall of the city (Neh. 3:3; 12:39)—suggests that the stretch north of the Ophel must have followed the line of the east wall on the temple hill, which had existed since the time of Solomon. If the term "outer" applies also to this section of the wall, it may have run slightly east of the old line—in which case the small section of wall discovered by Warren 15 m. (49 ft.) east of the Golden Gate[7] may mark its approximate location.

All this wall-building required much new stone, and the recent excavations can suggest its source. Wherever bedrock has been reached on the western hill, there is evidence of quarrying, and in many cases the quarries are sealed by deposits of roughly the last century of the Hebrew monarchy. Large quantities of pottery, as well as weights, figurines, etc., support this date and suggest the presence here of a large number of workers and, presumably, merchants to cater to their needs. But the absence of any structures that can be considered domestic, the lack of evidence for city walls, and particularly the quarrying itself (which would not be pursued within the limits of the city) all support the conclusion that the western hill remained outside the walled city of Jerusalem. The 1968–69 excavations appear to substantiate this.

[6] Kenyon, *PEQ,* 1965, pp. 14–15.

[7] Simons, p. 331.

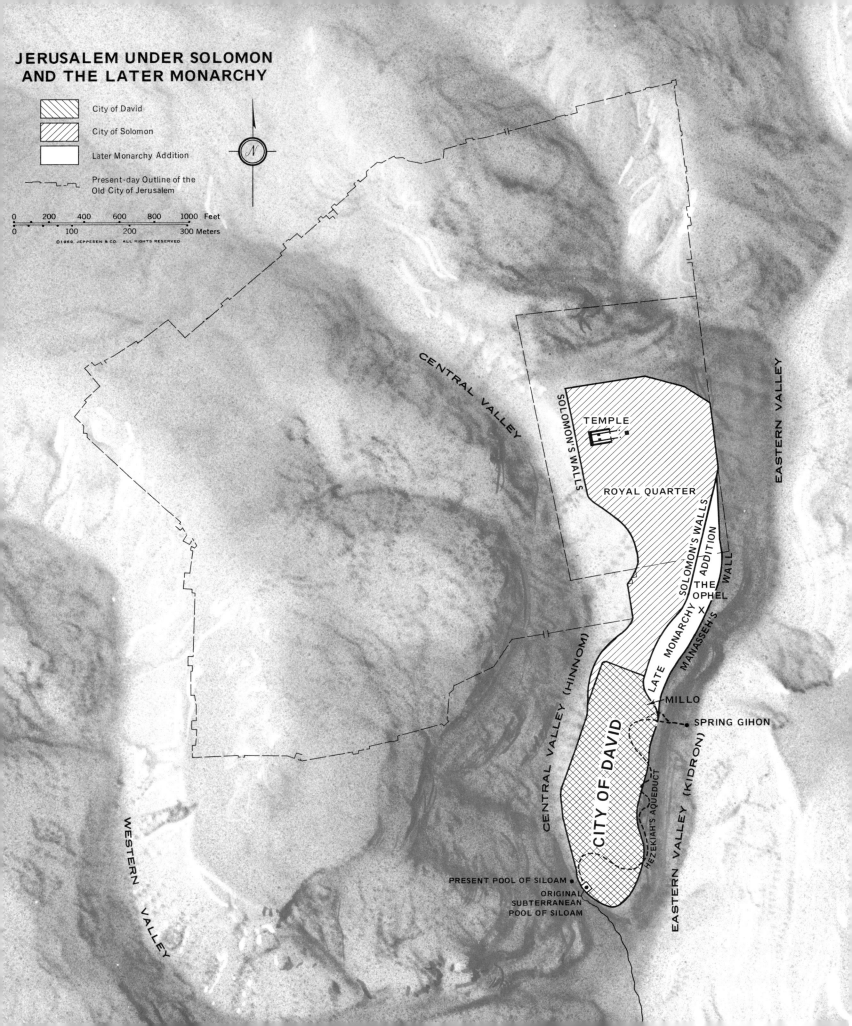

# JERUSALEM UNDER SOLOMON AND THE LATER MONARCHY

City of David
City of Solomon
Later Monarchy Addition
Present-day Outline of the Old City of Jerusalem

0   200   400   600   800   1000 Feet
0      100      200      300 Meters

©1968, JEPPESEN & CO. ALL RIGHTS RESERVED.

N

CENTRAL VALLEY

EASTERN VALLEY

SOLOMON'S WALLS

TEMPLE

ROYAL QUARTER

SOLOMON'S WALLS

LATE MONARCHY ADDITION

THE OPHEL
X

MANASSEH'S WALL

MILLO

SPRING GIHON

CENTRAL VALLEY (HINNOM)

CITY OF DAVID

HEZEKIAH'S AQUEDUCT

EASTERN VALLEY (KIDRON)

WESTERN VALLEY

PRESENT POOL OF SILOAM
ORIGINAL SUBTERRANEAN POOL OF SILOAM

A city quarter first referred to in the latter part of the seventh century B.C. during the reign of Josiah (II Kings 22:14; II Chron. 34:22; Zeph. 1:10) is the Mishneh ("Second Quarter," i.e., "annex" or "suburb"). Although no lo-cation is given, an identification with the newly incorporated Ophel district finds support in the fact that the Mish-neh was the home of Huldah, the prophetess, wife of Shallum, keeper of the (presumably priestly or High Priestly) wardrobe, and that the Ophel was the traditional living quarter of the temple servants (Neh. 3:26; 11:21). There is at least no evidence that the Mishneh was located anywhere but on the eastern ridge.

## Map 32

# JERUSALEM IN THE POST-EXILIC AND HASMONEAN PERIOD

For nearly a century and a half after Nebuchadnezzar's destruction of Jeru-salem, the city walls lay derelict. Al-though there is biblical evidence that there was an earlier rebuilding of the temple, it was Nehemiah who rebuilt the walls—and described the problems that he faced (Neh. 2:12–15; 3:1–32; 12:31, 37–39). In most cases, the old walls were merely rebuilt, but on the east slope this was impossible. Nehe-miah says, apparently of this area, "there was no place for the beast that was under me to pass," and this de-scription fits most vividly the utter de-struction discovered by the excavators on the slopes above the spring. On such an unstable base no wall could be founded; as a result the wall of Nehemiah retreated to the crest of the hill. The latest expedition has discov-ered a short length of his wall,[1] and it is probable that all the stretches of wall on the eastern crest of the south-east hill, discovered by earlier excava-tors, had their origin at this time.[2] This new line, moreover, can probably find literary support in Nehemiah's descrip-tion, which appears to presuppose two re-entrant angles in the east wall (Neh. 3:19–25), the southernmost where the wall ascends from its old line to the crest, the second—north of the place where the wall has recently been found —to the east.[3] The latter would be required if the wall were to enclose the Ophel (Neh. 3:26–27), and it is probable that it made a junction with the earlier wall of Manasseh. The wall discovered by Warren a century ago and called the Ophel Wall[4] can only suggest the line followed by Nehemiah's and later walls in this area.

For a century and a half after the time of Nehemiah we have little liter-ary or archaeological evidence bearing on the history of Judah or of its cap-ital, Jerusalem. It was probably, for the city, a period of gradual economic im-provement and increase of population, but there was no need for drastic change or expansion. It was but a small city in a far-off province of the great Persian empire. Even the meteoric ca-reer of Alexander the Great and, after his death, the struggles between the successor kingdoms ruled by his gen-erals brought little change. Culturally, it was another matter, for there grew up, against the orthodox Jewish party, another group who welcomed the new ways and the new thinking favored by their Greek rulers. The struggle be-tween these two groups came to a head soon after Antiochus Epiphanes came to the throne of Syria in 175 B.C.[5]

---

[1] Kenyon, *PEQ*, 1963, pp. 15–16.

[2] Simons, *op. cit.*, pp. 68 ff.

[3] M. Avi-Yonah, "The Walls of Nehemiah," *Israel Exploration Journal,* vol. 4 (1954), pp. 246 f.

[4] Simons, pp. 138 ff.

[5] For the period between 175 B.C. and the accession of John Hyrcanus in 134 B.C., our prime source is the book of I Maccabees. For the later period, down to the fall of Jerusalem in A.D. 70, we are dependent on Josephus, *The Jewish War* and *Antiquities of the Jews* (hereafter cited as *War* and *Antiq.* respectively). References to I Maccabees are based on the American Translation. Josephus is quoted from the Loeb Classical Library edition, translated by H. St. J. Thackeray and Ralph Marcus, vol. II–IX (London: William Heinemann Ltd., 1927–65).

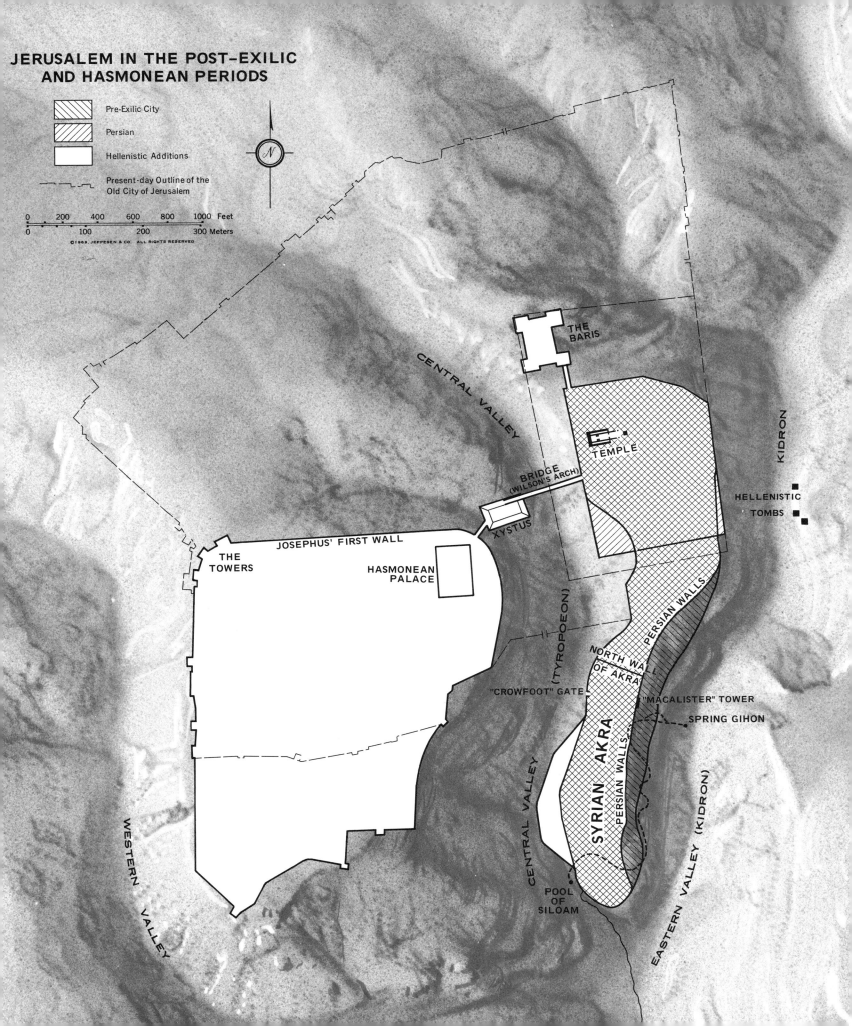

# JERUSALEM IN THE POST-EXILIC AND HASMONEAN PERIODS

Pre-Exilic City

Persian

Hellenistic Additions

Present-day Outline of the Old City of Jerusalem

0   200   400   600   800   1000 Feet
0      100      200      300 Meters

© 1969, JEPPESEN & CO.  ALL RIGHTS RESERVED

N

THE BARIS

CENTRAL VALLEY

KIDRON

TEMPLE

BRIDGE (WILSON'S ARCH)

HELLENISTIC TOMBS

XYSTUS

JOSEPHUS' FIRST WALL

THE TOWERS

HASMONEAN PALACE

PERSIAN WALLS

NORTH WALL OF AKRA

"CROWFOOT" GATE

CENTRAL VALLEY (TYROPOEON)

"MACALISTER" TOWER

SPRING GIHON

SYRIAN AKRA

PERSIAN WALLS

WESTERN VALLEY

POOL OF SILOAM

EASTERN VALLEY (KIDRON)

Antiochus entered Jerusalem at the end of 168 B.C., defiled and pillaged the temple, and plundered the city and set fire to it. To maintain his control, he fortified the City of David, the southeast hill, with a great wall and strong towers. This Syrian citadel (Akra) "became a great threat, and it proved a place of ambush against the sanctuary" (I Macc. 1:33–36; 2:31, etc.). It is possible that a portion of the Syrian Akra's northern wall has been discovered where it overlies the earlier north wall of the Jebusite and Davidic city. The wall is over 4 m. (13 ft.) thick and faces north. It is built of heavy stone rubble with a facing of cut blocks laid as headers—a structural characteristic of the Hellenistic period.[6] Although direct stratigraphic evidence for its dating is almost entirely lacking, no period of earlier or later defensive works better fits its construction than the one here suggested.[7]

Antiochus also proscribed the Jewish religion, an act which led directly to the Maccabean revolt under Judas and his brothers Jonathan and Simon. Even to purify the temple and, finally, to fortify it (I Macc. 4:36–43, 60–61) "as it was formerly" (6:7), Judas had to contain the Syrian troops and his Jewish opponents in the citadel with his troops. These temple walls and its stronghold (the predecessor of Herod's Antonia) were soon demolished by the Syrian general Lysias. Jonathan was permitted to refortify the temple mount (10:7–11) and, later, constructed a great mound between the citadel and the city, which was apparently intended to cut off the citadel, ritually, from the temple area but also served as a siege wall against it (12:36; 13:21, 49–52). The citadel, however, held out until 141 B.C., when it finally capitulated to Simon. Henceforth it was a Jewish fortress (13:52; 14:36–37; 15:28).[8] Other defensive works, in some cases initiated by Jonathan but finished by Simon (13:10), are described in I Macc. 12:35 ff. The new wall built to replace that by the ravine (the Kidron) which had collapsed (12:37) possibly included the rectangular tower discovered by Macalister and thought by him to be Jebusite and Davidic but now known to be Maccabean[9] as well as parts of the wall found along the eastern crest.[10] The so-called "Crowfoot" Gate in the west wall[11] was in use, if not built, in this period. The evidence is strong that Jerusalem was still confined, at this period, to its old site on the southeast hill and the temple mount.

Antiochus VII invaded Judah in 134 B.C., besieged Jerusalem, and, in spite of John Hyrcanus' capitulation, destroyed its fortifications once more.[12] After Antiochus' death in 129 B.C., however, Hyrcanus and his successors, Aristobulus and Alexander Jannaeus, took advantage of the political confusion and weakness of Syria and Egypt to extend Judah's boundaries to a reach not attained since the time of David, and established themselves as kings. Such new wealth and prosperity provided the conditions for the expansion and beautification of their capital but, strangely, the details of their work have not been preserved for us. We are merely told that John built the city's walls (I Macc. 16:23) and that he constructed the fortress (Baris) at the northwest corner of the temple which was later to be rebuilt by Herod the Great and called the Antonia.[13]

The first reference to the inclusion of part of the southwest hill within the walls of Jerusalem is found in Josephus' accounts of Pompey's attack in 63 B.C.[14] Pompey was admitted by one party into the "city," but, because the bridge joining it to the temple was broken down, he was forced to attack the temple from the north. The bridge, probably on the line of the viaduct across the central valley marked today by "Wilson's Arch,"[15] reached from the temple precincts to the "Xystus," a gymnasium in the valley, which was overlooked by the temple on the east (II Macc. 4:9–15) and by the palace of the Hasmoneans on the southwest hill.[16] Only in one passage does Josephus apparently state that a wall (his First Wall) crossed the central valley at

---

[6] See Kenyon, *PEQ*, 1963, plate IX A.

[7] See also Willis A. Shotwell, "The Problem of the Syrian Akra," *Bulletin of the American Schools of Oriental Research*, vol. 176 (Dec., 1964), pp. 10 ff.

[8] Josephus' statements (*Antiq.* XIII, 215 ff.; *War* V, 138–39) that Simon destroyed the citadel and that the population spent three years, working day and night, to lower the hill on which it stood that it might no longer be higher than the temple mount appear to be controverted by the preservation of the Jebusite north wall and subsequent structures in the same area. (See also *War* V, 253; VI, 355.)

[9] Kenyon, *PEQ*, 1962, pp. 76 ff.

[10] Simons, pp. 68 ff.

[11] *Ibid.*, pp. 88 ff.

[12] *Antiq.* XIII, 247.

[13] *Antiq.* XVIII, 91–92.

[14] *War* I, 141 ff.; *Antiq.* XIV, 57 ff.

[15] Simons, pp. 364 ff. "Wilson's Arch" is bonded into the Herodian west wall of the temple enclosure. The earlier bridge, while probably following the same course, probably started farther to the east.

[16] *War* II, 344; *Antiq.* XX, 189–90.

this point.[17] All other passages assume that the bridge was the only link (except, of course, for the later Second and Third Walls) between the two parts of the city right down to the destruction of the city by Titus (e.g., the towers at either end of it built by Simon and John,[18] and no certain trace of a wall on this line has ever been discovered.[19]

The new suburb on the southwest hill had its own circumvallation in addition to its natural defenses.[20] The north wall ran parallel to the cross-valley from the Xystus to the towers which guarded the neck of land joining the southwest hill to the northwest (discovered by Johns inside the present Citadel[21]). This is Josephus' First or Old Wall.[22] The west wall was also found by Johns and has probably been identified in the latest excavations;[23] this

too appears to be Maccabean. The southern and southeastern extent is not so easily established. The present south wall on the western hill can hardly be said to be protected by a valley.[24] Although definite evidence is lacking, it is probably best to assume that the line is marked by the scarp around the southern crest discovered by Maudslay and Bliss[25] projected to the northeast to follow the crest which still delimits the Jewish quarter of the city on the east and south. It could not have extended farther towards the southeast, for, outside this line, soundings have produced no evidence of occupation before the time of Herod Agrippa (A.D. 40–44[26]), while tombs of the Hasmonean period—which must have been outside the walls—have been found.[27] The east wall presumably followed the

crest above the Tyropoeon (Josephus' name for the central valley) to join the north wall near the palace of the Hasmoneans.

It seems highly probable, therefore, that the southwest hill was included within the defenses of Jerusalem first in the Maccabean period. To be more precise, the reigns of John Hyrcanus and his immediate successors provide the most likely occasion for such an extension, for it was at this time that Jerusalem, as the capital of a prosperous and confident state, would increase in population and would require the additional space, while the pride and wealth resulting from the new independence and expansion of territory would provide the incentive and means.

---

[17] *War* V, 144.

[18] *War* IV, 580–81; VI, 191, 377.

[19] Simons, pp. 255–56.

[20] *War* VI, 374.

[21] Simons, p. 267 ff.

[22] He says (*War* V, 142 ff.) that it dates from the time of David, Solomon, and their successors. This anachronistic statement is a result of his view—also wrong—that David's city was on the southwest hill (*Ibid.*, 137 ff.).

[23] Kenyon, *PEQ*, 1968, pp. 110–11.

[24] *Antiq.* XV, 410.

[25] Simons, pp. 257–58, 260.

[26] Kenyon, *PEQ*, 1962, pp. 84 ff.

[27] Simons, p. 274.

## Map 33

# JERUSALEM FROM HEROD THE GREAT TO THE CRUCIFIXION

Josephus devotes a great deal of space to the description of Herod the Great's building enterprises in Jerusalem. There is no new evidence bearing on the location of his theater, amphitheater, hippodrome, and other structures typical of a Hellenized city. But the recent excavations, if the discoveries are correctly interpreted, do provide some clues as to his wall-building and the construction of the great temple platform.

Josephus refers to a Second Wall in his description of the city as it was before the siege of Titus in A.D. 70. His First Wall is, of course, the north wall of the new quarter on the southwest hill, which has been described above. The Second Wall ran from the Gate Gennath in this wall to the fortress Antonia at the northwest corner of the temple and enclosed only a northern district[1]—including, obviously, the northern part of the central valley. This consisted, in part at least, of a market,[2] probably the Lower Market to distinguish it from the Upper Market on the western hill.[3] This Second Wall was probably built by Herod the Great, for it is not known before his time,[4] it assumes the existence of the Antonia fortress, and it must precede the Third Wall built by Herod Agrippa in A.D. 40–44. Its course is uncertain, but recent excavations at the point marked X on the plan have provided some evidence. Here a deep fill, dating from the time of Hadrian's rebuilding of the city in A.D. 135, extended down almost to the scarped bedrock.[5] The site, therefore, apparently lies in the cross-valley which, at this point, had been kept clear as a fosse against the First North Wall and/or the west face of the north-

south stretch of the Second Wall even after the construction of the Third Wall (see below). The Gate Gennath in the First North Wall, from which the Second Wall took its departure, must, therefore, lie east of this point. Assuming that the wall followed the most strategic line possible, it has been drawn on the plan following more or less the present street lines. While the exact course is hypothetical, there is no doubt that it excluded the traditional sites of Calvary and the Tomb of Jesus, now marked by the Church of the Holy Sepulcher. The archaeological evidence does not, of course, prove that these sites are the correct ones; it does, however, contradict any argument against their authenticity based on archaeology.

This was the first wall, to our knowledge, to join the new quarter on the southwest hill to the older part of the city, for there is no evidence that Josephus' First Wall crossed the central valley. But the construction of this wall on the north assumes that Herod also built a wall across the central valley farther south. This was probably a continuation, more or less directly eastward across the valley, of the Hasmonean south wall of the western hill to meet the old west wall of the eastern hill. South and east of the point of junction, Herod quarried away the rock,[6] presumably to obtain building material for the temple extensions, and destroyed, in the process, nearly all evidence of earlier occupation in this area.

The central valley, enclosed between the two new walls, was crossed by a bridge which replaced the earlier one and was supported, in part, by "Wilson's Arch."[7] Another bridge, or

---

[1] Josephus, *The Jewish War* V, 146.

[2] *Ibid.*, 331 ff.

[3] *Ibid.*, 137.

[4] There is no record of its existence in the accounts of the attacks on the city by Pompey (Josephus, *War* I, 141 ff.; *Antiquities of the Jews* XIV, 57 ff.) or Herod the Great (*War* I, 295 ff., 343 ff.; *Antiq.* XIV, 399 ff., 465 ff.).

[5] Kenyon, *PEQ,* 1964, p. 16.

[6] Kenyon, *PEQ,* 1968, pp. 101–02.

[7] *War* II, 344; VI, 325; etc.; Simons, *op. cit.,* pp. 365 ff.; William F. Stinespring, in *Biblical Archaeologist,* vol. 29 (1966), no. 1, and vol. 30 (1967), no. 1.

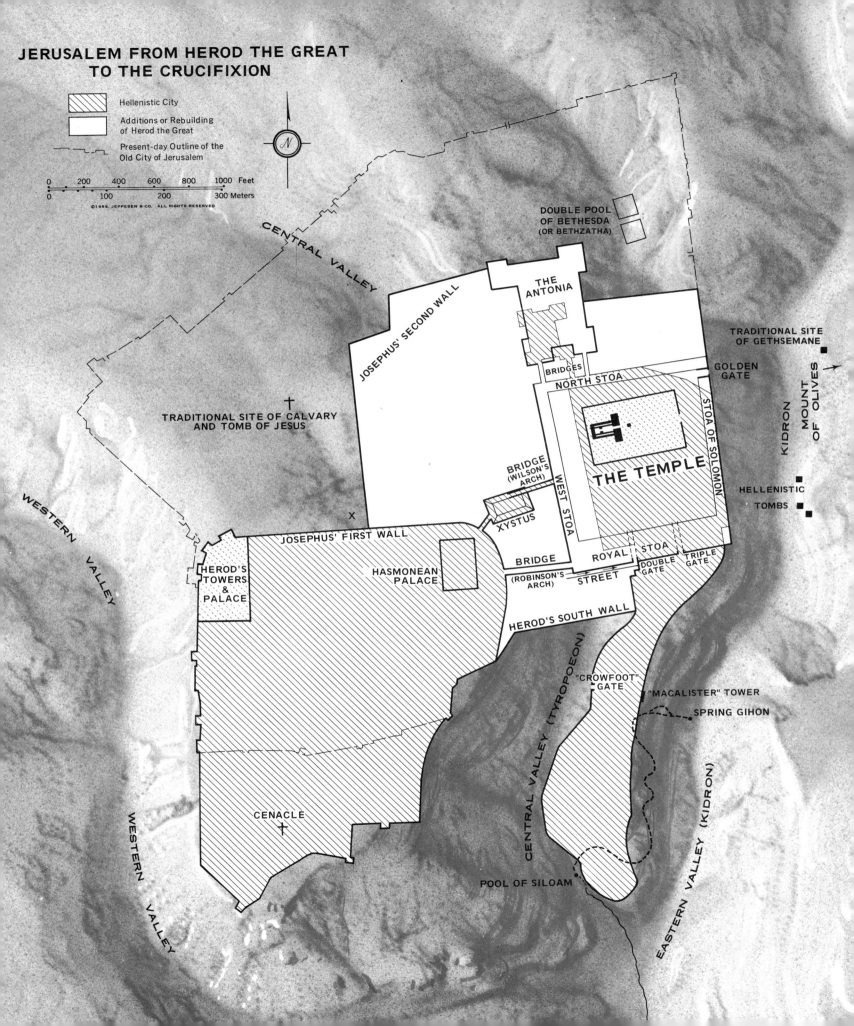

# JERUSALEM FROM HEROD THE GREAT TO THE CRUCIFIXION

Hellenistic City

Additions or Rebuilding of Herod the Great

Present-day Outline of the Old City of Jerusalem

| 0 | 200 | 400 | 600 | 800 | 1000 Feet |
| 0 | 100 | | 200 | | 300 Meters |

©1965, JEPPESEN & CO. ALL RIGHTS RESERVED

N

CENTRAL VALLEY

DOUBLE POOL OF BETHESDA (OR BETHZATHA)

THE ANTONIA

JOSEPHUS' SECOND WALL

BRIDGES

NORTH STOA

GOLDEN GATE

TRADITIONAL SITE OF GETHSEMANE

TRADITIONAL SITE OF CALVARY AND TOMB OF JESUS

STOA OF SOLOMON

THE TEMPLE

KIDRON

MOUNT OF OLIVES

HELLENISTIC TOMBS

BRIDGE (WILSON'S ARCH)

WEST STOA

XYSTUS

JOSEPHUS' FIRST WALL

HASMONEAN PALACE

HEROD'S TOWERS & PALACE

BRIDGE (ROBINSON'S ARCH)

ROYAL STOA

STREET

DOUBLE GATE

TRIPLE GATE

HEROD'S SOUTH WALL

WESTERN VALLEY

"CROWFOOT" GATE

"MACALISTER" TOWER

SPRING GIHON

CENTRAL VALLEY (TYROPOEON)

CENACLE

WESTERN VALLEY

POOL OF SILOAM

EASTERN VALLEY (KIDRON)

stepped viaduct, apparently crossed the valley further south and is today marked by "Robinson's Arch."[8]

Northwest of the temple, Herod rebuilt the fortress (Baris) first constructed by John Hyrcanus and gave it the name Antonia.[9] No new information on its plan or relationship to the temple proper is available. The reconstruction here proposed assumes that the walled temple was protected on the north—and separated from the Antonia—by the northern cross-valley and its continuance to the west by an artificial ditch. This assumption, in turn, requires that the northern end of the western wall of the Haram, which is offset 2.5 m. (8.2 ft.) to the west of the southern stretch, be interpreted as actually forming part of the west wall of the Antonia. Other features are based on the data assembled and used by Vincent.[10] The Antonia is one of the two possible locations for the trial of Jesus before Pilate.

Herod's rebuilding of the temple included the extension and beautification of its surrounding courts. It seems unlikely that his great platform included any major expansion to the north, for here was the natural boundary of the cross-valley. An extension to the southeast is demonstrated by the clean break in the masonry of the east Haram wall about 32 m. (105 ft.) north of the southeast corner and the existence of Warren's "Master Course,"[11] which runs from this point around the corner to the Double Gate (and includes the Triple Gate). It seems probable, also, that only under Herod was the platform extended to its present line on the west and southwest. Of the gates giving access to this platform, the Double Gate and the Triple Gate (with their associated ascending ramps) appear to be the best attested. Access to the former from the west was provided by an ascending street that flanked the south wall of the enclosure,[12] while visitors from the south and east could apparently enter through the latter.

The buildings which this great platform supported—the temple itself, the porticoes, parapets, and defensive walls —are only suggested in the plan, for no new evidence is at hand.

At the northwest corner of the western hill, Herod built the three great towers of Hippicus, Phasael, and Mariamne to replace the earlier structures of Maccabean times.[13] The base of one of these (probably Hippicus) is still preserved in the modern Citadel as the traditional "Tower of David." Excavations inside the Citadel have revealed traces of the other two towers and their connecting curtain walls.[14] To the south of these towers Herod built a magnificent new palace,[15] which according to some interpreters was the place where Jesus' trial before Pilate took place. Excavations some 250 m. (820 ft.) south of the Citadel have revealed no trace of this palace; it is probable, then, that it occupied a site farther north, roughly under the present Police Barracks.

If the south wall of Herod's city coincided with the proposed Maccabean line on the western ridge, it is possible to accept the authenticity of traditional sites in this area which are associated with events immediately preceding the Crucifixion or connected with the very early church: the Palace of the High Priest, Caiaphas, and the "Mother-Church" of Christendom, i.e., the house where the disciples were assembled at Pentecost (Acts 2:1–4), or, even earlier, for the Last Supper, now marked by the Cenacle. But without unambiguous dating evidence for this wall line, there can be no certainty.

[8] *Antiq.* XV, 410; Simons, pp. 362 ff.

[9] *War* I, 401; *Antiq.* XVIII, 91–92.

[10] Simons, pp. 374 ff.

[11] *Ibid.,* p. 357, figs. 48 and 50, and plate XXVI. 1.

[12] Kenyon, *PEQ,* 1962, pp. 88–89, plate XXV A.

[13] *War* V, 161 ff.

[14] Simons, pp. 265 ff.

[15] *War* V, 176 ff.

## Map 34

### JERUSALEM FROM THE CRUCIFIXION TO ITS DESTRUCTION IN A.D. 70

Jerusalem reached its greatest extent in the years immediately preceding the Jewish revolt which led to the city's partial destruction by the Romans under Titus in A.D. 70. Herod Agrippa (A.D. 40–44) was responsible for a new wall-building program, which has been proved by archaeological investigation to have been even more extensive than Josephus had led us to believe. This author describes how a new wall, outside the First and Second Walls, enclosed a large northern quarter including Bezetha, the hill north of the temple, and a district on the northwest hill.[1] The northern stretch of this Third Wall can now with certainty be identified with the present north wall of the city,[2] and it is probable that its returns to the older line of circumvallation—on the west to the tower of Hippicus,[3] and on the east along the Kidron Valley—followed very closely the lines of the present wall.

The city of Herod Agrippa also enclosed a large new area to the south, a fact not referred to specifically by Josephus—perhaps because he was particularly interested in the northern defenses against which the Romans made their most determined efforts. The evidence of the recent excavations demonstrates that the system of walls discovered more than seventy years ago running across the mouth of the central valley below the Pool of Siloam must be attributed to him. If so, it is possible that the pool itself—open to the sky as it still is—had for a long time remained outside the defenses of the city. It had long ceased to be all-important to its survival, for cisterns and an aqueduct provided the city with all the water it needed.

---

[1] Josephus, *The Jewish War* V, 147 ff.; Simons, *op. cit.,* pp. 491 ff.; Kenyon, *PEQ,* 1967, p. 69; E. W. Hamrick, "New Excavations at Sukenik's 'Third Wall,' " *Bulletin of the American Schools of Oriental Research,* vol. 183 (Oct. 1966), p. 19 ff., and "Further Notes on 'Third Wall,' " *ibid.,* vol. 192 (Dec. 1968), pp. 21 ff. The identification of Agrippa's wall with another line some 450 m. (1,476 ft.) farther north (the "Robinson-Sukenik Wall") must be abandoned. It does not fit Josephus' description, and excavation has proved it to be later than the time of Agrippa; its purpose and date, however, remain unclear.

[2] This western section must have enclosed the area of excavation marked X on the map. The presence here of a fill dating from A.D. 135 (*PEQ* 1964, p. 16) can only mean that the fosse outside the First North Wall was kept clear even after the Second and Third Walls were built. This assumption gains strength from the fact that Titus took the Third and Second Walls with relative ease but was forced to raise a siege wall outside the First Wall—in spite of which it withstood his attacks for four months.

[3] Simons, pp. 256 ff.; Kenyon, *PEQ,* 1962, pp. 84 ff.

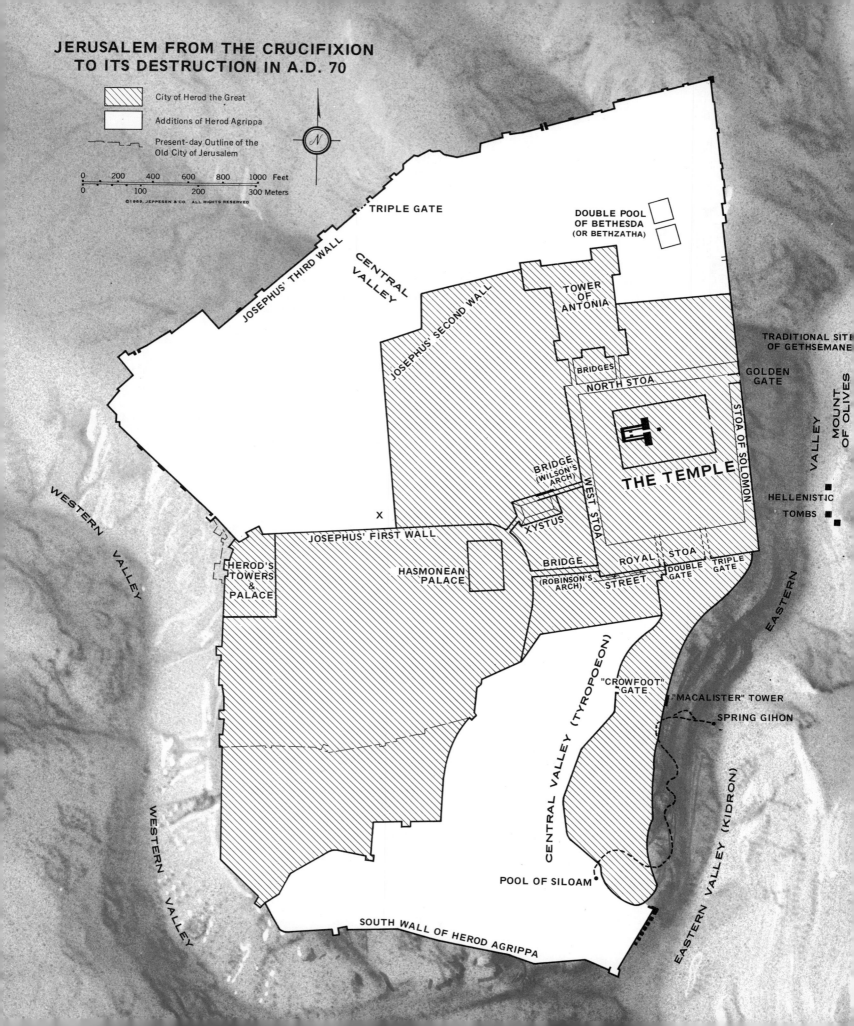

# JERUSALEM FROM THE CRUCIFIXION TO ITS DESTRUCTION IN A.D. 70

City of Herod the Great

Additions of Herod Agrippa

Present-day Outline of the Old City of Jerusalem

N

0  200  400  600  800  1000 Feet
0    100    200    300 Meters
©1969, JEPPESEN & CO.  ALL RIGHTS RESERVED

TRIPLE GATE

DOUBLE POOL OF BETHESDA (OR BETHZATHA)

CENTRAL VALLEY

JOSEPHUS' THIRD WALL

JOSEPHUS' SECOND WALL

TOWER OF ANTONIA

TRADITIONAL SITE OF GETHSEMANE

BRIDGES

NORTH STOA

GOLDEN GATE

VALLEY

MOUNT OF OLIVES

BRIDGE (WILSON'S ARCH)

WEST STOA

STOA OF SOLOMON

THE TEMPLE

HELLENISTIC TOMBS

X

XYSTUS

JOSEPHUS' FIRST WALL

HEROD'S TOWERS & PALACE

HASMONEAN PALACE

BRIDGE (ROBINSON'S ARCH)

ROYAL STOA

STREET

DOUBLE GATE

TRIPLE GATE

WESTERN VALLEY

EASTERN VALLEY

CENTRAL VALLEY (TYROPOEON)

"CROWFOOT" GATE

"MACALISTER" TOWER

SPRING GIHON

WESTERN VALLEY

POOL OF SILOAM

EASTERN VALLEY (KIDRON)

SOUTH WALL OF HEROD AGRIPPA

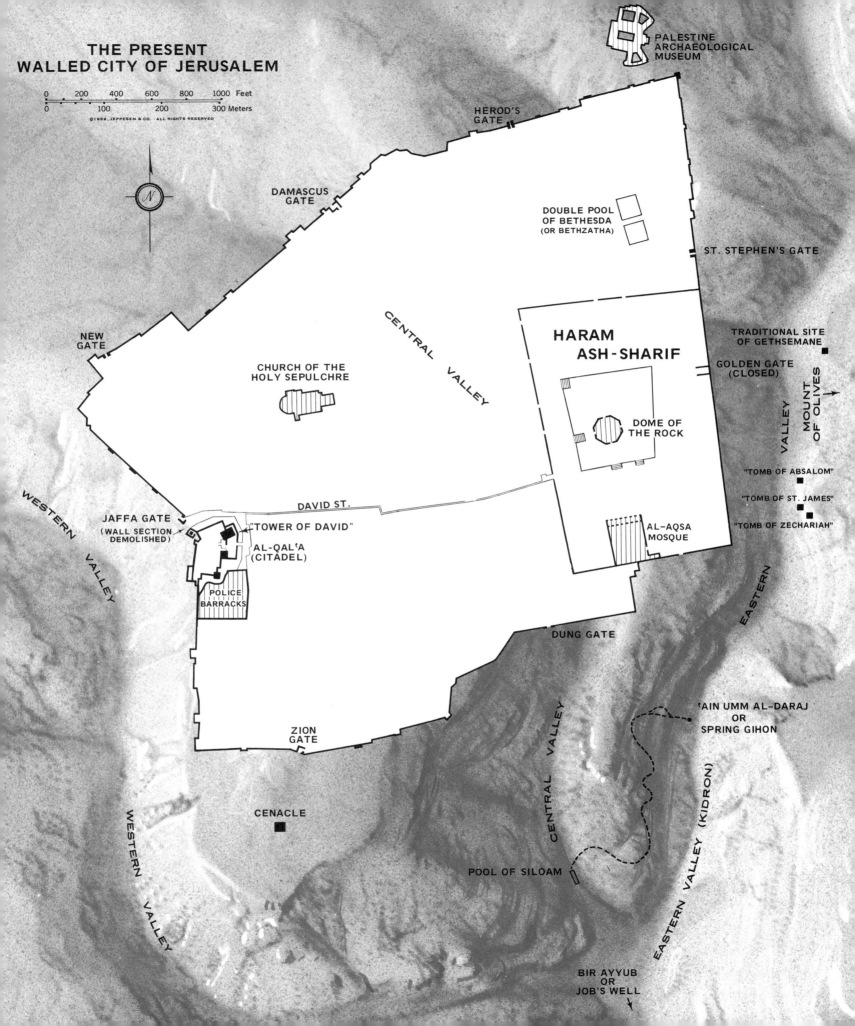

# THE PRESENT WALLED CITY OF JERUSALEM

0 200 400 600 800 1000 Feet
0 100 200 300 Meters
©1969. JEPPESEN & CO. ALL RIGHTS RESERVED

*N*

PALESTINE ARCHAEOLOGICAL MUSEUM

HEROD'S GATE

DAMASCUS GATE

DOUBLE POOL OF BETHESDA (OR BETHZATHA)

ST. STEPHEN'S GATE

NEW GATE

CENTRAL VALLEY

CHURCH OF THE HOLY SEPULCHRE

HARAM ASH-SHARIF

TRADITIONAL SITE OF GETHSEMANE

GOLDEN GATE (CLOSED)

MOUNT OF OLIVES

DOME OF THE ROCK

"TOMB OF ABSALOM"

"TOMB OF ST. JAMES"

DAVID ST.

JAFFA GATE (WALL SECTION DEMOLISHED)

"TOWER OF DAVID"

AL-QAL'A (CITADEL)

AL-AQSA MOSQUE

"TOMB OF ZECHARIAH"

EASTERN VALLEY (KIDRON)

POLICE BARRACKS

WESTERN VALLEY

DUNG GATE

ZION GATE

CENTRAL VALLEY

'AIN UMM AL-DARAJ OR SPRING GIHON

CENACLE

WESTERN VALLEY

POOL OF SILOAM

BIR AYYUB OR JOB'S WELL

# Map 35

# THE PRESENT
# WALLED CITY
# OF
# JERUSALEM

Jerusalem suffered again from the siege and destruction which followed the Second Jewish Revolt in A.D. 132–35. Then, in A.D. 135, the Emperor Hadrian rebuilt the city as a Roman colony with the new name of Aelia Capitolina to stamp out all emotional and political connections with its Jewish past. The new city had as its northern, eastern, and western lines the wall established by Herod Agrippa and his predecessors, but its old extension to the south was sharply curtailed. The south wall appears to have coincided almost exactly with the present south wall of the Old City, thus excluding the southern part of the southwest hill and, even more noteworthy, the whole of the southeast hill—the ancient City of David. In this area, the salient from the south wall of the Haram, which had marked the line of the west wall of this hill since the time of Solomon, now—with the destruction of the old east wall—became the southernmost portion of the east wall of the city.[1]

Jerusalem's history and the history of its walls and chief buildings did not, of course, end with Hadrian. At times, it expanded again—particularly in the prosperous Byzantine period—to include once more the southeast and southwest hills. But, since the final reconstruction of its walls by Sultan Suleiman the Magnificent in the sixteenth century, its limits have been those established by Hadrian. Over the last century, the city has expanded greatly, particularly in large extramural suburbs to the north and west. Although these now contain the bulk of the population and most of the city's amenities, there is no doubt that the walled Old City, with its nearly four thousand years of history, remains its heart and soul.

[1] Kenyon, *PEQ*, 1967, pp. 69–70; 1968, p. 102.

# PRINCIPLE MATERIALS CONSULTED IN THE PREPARATION OF THE MAPS

## GENERAL

### 1. Atlases

Aharoni, Yohanan, and Michael Avi-Yonah. *The Macmillan Bible Atlas.* New York: Macmillan Co., 1968.

*Atlas of the Arab World and the Middle East.* Intro. by C. F. Beckingham. New York: Macmillan Co., 1960.

*Atlas Climatique du Liban.* Beirut: Service Météorologique du Liban, with l'Observatoire de Ksara, 1966.

*Atlas of Israel.* In Hebrew. Jerusalem: Department of Surveys, Ministry of Labour, and the Bialik Institute, Jewish Agency, 1956.

*Atlas Mira* [Great Soviet World Atlas]. Moscow: Chief Administration of Geodesy and Cartography, Ministry of the Interior, 1954.

Beek, Martin A. *Atlas of Mesopotamia.* New York: Thomas Nelson and Sons, 1962.

*Climatological Atlas for Iraq.* Baghdad: Republic of Iraq, Ministry of Communications, no date.

*Edinburgh World Atlas.* 5th ed. Edinburgh: John Bartholomew, The Geographical Institute, 1966.

Grollenberg, Luc H. *Atlas of the Bible.* New York: Thomas Nelson and Sons, 1957.

————. *Shorter Atlas of the Bible.* New York: Thomas Nelson and Sons, 1961.

Kraeling, Emil G. *Rand McNally Bible Atlas.* Chicago: Rand McNally, 1956.

May, Herbert G., ed. *Oxford Bible Atlas.* New York: Oxford University Press, 1962.

*The Oxford Atlas.* London: Oxford University Press, 1951.

*Oxford Regional Economic Atlas: The Middle East and North Africa.* London: Oxford University Press, 1960.

*Physical-Geographical Atlas of the World.* Moscow: Chief Administration of Geodesy and Cartography, Academy of Sciences, 1964.

Shalash, ʿAli al-. *Rainfall Atlas of the Hashemite Kingdom of Jordan.* Amman: University of Jordan, 1964.

*The Times Atlas of the World.* Comprehensive ed. Boston: Houghton Mifflin Co., 1967.

### 2. Maps

*Arabian Peninsula.* 1:2,000,000. Compiled by the U.S. Geological Survey and the Arabian American Oil Co. Map I-270 B-2. Washington: U.S. Geological Survey, Department of the Interior, 1963.

*Archaeological Map of Iraq.* 1:1,000,000. Baghdad: Republic of Iraq, Directorate General of Antiquities, no date. Arabic ed., 1963.

*Archeological Map of the Hashemite Kingdom of the Jordan.* 1:250,000. 3 sheets. Department of Lands and Surveys of the Hashemite Kingdom of the Jordan, 1950.

*Bordure Orientale de la Méditerranée: Carte Lithologique.* 1:500,000. 2 sheets. Délégation Général au Levant de la France Combattante, Service des Travaux Publics, 1942.

*Carte Agricole du Liban.* 1:200,000. Prepared by Boulos F. Boulos. Beirut: Imprimerie Catholique, 1963.

*Carte Géologique Internationale de l'Afrique.* 1:5,000,000. Sheet no. 3. Prepared by Louis Dubertret. Paris: Association des Services Géologiques Africains, 1959.

*Carte Géologique du Liban.* 1:200,000. Prepared by Louis Dubertret. Lebanese Republic, Ministère des Travaux Publics, 1955.

*Carte Géologique: Liban, Syrie, et Bordure des Pays*

*Voisins.* 1:1,000,000. Prepared by Louis Dubertret. Paris: Muséum National de l'Histoire Naturelle, 1962.

*Carte Géologique du Moyen Orient.* 1:2,000,000. Prepared by Louis Dubertret. Service Géographique des F.F.L., 1942.

*Carte Pluviométrique du Liban.* 1:200,000. Prepared by J. Rey, S.J. Observatoire de Ksara, Lebanon, 1954.

*Europa: Vegetation Map.* 1:2,500,000. E. Ehlin and A. Soderlund. Stockholm: P. A. Norstedt & Soners Forlag, 1943.

*Geological Map of Iran.* 1:2,500,000. Teheran: National Iranian Oil Company, 1957.

*Geological Map of Jordan (East of the Rift Valley).* 1:250,000. 3 sheets. By A. Quennell. Amman: Government of the Hashemite Kingdom of the Jordan, 1959.

*Geological Map of Turkey.* 1:500,000. 18 sheets. Ankara: Institute of Mineral Research and Exploration, 1961.

*Geological Maps and Sections of South-West Persia.* London: British Petroleum Company, 1956.

*The Hashemite Kingdom of the Jordan.* 1:100,000. 15 sheets. In Arabic. Amman: Department of Lands and Surveys of the Hashemite Kingdom of the Jordan, 1951.

*The Hashemite Kingdom of the Jordan.* 1:250,000. 4 sheets. Amman: Department of Lands and Surveys of the Hashemite Kingdom of the Jordan, 1949.

*International Map of the World.* 1:1,000,000. GSGS 1301, etc. Revised Editions 1954–1963. Sheets E. 37, 38, 39, 40; F. 37, 38, 39, 40; G. 41; H. 37, 41; I. 41; J. 41. London: The War Office, 1954–63.

*Israel.* 1:100,000. 26 sheets. In Hebrew. Department of Surveys, Israel, 1962.

*Israel.* 1:250,000. 3 sheets. In Hebrew. Department of Surveys, Israel, 1951.

*Jet Navigation Charts.* 1:2,000,000. St. Louis: U.S. Aeronautical Chart and Information Center. Base revision dates 1963–1966.

*Landforms Map of the Near East.* 47 mi. per inch. Prepared for the Quartermaster General, U.S. Army. Boston: Irwin Raisz, 1951.

*Landforms Map of North Africa.* 1:4,500,000. Prepared for the Quartermaster General, U.S. Army. Boston: Irwin Raisz, 1952.

*Lands of the Bible Today.* 1:2,851,200. Washington, D.C.: National Geographic Society, 1956.

*Levant.* 1:200,000. 28 sheets. Paris: Institut Géographique National, 1949.

*Liban: Carte Touristique.* 1:100,000. Beirut. Direction des Affaires Géographiques, 1965.

*Middle East.* 1:4,000,000. Edinburgh: John Bartholomew, 1963.

*North-East Africa.* 1:4,000,000. Edinburgh: John Bartholomew, no date.

*Old Testament Palestine.* 1:500,000. Jerusalem: Department of Antiquities, Government of Palestine, n.d.

*Operational Navigation Charts.* 1:1,000,000. St. Louis: U.S. Aeronautical Chart and Information Center. Base revision dates 1963–1967.

*Palestine.* 1:100,000. 16 sheets. Jerusalem: Survey of Palestine, 1944.

*Pilotage Charts.* 1:500,000. St. Louis: U.S. Aeronautical Chart and Information Center. Base revision dates 1965, 1966.

*Roman Palestine.* 1:250,000. Jerusalem: Department of Antiquities, Government of Palestine, 1940.

*Syrie & Liban.* 1:1,000,000. Paris: Ministère des Travaux Publics et des Transports, 1945.

*Türkiye.* 1:800,000. 8 sheets. Ankara: Harita Umum Müdürlügü, 1956.

*Vegetation Map of Africa.* 1:10,000,000. Explanatory notes by R. W. J. Keay. Published for UNESCO. London: Oxford University Press, 1959.

*Vegetation Map of the U.S.S.R.* 1:4,000,000. Minsk: Jomarov Geobotanical Institute, 1955.

*The World.* 1:500,000. Sheets 322 C; 323–325 C, D; 338–342 A, B, C, D; 343 B, C; 424 B; 425 A; 426–429 A, B, C, D; 443–448 A, B, C, D; 543–544 A, B, C, D; 545 A, D; 546–547 A, B, C, D; 566 A, D; 567 A, B, C, D; 568 A, B; 669 B, C; 670 A, B, D; 686 A, B; 687 A, B, C, D; 789 B, C; 790 A, B, C, D; 791 A, D. London: War Office and Air Ministry, 1960–.

## 3. Books

Aharoni, Yohanan. *The Land of the Bible.* Translated by A. F. Rainey. Philadelphia: Westminster Press, 1967.

Baly, Denis. *Geographical Companion to the Bible.* New York: McGraw-Hill Book Co., 1963.

———. *The Geography of the Bible.* New York: Harper and Brothers, 1957.

Birot, Pierre, and Jean Dresch. *La Méditerranée et le Moyen-Orient.* Vol. 2, *La Méditerranée Orientale et le Moyen-Orient.* Paris: Presses Universitaires de France, 1955.

Cornfeld, Gaalyahu, ed. *Pictorial Biblical Encyclopedia.* New York: Macmillan Co., 1964.

Cressey, George B. *Crossroads: Land and Life in Southwest Asia.* Philadelphia: J. B. Lippincott Co., 1960.

Fisher, W. B. *The Middle East.* 5th ed. New York: E. P. Dutton, 1963.

George, Pierre. *U.R.S.S., Haute Asie–Iran.* Paris: Presses Universitaires de France, 1947.

Kopp, Clemens. *The Holy Places of the Gospels.* New York: Herder and Herder, 1963.

Noth, Martin. *The Old Testament World.* London: Black, 1966.

Pfeiffer, Charles F. *The Biblical World.* Grand Rapids, Mich.: Baker Book House, 1966.

———— and Howard F. Vos. *The Wycliffe Historical Geography of Bible Lands.* Chicago: Moody Press, 1967.

Simons, J. *The Geographical and Topographical Texts of the Old Testament.* Leiden: E. J. Brill, 1959.

## 4. Other Materials

Photographs. 2″ x 2″ color transparencies from Project Gemini and other space satellites. National Aeronautics and Space Administration, Washington, D.C.

## JERUSALEM

### 1. Maps

*Jerusalem.* Scale not indicated. Jerusalem: M. Gabrieli, 1967.

*Jerusalem: The Old City.* 1:2500. Originally compiled, drawn, and printed under the direction of F. J. Salmon, Commissioner for Lands and Surveys, Palestine, 1936. Revised from information supplied by the Department of Antiquities of Palestine, 1945; modified May 1947. Survey of Israel, 1954.

### 2. Books and Articles

Kenyon, Kathleen M. "Excavations in Jerusalem." *Palestine Exploration Quarterly,* 1962–1968.

Simons, J. *Jerusalem in the Old Testament.* Leiden: E. J. Brill, 1952.

Warren, Charles. *Plans, Elevations, Sections, etc. Shewing the Results of the Excavations at Jerusalem, 1867–70.* London: Palestine Exploration Fund, 1884.

———— and R. C. Conder. *Survey of Western Palestine: Jerusalem.* London: Palestine Exploration Fund, 1884.

# BASIC BIBLIOGRAPHY

This bibliography has been compiled with the help of the members of the Editorial Board, whose assistance in this matter is gratefully acknowledged. Atlases, biblical and other, are listed among the materials consulted in the preparation of the maps.

## 1. GENERAL MIDDLE EASTERN GEOGRAPHY AND ARCHAEOLOGY.

Birot, Pierre, and Jean Dresch. *La Méditerranée et le Moyen-Orient*. Vol. 2, *La Méditerranée Orientale et le Moyen-Orient*. Paris: Presses Universitaires de France, 1955.

Blanchard, Raoul. *Asie Occidentale*. Paris: Armand Colin, 1929.

Brice, William C. *South-West Asia: A Systematic Regional Geography*. London: University of London Press, 1966.

Cary, M., and E. H. Warmington. *The Ancient Explorers*. Baltimore: Penguin Books, 1963.

*Changes of Climate: Proceedings of the Rome Symposium Organized by UNESCO and the World Meteorological Organization*. Arid Zone Research. Paris: UNESCO, 1963.

Cornfeld, Gaalyahu. *Pictorial Biblical Encyclopedia*. Tel Aviv: Hamikra Baolam Publishing House; New York: Macmillan Co., 1964.

Cressey, George B. *Crossroads: Land and Life in Southwest Asia*. Philadelphia: J. B. Lipponcott Co., 1960.

Culican, William. *The First Merchant Venturers: The Ancient Levant in History and Commerce*. London: Thames and Hudson, 1966.

Fisher, W. B. *The Middle East: A Physical, Social, and Regional Geography*. 5th ed. New York: E. P. Dutton and Co., 1963.

Grant, Michael. *The Ancient Mediterranean*. London: Weidenfeld and Nicolson, 1969.

*Guides Bleus*. Paris: Librairie Hachette.
Baud, Marcelle, and Magdelaine Parisot, eds., *Egypte*. 1956.
Boulanger, Robert, ed. *Moyen-Orient*. 1956.
————. *Turquie*. 1965.

Hills, E. S., ed. *Arid Lands: A Geographical Appraisal*. Paris: UNESCO, 1966.

Longrigg, Stephen H. *The Middle East: A Social Geography*. Chicago: Aldine Publishing Co., 1963.

Meigs, Peveril. *Geography of Coastal Deserts*. Arid Zone Research, vol. 28. Paris: UNESCO, 1966.

Mongait, A. L. *Archaeology in the U.S.S.R.* Translated and adapted by M. W. Thompson. New York: Peter Smith, 1961.

Noth, Martin. *The Old Testament World*. New York: Fortress Press, 1965.

Pfeiffer, Charles F., and Howard F. Vos. *The Wycliffe Historical Geography of Bible Lands*. Chicago: Moody Press, 1967.

Phillips, E. D. *The Royal Hordes: Nomad Peoples of the Steppes*. London: Thames and Hudson, 1965.

Piggott, Stuart. *Prehistoric India*. New York: Barnes and Noble, 1950.

Pritchard, James B. *The Ancient Near East in Pictures Relating to the Old Testament*. Princeton: Princeton University Press, 1954.

————, ed. *Ancient Near Eastern Texts Relating to the Old Testament*. 2nd ed. Princeton: Princeton University Press, 1955.

Raikes, Robert. *Water, Weather and Prehistory*. London: John Baker, 1967.

Stamp, L. Dudley, ed. *A History of Land Use in Arid Regions.* Arid Zone Research, vol. 17. Paris: UNESCO, 1961.

Talbot Rice, Tamara. *The Scythians.* London: Thames and Hudson, 1957.

Thomas, D. Winton, ed. *Archaeology and Old Testament Study.* Oxford: At the Clarendon Press, 1967.

Walton, K. *The Arid Zones.* London: Hutchinson University Library, 1969.

## 2. THE ARABIAN PENINSULA.

*Aramco Handbook.* Dhahran, Saudi Arabia: Arabian American Oil Company, 1969.

Bell, Gertrude Lowthian. *Amurath to Amurath.* London: Heinemann, 1911.

———. *The Letters of Gertrude Bell.* Selected and edited by Lady Bell. 2 vols. New York: Boni and Liveright, 1927.

———. *Selected Letters of Gertrude Bell.* Selected by Lady Richmond from Lady Bell's Standard Edition. London: Penguin Books, 1953.

Blunt, Lady Anne. *A Pilgrim to Nejd.* 2 vols. 1881. Reprint, London: Cass and Co., 1968.

Burckhardt, J. L. *Travels in Arabia.* 1829. Reprint, London: Cass and Co., 1968.

Burton, Sir Richard F. *Personal Narrative of a Pilgrimage to Al-Madinah & Meccah.* London: G. Bell and Sons, 1906.

Dickson, Harold Richard Patrick. *The Arab of the Desert: A Glimpse into Badawin Life in Kuwait and Saʿudi Arabia.* 2nd ed. New York: Macmillan Co., 1951.

Doughty, Charles Montagu. *Travels in Arabia Deserta.* Cambridge: At the University Press, 1888.

———. *Travels in Arabia Deserta.* An Abridgement by Edward Garnett. Garden City, N.Y.: Doubleday and Co., 1955.

Ingrams, William Harold. *Arabia and the Isles.* London: John Murray, 1942.

Hansen, Thorkild. *Arabia Felix: The Danish Expedition of 1761–1767.* Trans. James and Kathleen McFarlane. New York: Harper and Row, 1964.

Meulen, Daniel van der. *Aden to the Hadhramaut: A Journey in Southern Arabia.* London: John Murray, 1947.

———. *The Wells of Ibn Saʿud.* New York: Frederick A. Praeger, 1957.

Musil, Alois. *The Northern Hegaz: A Topographical Itinerary.* New York: American Geographical Society, 1926.

———. *Northern Negd: A Topographical Itinerary.* New York: American Geographical Society, 1928.

Philby, H. St. John B. *Arabian Highlands.* Ithaca, N.Y.: Cornell University Press, for the Middle East Institute, 1952.

———. *The Empty Quarter.* New York: Henry Holt, 1933.

———. *Sheba's Daughters: Being a Record of Travel in Southern Arabia.* London: Methuen, 1939.

Rihani, Ameen F. *Arabian Peak and Desert.* Boston: Houghton Mifflin Co., 1930.

———. *Around the Coasts of Arabia.* Boston: Houghton Mifflin Co., 1930.

Scott, Hugh. *In the High Yemen.* London: John Murray, 1942.

Stark, Freya. *The Southern Gates of Arabia.* New York: E. P. Dutton and Co., 1936.

Thesiger, Wilfred. *Arabian Sands.* New York: Longmans, Green and Co., 1959.

Thomas, Bertram. *Arabia Felix: Across the "Empty Quarter."* New York: Charles Scribner's Sons, 1932.

Twitchell, K. S. *Saudi Arabia: With an Account of the Development of Its Natural Resources.* Princeton: Princeton University Press, 1958.

## 3. NORTH-EAST AFRICA

Aldred, Cyril. *The Egyptians.* New York: Frederick A. Praeger, 1961.

Barbour, Kenneth Michael. *The Republic of the Sudan: A Regional Geography.* New York: International Publications, 1961.

Emery, Walter B. *Archaic Egypt.* Baltimore: Penguin Books, 1961.

———. *Egypt in Nubia.* London: Hutchinson and Co., 1965.

Furon, Raymond. *Geology of Africa.* Translated by A. Hallam and L. A. Stevens. New York: Hafner, 1963.

Hurst, Harold Edwin. *The Nile: A General Account of the River and the Utilization of Its Waters.* Rev. ed. London: Constable and Co., 1957.

Kees, Hermann. *Ancient Egypt: A Cultural Topography.* Edited by T. G. H. James. London: Faber and Faber, 1961.

Luther, Ernest W. *Ethiopia Today.* Stanford: Stanford University Press, 1958.

Maurette, Fernand. *Afrique Equatoriale, Orientale et Australe.* Paris: Librairie Armand Colin, 1938.

Platt, Raye R., and Mohammad D. Hafny. *Egypt: A Compendium.* New York: The American Geographical Society, 1958.

Shinnie, P. L. *Meroe: A Civilization of the Sudan.* New York: Frederick A. Praeger, 1967.

Steindorff, George, and Keith C. Steele. *When Egypt Ruled the East.* Revised by Keith C. Steele. Chicago: University of Chicago Press, 1963.

Tregenza, L. A. *The Red Sea Mountains of Egypt.* Oxford: The University Press, 1955.

Wilson, John A. *The Culture of Ancient Egypt.* (Originally published as *The Burden of Egypt.* 1951.) Chicago: University of Chicago Press, 1956.

## 4. IRAN AND AFGHANISTAN.

Bartholomae, Christian. *Altiranisches Worterbuch.* 2 vols. 1904. Reprint, Berlin: W. de Gruyter, 1961.

Berghe, L. van den. *Archéologie de l'Iran Ancien.* Leiden: E. J. Brill, 1959.

British Naval Intelligence Division. *Persia.* Admiralty Handbook. London: His Majesty's Stationery Office, 1945.

Byron, Robert. *The Road to Oxiana.* 2nd ed. London: John Jehrman, 1950.

Cameron, George Glenn. *History of Early Iran.* Chicago: University of Chicago Press, 1936.

Christensen, Arthur Emanuel. *L'Iran sous les Sassanides.* Copenhagen: Levin and Munksgaard, 1944.

*Corpus Inscriptionum Iranicarum.* Edited by an international committee. London: P. Lund, Humphries, 1950–.

Curzon, George Nathaniel. *Persia and the Persian Question.* New York: Longmans, Green and Co., 1892.

Darmesteter, James, *Le Zendavesta: Traduction Nouvelle.* 1892–93. Reprint, Paris: Adrien-Maisonneuve, 1960.

Debevoise, Neilson Carel. *A Political History of Parthia.* Chicago: University of Chicago Press, 1938.

Fisher, W. B., ed. *The Land of Iran. The Cambridge History of Iran,* vol. 1. Cambridge: The University Press, 1968.

Fox, Ernest F. *Travels in Afghanistan, 1937–1938.* New York: Macmillan Co., 1943.

Frye, Richard N. *The Heritage of Persia.* Cleveland: The World Publishing Company, 1962.

———. *Iran.* New York: Holt, Rinehart and Winston, 1953.

George, Pierre. *U.S.S.R., Haute Asie, Iran.* Paris: Presses Universitaires de France, 1947.

Ghirshman, R. *Iran.* London: Penguin Books, 1954.

Kammenhuber, A. *Die Arier im Vorderen Orient.* Heidelberg: C. Winter Verlag, 1968.

Kent, R. *Old Persian: Grammar, Texts, Lexicon.* New Haven: American Oriental Society, 1953.

Markwart, Josef (originally Marquart). *The Provincial Capitals of Eranshahr.* Rome: Istituto Pontifico Biblico, 1931.

———. *Eransahr nach der Geographie des ps. Moses Xorenac'i.* Berlin: Weidmann, 1901.

Nawabi, Y. M. *A Bibliography of Iran.* Vol 1, *Ancient Iran.* Tehran, 1969.

Olmstead, A. T. *History of the Persian Empire.* Chicago: University of Chicago Press, 1948.

Schwarz, Paul. *Iran im Mittelalter nach den Arabischen Geographen.* 9 vols. Leipzig: O. Harrassowitz, 1929–1936.

Spiegel, Friedrich von. *Eranische Altertumskunde.* 3 vols. Leipzig: W. Engelmann, 1871–78.

Spuler, Bertold, ed. *Handbuch der Orientalistik, Iranistik.* Leiden: E. J. Brill, 1958.

Sykes, Sir Percy. *A History of Persia.* 3rd ed. Vol. 1. New York: St. Martin's Press, 1930.

Tolstov, Sergei Pavlovich, ed. *Narody Perednei Azii* [The Peoples of the Near East]. Moscow: Izdatelstvo Akademii Nauk, 1957.

Wilber, Donald H., ed. *Afghanistan.* New Haven: Human Relations Area Files, 1956.

## 5. JERUSALEM.

Avi-Yonah, M. "The Walls of Nehemiah," *Israel Exploration Journal* 4 (1954): 246 ff.

Avnimelech, M. "Influence of Geological Conditions on the Development of Jerusalem," *Bulletin of the American Schools of Oriental Research,* no. 181 (Feb. 1966), pp. 23 ff.

Bliss, F. J., and A. C. Dickie. *Excavations at Jerusalem, 1894–97.* London: Palestine Exploration Fund, 1898.

Crowfoot, J. W., and G. M. Fitzgerald. *Excavations in the Tyropoeon Valley, 1927.* Annual of the Palestine Exploration Fund, 5. London, 1929.

Hamilton, R. W. "Street Levels in the Tyropoeon Valley," *Quarterly of the Department of Antiquities of*

*Palestine,* 1:103 ff.; 2:34 ff.

—————. "Excavations Against the North Wall of Jerusalem, 1937–38," *Quarterly of the Department of Antiquities of Palestine,* 10:1 ff.

Jeremias, Joachim. *Jerusalem in the Time of Jesus: An Investigation into Economic and Social Conditions during the New Testament Period.* Philadelphia: Fortress Press, 1969.

Johns, C. N. "The Citadel, Jerusalem: A Summary of Work since 1935," *Quarterly of the Department of Antiquities of Palestine,* 14:121 ff.

Josephus, Flavius. *The Works of Flavius Josephus.* Loeb Classical Library Edition. Translated by H. St. J. Thackeray and Ralph Marcus. New York: G. P. Putnam, 1926–65.

Kenyon, Kathleen M. *Jerusalem: Excavating 3000 Years of History.* London: Thames and Hudson, 1967.

—————. Preliminary Reports in *Palestine Exploration Quarterly.* 1962, pp. 72 ff.; 1963, pp. 7 ff.; 1964, pp. 7 ff.; 1965, pp. 9 ff.; 1966, pp. 73 ff.; 1967, pp. 65 ff.; 1968, pp. 97 ff.

Macalister, R. A. S., and J. G. Duncan. *Excavations on the Hill of Ophel, Jerusalem, 1923–25.* Annual of the Palestine Exploration Fund, 4. London, 1926.

Simons, J. *Jerusalem in the Old Testament.* Leiden: E. J. Brill, 1952.

Sukenik, E. L., and L. A. Mayer. *The Third Wall of Jerusalem: An Account of Excavations.* London: Oxford University Press, 1930.

Vincent, L-H. *Jérusalem sous terre.* London: H. Cox, 1911.

—————. *Jérusalem: recherches de topographie, d'archéologie et d'histoire.* Vol. 1, *Jérusalem Antique.* Paris: Gabalda, 1912. Vol. 2, *Jérusalem Nouvelle* (with F. M. Abel). Paris: Gabalda, 1914–26.

Warren, Charles. *Underground Jerusalem.* London: R. Bentley and Son, 1876.

—————. *Plans, Elevations, Sections, etc. Shewing the Results of the Excavations at Jerusalem, 1867–70.* London: Palestine Exploration Fund, 1884.

—————, and C. R. Conder. *The Survey of Western Palestine: Jerusalem.* London: Palestine Exploration Fund, 1884.

Weill, R. *La Cité de David.* Vol. 1. Paris: Geuthner, 1920. Vol. 2. Institut francais d'archéologie de Beyrouth, Bibliothèque archéologique et historique, vol. 44. Paris: Geuthner, 1947.

Yeivin, S. "The Sepulchres of the Kings of the House of David," *Journal of Near Eastern Studies,* VII, 1948, 30 ff.

## 6. MESOPOTAMIA.

Adams, Robert McC. *Land Behind Baghdad: A History of Settlement on the Diyala Plains.* Chicago: University of Chicago Press, 1965.

Brinkman, J. A. *A Political History of Post-Kassite Babylonia.* Analecta Orientalia, 43. Rome, 1969.

British Naval Intelligence Division. *Iraq and the Persian Gulf.* Admiralty Handbook. London: His Majesty's Stationery Office, 1944.

*Cambridge Ancient History.* 12 vols. Cambridge: The University Press, 1926–1939. 2nd ed., vols. 1 and 2 now appearing in fascicles.

Dossin, G., et al. *Archives Royales de Mari.* Paris: Imprimerie Nationale, 1950–.

Edzard, D. O. *Die Zweite Zwischenschaft Babyloniens.* Wiesbaden: Otto Harrasowitz, 1957.

Frankfort, H. A. *Art and Architecture of the Ancient Orient.* Baltimore: Penguin Books, 1954.

Jones, A. H. M. *Cities of the Eastern Roman Empire.* Oxford: Oxford University Press, 1937.

Kramer, S. N. *The Sumerians.* Chicago: University of Chicago Press, 1964.

Laessøe, Jørgen. *People of Ancient Assyria: Their Inscriptions and Correspondence.* Translated by F. S. Leigh-Browne. London: Routledge and Kegan Paul, 1963.

Lloyd, Seton. *Twin Rivers.* 2nd ed. Oxford: The University Press, 1947.

Luckenbill, Daniel David. *Ancient Records of Assyria and Babylonia.* Chicago: University of Chicago Press, 1926.

Neusner, Jacob. *History of the Jews in Babylonia.* Leiden: E. J. Brill, 1968.

Oates, David. *Studies in the Ancient History of Northern Iraq.* London: Oxford University Press, for the British Academy, 1968.

Oppenheim, A. Leo. *Ancient Mesopotamia.* Chicago: University of Chicago Press, 1964.

Rostovtzeff, M. I. *Social and Economic History of the Hellenistic Period.* Oxford: The University Press, 1941.

—————. *Social and Economic History of the Roman Empire.* 2nd ed. Revised by P. M. Fraser. Oxford: The University Press, 1957.

Saggs, H. W. F. *The Greatness That Was Babylon.* New York: Hawthorne, 1962.

Thesiger, Wilfred. *Marsh Arabs.* New York: E. P. Dutton and Co., 1964.

## 7. PALESTINE AND THE LEVANT.

To conserve space, books on the Palestinian area published before 1957 are not listed here. The reader is referred to the bibliography in Denis Baly, *The Geography of the Bible* (New York: Harper and Row, 1957).

Abel, F. M. *Géographie de la Palestine*. 2 vols. 1933–38. Reprint, Paris: Librairie Lecoffre, 1967.

Aharoni, Y. *The Land of the Bible: A Historical Geography*. Translated by A. F. Rainey. Philadelphia: The Westminster Press, 1967.

Ashbel, D. *The Sunny Climate of Jerusalem, 1860–1964*. Jerusalem: The Hebrew University, no date.

Avi-Yonah, M. *The Holy Land from the Persians to the Arab Conquest: A Historical Geography*. Grand Rapids: Baker Book House, 1966.

Baly, Denis. *Geographical Companion to the Bible*. New York: McGraw-Hill Book Co., 1963.

Bodenheimer, F. S. *Animal and Man in Bible Lands*. Leiden: E. J. Brill, 1960.

Burdon, David J. *Handbook of the Geology of Jordan*. Amman: Government of the Hashemite Kingdom of Jordan, 1959.

Dubertret, L. *Aperçu de géographie physique sur le Liban, l'Anti-Liban et la Damascène*. 4 vols. Beirut: Imprimerie Catholique, 1945–1948.

du Buit, M. *Géographie de la Terre Sainte*. 2 vols. Paris: Editions du Cerf, 1958.

Glueck, Nelson. *Deities and Dolphins*. New York: Farrar, Straus and Giroux, 1965.

———. *Rivers in the Desert: A History of the Negev*. New York: Farrar, Straus and Cudahy, 1959.

Gray, John. *Archaeology and the Old Testament World*. New York: Thomas Nelson and Sons, 1962; Harper and Row, Harper Torchbooks, 1965.

Harden, Donald. *The Phoenicians*. New York: Frederick A. Praeger, 1962.

Harding, G. Lankaster. *The Antiquities of Jordan*. London: Lutterworth Press, 1959. Rev. ed. 1967.

Kenyon, Kathleen M. *Archaeology in the Holy Land*. New York: Frederick A. Praeger, 1960.

Kopp, Clemens. *The Holy Places of the Gospels*. New York: Herder and Herder, 1963.

Orni, Efraim, and Elisha Efrat. *Geography of Israel*. 2nd ed. Jerusalem: Program for Scientific Translations, 1966.

Reifenberg, A. *The Struggle between the Desert and the Sown: Rise and Fall of Agriculture in the Levant*.

Jerusalem. Publishing Department of the Jewish Agency, 1955.

Smith, George Adam. *The Historical Geography of the Holy Land*. 25th ed. 1931. Rev. ed., with intro. by H. H. Rowley. New York: Harper and Row, Harper Torchbooks, 1966.

Thoumin, R. *Géographie Humaine de la Syrie Centrale*. Tours, 1936.

Vaumas, Etienne de. *Le Liban: Etude de Géographie Physique*. 3 vols. Paris: Firmin-Didot, 1954.

Weulersse, J. *Le Pays des Alouites*. Tours, 1940.

Wolfart, R. *Geologie von Syrien und dem Libanon*. Beitrage zur regionalen Geologie der Erde. Berlin: Gebrüder Borntraeger, 1967.

## 8. TURKEY.

Akurgal, E. *The Art of the Hittites*. New York: Abrams, 1962.

———. *Die Kunst Anatoliens von Homer bis Alexander*. Berlin: de Gruyter, 1961.

———, C. Mango, and R. Ettinghausen. *Treasures of Turkey*. Geneva: Skira, 1967.

Bean, G. E. *Aegean Turkey: An Archaeological Guide*. London: Benn, 1966.

———. *Turkey's Southern Shore: An Archaeological Guide*. New York: Frederick A. Praeger, 1968.

Bossert, H. T. *Altanatolien*. Berlin: Wasmuth, 1942.

Cook, J. M. *The Greeks in Ionia and the East*. London: Thames and Hudson, 1962.

Garstang, J. *The Hittite Empire*. New York: Smith, 1930.

———. *The Land of the Hittites*. London: Constable, 1910.

———, and O. R. Gurney. *The Geography of the Hittite Empire*. Ankara: The British Institute of Archaeology, 1959.

Gurney, O. R. *The Hittites*. Baltimore: Penguin Books, 1952.

Lloyd, Seton. *Early Anatolia: The Archaeology of Asia Minor before the Greeks*. London: Penguin Books, 1956.

———. *Early Highland Peoples of Anatolia*. New York: McGraw-Hill Book Co., 1967.

Magie, David. *Roman Rule in Asia Minor to the End of the Third Century after Christ*. Princeton: Princeton University Press, 1950.

Mellaart, J. *The Chalcolithic and Early Bronze Ages in the Near East and Anatolia*. Mystic, Conn.: Lawrence Verry, 1966.

————. *Earliest Civilizations in the Near East.* New York: McGraw-Hill Book Co., 1966.

Piotrovskii, B. B. *Urartu: The Kingdom of Van and Its Art.* London: Adams, 1967.

Stark, Freya. *Alexander's Path, from Caria to Lycia.* New York: Harcourt, Brace and World, 1958.

————. *Ionia: A Quest.* London: Murray, 1954.

————. *The Lycian Shore.* London: Murray, 1956.

————. *Rome on the Euphrates: The Story of a Frontier.* New York: Harcourt, Brace and World, 1966.

van Loon, M. N. *Urartian Art: Its Distinctive Traits in the Light of New Excavations.* Istanbul: Nederlands Historisch-Archaeologisch Instituut, 1966.

# Index to the Text

NB. Figures in italics refer to photographs. Roman numerals indicate color plates, and Arabic numerals black and white plates.

# Index to the Maps

This index contains all the place names which occur on the maps or diagrams. Roman numerals indicate the colored maps; Arabic numerals the black and white maps; and Arabic numerals in italics the page numbers of the sketch-maps in the text. Arabic names beginning with the definite article el-, or its elided forms, en-, es-, et-, etc., are listed under the first letter of the noun. Thus el-Leja is to be found under L. Though the common form el- is used here, it should be made clear for those who do not know Arabic that this is the same as the technically more correct al-, and that both forms are now so common that they have become almost interchangeable in western usage.

Wherever possible, the modern equivalent of an ancient name is given. However, it must be recognized that the majority of biblical sites have not yet been identified with certainty, and for many the identification is at present very tentative. This is especially true of the places mentioned in the accounts of the wanderings in the wilderness during the period of the Exodus, and here identification is closely related to the very vexed question of the site of Mount Sinai (see the description of Map 18). Yet, to show only those places of which we are fairly certain would have meant leaving large blank spaces, and this itself would have been misleading. Consequently, wherever it has been possible to make a reasonable, even though tentative, identification, this place has been shown on one of the maps or diagrams. Occasionally alternative sites are listed in the index, and in these cases the first site listed in the index is the one shown on the map.

In some cases a biblical place name, mentioned only in a list of names, is not shown on any maps if it cannot be identified with certainty. For these the indication of the location of a possible site in relation to some place which does appear in the Atlas is given, wherever possible.

The following commonly used technical terms occur frequently in the index, and so their meanings are given here. Where they precede the main noun, as in *jebel Jarmuk*, or *wadi Sirhan*, the place is indexed under the first letter of the main noun, in these two cases under J and S.

*Jebel* (Arabic). A very general term meaning a hill or mountain.

*Khirbeh* (Kh.) (Arabic). A ruin. When it precedes a vowel, it is pronounced "khirbet."

*Nahr* (Arabic). River or stream.

*Su* (Turkish). River.

*Tell* (T.). In Arabic this means any little rounded hill, and in southern Syria is used for the low volcanic cones on the plateau, but it has come to be a technical term in archaeology for the hill which is formed when one town is built on the ruins of another (see plate X).

*Tepe*. In Turkey and Iran this is the equivalent of the Arabic *tell*.

*Wadi*. In Arabic this means any kind of valley, but in geography it is a technical term used for a dry valley, in which there is a stream only after rain.

(2.) Num. 21:16. A place in Moab. Unknown.

Beer-elim. A place in Moab, perhaps the same as Beer 2.

Beer-lahai-roi. An oasis near Kadesh Barnea. Unknown.

Beeroth. (1.) A place in Benjamin. *el-Bireh*, or possibly a tell nearby. *Ras at-Tahuneh* and *Kh. Raddana* have been suggested. 19:C5, 20:D1, 26:C5, *128*. (2.) Deut. 10:6. A stopping place during the Exodus, probably the same as Bene-jaakan, q.v.

Beersheba. *T. as-Saba*ᶜ. X:E2, XIII:B6, XIV:B6, 16:B6, 17:B3, 18:E2, 19:B6, 20:C4, 21:B6, 26:B6, *114, 120, 128*.

Beersheba-Zered Depression. Modern geographical term. 3:B6.

Beerzeth. *Bir Zeit*. 26:C5.

Be-eshterah. See Ashtaroth.

Behistun. *Bisutun*. IV:B3, VI:G5, 24:C2.

Beihan. Modern name of place in Arabia. IX:D5.

Beit el-Faqih. Modern name of place in Arabia. IX:C5.

Beit Rehob. More correctly Beth-rehob, q.v. XII:C4.

Bela. (1.) Modern name of town in Pakistan. 25:E3. (2.) See Cities of the Plain.

Bene-berak. *Ibn Ibraq*. 115.

Bene-jaakan. *Birein*. 18:E3.

Beni-hasan. Modern name of town on the Nile. X:C4.

Benjamin. Tribe. XIII:C5, 20:D1, *114*.

Beon. See Baal-meon.

Beqaᶜa, the. A regional name used today to describe the valley between the Lebanon and Anti-Lebanon, but also for many other lowland regions.

Berachah, valley of. *Wadi Ghar?* 20:E3.

Berea. (1.) The same as Beroea, q.v. *Verria*. 28a:A1. (2.) I Macc. 9:4. The same as Beeroth 1.

Bered. A place near Kadesh-barnea. Unknown.

Berenike. A port on the Red Sea. VIII:B3, X:E6.

Beroea. *Verria*. V:A2.

Berothah, Berothai. Town in Lebanon, possibly *Bereitan* in the Beqaᶜa, q.v.

Bersabe. (1.) See Beersheba. (2.) In Galilee. *Kh. Abu esh-Sheba*ᶜ. 10 km. (6 mi.) southwest of Meroth.

Berytus. *Beirut*. XIV:D1, 15:B3.

Besara. *Kh. Bir el-Beidar*. 27:B2.

Besor, brook. *Wadi Ghazzeh*, entering the sea near Gaza.

Beten. A place in Asher. *Kh. Ibtin*. 115.

Bethabara. Name given in some manuscripts to Bethany beyond Jordan.

Beth-anath. *el-Ba*ᶜ*neh*, or possibly *Safad el-Battikh*. 19:C3, 115.

Bethania. See Bethany.

Beth-anoth. A town in Judah. *Kh. Beit* ᶜ*Anun*. 114.

Bethany, *el-*ᶜ*Azariyeh*. XIV:C5.

Bethany beyond Jordan. Unknown.

Beth-aphra. See Beth-le-Aphrah.

Beth-Arabah. A town in Judah. ᶜ*Ain Gharbeh?* 114.

Beth-arbel. The same as Arbela 2.

Bethaven. The same as Bethel 1.

Beth-azmaveth. See Azmaveth.

Beth-baal-meon. See Beth-meon.

Beth-bamoth. See Bamoth.

Bethbarah. A place in the Jordan valley. Unknown.

Bethbasi. *Kh. Beit Bassa*. 26:C5.

Beth-birei. A town in Simeon. Unknown.

Beth-car. Beth-char. Perhaps the same as Beth-horon the Lower.

Beth-dagon. (1.) *Kh. Dajun*. 19:B4. (2.) A town in Asher. Unknown.

Beth-diblathaim. *Deleilat esh-sharqiyeh*. 21:C6.

Beth-eden. See Bit-adini.

Beth-eglaim. *T. el-*ᶜ*Ajjul*. 16:B6, 20:A3.

Beth-eked. Near Jezreel. Unknown.

Bethel. (1.) *Beitin*. XIII:C5, 16:C6, 18:F2, 19:C5, 20:E1, 21:C6, 26:C5, *114, 115, 120, 128*. (2.) I Sam. 30:27. Probably the same as Bethul, q.v.

Bethel, Mount. The region round Bethel 1.

Beth-emek. A place in Asher. *T. Mimas*. 115.

Bethesda, pool of. See under Jerusalem.

Beth-ezel. A place in Judah. *Deir el-*ᶜ*Asal*. 8 km. (5 mi.) northeast of Debir.

Beth-gader. See Gedor 1.

Beth-gamul. A town in Moab. *Kh. el-Jumeil*, 11 km. (7 mi.) east of Aroer?

Beth-gilgal. See Gilgal 1. *128*.

Beth-haccerem. *Kh. Salih* near Ramat Rahel. *128*.

Beth-haggan. See En-gannim.

Beth-haram, Beth-haran. *T. Iktanu*. 20:F1, *115*.

Beth-hoglah. *Deir Hajlah*. 20:F1, *114*.

Beth-horon (Lower). *Beit* ᶜ*Ur et-Tahta*. 19:C5, 20:D1, *114, 120*.

Beth-horon (Upper). *Beit* ᶜ*Ur el-Fauqa*. 19:C5, 20:D1, *115*.

Beth-jeshimoth. *T. el-*ᶜ*Azeimeh*. 18:F2, 19:D5, 20:F1.

Beth-le-Aphrah. Possibly *et-Taiyebeh* near Hebron.

Beth-lebaoth. A place in Simeon. Unknown.

Bethlehem. (1.) *Beit Lahm*. XIV:C5, 19:C5, 20:D2, 21:C6, *114, 128*. (2.) In Galilee. *Beit Lahm*. Josh. 19:15; Jud. 12:8. 19:C3, *115*.

Beth-maacah. The same as Abel-beth-maacah.

Beth-maon. See Beth-meon.

Beth-marcaboth. A town in Simeon near Ziklag, possibly the same as Madmennah.

Beth-meon. *Ma*ᶜ*in*. 19:D5, 20:F2.

Beth-millo. See Millo.

Beth-nimrah. *T. al-Bleibil*. 19:D5, 20:F1.

Beth-pazzez. A town in Issachar. Unknown.

Bethpelet. A town in the Negeb. Possibly *Kh. el-Meshash* or *T. es-Saqati*. *128*.

Beth-peor. *T. Iktanu?* The same as Baal-peor. 20:F1, *115*.

Bethpage. Uncertain, possibly *Kefr et-Tur*.

Beth-rehob. *Banias*. 21:C4.

Beth-rehob, kingdom of. XII:C4, 21:C4.

Bethsaida, Bethsaida Julias. *el-*ᶜ*Araj*. XIV:D3, 27:C2.

Beth-shan, Beth-shean. *T. el-Husn*. XIII:D4, 16:C5, 19:D4, 21:C5, *115, 120*.

Beth-shemesh. (1.) In Judah. *T. el-Rumeileh*. 19:B5, 20:C2, *120*. (2.) In Issachar. Josh. 19:22. Uncertain, perhaps *el-*ᶜ*Abeidiyeh*,

or *Kh. Sheikh esh-Shamsawi*. (3.) In Naphtali. Josh. 19:38; Jud. 1:33. Uncertain, perhaps *Kh. Tell er-Ruweisi*. 115. (4.) In Egypt. Jer. 43:13 (KJV). See Heliopolis 1.

Beth-shittah. Uncertain, perhaps *Shattah* east of the spring of Harod.

Bethshur, Bethsura. *Kh. Tubeiqa*. See Bethzur.

Beth-Tappuah. *Taffuh*. A town in Judah. *114*.

Beth-togarmah. Unknown.

Bethuel, Bethul. A town in Simeon. *Kh. er-Ras?* *114*.

Beth-yerah. *Kh. el-Kerak*. 26:D3.

Beth-zaith. *Beit Z*ᶜ*ita*. 26:C5.

Beth-zatha. See Jerusalem, Bethesda.

Beth-zechariah. *Kh. Beit Zakariyeh*. 26:C5.

Bethzur. *Kh. Tubeiqa*. 19:C5, 20:D2, 26:C5, *128*.

Betonim. *Kh. Batneh*. 19:D4, *115*.

Beyond the River. A regional name meaning "beyond the Euphrates."

Bezek. (1.) I Sam. 11:8. *Kh. Buzqa*, 6 km (4 mi.) northeast of Gezer? (2.) Jud. 1:4 ff. *Kh. Bezqa* on the coast plain, or it may be the same as Bezek 1.

Bezer. (1.) In Reuben. *Umm el-*ᶜ*Amad*. 19:D5, 21:C6. (2.) In Bashan. See Bostra.

Bezeth. See Beth-zaith.

Bilas, jebel. Modern name for range of hills in Syria. 15:F1.

Bileam. See Ibleam.

Bilhah. See Baalah 1.

Bingöl Mountains. Mountain range in eastern Anatolia. VI:E3.

Birecik. Modern name of town on the Euphrates. VI:C4.

Bisha. Modern name of town in Arabia. IX:C3.

Bisutun. See Behistun. VII:F3.

Bit-adani. Region and kingdom. XII:F1, 21:F1, 22:C2.

Bithron. Valley on the eastern plateau scarp. Unknown.

Bithynia. Regional name. V:E2, 28a:C1.

Bitter Lakes. Modern name for lakes on route of Suez Canal. 18:C3.

Biziothiah (RSV), Bizjothjah (KJV). Town in the Negeb of Judah. Unknown.

Black Sea. I, II, III:B1, V:D1, VI:C2, 1:B1, 22:C1, 23:C1, 24:B1, 25:B1, 28a:C1, 28b:F1, *16*.

Blessing, valley of. See Berachah.

Bochim. See Allon-Bachuth.

Bohan, stone of. Unknown. Perhaps *Hajar el-Asbah*.

Bojnurd. Modern name of town in Iran. 25:D3.

Bokhara. Modern name of town in Turkestan. III:E2, IV:E2, 25:E2.

Borashan. See Ashan.

Borsippa. *Birs Nimrud*. VII:E4, 17:D3, 22:D3, 23:D3.

Bosor. *Busr el-Hariri*. 15:C5, 26:E3.

Bosora, Bostra. *Bosra eski-Sham*. 26:E3.

Bozkath. *Dawa* ᶜ*imeh*. 20:C2.

Bozrah. (1.) *Buseireh* in Edom. XII:C7, 16:C7. (2.) The same as Bezer in Moab. 20:C6.

Brak, Tell. Excavated site in northern Iraq. VI:D4, VII:C2, 17:D2.

Bridge of Jacob's Daughters. *Jisr Banat Ya*ᶜ*qub*. 15:B4.

Bsharreh. Modern name of town in the Lebanon. 15:C2.

Bubastis. *T. Basta.* X:C2, 18:B3, 22:B3, 23:B3.

Buhen. Fortress on the Upper Nile. III:B3, X:C7.

Bureidah. Modern name of town in Arabia. VIII:C2.

Busiris. *Abu Sir.* X:C2, 18:B3.

Buz. Region in Arabia. VIII:B2.

Byblos. *Jubeil.* XII:C4, 15:B2.

Byzantium. *Istanbul.* V:D2, 23:A1, 24:A1.

Cabbon. A town in Judah. Uncertain, perhaps *Kh. Habra* east of Lachish. *114.*

Cabul. *Kabul.* 19:C3, 21:C5, *115.*

Cadasa. *Qadas.* 27:C1.

Cades. See Kedesh-Naphtali.

Caesarea. (1.) *Qaisariyeh.* XIV:B3, 27:A2, 28a: D3, 28b:G3. (2.) In Cappadocia. *Kaiseri.* V:G3.

Caesarea-Philippi. *Banias.* XIV:D2, 15:B4, 27: C1.

Cain. See Kain.

Calah. *Nimrud.* VII:D2, 17:D2, 22:D2.

Callirhoe. *Zarah.* 26:D5.

Calneh. (1.) Gen. 10:10 (KJV). Probably not a place name. (2.) Also Calno. *Kullanköy.* 21:E1, 22:C2.

Calvary. See under Jerusalem.

Cana. *Kh. Qana.* XIV:C3, 27:B2.

Canaan. Regional name for Palestine before the Israelite kingdom.

Canaanites. Name of a people. 16:C5.

Canneh. *Qanah Bir ʿAli.* VIII:D5, IX:E6.

Capernaum. *Tell Hum.* XIV:D3, 27:C2.

Capharsaba. *Kh. Sabyeh.* 26:B4.

Capharsalama. *Kh. Irha,* or *Kh. Salameh.* 26: C5.

Caphtor. *Crete.* III:A2.

Cappadocia. Region in central Anatolia. V: G3, 24:B2.

Carchemish. *Jerablus.* VI:B4, VII:A2, XII:E1, 14:E1, 16:F1, 17:C2, 20:F1, 22:C2, 23:C2.

Caria. Regional name. 23:A2.

Carmania. Regional name. IV:D4, 24:D3.

Carmel. *Kh. el-Karmil.* Josh. 15:55; I Sam. 25:2 ff. 19:C6, 20:D3, *114.*

Carmel, Mount. X:E1, XIII:C3, 3:C5, 7:B5, 27:B2, *115.*

Carnaim. *Sheikh Saʿad.* 26:E3.

Casiphia. In Babylonia. Unknown.

Casphor. *Khisfin,* east of the Lake of Galilee. See Chaspho.

Caspian Sea. I, II, III:C1, IV:B1, VI:H1, VII:HI, 1:C1, 17:F1, 22:F1, 23:F1, 25:C1.

Cassius Mountains. XII:D1, 3:D1.

Çatal Hüyük. Excavated site in central Anatolia. V:F4.

Caucasus Mountains. I, IV:B1, VI:E1, *16.*

Cauda. *Gavdos.* V:B5, 28b:D3.

Cedron. See Kidron.

Cenchreae. *Kechries.* V:A4.

Cerasus. *Giresun.* VI:C2.

Chabulon. *Kabul.* 27:B2. The same as Cabul.

Chagar Bazar. Excavated site in Mesopotamia. VII:C2.

Chalcedon. *Kadiköy.* V:D2.

Chaldea. Regional name. The same as Babylonia, q.v.

Chaldeans. Name of a people. 22:E3.

Characa, Charax. II Macc. 12:17. A common name for a camp.

Charachmoba. *el-Kerak.* The same as Kirhareseth. 26:D6.

Charax. *Mohammerah.* 25:C2.

Chaspho. *Khisfin.* 26:D3.

Chebar, river. A canal near Babylon, called *Naru Kabari* in ancient texts.

Chephar-ammoni, Chephar-haammoni. *Kefr ʿAna.* A town in Benjamin. *114.*

Chephirah. *Kh. el-Kefireh.* 20:D1, *128.*

Chephirim. Neh. 6:2 (KJV) should probably be translated "one of the villages."

Cherith, brook. A stream east of the Jordan, possibly the *Wadi Yabis.*

Cherub. Ezra 2:59; Neh. 7:61. A place in Babylonia. Unknown.

Chesalon. A place in Judah. *Kesla. 114.*

Chesil. A town in the Negeb, perhaps *Kh. el-Qaryatein.*

Chesulloth. A town near Jezreel. *Iksal. 115.*

Chezib. *T. el-Beida.* The same as Achzib 2. 16:B6.

Chinnereth. *T. el-ʿUreimeh.* 19:D3, *115.*

Chinnereth, Sea of. Lake of Galilee.

Chinneroth. See Chinnereth.

Chios. Island in the Aegean Sea. V:C3, 28a: B2.

Chisloth-tabor. See Chesulloth.

Chitlish. *Kh. el-Maghaz.* A place in Judah. *114.*

Choga Zambil. An excavated site in southwestern Iran. VII:G5.

Chorasmia. Regional name. IV:E1, 24:E1.

Chorazin. *Kh. Kerazeh.* XIV:D3, 27:C2.

Cilicia. Reignal name. 5:F4, 28a:D2, 28b:G2.

Cilician Gates. A pass in the Taurus mountains. V:G4.

Cilician Gulf. XI.

Cilician Plain. Regional name. XII:C1.

Cities of the Plain. These were Admah, Bela, Gomorrah, Sodom, Zeboiim. They may be under the southern end of the Dead Sea, but there is no direct evidence of this.

Citium. *Larnaca.* V:F5, XII:A3, 24:B2.

City of Salt. *Kh. Qumran. 114.*

Clysma. Port at the head of the Gulf of Suez. X:D2.

Cnidus. Near Cape Krio. 28b:E2.

Cnydus, river. Near Tarsus.

Coele-Syria. The *Beqaʿa* of Lebanon. 15:B3.

Colossae. Near *Khonai.* V:D4, 28a:B2.

Commagene. Regional name. 24:B2.

Corinth. *Korinthos.* V:A4, 24:A2, 28a:A2.

Corruption, Mount of. See Jerusalem: Offence, Mount of.

Çoruh, river. Modern name of river in Anatolia. VI:D2.

Cos. Island in the Aegean Sea. V:C4, 28a:B2.

Craftsmen, valley of. Possibly *Wadi ash-Shellal,* near Lod.

Crete. Island in the Mediterranean Sea. V:B5, 24:A2, 28a:A2, 28b:E2, *16.*

Crocodile River. *Wadi Mifjir* in the north of Sharon.

Crocodilopolis. *Madinet el-Fayum.* 18:E4.

Ctesiphon. *Taq-i-Kisra.* IV:A3, VII:E4.

Cush. Region on the Upper Nile. 24:B3.

Cuthah. *T. Ibrahim.* 22:D3, 23:D3.

Cyprus. Island in the eastern Mediterranean. V:F5, XII:A2, 28a:C3, 28b:F3, *16.*

Cyprus-Antioch Depression. Modern geographical term. 3:B2.

Cyrene. Regional name for what is now eastern Libya.

Cyropolis. *Ura-Tyube.* IV:F1.

Cyrus, river. River *Kura.* IV:B1, VI:G2, 24:C1.

Dabaloth. *Kh. Deleilat esh-Sharqiyeh.* 26:D5.

Dabareh, Dabaritta. See Daberath.

Dabbesheth. A border town of Zebulun and Issachar. *T. esh-Shammam. 115.*

Daberath. A town in Issachar. *Deburriyeh. 115.*

Daghestan. Modern regional name. VI:G1.

Dahnaʿ. Modern Geographical term. VIII:D2.

ad-Dakhla. Modern name of oasis in the Sahara. X:B5.

Dalmanutha. Probably the same as Magdala, q.v.

Damascus. *esh-Sham.* III:B2, XII:D4, XIII:E1, XIV:E1, 7:D4, 8:D4, 14:D4, 15:C3, 16:D4, 17:C3, 19:E1, 21:D4, 22:C3, 23:C3, 24:B2, 25:B2, 26:E1, 27:D1.

Damghan. Modern name of town in Iran. 24:D2.

Damietta. One of the two major mouths of the Nile. X:C2.

Dan. *T. el-Qadi.* XIII:D2, 15:B4, 19:D2, 21: C4, *115, 120.*

Dan, camp of. See Mahaneh-dan.

Dan, tribe of. XII:D2, *114, 115.* N.B. At the time of the entry into Canaan the territory was in the south, but Philistine pressure forced the tribe to move north.

Dan-jaan. II Sam. 24:6 (KJV). Probably the same as Dan.

Dannah. A town in Judah, perhaps *Deir esh-Shamash. 114.*

Danos. *T. el-Qadi.* 27:C1.

Danube, river. V:B1.

Daphne. (1.) In Egypt. *T. Dafanneh.* X:D2. (2.) *Kh. Dafneh,* just south of Dan. (3.) *Harbiye,* five miles west of Antioch 1.

Dascylium. 25:A1.

Dasht-i-Kavir. Modern name of northern section of the Great Iranian Desert. IV:C3.

Dasht-i-Lut. Modern name of southern section of Great Iranian Desert. IV:D3.

Dashur. Modern name for site on the Nile. X:C3.

Dathema. *T. Hamad,* or perhaps *T. er-Ramat.* 26:E3.

Dead Sea. XIII:C6, 7:C6, 19:C6, 20:E3, *114.*

Debir. (1.) Usually identified with *T. Beit Mirsim,* and so placed in this atlas, but some scholars would now place it at *Kh. Rabud,* 13 km. (8 mi.) east of Hebron. 19:B6, 20:C3, *114.* (2.) Josh. 15:7. *Thoghret ed-Debr.* 20:E1, *114.* (3.) In Gad. Josh. 13:26. Probably the same as Lodebar, q.v. *115.*

Decapolis. Regional name. XIV:D4, 27:C3.

Dedan. (1.) *el-ʿUla.* VIII:B2, 17:C4, 22:C4, 23: C4, 24:B3. (2.) The region round Dedan 1. VIII:B2.

Delos. Island in the Aegean Sea. V:B4.

Delphi. Sanctuary of Apollo in Greece. V:A3, 24:A2.

Demavand, Mount. Modern name of extinct volcano in Elburz mountains. IV:C2.

Kabul. (1.) Modern name of city in Afghanistan. III:E2, IV:F3, 25:E2. (2.) In Palestine. See Cabul.

Kabzeel. *Kh. Hura.* 20:C3, 26:B6, *114.*

Kadesh. (1.) On the Orontes. *T. Nebi Mend.* V:H5, 14:D3, 15:D1, 16:D3, 17:C3, 21:D3, 22:C3, 23:C3. (2.) Gen. 20:1; Num. 13:26; 20:16. See Kadesh Barnea. (3.) I Macc. 11:63. The same as Kedesh 1. 26:D2.

Kadesh Barnea. *'Ain Qudeirat,* or possibly *'Ain Qudeis.* 16:B7, 18:E3, 21:B7.

Kain. A place in Judah. *Kh. Yaqin. 114.*

Kalabsha. The site of a temple on the Upper Nile. X:D6.

Kamon. *Qamm,* or *Qamim.* 19:D3.

Kanah. A place in Asher. Josh 19:28. Perhaps *Qana* southeast of Tyre. *115.*

Kanah, river. *Wadi Qanah. 115.*

Kanata. *Qanawat.* XIV:F3.

Kandahar. Modern name of city in Afghanistan. IV:F3, 25:E2.

Kanish. *Kultepe.* V:G3, VI:A3, 17:C2.

Kara Kum. Modern regional name. III:D1, IV:D2.

Karasu. (1.) Modern name of river in Anatolia. VI:C3. (2.) Modern name of tributary of the Orontes, just east of the Amanus Mountains.

Karatepe. Excavated site in Turkey. V:H4, VI:B4.

Karem. Josh. 15:59 (LXX). A place in Judah, perhaps the same as Beth-haccerem, q.v.

Karka, Karkaa. A place in southern Judah. Unknown.

Karkor. A place in Gad. Uncertain. Perhaps *Qarqar* in eastern desert of the Hashemite Kingdom of Jordan.

Karmir Blur. Urartu fortress north of Mount Ararat. VI:F2.

Karnaim. *Sheikh Sa'ad.* 15:C5, 16:D5, 19:E3, 21:D5.

Karnak. Site of great temple in the region of Thebes, just north of Luxor. X:D5.

Kars. Modern name of city in eastern Turkey. VI:E2.

Kartah. A place in Zebulun. Unknown.

Kartan. A place in Naphtali. Unknown.

Karun, river. Modern name of river flowing into the Persian Gulf. VII:G5.

Kashan. Modern name of city in Iran. III:D2.

Kassites. Name of a people VII:F4.

Kattath. A place in Zebulun. Unknown.

Kedar. Regional name. VIII:B2, 17:C3.

Kedemoth. Perhaps *Qasr ez-Za'feran.* 19:D5.

Kedesh. (1.) In Naphtali. *T. Qadas.* 15:B4, 19:D2, 21:C4, *115.* (2.) In Issachar. I Chr. 6:72, and probably Jud. 4:11, although Jud. 4:6 is Kedesh 1. Uncertain, but *T. Qisan* at the foot of Mount Tabor, or *T. Abu Qudeis* 5 km. (3 mi.) southeast of Megiddo, have been suggested. (3.) Josh. 15:23. See Kadesh-barnea.

Kedesh-naphtali. See Kedesh 1.

Kedron. *Qatra.* 26:B5.

Kehelathah. Num. 33:22. *Kuntillet Jeraya.* 18:E3.

Keilah. *T. Qila.* 19:B5, 20:D2, *128.*

Kelkit, river. Modern name of river in Anatolia. V:H2, VI:B2.

Kenath. *Qanawat.* 15:D5.

Kerioth. (1.) Jer. 48:24; Amos 2:2. *Saliyeh,*

or possibly *el-Qereiyat,* in Moab. (2.) Josh. 15:25 (KJV). See Kerioth-hezron.

Kerioth-hezron. *Kh. el-Qaryatein.* 20:D3.

Kerman. Modern name of city in Iran. III:D2, IV:D3, 24:D2.

Keziz, valley of. See Emek-keziz.

Khabur, river. Modern name of tributary of the Euphrates. VII:C3.

Khaibar. Modern name of oasis in Arabia. 22:C4, 23:C4.

Khalab. The same as Halab (Aleppo). VII:A2.

Khalab, kingdom of. XII:E1.

Khanazir, jebel. Modern name of hills in Syria. 7:E3.

al-Kharga. Modern name of oasis in the Sahara. X:C5.

al-Kharj. Modern name of oasis in Arabia. VIII:D3.

Khazazu. *'Azaz.* 23:C2.

Khilakku. The same as Cilicia. 22:B2.

Khindanu. Regional name. 22:D3, 23:D3.

Khurasan Divide. Modern geographical term. IV:D3.

Khyber Pass. Modern name of pass leading from Kabul 1 to Pakistan. III:F2.

Kibroth-hataavah. Possibly *Rueis el-Eberig.* 18:E5.

Kibzaim. A place in Ephraim. Unknown.

Kidron Valley. See under Jerusalem.

Kinah. A place near Arad. Unknown.

King's Highway. *Tariq es-Sultan.* 14:C6.

King's Vale. See Shaveh.

Kir. Is. 15:1. See Kir Hareseth.

Kir Hareseth. *el-Kerak.* XII:C6, XIII:D6, 18:F2, 19:D6, 20:F4, 21:C6, *120.*

Kir Haresh, Kir Heres. See Kir Hareseth.

Kiriath. See Kiriath-jearim.

Kiriathaim. (1.) East of the Jordan. *Kh. el-Qureiyeh.* 16:C6, 19:D5, 20:F2. (2.) In Naphtali. Probably the same as Kartan. Unknown.

Kiriath-arba. See Hebron.

Kiriatharim. See Kiriath-jearim.

Kiriath-baal. See Kiriath-jearim. *114.*

Kiriath-huzoth. Num. 22:39. Unknown.

Kiriath-jearim. *Kiriat el-'Anab, T. el-Azhar.* 19:C5, 20:D1, *128.*

Kiriath-sannah. See Debir 1.

Kiriath-sepher. See Debir 1.

Kirjath, Kirjathaim, Kirjath-arba, etc. (KJV). See Kiriath, Kiriathaim, etc.

Kirshu. *Mut.* 23:B2.

Kish. *T. el-Ukheimir.* VII:E4.

Kishion. A place in Issachar. The same as Kedesh 2?

Kishon, river. *Nahr el-Muqatta',* draining the plain of Esdraelon from Megiddo northwestwards.

Kithlish. See Chitlish.

Kitron. See Kattath.

Kittim. *Cyprus.* III:B2, XII:A2, 17:B2, 21:A2, 23:B2.

Kizzuwatna. The same as Cilicia. 17:C2.

Knossos. The capital of Crete in Minoan times. V:B5.

Kom Ombo. Modern name for site of temple in Egypt. X:D5.

Kopet Dagh. Modern name for mountains southeast of the Caspian Sea. IV:D2, *16.*

Kue. The same as Cilicia. V:G4, XII:C1, 21:C1, 22:C2, 23:C2.

Kuh Rud. Modern name of volcanic mountain range in Iran. IV:C3.

Kush. The same as Cush. X:C7.

Kuwait. Modern name of city on the Persian Gulf. VIII:D2.

Kyrenia Range. Modern name of mountain range in Northern Cyprus. 3:A2.

Kysyl Kum. Modern regional name. III:E1.

Laban. Deut. 1:1. Unknown.

Lachish. *T. ad-Duweir.* XIII:B5, 14:B6, 19:B5, 20:C2, 21:B6, 22:B3, 23:B3, *114, 128.*

Ladder of Tyre. *Ras en-Naqurah.* 27:B1.

Lagash. *Telloh.* VII:F5, 17:E2.

Lahmam. *Kh. el-Lahm. 114.*

Laish. (1.) *T. el-Qadi.* This was the old name of Dan. (2.) Is. 10:20 (KJV). See Laishah.

Laishah. A place just north of Jerusalem. *el-'Issawiyeh.*

Lakkum, Lakum. A place on the border of Naphtali. *Kh. el-Mansurah. 115.*

Laodicea. (1.) In Syria. *Lattaqieh.* V:G5. (2.) In Anatolia. *Eskihisar.* V:D4, 28a:B2.

Larsa. *Senkereh.* VII:E5, 17:E2, 22:E3.

Lasea. A small coastal town in Crete, near Fair Havens. 28b:D2.

Lasha. A place near the Cities of the Plain. Gen. 10:19. Unknown.

Lasharon. Josh. 12:18. Text uncertain. See Sharon.

Lebanon, valley of. Regional name. *el-Beqa'a.* XIII:D1.

Lebanon Depression. A modern geographical term. 3:D3.

Lebanon Mountains. XIII:D1, 15:B3.

Lebaoth. A place in southern Judah. Unknown.

Lebo Hamath. Usually identified with *Lebweh,* but it is not impossible that it is a regional term. 15:C2, 16:D3, 21:D3.

Lebonah. *Lubban.* 19:C4.

Lehi. A place in Judah. Perhaps *Beit 'Itab,* 10 km. (6 mi.) east of Beth-shemesh.

el-Leja. Modern regional name. XIII:E2, 15:C5.

Leontes, river. *Nahr el-Litani.* 27:B1.

Leshem. See Laish 1.

Lessau. II Macc. 14:16 A place near Jerusalem. Unknown.

Levant Coast. Modern geographical term for the coastal area extending from Cilicia to Egypt.

Libba. *Kh. Libb.* 26:D5.

Libnah. (1.) Usually identified with *T. es-Safi,* but recent evidence suggests that it should be placed at *T. Bornat,* 8 km. (5 mi.) farther south. XIII:B5, 19:B5, 20:C2, *114, 120, 128.* (2.) Num. 33:20, 21. A place in Sinai. Unknown.

Libya. Regional name for the coastal areas west of the Nile Delta.

Lidebir. Josh. 13:26 (KJV). See Lo-debar.

Lisan, the. Modern name of the peninsula in the Dead Sea. 20:E3.

Litani, river. Modern name of river in southern Lebanon. 15:A4, 19:C2.

Lod. *Lod (Lydda).* 20:C1, 26:B5, *128.*

Lo-debar. *Umm ed-Debar.* 21:C5.

Lower Sea. The Persian Gulf. 22:F4, 24:D3.

Lubim. See Libya.

Lud. See Lydia.

Perga. *Murtana.* V:E4, 25:B2, 28a:C2.
Pergamum. *Bergama.* V:C3, 28a:B2.
Persepolis. *Takht-i-Jamshid.* III:D3, IV:C4, 24:D3, 25:D3.
Persia. Regional name. *Fars.* IV:C4, VII:H4, VIII:E2, 23:F4.
Persian Gulf. Modern name. I, II, III:D3, IV:C4, VII:G6, VIII:E2, 17:F4, 23:F4, 25:D3, *16.*
Persian Plateau. Modern geographical term. I, *16.*
Persis. The same as Persia. 24:D3.
Pethor. Perhaps *T. Ahmar.* 16:F1.
Petra. *Wadi Musa.* III:B2, VIII:B1, X:E2.
Pharathon. The same as Pirathon. *Far'ata.* 26:C4.
Pharpar, river. *Nahr el-'Awaj,* one of the wadis on the east side of Mount Hermon, near Damascus.
Phasaelis. (1.) *Kh. Fasa'il* in the Jordan valley south of Alexandrium. (2.) *Tekirova.* 25:B2.
Phasis. *Poti.* 24:C1.
Phenice. A city in Crete. 28b:D2.
Philadelphia. (1.) Roman name of *'Amman* (Rabbah in O.T.) XIV:D5, 26:D5. (2.) *Alaşehir.* V:D3, 28a:B2.
Philae. Island in the Nile just above Aswan. X:D6.
Philippi. *Filibedjik.* V:B2, 28a:A1.
Philistia, Philistines. Region and people. XII:B6, XIII:B5, 19:B5, 20:B2, 21:B6, 26:B5, *114.*
Philoteria. *Kh. el-Kerak.* 27:C2.
Phoenicia. Regional name. XII:C4, XIII:C2, 15:A4, 21:C4, 22:C3, 24:B2, 27:B1, 28a:D3.
Phrygia. Regional name. V:E3, 22:B2, 24:B2, 28a:C2.
Pi-beseth. See Bubastis.
Pi-hahiroth. A place on the Egyptian border. Unknown.
Pirathon. *Far'ata.* 19:C4.
Pirindu. Regional name. 23:B2.
Pisgah, the. The edge of the Trans-Jordan plateau. XIII:D5.
Pishon, river. One of the distributaries of the Tigris or Euphrates.
Pisidia. Regional name. V:D4, 28a:C2.
Pison, river. See Pishon.
Pithom. Usually identified with *T. Retabeh,* but others would equate it with Heliopolis 1. X:D2, 18:C3.
Pitusu. *Karginçik Island.* 23:B2.
Plain, sea of the. See Dead Sea.
Pontic Mountains. Modern name of mountain range in Anatolia. V:F2.
Pontus. Regional name. 28a:C1.
Prophthasia. *Qala-i-Kang.* 25:E2.
Prusa. *Bursa.* V:D2.
Ptolemais. (1.) *Acre.* I Macc. 5:22; 11:22,24; 12:45,48; Acts 21:7. XIV:C3, 26:C3, 27:B2, 28a:D3. (2.) In Egypt. *el-Menshiyeh.* X:C4.
Ptolemais Theron. A port on the Red Sea. III:B4.
Punon. *Feinan.* 21:C7.
Punt. A region either in Abyssinia, or somewhere on the East African coast. IX:B6, E7.
Pura. *Fahraj.* 24:D3.
Put. Regional name. The area west of the Nile delta.
Puteoli. *Puzzuoli.* 28b:B1.

Qarqar. *Kh. Qarqur.* 14:D2, 21:D2, 22:C2.
Qatabah. Modern name of town in southwest Arabia. IX:D6.
Qataban. Region in southwest Arabia. IX:D5.
Qatna. *T. el-Mishrifiyeh.* 16:D3.
Qattara Depression. Modern geographical term. X:A3.
Qidri. Akkadian form of Kedar, q.v. 22:C3.
Qizan. Modern name of town in southwest Arabia. IX:C4.
Quetta. Modern name of city in West Pakistan. III:E2, IV:F3.
Qum. Modern name of city in Iran. IV:C3.
Qumran. Site of the monastery, and of the discovery, of the Dead Sea Scrolls. XIV:C5, 26:C5.
Quramati. *Qal'at Jaber.* 23:C2.
Quseir. Port on the Red Sea, known in classical times as Myos Hormos. X:E4.

Raamah. A place in Arabia. Unknown.
Raamses. Usually placed at *San al-Hagar,* but others would identify it with *Qantar-Khata'na.* X:C2, 18:B2.
Rabbah. (1.) Rabbath ha-Ammoni. *el-Qala'* in *'Amman.* VIII:B1, X:E2, XII:C6, XIII:D5, 14:C6, 16:C6, 18:F2, 19:D5, 21:C6, *120.* (2.) In Judah. Josh. 15:60. A place near *Suba.* Unknown.
Rabbath-Ammon. See Rabbah 1.
Rabbith. A place in Issachar. Unknown.
Rabboth-Ammon. See Rabbah 1.
Rages. See Rhagae.
Rahab. A name given to Egypt. Ps. 87:4; 89:10; Is. 51:9.
Rakkath. A place in Naphtali. *115.*
Rakkon. A place in the original territory of Dan. Unknown.
Rama. Matt. 2:18 (KJV). See Ramah 1.
Ramah. (1.) *er-Ram.* 20:E1, *128.* (2.) In Asher. Josh. 19:29. A place on the boundary of Asher. *115.* (3.) In Naphtali *er-Rameh.* Josh. 19:36. *115.* (4.) I Sam. 1:19; 2:11; 7:17; 8:4. May be the same as Ramathaim-zophim, i.e. *Rentis,* or it may be the same as Ramah 1. (5.) The same as Ramoth Gilead. *T. Ramith.* (6.) In the Negeb. Josh. 19:8. Unknown.
Ramath. Josh. 19:8 (KJV). See Ramah 6.
Ramathaim-zophim. *Rentis.* 19:C4.
Ramath-lehi. A place in the Shephelah. Unknown.
Ramath-mizpeh. See Mizpah 3. *115.*
Ramlat Sabatein. Modern regional name. IX:E5.
Ramoth. (1.) See Ramoth-gilead. (2.) In Manasseh. I Chr. 6:73. *Kaukab el- Hawa.* The same as Remeth, q.v. (3.) I Sam. 30:27. See Ramah 6.
Ramoth-gilead. *T. Ramith.* XIII:D3, 19:D3, 21:D5, *115, 120.*
Ramoth of the Negeb. See Ramah 6.
Raphana. The same as Raphon. *er-Rafeh.* XIV:E3, 27:C2.
Raphia. *Rafah.* 21:B6, 26:A6.
Raphon. *er-Rafeh.* 15:C5, 26:E3.
Ras Shamra. Excavated site in northern Syria. See Ugarit.
Rathamin. *Rentis.* 26:C4.
Recah, Rechah. I Chr. 4:12. A place in Judah. Unknown.

Red Sea. (1.) In the Exodus story this should be translated ''Reed Sea,'' and probably indicates the marshes near the Great Bitter Lake, in the region where the Suez Canal now is. (2.) The large body of water occupying the rift valley between Arabia and North Africa. I, III:B3, VIII:B3, IX:A3, X:E5, 1:B3, 17:C4, 18:E6, 22:C4, 23:C4, 24:B3, 25:B3, *16.*
Rehob. (1.) In Asher. *T. al-Gharbi.* *115.* (2.) On the border of Asher. Josh. 19:28. *Kh. el-'Amri.* 19:C3, *115.* (3.) In Egyptian records. *T. es-Sarem,* south of Beth-shan.
Rehoboth. (1.) Gen. 26:22. *Kh. Ruheibeh.* 16:B6, 20:B4, (2.) Gen. 36:37; I Chr. 1:48. On the Euphrates. Unknown. (3.) Gen. 10:11 (KJV). See Rehoboth-ir.
Rehoboth-ir. A place near Nineveh. Unknown.
Rekem. A place in Benjamin. Unknown.
Remeth. A place in Issachar. Perhaps *Kaukab el-Hawa.* *115.*
Rephaim, valley of. *el-Buqei'a,* just west of Jerusalem.
Rephidim. A stopping place in the Exodus. Perhaps *Wadi Refayid.* 18:D5.
Resen. A place near Nineveh. Unknown.
Reuben. Tribe. XIII:D5, *115.*
Rezaiyeh. Modern name of town in Iran. VI:F4.
Rezeph. A city in Assyria. Uncertain.
Rhagae. *Reyy.* III:D2, IV:C2, VII:H3, 22:F2, 23:F2, 24:D2, 25:D2.
Rhegium. *Reggio.* 28b:C2.
Rhodes. (1.) City. V:D4, 23:A2. (2.) Island. V:C4, 24:A2, 28a:B2.
Rhodope Mountains. Modern name of mountains in southern Bulgaria. V:B2.
Riblah. *Ribleh.* 15:D2, 23:C3.
Rimah. Excavated site in Iraq. VII:D2, 22:D2.
Rimmon. (1.) In Zebulun. Josh. 19:13; I Chr. 6:77. *Rummaneh.* 19:C3, *115.* (2.) Josh. 15:32. See En-rimmon. (3.) ''Rock of Rimmon.'' Jud. 20:45; Is. 10:27 (RSV). *Rammun,* east of Bethel.
Rimmon-perez. Perhaps *Naqb el-Biyar.* 18:E4.
Rissah. Perhaps *el-Kuntilla.* 18:E4.
Rithmah. Perhaps *Bir es-Saura.* 18:E4.
Riyadh. Modern name of city in Arabia. VIII:D3.
Rogel, spring of. See Jerusalem: En-Rogel.
Rogelim. A place in Gilead. Perhaps *Bersynia,* 14 km. (9 mi.) southwest of Irbid, i.e. Arbela 2.
Rome. *Roma.* 28b:B1.
Rosetta. One of the mouths of the Nile. X:C2.
Ruba' al-Khali. Modern name for great sand desert of southern Arabia. I, III:C4, VIII:E3, IX:E3, *16.*
Rumah. II Kings 23:36. Uncertain. Perhaps *Kh. Rumeh,* just northwest of Rimmon 1.

Saab. A place mentioned by Josephus. *Sha'b.* 27:B2.
Sa'da. Modern name of town in Arabia. IX:C4.
as-Safa. Modern name of basalt region in Syria. XIII:F2, 15:D4.
Safid, river. *Safid Rud.* VI:H4.
Sagartia. Regional name. IV:C3.

that the translation should be "one of the settlers in Gilead." See RSV margin.

Tob. *et-Taiyibeh.* XII:D5, 19:D3, 21:C5.

Tob, kingdom of. XII:D5.

Tobie. See Tob.

Togarmah. *Gürün.* 22:C2.

Tolad. See Eltolad.

Tophel. *Tafileh.* 18:F3, 19:D7, 20:F5, 21:C7.

Topheth. A district in Jerusalem, possibly to be equated with the Valley of Hinnom. See under Jerusalem.

Trachonitis. Regional name. *el-Leja.* XIV:F2, 27:D1.

Trans-Caucasian Depression. Modern geographical term. VI:G2.

Trapezus. *Trabzon.* VI:C2, 23:C1, 24:B1.

Tripolis. *Tripoli.* 15:B2, 25:B2.

Troas. *Eskistanbul.* V:C3, 28a:B2.

Trogyllium. A promontory on the west coast of Asia Minor, close to Samos. 28a:B2.

Troodos Mountains. Modern name of mountains in Cyprus. 3:A3.

Troy. *Truva.* 25:A2.

Trunk Road. Modern geographical term. 14:A6, D2.

Tubal. Region and people in Anatolia. 22:C2.

Turkestan. Modern name of region in Russian Central Asia. 1, *16.*

Turushpa. *Van.* VII:D1, 22:D2.

Tus. A town in Iran near the modern Meshed. IV:D2, 24:D2.

Tuspa. *Van.* VI:E3.

Tutub. *Khafaja.* VII:E4.

Tuz Gölü. Modern name of lake in Anatolia. V:F3.

Tyana. *Kizli Hisar.* 25:B2.

Tyre. *Tsur.* III:B2, XII:C4, XIII:C2, XIV:C2, 3:C4, 14:C4, 15:A4, 16:C4, 17:C3, 19:C2, 22:C3, 23:C3, 24:B2, 25:B2, 26:C2, 27:B1, 28a:D3, *120.*

Tyropoeon Valley. See under Jerusalem.

Ubaid. *T. el-ʿUbaid.* VII:F5.

Ugarit. *Ras Shamra.* V:G5, XII:C2, 16:C2, 17:C2, 21:C2.

Ulai. A river near Susa. Unknown.

Ummah. A place in Asher. Perhaps the same as Acco.

Unqi. A region in Syria. *Biqaʿat ʿAmuq.* XII:D1.

Uphaz. Perhaps Ophir, q.v.

Upper Sea. The Mediterranean Sea. 22:B3, 24:A2.

ʿUqair. Modern name of town on the Persian Gulf. III:D3, VIII:E2.

Ur. *el-Muqeiyar.* III:C2, IV:B3, VII:F5, VIII:D1, 17:E3, 22:E3, 23:E3, 24:C2.

Urartu. Region and kingdom in eastern Anatolia. I, IV:A2, VI:E3, VII:E1, 17:D2, 22:D2, 23:D2.

Urmia, lake. Modern name of lake in Iran,

also called Lake Rezaiyeh. IV:B2, VI:F4, VII:E2, 17:E2, 22:E2, 23:E2.

Usiana. City and region in Anatolia. 22:B2.

Uz. Probably a name for Edom, or else a region in Arabia close to Edom.

Uzal. *Sanaʿ.* VIII:C4.

Uzu. *T. Rashidiyeh,* near Tyre. *115.*

Uzzen-sheerah, Uzzen-sherah. Unknown.

Van, lake. Modern name of lake in eastern Turkey. IV:A2, VI:E3, VII:D1, 17:D2, 22:D2, 23:D2.

Vardar, river. Modern name of river in Yugoslavia. V:A2.

Wadian. Modern regional name. VII:C5.

Way of the Philistines. Road along the coast from Palestine to Egypt.

Way of the Wilderness of Shur. Way to Egypt from Beersheba through central Sinai.

Western Sea. The Mediterranean Sea. 22:B3.

Willows, brook of the. See Zered. river.

Xanthus. *Kınık.* 24:A2, 25:A2.

Yanoam. See Janoah.

Yarim. Modern name of town in southwest Arabia. IX:D5.

Yarmuq, river. Modern name of tributary of the Jordan. XIII:D3, 19:D3, 27:C2.

Yathrib. *Medina.* VIII:B3, 22:C5, 23:C5, 24:A3.

Yazd. Modern name of city in Iran. III:D2, IV:C3, 24:D2.

Yeb. The same as Elephantine. *Aswan.* 24:A3.

Yemen. Modern name for southwest Arabia. I, VIII:C5, *16.*

Yiron. A place in Naphtali. *Yarun. 115.*

Yishub. *Kh. Kafr Sib.* 27:B3.

Zaanaim, plain of. Jud. 4:11 (KJV). Translated "the oak in Zaaninnim" in RSV.

Zaanan. See Zenan.

Zaaninnim. A place in Naphtali. *Khan et-Tujjar. 115.*

Zab, Great. Modern name of tributary of the Tigris. *Zab el-ʿAla.* VII:E2.

Zab, Little. Modern name of tributary of the Tigris. *Zab es-Saghir.* VII:D3.

Zadrakarta. *Gorgan (Astrabad).* 24:D2, 25:D2.

Zagros Mountains. Modern name of ranges between Iran and Iraq. I, IV:B3, VII:F3, VIII:E1, *16.*

Zahle. Modern name of town in Beqaʿa of Lebanon. 15:B3.

Zahran. Modern name of town in southwest Arabia. IX:C4.

Zair. II Kings 8:21. See Zior.

Zalmon. In Judges 9:48 it appears to be a hill or mountain near Shechem, but in

Psalm 68:14 it must be the *Jebel Druze,* i.e., the "black mountain," as opposed to Lebanon, the "white mountain."

Zalmonah. A stopping place in the Exodus. Perhaps *Bir Malkhur.* 18:F3.

Zanoah. (1.) *Kh. Zanuʿ.* 19:C5, 20:D2, *128.* (2.) Josh. 15:56. A place in the hill country of Judah. *Kh. Zanuta. 114, 128.*

Zaphon. A place in Gad. *T. el-Qos. 115.*

Zarephath. *Sarafand.* 21:C4.

Zaretan, Zarethan. *T. es-Saʿidiyeh.* 19:D4, *120.*

Zareth-shahar. See Zereth-shahar.

Zeboiim. See Cities of the Plain.

Zeboim. I Sam. 13:8; Neh. 11:34. Unknown.

Zebulun. Tribe. XIII:C3.

Zedad. *Sadad.* 15:D2, 21:D3.

Zela. A place in Benjamin. *Kh. Salah. 114.*

Zelzah. A place in Benjamin. Unknown.

Zemaraim. *Ras ez-Zeimara.* 20:E1.

Zenan. A place in the Shephelah of Judah. Unknown.

Zephath. See Hormah.

Zephathah, valley of. *Wadi es-Safiyeh.* This is the wadi leading northwestwards from Lachish to the coast.

Zer. A place in Naphtali. Perhaps *Qarn Hattin. 115.*

Zered, river. Wadi *el-Hesa.* XIII:D7, 19:D7, 20:F5.

Zeredah. (1.) I Kings 2:26. *Deir Ghassaneh,* about 5 km. (3 mi.) north of Timnath-serah. (2.) II Chr. 4:17. See Zarethan.

Zererah. See Zarethan.

Zereth-shahar. *Zarah.* 19:D5, 20:F2.

Ziddim. A place in Naphtali. *Kadish. 115.*

Ziklag. *T. el-Khuweilfeh.* 19:B6, 20:C3, 26:B6, *128.*

Zin, wilderness of. Regional name. 18:E3.

Zion. A name given to Jerusalem. Also Mount Zion. See under Jerusalem.

Zior. A place in Judah. *Siʿir. 114.*

Ziph. (1.) In the hill country of Judah. *T. Zif.* 19:C6, 20:D3. (2.) Josh. 15:24. In the south of Judah. *T. Zif.* 19:C7, 20:D4, *114.*

Ziph, wilderness of. Desert region east of Ziph 1.

Ziphron. A place in Syria. Unknown.

Ziz, ascent of. *Wadi Hasasah.* 20:E2.

Zoan. See Raamses. 22:B3, 23:B3, 24:B2.

Zoar. *Kh. Sheikh ʿIsa.* 16:C6, 20:E4.

Zobah. Possibly *Homs.* XII:D3.

Zobah, kingdom of. XII:D3.

Zoheleth, stone of. I Kings 1:9 (KJV). "Serpent's Stone" (RSV). A stone near En-Rogel. See Jerusalem: En-Rogel.

Zophim, field of. Num. 23:14. Somewhere on the edge of the plateau of Moab.

Zorah. *Sarʿah.* 19:B5, 20:C1, *114, 128.*

Zuph, land of. A district near Ramathaim-Zophim.